D1124041

The Feminine Gaze

A Canadian Compendium of Non-Fiction Women Authors and Their Books, 1836-1945

Anne Innis Dagg

Wilfrid Laurier University Press

We acknowledge the support of the Canada Council for the Arts for our publishing program. We acknowledge the financial support of the Government of Canada through the Book Publishing Industry Development Program for our publishing activities.

National Library of Canada Cataloguing in Publication Data

Dagg, Anne Innis
    The feminine gaze: a Canadian compendium of non-fiction women authors and their books, 1836-1945

Includes bibliographical references and index.
ISBN 0-88920-355-5

1. Women authors, Canadian (English)—Biography.* 2. Canadian prose literature (English)—Women authors—Bio-bibliography.* 3. Canada—Bio-bibliography I. Title.

Z1376.W65D33 2001   016.818′08   C2001-930470-6

© 2001 Wilfrid Laurier University Press
     Waterloo, Ontario   N2L 3C5

Cover design by Leslie Macredie. Family photos courtesy of Carroll Klein and Jacqueline Larson.

∞

Printed in Canada

*Dedicated to
Mary Quayle Innis
and Edna Staebler,
authors and friends*

CONTENTS

FOREWORD

From Lady Aberdeen, the governor general's wife who wrote of her photographic adventures in *Through Canada with a Kodak* to Anahareo, Grey Owl's companion who told her side of the story in *Devil in Deerskins*, from Kootenay historian Clara Graham to Helen MacMurchy, medical doctor and health activist, from the famous pioneering Strickland sisters to the feminist activist and judge Emily Murphy, this compendium of women non-fiction writers is a unique collection. Anne Innis Dagg has produced a wide-ranging and varied collection of individual entries on women whose non-fiction work has been an ever present but often little noticed part of our culture for almost two centuries.

This book will prove of great practical use to researchers who wish to use it as an encyclopedia of women's non-fiction writing; its excellent cross-referenced index, which will help the reader find whole groups of women interested in the same subject, from education through immigration to agriculture, is particularly helpful. However, I found its most profound effect came from browsing through the entries without seeking a specific focus. The cumulative effect of reading the entries is to discover a collage of the cultural history of women and their accomplishments in Canada over two centuries.

Women in Canada have used a multitude of ways to write themselves into being. In the early days their writing ranged from botany to travel writing to religion. Later, areas such as business, science and politics began to open to them. Each bio-bibliographical entry, even the ones where only limited facts are available, tells the story of a woman reaching out from the private world to which, it would seem, culture has relegated her, to a public world where her particular expertise would have its chance to affirm, shape or change the larger culture.

This collection contradicts the truism that women have not been part of public culture in Canada's past. Perhaps closer to the truth is that they have been, by and large, edited out of the public history of our culture. This book works at correcting that omission. Here we see women who enter the public domain in a variety of endeavours, some of them as surprising as exploration and economics. Although first-wave feminism at the turn of the twentieth century offered many more women the opportunity to enter the public forum, this book makes it clear that women's cultural texts by no means began with feminism. Reading the entries shows that a large number of these women did not hold particularly feminist viewpoints. Indeed, they seek their authority to speak by becoming expert at the very patriarchal modes of discourse (for example, religion, history and science) that would normally exclude them. Yet, even though some of the individual voices of these women may not sound very different from those of their male counterparts, the cumulative effect of reading their lives and their achievements is. We can read in the way they negotiate—and sometimes even subtly undermine and subvert while seeming to obey—the norms and values of their contemporary societies.

Discoveries await the reader of this book. The entry on Susan Allison, who gave birth to and raised fourteen children in the Similkameen and Okanagan districts before it was settled by other white women and men, may well make you want to read her memoirs and those of a multitude of other early women whose entries refer to their first-hand accounts of pioneering days. The number of women who found journalistic writing the way into the public market is surprising at first, but quickly reminds us that women such as Nellie McClung and Madge Macbeth found newspapers and magazines—the literature most likely to enter the home and get into the hands of busy wives and mothers—the most readily available format for their ideas. The entries introduce us to the possibility that their book-length works may be only the tip of the iceberg in rediscovering women's cultural artifacts.

Anne Innis Dagg's compendium makes space for the enormous variety of women non-fiction writers in Canada. She is as fair to the women who wrote of men's adventures, who authored men's biographies or who wrote on safe "feminine" subjects such as gardening and mothering as she is to rebels who spoke against established views, or those who ventured into male preserves such as business and politics. This book will be an excellent research aid to those seeking biographical and topical information on women non-fiction writers; it will also be immensely appealing to anyone interested in women's publications and women's cultural place in Canada.

Helen M. Buss, University of Calgary

INTRODUCTION

By writing this compendium I hope to bring back to public consciousness the many anglophone women associated with Canada's early culture who wrote non-fiction books. I originally planned to include books in French, but this project has become so large that time and energy have run out. I hope that this compendium will encourage a French Canadian to give visibility to early non-fiction books by francophone women.

A great deal has been published about Canadian women fiction writers and poets, but little attention has been paid to most of the 476 or more anglophone non-fiction women authors in Canada's past. In addition, my goal is to publicize the books they wrote, so that future studies of early Canadian culture can also take them into account. This work greatly expands the project I began in 1985, on which I published a preliminary paper in the *Journal of Canadian Studies*: "Canadian voices of authority: Non-fiction and early women writers" (Dagg 1992).

Who were these women? The first and larger category is that of women who lived in what is now Canada and wrote about their own lives or other interests, most of which centred in Canada. The second is that of women who were not Canadians, but wrote about the country or its inhabitants; most in this category were tourists or journalists from Great Britain or the United States.

Why should we remember these women and their books? Because this information could redress in part the disproportionate extent to which Canada in the past has been seen and described through male eyes (Waite 1995). If we are to know our country properly, it is essential that the contribution of women writers, which often focused on women's needs and interests previously ignored by men, be given proper weight. For example, whereas early immigrants to Canada were generally thought to have had a "garrison mentality," analysis indicates that men may have had such a perspective, but to many women, their lives in Canada were much more free than they would have been in Europe (Buss 1990).

By remembering these authors, we also salute their memory. They are important because they reached beyond the private sphere allotted to them by society and into the public sphere, becoming voices of authority in their own right at a time when women's autonomy and influence were rare.

By remembering their books, our knowledge of Canada, Canadian culture and other topics is expanded. The comprehensive index of this compendium indicates the broad array of subject matter that women addressed; it will be useful to help readers discover a feminine perspective on topics that previously may have been covered only by men.

Why these women and their books were so often forgotten is a complex topic I have not addressed. However, much of the agenda of this work is driven by a feminist perspective, in that the cultural forgetting of women writers' contributions to society strikes me as an example of the silencing of their voices in so many realms. Few of the contributions of these 476 women and their 677 or more books are remembered, yet not only were many of the books published remarkable, but their sales and popularity at the time were also often impressive.

To gather the material for this work, I compiled a list of as many early women writers and their books as possible, gleaned largely from the sources listed in the General Bibliography. Over a period of fifteen years, I perused the books (either in book form or in microfiche) at ten large libraries, beginning at the University of Waterloo (where the Aberdeen Library Collection of books by women is housed), the National Library of Canada and the Metro Toronto Reference Library. I then visited the libraries of the following universities: British Columbia, Guelph, Queen's, McGill, Saskatchewan, Wilfrid Laurier and Toronto. To locate books unavailable at any of these libraries, I resorted to inter-library loans through the kindness of the University of Waterloo.

I also hunted for information about the women themselves. This was sometimes available in the books they wrote and in the sources I have listed in the General Bibliography, but also in a wide variety of other books and articles; if the information came from a particular work rather than a compendium, this is listed in the bibliographic information after a woman's entry. For all too many women, however, I could find no information at all, although this may exist in private collections or other sources beyond my research; this means that the first paragraph of an entry may consist of only a single self-evident sentence. I would be grateful if readers would alert me to information I have been unable to discover.

Information about women was harder to unearth than it would have been about men. In the past many more books were written by men than women, and they dealt far more often with men's rather than women's activities and interests. Sometimes a woman was identified only by her husband's name; if he had two or more wives, these seem interchangeable; if a woman married, she changed her name and may not be traceable. Women's dates of birth and death are also often difficult to establish: many women refused to divulge their birth date, as did Alice Massey, presumably because she was eight or nine years older than her husband; Lilian Whiting reduced her age by twelve years because she did not want to grow old. Death dates are often unknown because obituaries were reported only locally.

Sometimes different accounts of writers' lives are contradictory in some details, occasionally because authors themselves, such as Anna Leonowens, gave out incorrect information. Other inaccuracies appear in edited versions; for example, in one source the author Mary Quayle Innis, who edited *The Clear Spirit*, is identified as Inns, editor of *The Clean Spirit*. In different sources the number of a woman's children often varies, which is not surprising as many children died when young and may or may not have been counted. I have in general assumed that the more recent accounts are the more accurate, and where possible have depended on *The Dictionary of Literary Biography*, *The Dictionary of Canadian Biography* and biographies.

To make this project feasible, I set the following guidelines:
• I did not include the scores of women who wrote only cookbooks, how-to books, manuals, workbooks or school primers, because these involve a different sort of creativity than that needed for more literary works. (Elizabeth Driver has compiled a forthcoming bibliography of Canadian cookbooks up to 1950.)
• If a woman wrote books after 1945, this may be mentioned in the text, but the books are not described. I used this cut-off date because after that time, Canadian publishers increasingly included non-Canadian books in their lists, and it was difficult to distinguish these from Canadian books.
• A book is defined as having more than forty-eight pages (UNESCO definition); if a visiting woman wrote a travel book about a number of countries, it is included here only if the portion about Canada exceeds forty-eight pages.
• Women who grew up in Canada but moved elsewhere as adults and then wrote books are not included, unless the books are about Canada (which they sometimes were, such as books by Constance Skinner and Agnes Laut). Public figures such as Marie Dressler, Mary Pickford, Maud Allan

and Emma Albani, who were born in Canada but spent their adult years largely elsewhere, *are* considered as Canadians, because many Canadians like to remember them in this way.

- Each entry gives, in the first paragraph, the main facts I found about the woman's life. If this paragraph is small, as too often it is, this is because I could discover little about the author. In my brief synopsis of each book, I include details that interested me, such as information on the woman as a writer, the presence of a network among women authors (with friends noted in bold type in the text), how each author is presented by the publishers (whether her name is given on the title page, whether she uses her own name, initials or her husband's name, etc.), comments about Canada and anecdotes that reveal something about her personality or the conditions under which she lived.
- Sometimes the line between fiction and non-fiction was unclear; I included rather than excluded borderline books.

I used the following format in this compendium:

- All books that I have seen are indicated by a bullet; each lists the information given on the title page in the bibliographic citation for each woman—thus, some books may list the author by a pseudonym and others by a married or maiden name.
- The name by which each woman is listed is the name she used as an author; if she was known by another name, this is indicated.
- If quotations from the book are cited, no page number is given if they come from the preface, foreword or introduction.
- The edition of any book perused is the one cited in the bibliography of each entry. If the book had an earlier copyright, this is noted in brackets where known.
- Bibliographies at the end of each entry cite not only books by the author but where possible her autobiography and other works about her as further reference sources.
- References cited in the text devoted to a woman are included in her bibliography unless they are also included in the entry for another woman; then they appear in the General Bibliography at the end of the compendium.

I am grateful to all the libraries that gave me access to non-fiction books by women and to the librarians who were invariably helpful. I especially thank Susan Bellingham, Diane Fitzpatrick, Jane Forgay, Ruth Lamb and Dianne Seager from the University of Waterloo library for their friendly assistance; Mary Williamson, Elaine Auerbach and John Meisel who provided valuable information on specific women; Alan Cairns who gave useful editorial suggestions; Carroll Klein who edited the manuscript with careful attention; Brian Henderson the current director of Wilfrid Laurier University Press and Sandra Woolfrey, his predecessor, who was responsible for having my manuscript accepted for publication.

Interpretive Commentary

Throughout this compendium there are multiple themes related to the women authors, such as who wrote non-fiction, what they wrote about, their feelings about their writing, their friends who were also authors, their observations that mirror present-day concerns, information about the publishing process, the authors' perspectives and their ideas about the future. These themes will be discussed in this interpretive commentary.

Who Wrote Non-Fiction Books?

Most of the books included in this compendium were written by the elite— in the early days by the daughters, sisters and wives of lawyers, doctors, aristocrats, ministers, educators and businessmen, and later as well by professional women and other women successful in their own right. Unfortunately, we have no books by the non-literate who made up most of the population of early Canada, and almost none by non-Anglo immigrants, working-class people, Native women and members of other marginalized groups. To write a book and have it published, a person had to have time, opportunity, drive, persistence, self-confidence and often money as well. Many of the authors were single, but many were married, too. The list even includes Canadian aristocrats, such as Lady Matilda Edgar and Lady Marjory Willison.

Some women worked closely with their husbands in writing their books. For example, Mary Guillet (1939) and Ethel Jeanneret (1941) co-authored books with their husbands (Marcel Jeanneret worked for the firm that published their book), while others wrote books at their husbands' request to further their husbands' work: Mary Quayle Innis (1936) wrote a text for her husband's university economics course, and Annie Stephenson (1925) published a Methodist mission history for the church groups of young people organized by her husband. Eileen Jenness's (1933) book on Indian tribes was based on her husband's primary research on the same topic. Some women, such as Martha Black, Kathrine Brinley, Dorothy Hogner and Florence Jaques, had their books illustrated by their husbands.

Other women had to follow their husbands' agendas in ways that surely bothered them. At least two left young children behind when they immigrated to Canada, in one case (Geraldine Ball) a baby girl given against her will to her sister-in-law; she would not see the child again.

Women's success as writers gave them access to other women writers, so that many of these authors were friends, as noted in bold type in the text.

A number of these women founded and joined clubs for writers, such as the Canadian Women's Press Club, the Toronto Heliconian Club (women only) and the Canadian Authors Association; such clubs were vital in reducing feelings of isolation for the writers and in encouraging young people to become authors (Tippett 1990, 6).

Women authors were often exceptional writers. Six early authors would win Governor General's Awards, inaugurated in 1936, for non-fiction: Laura Salverson in 1939, Emily Carr in 1941, Dorothy Duncan in 1944, Evelyn Richardson in 1945 and later Marjorie Campbell in 1950 and Grace MacInnis in 1953. Mazo de la Roche and Marshall Saunders (who each wrote one book of non-fiction) were world famous as authors, the latter being the first Canadian to sell over a million copies of a book, *Beautiful Joe*. Agnes Laut was so successful with her books about Canadian history, written using primary sources, that she was given 20 percent royalties from her Toronto publisher. At least eighty-seven of the books have been republished or reprinted, sometimes by university presses which added extensive introductions, attesting to their importance. Many authors were awarded honorary degrees from universities (Appendix A); however, in nearly all cases this was not primarily because of their non-fiction books but rather because of the authors' other commendable achievements.

Many of the authors were old when they wrote books. Emily Carr and Edith Archibald published their first books when seventy, Elizabeth Johnston when seventy-two, Susan Sibbald when over seventy-two, Maud Henderson Miller when seventy-four and Anne Langton and Margaret Ross when seventy-seven. Susan Allison published her autobiography when eighty-six and Alice Ravenhill hers when ninety-two.

Despite their status as upper- or middle-class women, those who wrote non-fiction books represented a diverse background. There were at least 476 of them, the number included in this compendium whose books I was able to locate, and there may be more. Before 1946 they wrote at least 677 non-fiction books among them. Most authors published only one book, but some, usually professional writers, wrote a number, including sometimes novels which may be mentioned in this work.

As I read and examined the books included in this compendium, I found that most of the authors (but certainly not all) could be grouped into five categories: professional women; professional writers; religious women; visiting British women; and high-profile women in society. A few women, of course, are included in more than one of these categories.

Professional Women

Many of the professional women were scholars. Women were not allowed into universities in Canada until the 1880s, but once they were, a number went on to obtain doctoral degrees. Many of these, at least in the humanities and social sciences, published their revised theses as books which are included in this survey. (No scientist wrote a book based on her doctoral thesis, which is not surprising given the nature of the science disciplines, but there were many women with PhDs in science. Ford (1984, 46) indicates that the first twenty-eight out of thirty doctoral theses written at the University of Toronto by women were in science or mathematics.) Nine women wrote their books/doctoral theses on Canada, but all did so at non-Canadian universities; at least seventeen Canadian authors in total were awarded PhDs (Appendix B), while at least twenty-two earned master's degrees.

Fifteen of the authors were university professors—in 1931 there were proportionately almost as many women teaching at Canadian universities (19 percent) as there are today (Dagg and Thompson 1988, 65; current Statistics Canada data). Eleven of these taught at Canadian universities in a wide variety of disciplines (Appendix B).

Other professional women who wrote non-fiction books, often autobiographical, included five doctors and seven nurses (Appendix B). Few women were lawyers before 1945, and those included here, Dorothy Heneker and Janet MacKay, both faced sexual discrimination. By contrast, although Helen McGill and Emily Murphy were not lawyers, both became judges because of their long-term concern with social issues, especially those concerning women.

At least forty-three of the authors were schoolteachers at some point in their lives, which was an accepted occupation for young women, but these women did not write autobiographies describing their teaching experiences. Some continued to write in the educational field, but most went on to other adventures and wrote about other subjects.

Professional Writers

Book authors who wrote articles for money, such as journalists or freelance authors, numbered at least forty-three. Some of these had a lifetime career as journalists (Kit Coleman), some had columns in magazines and newspapers (and sometimes published collections of these as books—as did Kit Coleman, Margaret Currie, Dora Farncomb, Nellie McClung, Gertrude Pringle and Gertrude Watt) and some published occasional articles or series of articles where they could. At least fourteen women were editors of books, journals or newspapers, and at least ten gave paid public lectures on their areas of expertise. Some, such as Madge Macbeth, supported themselves and their children with their writing.

Religious Women

Religion was a great interest for women, an area in which they could have authority without needing an education denied them in early years because of their sex. Eleven of the women considered in this compendium were nuns. The religious life allowed them the chance to write and publish books denied to most women. Common topics were the biographies of founders of their orders (three about Marguerite Bourgeoys and one about Mother d'Youville) and histories of orders or convents (four, written by four nuns).

As well as nuns, other devout Catholic authors, such as Katherine Burton, Ruth Mugglebee, Agnes Repplier and Mary Anne Sadlier, wrote biographies of religious individuals specifically to promote their religion. As the index indicates, twenty-four in all wrote about religion (mostly Christianity). A number of early women ruminated on their relationship with God for the edification of others, while later women were more likely to prepare books on religious themes to act as guidebooks for church discussion groups.

Visiting British Women

This category includes mainly two types of women, those who were wealthy and aristocratic, and those who wrote about their travels in Canada to make money and to encourage (and in one case discourage: Catherine Johnstone) immigration.

The wealthy women were sometimes related to the current governors general of Canada: Lady Aberdeen, Anna Buchan, Viscountess Byng, Lady Dufferin and Frances Monck; under the auspices of their eminent relatives they could meet important people, travel in style and discuss these experiences in their autobiographies. Seven of the authors indicated their rank of Lady in their books, so that readers would know of their high status.

Authors who toured Canada in order to write a book about their adventures were so numerous that Frances Douglas and Thelma Lecocq (1934) wrote a satire on their methods in their description of England. Twelve women did so, some having their way paid in part by the Canadian government and/or by Canadian railways, which wanted to encourage immigration.

High-Profile Women

This category can be divided into feminists/activists and other well-known women. Probably scores of women authors acted as feminists, but eighteen were outspokenly so, often devoting their lives not only to writing about the cause of women but spending their days working for women through such means as women's suffrage groups, National and Local Councils of Women, the Victorian Order of Nurses, Women's Institutes, the Woman's Christian Temperance Union, and the Young Women's Christian Association. Mostly these women were maternal feminists, rather than feminists as we know them today. Among them they tried to change society with their books (as did Nellie McClung and Emily Murphy), wrote books about laws to indicate inequalities between the sexes (as did Henrietta Edwards and Helen MacGill) and wrote their autobiographies to inspire other women (as did Alice Chown and Letitia Youmans). Other women wrote books unusual at the time in that they consciously highlighted women (as did Sophy Elliott, Mabel McKinley, Mary Pepper and Isabel Skelton). Only a few women were anti-feminist (Maud Allan, Marion Angus and Jessie Saxby).

Well-known women who probably wrote books because they knew they would sell and make money, as well as increase their fame, included Maud Allan, the dancer, Mary Pickford, the actor, Dame Emma Albani, the opera singer and Marie Dressler, the actor.

What Did Women Write About?

Simplistic theory indicates that until recently, women in Canada were restricted to the private sphere, while men controlled the public sphere. However, the subject matter of books by women indicates that this was by no means true. By the time of the First World War, women were writing books about global peace and government, and about laws and women's place in the new society. When the Great Depression struck in the 1930s, women produced books on how the economy worked and discussed political solutions. However, they did not address some topics in the male domain, such as physics, architecture and engineering, nor those in socially taboo areas, such as sexuality, sexual abuse, prostitution, incest and lesbianism. Presumably many of these women had erotic sex lives, as was described by Peter Gay (1984) for other bourgeois women living before 1914, but you would not know this from their books. Nor were there many books about professional subjects, since few women in early times were allowed to become professionals.

The books women did write can be grouped into ten categories as discussed below, with the number in virtually all the categories increasing as the years passed. The first non-fiction books were published in 1836, long after novels by Canadian women had appeared. The first novel, by Frances Brooke, was published in 1769; perhaps because fiction by women was more acceptable culturally, it served to pave the way for women's non-fiction. While there were only fourteen non-fiction books written by women between 1836 and 1856, there were about three hundred published between 1931 and 1945, even though these latter years encompass both the Great Depression and the Second World War.

The types of non-fiction published also changed over the years, as will be discussed below in detail. Before 1870, autobiography and history were more common than other kinds of books. During the next thirty years, travel books and biography became increasingly important, too. By the twentieth century, when many women had obtained university degrees and more freedom than ever before, there was an increase of books on these topics as well as on religion and social issues, and to a lesser extent on science and medicine. By 1945, books on education and on the arts were also numerous.

The following categories are presented in numerical order, with the most common first.

History

Women wrote more books of history than any other kind; these can largely be divided into three categories. One was the history of local regions, of extended families, of institutions or of individual churches, using archives, letters, newspaper reports, interviews and other material obtainable close to hand. A second category was academic histories, heavily footnoted, and often derived from theses written for doctoral or master's degrees; these required years of work and visits to public archives and other primary sources. Finally, many women wrote about the early history of Canada as a whole, using mainly secondary sources; they focused particularly on explorers and the fur trade, often aiming their work at young readers. Helen Palk states that she specifically omitted information on Confederation and other topics that would be of little interest to children; Mabel McKinley agreed with this approach in her book, declaring "differences of theory and opinion, official mistakes and shortcomings, are purposely left out." The large number of women teachers gave them an entrée into this educational market. For example, The Children's Study series, published by the Toronto firm Briggs about 1900, comprised books about nine countries of the world, seven of which were written by women, including Canada's J.N. McIlwraith. At least one woman, Robina Lizars, claimed that she was not writing history at all in her books about early Upper Canada, but rather the stories of families that could in turn form the foundation for general histories; she did not include footnotes, finding them unsightly.

Autobiography

Autobiography was the second most common category of books written by women; even if they did not have the education or resources to pursue other topics, women could always write about their own experiences. These autobiographies were not consciously informed by the desire to present a woman's point of view, nor presented as a contrast to the far greater number of autobiographies written by men. Even so, from a contemporary perspective we can learn much about women's lives before 1946. Women wrote autobiography in increasing numbers beginning with Traill's account of her early life in backwoods Upper Canada in 1836. Some of these women lived uneventful lives, but wanted their children and grandchildren to understand about pioneer life in Canada. Others had adventures which they wanted to share for various reasons—to enhance their fame, to increase immigration to Canada, to spread their religious beliefs, to further a personal cause, to make money. These books were important in making readers more aware of ways of living which went beyond domesticity. Unfortunately, some of the authors apparently felt it necessary to omit or to change place names and dates from their accounts to protect identities, thereby decreasing the historical value of their stories. Others chose to omit negative experiences, as Emma Graham did in her 1895 book about being a minister's wife.

Travel and Description

A large number of women throughout Canada's history travelled in Canada or abroad from Canada and wrote books describing the places they visited and their adventures. At first, travellers were often aristocrats who had the money, leisure and opportunity for long trips; later, even single working women took journeys to various destinations and wrote about their experiences, often with a wit and style still compelling today. These travel books, which usually included information on geography, history and present conditions, were popular with armchair readers and invaluable for other travellers who wanted to visit the same places. Especially popular were travel books about trips across Canada that would be read by prospective immigrants. These were usually undertaken by British authors who could bring a woman's perspective to their writing; their expenses were sometimes paid by the Canadian government or by a Canadian railway. A number of women wrote positively about their visits to the north of Canada, having either lived there for years or visited for a few months. Also popular were books about Quebec, which seemed exotic to readers, but was near enough for both English-speaking Canadians and Americans to visit without too much effort.

Biography

Biography came into its own especially toward the end of the period considered in this work. In the early years, women often wrote about relatives whose papers would have been readily available and whose stories might have otherwise remained untold; twenty-seven (including three about women) of the hundred biographies written were of relatives of the authors. Wilhelmina Gordon notes that a male author stated that "a biography written by a son is only one degree less contemptible than one written by a daughter," but these women did not let this attitude stop them. They wrote their biographies to keep alive the memory of someone close to them. Later, authors were more likely to write biographies of unrelated individuals using material more difficult to collect. They seem more likely to write biographies of women than men would have been, with twenty-eight of the one hundred biographies having female subjects.

Social Issues

This category became important only in this century, when women had the education and authority to comment on social issues. Some of the books dealt with women—laws concerning women, women and work, women and war and advice for young women; some dealt with Native people, especially their legends; some considered issues of economics or politics; and some focused on other societies entirely.

Religion

Many authors were consumed with religion, writing about missionary experiences, the history of missionary enterprises and descriptions of individual churches or groups of churches. However, the two earliest books on religion were diaries of religious thoughts and Christian beliefs (Mary Bradley and Eliza Chipman), published for the edification of readers and suitable for women authors who were writing from the private sphere. Other books dealt with prayer, Christian writings and interpretations (especially by Lily Dougall and Mary Anne Sadlier), and material to be used as study guides for church groups. One author wrote about eastern religions (Lily Beck) and four wrote about spiritism or the occult, which was popular between the wars. Religion gave nuns the opportunity to write books they might not otherwise have had.

Science and Medicine

Aside from three works by Catharine Parr Traill, books in this category were not published until the twentieth century. Most books were about plants, a subject seen as suitable for women's study (Bennett 1991), followed by books about animals, especially birds. Helen MacMurchy, employed by the Ontario and then the federal governments, was the only author to focus on health concerns.

Arts

This category became popular only after the First World War, when authors and experts began exploring areas of art, music, crafts (Native and non-Native) and especially literature.

Education

Although many thousands of women have been teachers in Canada over the last 150 years, few of them have been in a position to write books about education other than histories for schoolchildren and school readers (which are not included in this compendium). One of the most prolific of these women was Dr Donalda Dickie, who taught or supervised teachers all her life in the public education system of Alberta. Most of the books included in this category were written by women involved with the Institute of Child Study at the University of Toronto.

Essays

This category includes only books published in the twentieth century; they were most often collections of columns which had appeared in local magazines or newspapers.

Why Did Women Say They Wrote Books?

One way authors counteracted possible adverse reaction to their temerity in writing books was to include in their preface comments indicating that the work was not originally intended for publication, or that it was undertaken only at the urging of friends/children/grandchildren/great-grandchildren/husbands/nephews and nieces/readers/ex-pupils/publishers/editors and even God. Kit Coleman states she was obeying "the commands of certain shadows who . . . have written over vague signatures," asking that her letters be made into a book. These entreaties indicated that the author was only obeying the wishes of others, as befitted a proper woman.

Other reasons for writing books were given, too. Some authors claimed that there was great interest in their topic and thus a pressing need for more information, while others stated that too little was known about their subject, which required them to rectify this lack. Some felt driven to write their books to purge an idea that consumed them (Marjorie Campbell), to bring fresh air to troubled readers (Mary Schäfer) or to divert their thoughts from the oppressive years of the Second World War (Anna Buchan, Kathleen Cannell, Raïssa Maritain). Others wanted to bring their readers closer to the love of God.

Ambition vs Humility

It took a great deal of ambition for an early woman to write a book and have it published; an autobiography was particularly audacious, because it destroyed a woman's exalted privacy. To write a book of non-fiction indicated that a woman felt her ideas and information should reach a wider audience than the friends and relatives who made up her private sphere. Yet women were socialized to believe their place was in the home. Women authors circumvented this problem of being ambitious by seeming not to be so in a number of ways, as the following examples indicate.

Naming Authors

Early on, women sometimes retained their propriety by leaving their name off their books entirely. Miss L.M. Godfrey's 1855 book, for example, notes that it was written "By a Provincial," yet despite this coyness it has a huge agenda as noted by its subtitle (*Nova Scotia as it Was, as it Is, and as it May Be*) and was published by the author herself. Agnes Machar's name was omitted from her first book in 1859, as was that of Elizabeth Frame, "A Nova Scotian," on her 1864 book. "An Emigrant Lady," who published in 1878 a compilation of her letters from Muskoka, remains unknown today. Even a pseudonym was lacking for Margaret Wetherell's 1898 book. Bliss Carman (1908) writes in *The Making of Personality* that his co-worker, Mary Perry King, was responsible for the substance of the book, but as she refused joint signature on the titlepage, she is unknown as an author.

Soon women writers were bolder, allowing their initials but not their full names to appear on their books. Charlotte Bompas had no name on the title page of her first book in 1886, but ended it with her initials, C.S.B. About the same time two other reticent authors wrote travel books about Canada, an English woman, known only as A.S., and an American, Eliza Brown Chase, who gave only the musical notes for E, B and C on the title page. Bertha Carr-Harris published her first book in 1892, before she married, under her initials B.H.W., and in 1901, Carrie Derick had her book of botany published under her initials, C.M.D., even though she was at the time a faculty member in botany at McGill University.

Sometimes an author's name was omitted from the title page but present elsewhere in her book. This was true for Mrs A. McDougall, who wrote about her trip to Ireland in 1882. In 1892, Janet Carnochan, a Niagara historian, did not have her name on the title page of her first book, but it was mentioned in the preface by three church officials (who also praised her for writing the book without pay).

Other authors used their husband's name on their books (a practice that makes cataloguing the books highly problematic for librarians). The author "Mrs Edward Copleston" notes in the preface of her 1861 account of Canada that she had wanted her sketches published anonymously, but that her wish had been overruled by an archbishop. In 1880, Mrs P.A. Henry wrote under her husband's name, as did Mrs E.A. McCulloch and Mrs Tom Manning as recently as 1942 and 1945, respectively. The biography of John Lewis is noted on the title page as being not by Ada Lewis, but by "His Wife," even though this woman was assertive enough in her early life to have founded a series of homes for needy young women.

Emily Murphy chose to publish her early books under her maiden name, Ferguson, and later under her pseudonym, Janey Canuck, before she used her married name, Emily Murphy. Her maiden name probably provided her with some anonymity, given that she married young.

Writing a book gave women confidence, because even if a first book was published anonymously, subsequent books usually were not. Thus in 1877

Maria Lauder published a book under the pseudonym "Toofie," but when it was republished in 1884 it carried her real name. Janet Carnochan published her later books under her own name, as did Agnes Maule Machar.

By the twentieth century almost all women published under their own complete name, with a few exceptions: I.A. Caldwell and E. Barwick used their initials, perhaps because they wrote about male-oriented subjects, money and inventions; Elsie Pomeroy used her initials on her laudatory book about C.G.D. Roberts at his insistence so that there would be no gossip; and Charlotte Whitton's name is omitted entirely from one title page, presumably because she wrote her book about forestry on contract. Kathrine Brinley published her four travel books under her second name, Gordon Brinley, so that she seemed to be a male; similarly, Lily Beck published her books under the name L. Adams Beck. Sophie Hensley's pseudonym was Gordon Hart.

High Friends

Another way to counter possible censure was to dedicate a work to an aristocrat, with his or her permission. Many early women writers did this, while some later authors had famous men write forewords, such as former Prime Minister Robert Borden for one of Clara Dennis's books on Nova Scotia and the Dominion Naturalist John Macoun for Julia Henshaw's flower guides.

Humble Protestations

One way to soften a woman's authorship was to state that it was written at the request of others, which has been mentioned earlier. Another way was to undercut the importance of their own work; many authors referred to their "little" book even if it had as many as 428 pages (Monica Taylor). Jennet Roy referred to her book as a "little work," although it had 278 pages and would go into at least six editions. Grace Nute, who was a professor with a PhD, nevertheless alluded in 1931 to her first 289-page book as "little." Lady Aberdeen commented that her sketches were "superficial notes" that were "scarcely worthy" of being collected, Miss M.A. Nannary that her biography was an "imperfect sketch," Anna Ross that her "little" book was not a biography but only an attempt to preserve a memory, and the Lizars sisters that their books were not history but rather accumulations of historical details as if collected by "the humble ant." Some men reinforced this deprecating attitude: a professor referred to Rosa Langstone's 241-page book as "little" although also "excellent," while a parish priest twice wrote of Mary Hoskin's history of her parish (172 pp.) that it was a "little" book, as well as a "pretty book" and a "charming record."

Still other authors disparaged their own literary skill. Elizabeth McCully notes in her biography of a fellow missionary that it should have been written by a master pen rather than by a novice, but that no master was available. The Duchess of St Maur comments on her own lack of literary skill, and Harriet Youmans, writing about Grimsby Park, states that it has "a noble past which these imperfect pages have utterly failed to depict."

Assertive Protestations

Despite the humility of many, a few women refused to be apologetic about their efforts. Kit Coleman wrote that she did not edit her book about Queen Victoria's jubilee in case it would seem less immediate, while Rosalind Goforth noted she was too old to rewrite her text; both women had considerable reputations as authors, which allowed them this freedom. Lady Murray likewise acknowledged that her published letters "were hastily written, sent off by post uncopied, and generally uncorrected," but merely hopes that the reader will be indulgent.

Publishing and Critical Support of the Author

Most books were produced after being submitted to a publisher, over half to two-thirds of which were Canadian. (See Appendix C for further information on publishing and support of authors.) Virtually all other publishers were British or American (Doyle 1990). If a book proved successful, the publisher urged the author to write more books. Sometimes authors raised money by subscription, asking future buyers to give their money before publication to ensure there was no financial loss on their book. Others paid for the printing of their books themselves.

Most women lacked financial support for their writing, but some benefitted by scholarships for research, by government encouragement and by competitions. Publication was underwritten in some cases by commercial concerns, by governments, by interest groups, and by local committees (see Appendix C).

Perspective

Many authors wrote about the status of women, or women as individuals (in biographies and autobiographies) or groups of women as mentioned earlier, which is one reason why their books are so important; if they had not been written, we would know far less about women than we now do. Many authors also mentioned explicitly that they were writing from a woman's point of view, or with a female audience in mind.

The women writers in this compendium shared with Canadians in general the task of positioning Canada in the North Atlantic triangle of Canada, the United States and Britain, the three countries in which virtually all the books were published. They too had to make sense of a history that oriented Canada to Europe, but a geography that connected her to the United States. The imperialist tradition was upheld by both British and

Canadian women. Those who were British included Lady Hardy (1881), who praised the loyalty of Canadians to the monarchy; Eda Green (1915), who wrote, "Let us never forget that the soul of Imperialism is the religion of Jesus Christ"; Bessie Pullen-Burry (1912), who described herself as "first an Imperialist, then a traveller"; and Evelyn Springett (1937), who married a Canadian but revered her forebears who belonged "to that upper middle class of England which, with its fine manners, sound morals, loyalty and energy, has done so much to maintain and extend the Empire."

Other women who favoured imperialism were Canadian. Agnes Machar (1913) stated that the British Empire was so great that it had a divine purpose. Edith Marsh (1923) writes that "So long as her people are loyal to the good old Union Jack and true to the highest aims of life will the Canadian West be a great and glorious part of the Empire that girdles the Globe." Mabel Clint (1934) believed that Canada should remain secondary to the Empire, while Vivian Hill (1940) was equally keen on the British Empire.

Needless to say, those who emphasized America as Canada's closest ally were often Americans. They were visitors to Canada, especially Quebec, and authors who wrote books to explain Canada to the Americans, such as Agnes Laut (1909, 1915, 1921), Louisa Peat (1945), Leila Harris (1939), Anne Peck (1943), Dorothy Duncan (1941), who married Hugh MacLennan the novelist and Mary Bonner (1943), who stated that Canada "is such a vast and sparsely settled country, that each section knows only its own songs." However, Canadian-born Mary Alloway (1899) was also keen on the United States, arguing surprisingly that "the early histories of Canada and the United States are so closely connected that they may be considered identical." By aiming at two national markets, authors surely hoped for increased sales of their books.

Other writers were more nationalistic, putting Canada first. In the 1860s, Catherine Day strongly urged the need of a national literature to strengthen the country, while Catharine Parr Traill and her niece, out of patriotic pride, arranged to have their book on wildflowers published in Canada, even though the quality of the work might prove inferior. Because of patriotism, Mary Anne FitzGibbon also had her 1894 biography published in Canada. About that time, and for the next thirty years, many of the books reviewed for this compendium used American spelling ("honor") even when published in Canada. British spelling ("honour") became more common with the increasing importance after the First World War of the Ryerson Press, which focused on Canadian history and Canadian content (Campbell 1995). Nationalism in general became widespread in Canada during the 1920s (Creighton 1958, 454 ff). Between the world wars,

Donalda Dickie commented on the lack of Canadian books for children, a gap that she helped fill with her own books.

Racial Perspective

Many authors commented upon Native peoples living in Canada, some assuming the negative stereotypes common at their time (Charlotte Bompas, 1886; Lady Hardy, 1881; Maria Lawson, 1906; Bertha Price, 1923; Donalda Dickie, 1925; Isabel Mackay 1930). Others such as Emily Carr were far more positive, although a recent controversy has surfaced over whether Carr should be accused of voice and cultural appropriation. (For competing views see Crosby 1991 and Fulford 1993.) Charlotte Bompas (1886), as well as Edith Marsh (1923), noted how much better adapted to the north woods Indians were compared with Europeans, and Maude Abbott (1931) approved some Indian medical practices. Only two Native women spoke for themselves in publishing books—Pauline Johnson and Anahareo. A number of women wrote about Native legends, but they did so usually from a white perspective. Margaret Bemister, for example, thanks five men for their help with her book of legends, but only one has a stated Native connection. Mabel Burkholder writes that she included only "attractive and important legends," and omitted those which were meaningless. "Some are foolish and unimportant, merely relating the pranks of animals. Not a few are repulsive, bestial, hideous."

Authors often treated indigenous Native peoples and non-Western peoples more generally in a dismissive and condescending way. Missionaries by definition had to believe at a minimum in the moral and religious inferiority of those they tried to convert to Christianity. Minna Forsyth Grant (1888) was explicit about work in Hawaii, referring to "the noble efforts of missionaries to civilize and christianize a savage and voluptuous race." Pejorative comments about blacks (Lady A. Murray 1856) and Chinese men (Jessie Saxby 1890) indicate the ethnocentric assumptions that run through many of the works of this early period.

Some writers commented on "the nation-building" problem they detected in the diverse ethnic backgrounds of a population with two founding races (Aboriginal peoples were not considered as such) that was constantly fed by waves of immigrants from various other European nations. Catherine Day (1867) was for a Canadian literature in part because it would bind Canadians of all races together. Agnes Machar (1893) urged that Norman, Saxon and Celt merge together as Canadians, perhaps because of what Nellie Spence referred to in 1897 as the current "absurdly strong" racial prejudice against French-Canadians. Georgina Binnie-Clark, writing in 1910 and 1914, noted that British people such as herself were then unpopular on the prairies. A fairly standard position was taken by the president of the Royal Society of Canada in a foreword to Kate Foster's 1926 book: he stated that the general consensus was that only readily assimilable races should be admitted to Canada, namely people of Anglo-Saxon, Teutonic, Scandinavian and northern Celtic stock.

Crystal Ball

To end this commentary, it is interesting to consider observations in these books from the perspective of today. Some have turned out to be wildly wrong. Jean McIlwraith wrote in 1899 that "the time is at hand when French and English will remember only that they are Canadians, will glory alike in the deeds that the ancestors of either tongue have done upon this continent." Lilian Hendrie believed in 1915 that Canada's future was "indissolubly bound up with that of the British Empire." Donalda Dickie wrote in 1925 that after the battle of 1759, the new Quebec and the British joined hands, together "inheriting the glory of the past and looking courageously toward the unknown future." Annie Stephenson and Sara Vance (1929) expect that the church will eliminate racism in Canada. Marion Royce (1945) looks forward to a time when men and women will be fully equal, which now seems beyond hope, given the increasing feminization of poverty worldwide.

Other observations have been shrewdly correct. As a minor example, Lillian Barker, writing in 1941, predicted that the Dionne quintuplets would have problems settling in with their other siblings, which is what happened. Other writers, such as Mary Alloway (1899), Hazel Boswell (1938), Sister Helen Morrissey (1940) and Sophy Elliott (1941), emphasized the importance of Quebec and its history to Canada. Jane Turnbull argued that by 1938 Quebec poets had already developed a unique literature through "one absorbing purpose . . . namely, the creation as well as the preservation of a national consciousness." Hilda Neatby (1937) and Elizabeth Armstrong (1937) were both cognizant of Quebec's importance when they wrote their doctoral theses on Quebec topics. Still other comments in books give the reader the sensation of déjà vu. Elizabeth Frame aimed her 1864 book at the youth of Nova Scotia, in the hope of persuading them of the value of their province so that they would not leave home. Lady Amelia Murray noted in 1856 the bizarre circumstance whereby the parliament of the United Province of Canada was bilingual, but many of the members were unilingual. Mabel Ringland, who was an advisor to the T. Eaton Company between the wars, complained because the advertising industry treated women as "morons" and did not take their complaints seriously. And Quebec and its concerns, then as now, was the subject of a large number of books.

I began this work believing, in keeping with the private/public sphere dichotomy for the sexes apparently in place in early middle-class Canada, that there would be few women writing non-fiction, setting themselves up as voices of authority, especially before the First World War. As this compendium shows, this was not true. In fact, women were writing non-fiction books in great numbers. There were social constraints against women in public life, but as we have seen, hundreds of women found ways to evade them. Although many writers focused on subject matter in the women's domain, a surprising number discussed "big" issues such as war, nationalism, imperialism, women's status and Quebec. The extent of this focus is impressive, given that women did not get the vote until 1918, and by 1945, the end date for this study, only a few women had been elected to federal and provincial legislatures.

Abbott, Maude Elizabeth Seymour Babin BA MD CM LLD 1869-1940. Maude Abbott was born at St Andrews East, Quebec, and with her sister, raised by her grandmother after her father's desertion and her mother's death. The grandmother had their name changed to hers, Abbott, by an Act of Parliament; it was a prestigious name carried by their cousin who would be prime minister of Canada (1891-92). Abbott was educated by a governess and, when she was fifteen, at a private school in Montreal. In 1890, after she earned a BA and gold medal at McGill University (where she formed a lifelong friendship with classmate and later professor **Carrie Derick**), she applied to medical school at McGill University, but was refused admission because she was a woman. Instead, she studied to be a doctor at Bishop's College, graduating in 1894 with high honours. She then studied for three years abroad. Despite its repudiation of her earlier, she worked at McGill for most of the rest of her life, in 1910 and 1936 being given honorary degrees there. Although eventually world famous, she was never promoted above assistant professor; she used her small salary to support not only herself but her mentally ill sister who needed two full-time helpers. She was founder of the McGill Medical Museum, an expert on congenital heart disease, and author of over 140 scientific papers. She co-founded (with **Dr Helen MacMurchy**) and was the first president of the Canadian Federation of Medical Women, and one of the first sixteen people to be inducted into the Canadian Science and Engineering Hall of Fame.

Abbott's *An Historical Sketch of the Medical Faculty of McGill University* meticulously documents the story of the various medical buildings and ends with nineteen appendices. One appendix deals with The Female Benevolent Society, which announced that Montreal women formed this group in 1816 "for relieving indigent women with small children, the sick, the aged and the infirm." She notes that by 1819 the society was looking after "the convalescents whom the physicians are often obliged to dismiss before their perfect recovery, in order to make more room for more pressing cases," a statement that echoes in our own times.

Florence Nightingale is dedicated "To those noble women who have followed in the footsteps of Miss Nightingale, and have thereby raised the profession of Nursing to the high place it now occupies, and who maintain it therein above the dust of commercialism." The book was adapted from an address on Nightingale (1820-1910) delivered to the Harvard Historical Club in 1915 and centring around pictures of the subject. Abbott emphasizes the importance of Nightingale's work not only during the Crimean War but afterward, when extensive military reforms were largely initiated and directed under her efficient influence. These reforms focused on hygiene in the British army, sanitary science both in the East and West, hospital construction, and the "gentle art of nursing." Abbott herself sold a thousand copies of her book, donating the proceeds to the Canadian Red Cross.

History of Medicine in the Province of Quebec, Abbott's study of medical education in Quebec, was based on her research at the Dominion Archives and elsewhere on behalf of the Montreal General Hospital and McGill University. She begins the work with a discussion of early Indian medicine, noting that "As in all savage nations their efforts to combat disease and death were not confined to the use of natural remedies, in which they had considerable skill, but constituted an integral part of their religious practice, being inextricably interwoven with their ideas of the supernatural."

Bibliography
- Waugh, Douglas. 1992. *Maudie of McGill*. Toronto: Dundurn Press.
- Abbott, Maude E., BA, MD. 1902. *An Historical Sketch of the Medical Faculty of McGill University*. Montreal: Gazette, 111 pp.
- Abbott, Maude E. Seymour, BA, MD. 1916. *Florence Nightingale as Seen in Her Portraits with a Sketch of Her Life, and an Account of Her Relation to the Origin of the Red Cross Society*. Boston: n.p., 78 pp.
- Abbott, Maude E., BA, MD. 1931. *History of Medicine in the Province of Quebec*. Montreal: McGill University, 97 pp.

Aberdeen and Temair, Ishbel Maria Marjoribanks Gordon, Marchioness of LLD 1857-1939.   Ishbel Maria Marjoribanks (pronounced Marchbanks) was born in London, the daughter of politically active and very wealthy parents. In 1877 she married the Earl of Aberdeen, with whom she would have five children. She accompanied him to Canada for two visits shortly before he became Governor General of Canada from 1893 to 1898. On the first, taken in part to visit women for whom she had helped arrange immigration to Canada, she met **Annie Macpherson**, who similarly looked after child immigrants. Lady Aberdeen would be of great importance to women in Canada, founding a Canadian branch of the National Council of Women because she believed that women were potentially an enormous but underutilized resource for their pioneering country. As an aristocrat with democratic ideals, she did what she could to undermine the racial and religious bigotry of the 1890s, but her efforts were disparaged by the local establishment, which resisted change. She urged the initial collection of books by women that is now housed as the Lady Aberdeen Collection in the University of Waterloo library. She was awarded an LLD by Queen's University in 1897, the first time a woman had been so honoured in Canada.

Lady Aberdeen's *Through Canada with a Kodak* is a chatty account of her 1890 and 1891 trips across the country written for the magazine of the

Onward and Upward Association of Great Britain, which she had earlier founded for the promotion of women's more sisterly interest in each other, especially between women and their household help. She writes about the trips:

> They are merely the passing and superficial notes of a traveller journeying rapidly through the country, and desirous of conveying some impressions of the rich and varied attractions presented by "the Dominion," and which appear to be but very imperfectly realised by those at home, whether by the holiday seeker or the intending settler.

She demurs that her sketches and photographic views "appear to her to be scarcely worthy of being thus collected in the form of a volume. As, however, both publisher and many kind readers of these jottings in their previous form have desired to see them thus gathered together, their wishes have been deferred to." The public demand for her book was great, with three editions appearing in its first seven years. It stimulated both interest in Canada and in amateur photography, which was in its infancy; the first simple camera backed up by commercial processing of film was sold by Eastman in 1889.

Despite fierce opposition from the medical establishment, to commemorate Queen Victoria's diamond jubilee Lady Aberdeen founded the Victorian Order of Nurses in 1897 and wrote a book about its early work: *What Is the Use of the Victorian Order of Nurses?* During her trip across Canada she had noted the lack of medical care for the poor in much of the country, and realized the need for practical nursing help.

Together, long after they had returned from Canada to Britain, Lady Aberdeen and her husband wrote *We Twa*, an account of their reminiscences which includes a large section on their Canadian experiences.

Bibliography
•French, Doris. 1988. *Ishbel and the Empire: A Biography of Lady Aberdeen.* Toronto: Dundurn Press, 346 pp.
•Aberdeen, Countess of. 1994 [1893]. *Through Canada with a Kodak.* Toronto: University of Toronto Press, 285 pp. Introduction by Marjory Harper.
•_____. 1900. *What Is the Use of the Victorian Order of Nurses?* Ottawa: Mortimer, 73 pp.
•Aberdeen, Lord and Lady. 1925. *"We Twa": Reminiscences of Lord and Lady Aberdeen.* London: Collins, 2 vols, 358 and 353 pp.

Aberdein, Jennie Watson BA 1896-? Jennie Aberdein was a British scholar who studied at the University of Aberdeen.

Aberdein wrote the biography *John Galt* because she felt Galt (1779-1839) received too little credit for his accomplishments, which included helping British immigrants settle in Canada. She carried out her research in archives and libraries in Scotland, England and Canada, supported financially by the Carnegie Trust which generously guaranteed a sum of seventy-five pounds against possible loss on the sale of her book.

Bibliography

• Aberdein, Jennie W. 1936. *John Galt*. London: Oxford University Press, 209 pp.

Abraham, Dorothy E. 1894-? Dorothy Abraham came from England to Vancouver Island as a war bride to homestead after the First World War.

Lone Cone describes in entertaining narrative style Abraham's eleven years first farming on Vargas Island, and then near Tofino and Lone Cone Mountain, an extinct volcano whose name she used for her book's title. *Lone Cone* was so popular that it went into four editions by 1952. She and her husband later moved to Victoria, where she wrote a book entitled *Romantic Vancouver Island*, which was popular enough to have a fourth edition in 1964.

Bibliography

• Abraham, Dorothy. 1945. *Lone Cone: A Journal of Life on the West Coast of Vancouver Island, B.C.* Vancouver: private, 100 pp.

Adair, Mary. Mary Adair was a scholar of English literature.

Adair's book *Short Story Studies*, formulated to interest teachers in Canada and the United States about literature, focuses on story-telling: "The Story belongs to all nations and to all crafts, inspires Architect, Potter, Sculptor, Painter, Poet Musician, Actor Priest, and no other appeal can so successfully lure the child from play, youth from the open road, maturity from the pursuit of wealth, and age from the fireside." It includes stories and poems for children of all ages as well as discussions on humour, national celebrations, folk lore, mythology, fables and allegories.

Bibliography

• Adair, Mary. 1930. *Short Story Studies in Short Story Classics—Story-Telling, and Appreciation*. Boston: Gorham Press, 344 pp.

Albani, Dame Emma OBE 1847-1930 (Mme Marie Louise Emma Cécile Lajeunesse Gye). Dame Emma Albani from Chambly, Quebec, was Canada's first international celebrity, and one of the most famous operatic sopranos of the last century. She was raised in a musical family that moved when she was fifteen to Albany, New York (a name later reflected in her stage name). Seven years after her operatic debut in Italy in 1870, she had one of her greatest triumphs at a Handel Festival, where over 22,000 people at the Crystal Palace heard her sing in the *Messiah*. She later sang at Queen Victoria's funeral. Sadly, some of her last years in London after her husband's death were spent teaching music to make ends meet.

Albani's autobiography *Forty Year of Song* (in which her birth date is given as 1852 rather than 1847) was published in 1911, the year she retired. She introduces it: "After forty years before the Public, it is thirty nine years since I made my debut in England at Covent Garden Theatre, and after having sung in nearly every country in the world, I venture to offer an account of my career hoping that my many friends may find it interesting."

Bibliography

•MacDonald, Cheryl. 1984. *Emma Albani, Victorian Diva*. Toronto: Dundurn Press, 205 pp.
•Albani, Emma. 1977 [1911]. *Forty Years of Song*. New York: Arno Press, 285 pp.

Allan, Maud Durrant 1880-1956. Maud Durrant was born in Toronto, the daughter of two doctors, but grew up largely in California, where her brother would later be executed for murdering two young women. She studied music, art and literature in Berlin before deciding to give public performances from 1903 to 1936 as a barefoot dancer. She was noted for the gauzy draperies she wore while dancing *Salome*, and for performing for King Edward in 1907. In her prime, Allan attracted a larger audience than her contemporary, Isadora Duncan. During the Battle of Britain when Allan was in her sixties, she drove an ambulance in England, then returned to California in 1941 to continue war work.

Allan's autobiography, *My Life and Dancing*, focuses on her early life in dance; she did not favour ballet, which she considered artificial and constrained, but free-flowing movements from the heart. She was against votes for women, stating that "men have in the past, step by step, removed many obstacles that have stood in the way of woman's freedom. Our condition has changed immeasurably for the better, as witness the educational question on which my heart is set. Much yet remains to be done, and men will do it" (p. 119).

Bibliography

•Cherniavsky, Felix. 1991. *The Salome Dancer: The Life and Times of Maud Allan*. Toronto: McClelland and Stewart, 308 pp.
•Allan, Maud. 1908. *My Life and Dancing*. London: Everett, 128 pp.

Allison, Susan Louisa Moir 1845-1937. Susan Moir came with her family from Britain to settle near Hope, British Columbia, when she was fifteen. On her marriage to a miner and rancher in 1868, she moved with him to the Similkameen area near Princeton and later to the Okanagan Valley, running their home and bearing fourteen children, who all lived to maturity. When her children no longer needed her attention, she began to write stories about her life and about the local Natives. When she was eighty, Allison began spending the winters in Vancouver with her daughter before moving there permanently.

On hearing of her pioneering early life, the editor of the magazine section of the *Vancouver Daily Province* urged Allison to write her memoirs, which she agreed to do; they appeared in thirteen issues of this magazine in 1931, and were collected in book form as *A Pioneer Gentlewoman in British Columbia.*

Bibliography

• Allison, Susan. 1976 [1931]. *A Pioneer Gentlewoman in British Columbia: The Recollections of Susan Allison.* Edited by Margaret A. Ormsby. Vancouver: University of British Columbia Press, 144 pp.

Alloway, Mary H. Wilson 1848-1919. Mary Wilson, of Irish descent, was born and educated in Montreal, where in 1877 she married a veterinary surgeon, Dr Clement Alloway. She was well-known for her fiction, including her novel *Crossed Swords: A Canadian-American Tale of Love and Valor* (1912).

Besides historical fiction and articles, Alloway wrote a book of Canadian history, *Famous Firesides.* She states in its preface: "In offering this little volume [217 pp.!] to the kind consideration of Canadian and American readers, it is the earnest wish of the Author that it may commend itself to the interest of both, as the early histories of Canada and the United States are so closely connected that they may be considered identical." She ends her book: "What nation can boast of a purer or more glorious origin? May the future of Canada be worthy of its noble past."

Bibliography

• Alloway, Mary Wilson. 1899. *Famous Firesides of French Canada.* Montreal: Lovell, 217 pp.

Anahareo (Gertrude Bernard) 1906-1986. Anahareo, one of Canada's few early Native authors, was born in Mattawa, Ontario, her Iroquois father "a trapper, guide, carpenter, logger and river driver." She met Grey Owl in Temagami, Ontario, when she was eighteen. He appeared to be an aboriginal man, and although eighteen years her senior, she joined him in northern Quebec the following year, the beginning of a ten-year marriage. She swore off trapping in 1928 when she encountered a starving lynx trapped by one leg who in anguish had gnawed its flesh to the bone. In 1932, she and Grey Owl moved as caretakers to Prince Albert National Park in Saskatchewan, where their daughter Shirley Dawn was born. They all lived in a small shack with an active beaver lodge in the living room. After Grey Owl's death in 1938 following several exhausting lecture tours in Britain, she married Count Eric Moltke Huitfeldt of Sweden. In 1979, the League of Animal Rights based in Paris awarded her the Order of Nature. She died near Kamloops at eighty years of age.

Her autobiography *Devil in Deerskins* tells the story of their ten years together in the bush. Anahareo is especially important because she persuaded Grey Owl, who was actually an Englishman named Archie Belaney, to abandon trapping and killing of animals and instead work for their preservation. He did this by writing several best-selling books about nature and beavers. She, Grey Owl and their daughter are buried near the cabin they lived in with their beavers.

Bibliography
- Anahareo. 1972 [1940]. *Devil in Deerskins: My Life with Grey Owl*. Toronto: New Press, 190 pp.

Angus, Marion Isabel Hand 1902-1951. Marion Angus was primarily a poet, but also wrote one misogynist book, really a long essay.

Woman Unveiled is depressing because it is so stereotypical. We learn that "Fundamentally, women are the prey of their emotions" (p. 33), and that the feminine mind is "peculiar" with "illogical workings" (p. 67). She presents historical and anecdotal evidence to show that their right to vote has done little for the world: "Have they gained a living wage for all industrial workers, regardless of sex, age or color? Have they eradicated disease and social evils? Have they entirely wiped out the possibility of war, either internal or external?" she asks. Obviously, the answer is no. Although women have more rights and freedoms than they had in the past, she believes that these have not made them happy. "Woman has acquired all the rights of men, but in doing so, she has lost all the delightful feminine privileges and prerogatives that have been hers for centuries."

Bibliography
- Angus, Marion Isabel. 1932. *Woman Unveiled*. Vancouver: Vancouver Bindery, 95 pp.

Angus, Mary Edith Dunckley 1850-1936. Mary Dunckley was born and educated in Manchester, the daughter of a minister and his wife. She visited Germany to learn German, and tutored students before marrying William Angus when she was thirty. They moved to Canada in 1883, settling in Victoria where she gave birth to their son Henry in 1891, the year before her husband died; from then on her life revolved around Henry as well as tutoring students and writing articles. She took him to Europe for a lengthy tour, moved to Montreal when he attended McGill University, and moved again to England while he studied at Oxford University to become a lawyer.

After her son's service in the First World War, she settled with him and his family in Vancouver.

Diary of M.E. Angus 1914-1918, dedicated to her grandson and his generation, describes the war years which Angus spent in London, beginning with the enlistment of her son. She recounts mainly her volunteer work and other incidents in wartime Britain, but also notes Canadian accomplishments in the war and food parcels received from Montreal.

Chapters of Life, which notes that it was intended for private circulation only, is Angus's autobiography, discussing in detail the information supplied above.

Bibliography

•Angus, M.E. 1926. *Diary of M.E. Angus 1914-1918*. Vancouver: private, 73 pp.
•_____. 1929. *Chapters of Life: An Autobiography*. N.p.: private, 320 pp.

Archibald, Edith Jessie Mortimer 1854-1936. Edith Archibald was born in St John's, Newfoundland, to the then Attorney General and his wife. She was educated in New York and London before marriage at sixteen to her cousin, an engineer, with the same last name. They settled in Halifax where she raised a family and worked for the national and provincial Woman's Christian Temperance Union, the national and local Council of Women, the Halifax Victorian Order of Nurses, the Ladies' Musical Club and the Nova Scotia Red Cross. She helped to bring relief to the wives and children of men serving in the Boer War and to organize local support for sick, delinquent and feeble-minded children. Later in life she wrote several novels, including *The Token: A Tale of Cape Breton* (1930).

As the youngest daughter and sole survivor of her birth family, Archibald inherited the extensive papers of her father, Sir Edward Mortimer Archibald (1810-84); he had grown up in Nova Scotia, the son of a provincial politician, and played an important role in public service and international politics, working to prevent a more democratic government. (He felt that well-to-do men knew what was best for the common people.) Archibald was urged by her father's friends to prepare his papers for publication, but as a busy woman "much occupied with many outside interests besides the care of a growing family," she deferred the task until she had more leisure time. *Life and Letters of Sir Edward Mortimer Archibald* was finally published when she was seventy, long after his death.

Bibliography

•Archibald, Edith J. by his daughter. 1924. *Life and Letters of Sir Edward Mortimer Archibald KCMG, CB*. Toronto: Morang, 266 pp.

Archibald, Mabel Evangeline BA MA 1871-1955. Mabel Archibald, the daughter of a minister and his wife, belonged to a distinguished Baptist extended family with members in the mission field in India, where she herself would spend thirty-five years of her life. She graduated from Acadia University in 1895, received a master's degree, and travelled to India in 1897 to minister to the Telugus, most notably establishing evangelistic schools for Indian girls and boys.

Glimpses and Gleams of India and Bolivia comprises Archibald's information on India and Louise May Mitchell's short section on Bolivian missions (where she and her husband worked as missionaries for seventeen years). In her larger section of this book, Archibald discusses in detail twenty-one Canadian Baptist mission fields in India, including those of pioneering fellow-authors **K.S. McLaurin**, **Flora Clarke** and **Matilda Churchill**, written in her "characteristically racy and attractive style." For each field she gives a cheerful introduction to appeal to Canadian children ("Vuyyuru–Well, that is a queer name! Say, how do you pronounce it? Wee-your-ou," etc.) followed by a description of the place and of the mission work done there in the past and the present. She describes the activities of Canadian missionaries (such as those mentioned above), and lauds their accomplishments for Indian people in the areas of health, education and Christianity. Chapters, called "Lessons," end with review questions, poems and/or prayers. This book was so popular that is sold three thousand copies in three months.

Archibald revised and enlarged somewhat the India part of this book (while at the Missionary Rest Home in Toronto and en route from London to Bombay) to produce *Glimpses and Gleams of Our Own India*, published nine years later. Like its predecessor, it was aimed especially at children belonging to missionary societies, guilds and bands, and urges readers to give money for overseas missions or to become missionaries themselves.

Bibliography
•Archibald, Mabel Evangeline MA and Mrs Louise May Mitchell. 1923. *Glimpses and Gleams of India and Bolivia: The Jubilee Book for Mission Bands*. Toronto: Baptist Women's Missionary Societies of Canada.
•Archibald, Mabel Evangeline MA. 1932. *Glimpses and Gleams of Our Own India*. Kentville, Nova Scotia: United Baptist Women's Missionary Union of the Maritime Provinces, 272 pp.

Armstrong, Elizabeth Howard BA PhD 1898-? Elizabeth Armstrong was an American scholar who obtained her PhD in history from Columbia University. She studied under the prominent Canadian professor J.B. Brebner, who moved to Columbia University from the University of Toronto in 1925.

Armstrong's scholarly book *The Crisis of Quebec 1914-18* is adapted from her PhD thesis. It discusses in a perspective sympathetic to the French the change of French Canadians from a pro-war faction in 1914 to an anti-war faction by the war's end. This period also saw the rise of French-Canadian "nationalism." Her research was largely undertaken in Ottawa and in the province of Quebec.

Bibliography

• Armstrong, Elizabeth H. 1937. *The Crisis of Quebec 1914-18*. Toronto: McClelland and Stewart, 270 pp.

Arndt, Ruth Spence See Spence, Ruth.

Arnold, Mary Ellicott. Career woman Mary Arnold, who had studied co-operative projects in Europe and America, became in 1919 the treasurer and general manager of Consumers' Co-operative Services in New York and in 1922 the treasurer and a director of The Cooperative League of the United States. She was involved in building and managing co-op apartments in New York City. In 1937, Arnold came to Cape Breton to acquaint herself with the Adult Education Program that had been started in 1929 by St Francis Xavier University in Antigonish. The program had promoted co-operative stores and credit unions to improve the life of local people. A group of miners in Cape Breton had decided to study co-operative housing and then to build their own homes. She remained in Canada to oversee this project, which was named after Dr J.J. Tompkins, a popular parish priest at Reserve Mines.

Arnold describes in *The Story of Tompkinsville* how this community came into being, and offers information on other possible housing projects. When her book was written, ten houses had been completed by the miners and more buildings were planned, showing what could be accomplished by co-operative effort.

Bibliography

• Arnold, Mary Ellicott. 1940. *The Story of Tompkinsville*. New York: The Cooperative League, 102 pp.

Averill, Esther Holden BA 1902-1992. Esther Averill was born in Connecticut to an engineer and his wife. After graduating from Vassar College in 1923, she became a magazine editor in women's fashion, then moved to Paris for ten years to work in the same field. She founded Domina Press, which published a number of her books, many of them which she illustrated herself. When she returned to the United States, she worked in the children's section of the New York Public Library.

Averill's well-illustrated children's book *The Voyages of Jacques Cartier* contains quotations and descriptions of events taken from the logbook records of Jacques Cartier and from other historical documents, although she also includes imaginary conversations that might have taken place during his explorations. She ends her work by supporting his reputation, which had been unfairly discredited: "When the 'gold and diamonds' [he brought back from Canada] were tested in France, they proved to be copper and mica. A saying sprang into usage: 'False as a diamond of Canada,' and the laughter and mockery that followed brought Cartier's career as an explorer to an end."

Bibliography
• Averill, Esther. 1937. *The Voyages of Jacques Cartier Retold by Esther Averill*. New York: Domina Press, 95 pp.

Awdry, Frances See Green, Eda entry.

Ayre, Agnes Marian Miller 1890-? Agnes Ayre was a botanist who lived in Newfoundland. She worked closely with a university professor who helped her with the scientific names of the plants in which she was interested.

Ayre's small-format *Wild Flowers of Newfoundland* devotes one page to each species (or to closely related species) of the groups named in the title, as well as to a few well-known introduced plants. For each it gives common and scientific names, a brief description, a short note on habitat and distribution and a little black-and-white drawing; only forty words per page were allowed, so information was omitted on locality and on who discovered which plants when, a strange exclusion when each page contains unused space. Four similar books were planned to deal with the other Newfoundland groups of wild flowers.

Bibliography
• Ayre, A.M. 1935. *Wild Flowers of Newfoundland, Mainly Orchis–Willow–Buttercup–Mustard–Rose*. Part III. St John's, NF: private, 231 pp.

Baldwin, Alice Sharples See Sharples, Alice entry.

Ball, Geraldine F. The author grew up in England in a well-to-do family of eight children. She married in 1884, but had little authority in the marriage where she and her husband lived with his sisters. When her husband decided about 1888 that they should emigrate to Canada, she was forced, not wanting to "rock the boat," to leave her new baby behind to keep one of his sisters happy, and to take a second sister with them because she was "weak-minded." They homesteaded near Grenfell in southern Saskatchewan where her husband's brother lived.

Some Extracts and Reminiscences of a Lifetime, dedicated by Geraldine Ball to her children, is a series of stories about her life, told with much conversation. It begins with her and her brother playing on a beach in Cornwall, England; they have their shoes stolen by a woman who then comes to their house for a reward for returning the shoes, which she is denied by their lawyer father. After the author married and moved into her husband's family, she "realized when too late that I am simply nowhere and nobody in the house" (p. 125), with nothing to do day after day. Her boredom was assuaged when she was able to establish her own family home in Canada. The book ends in 1919 when her other children were grown and ready to marry and have families of their own.

Bibliography

•Ball, Geraldine F. 1922. *Some Extracts and Reminiscences of a Lifetime*. Regina: Leader Publishing, 165 pp. Printed for private circulation.

Barker, Lillian. Lillian Barker was a bilingual American reporter from New York who sided with Oliva and Elzire Dionne's point of view in the controversy over their family—that their quintuplets should not be housed in their own hospital, tended by nurses although they were not sick, and raised separately from the rest of the Dionne children.

Barker's book *The Quints Have a Family*, published when the Dionne quintuplets were seven, begins with an account of their day of First Communion. The other twenty-one chapters discuss the five sisters individually and from the perspective of their history, their family and the world. There is emphasis on the division of the Dionne children between the quints and the other brothers and sisters. The last chapter, "What does the future hold?" considers whether all the Dionnes will finally be reunited in one house and whether it may be too late for the family to be fully integrated; this proved to be the case, as the three surviving quintuplets describe in their 1995 book *Family Secrets*.

Bibliography

•Soucy, Jean-Yves, with Annette, Cécile and Yvonne Dionne. 1995. *Family Secrets*. Toronto: Stoddart.
•Barker, Lillian. 1941. *The Quints Have a Family*. New York: Sheed and Ward, 199 pp.

Barwick, E. Buller 1882-? E. Buller Barwick was an author interested in inventions.

Barwick notes in the introduction to *Man's Genius* that she has gathered information from every available source (largely books and encyclopedias) and has written it "in a spirit of absolute impartiality. The inventions have been arranged in order of date, making a continued story of the march of progress in the past two centuries till, in 1932, we find ourselves accepting, as a matter of course, the miracles of this scientific age." Each readable chapter is devoted to an invention, starting with James Watt's steam engine and ending (chap. 23) with aviation. Barwick's sex is not given away on the title page; her first name is indicated by an initial.

Bibliography
•Barwick, E. Buller. 1932. *Man's Genius: The Story of Famous Inventions and Their Development.* Toronto: Dent, 199 pp.

Baskine, Gertrude BA MA. Gertrude Baskine was a writer and social worker who, during the Second World War, lectured across Canada to encourage women's rights. Because of her interest in the north, she wanted to study the conditions of life in the Yukon and in Alaska so that she could write and lecture on the way men and women there had adapted to pioneering circumstances. She was the first woman to receive a military permit to travel along the Alaska Military Highway while it was still under construction.

In *Hitch-Hiking the Alaska Highway*, Baskine describes in detail her experiences of setting out from Edmonton and following the 1,630-mile route northwest until she reached Fairbanks. She then returned by air to Whitehorse and Edmonton.

Bibliography
•Baskine, Gertrude, MA, Fellow of RCGS. 1946 [1944]. *Hitch-Hiking the Alaska Highway.* Toronto: Macmillan, 317 pp.

Beaton, Maude Pettit Hill 1877-? After Maude Beaton's wealthy husband died, she decided to leave Toronto and travel around the world with her two grown daughters. Before the trip began, however, one daughter decided to marry instead and would soon produce her own daughter, Carolyn. Beaton therefore travelled with her other daughter.

Beaton wrote up their journey not only as articles, but as a book, *From Cairo to Khyber to Célebes*, which was addressed to her new granddaughter, Carolyn. The two women sailed by ship through the Suez Canal after visiting Egypt and the Holy Land, then drove their car in India from Bombay to the Khyber Pass. When her second daughter left her to be married in

New Zealand, taking the car (a Morris) with her, the enterprising Beaton carried on by herself or with shipboard friends, visiting Ceylon, Singapore, Borneo, Philippines, Hong Kong, China (for a long stay), Korea and Japan before returning to Canada. Shortly after this she sailed again to New Zealand to spend some months touring and helping her second daughter with the birth and care of her son.

Bibliography
•Beaton, Maude Hill. 1942. *From Cairo to Khyber to Célebes*. New York: Liveright Publishing, 261 pp.

Beaton, Muriel Elva 1914-? Muriel Beaton was born in Toronto to Kenneth and Mary Beaton the year they sailed as missionaries to West China, where she was raised. She married Rev. Frank G. Patterson and settled down with him in North Vancouver rather than remain in China, but she retained fond memories of this country.

Lanterns in the China Sky comprises true stories with pictures and much conversation "of Chinese boys and girls who have grown up in our West China Mission, where they learned to use their gifts to help others. They hold their lanterns high, to guide the feet of other travellers on the road of life." She writes in her Preface, "I hope that the Canadian boys and girls, as they meet these new Chinese friends, will enjoy their friendship as much as the author, who has had the privilege of living amongst them and now of writing about them." The chapters have upbeat titles such as "Duan Deh finds the royal road to learning," "From slave girl to teacher," and "Nurse Lin gave her free time." The children depicted continued as adults to serve the Church of Christ in China. Her father, Kenneth Beaton, also an author, was the Secretary of the Committee on Missionary Education, which co-published her book.

Bibliography
•Beaton, Muriel E. 1941. *Lanterns in the China Sky*. Toronto: Committee on Missionary Education/Woman's Missionary Society, 58 pp.

Beavan, Emily Elizabeth Shaw b. circa 1820. Emily Shaw was born in Belfast to a sea captain and his wife. As a young woman, she sailed with her father about 1836 to New Brunswick, probably to stay there with relatives; her name appears in school records, first as a pupil and then as a teacher. Two years later she married a surgeon and teacher, Frederick Beavan. She was well-known for her stories and poems, which were published in the monthly magazine *Amaranth* under her modest signature "Mrs B—n."

In 1843, Beavan and her husband returned to Ireland, where two years later she published *Sketches and Tales* about her stay in New Brunswick.

Her aim was to give prospective immigrants pertinent information about the province, which she was highly successful in doing.

> Not only is information presented more systematically and objectively in Mrs Beavan's book [than in other books such as *Roughing it in the Bush*], but it covers a much wider range of settlement life, extending to such areas as education, religion, the details of farming and lumbering operations and the reasons why they are so conducted, the significance of the timber trade, the consequences of the imposition of copyright regulations in British North America, the effect of the frontier upon speech patterns and of the climate upon women's skins. (Cogswell 1988)

Bibliography

•Cogswell, Fred. 1988. Emily Elizabeth Shaw (Beavan). *Dictionary of Canadian Biography*, s.v. Shaw, (Beavan), Emily Elizabeth.

Beavan, Emily. 1980 [1845]. *Sketches and Tales Illustrative of Life in the Backwoods of New Brunswick, North America*. St Stephen, NB: Print'n Press.

Beck, Lily Adams Moresby d. 1931. Lily Moresby was the daughter of Admiral John Moresby and granddaughter of Admiral of the Fleet Sir Fairfax Moresby; her grandfather had served under Admiral Nelson and her grandmother had known Lord Byron, both great men about whom Beck would write novels. She became enamoured of the Far East when her father was stationed there, visiting Japan, China, Egypt, Ceylon, Java, Burma, India and Tibet and investigating oriental languages and beliefs. In 1919 she settled in Victoria, British Columbia, where she began writing, first short stories and then thirty books, mostly novels such as *Exquisite Perdita* (1926), about the mistress of King George IV, but also some non-fiction. As well as her own name she used the pseudonyms E. Barrington and Louis Moresby. She continued travelling to the end of her life, dying in Kyoto, Japan, where she had been studying Zen Buddhism.

In *The Splendor of Asia*, Beck endeavoured "to make not only the story but the teaching of the Buddha intelligible and human, so that those who wish to understand one of the greatest facts in history may not find themselves entangled in the mazes of scholastic terms, and may perhaps be enabled to realize its strange coincidences with modern psychology and certain scientific verities." She emphasizes how important "knowledge of this high faith and philosophy is to leaven the materialism of the West." She consulted all available Scriptures for her book as well as Asian experts. She ends her preface: "I can scarcely hope to satisfy scholars and the general public. But if I succeed in interesting some of the latter, the former, will, I think, recognize that my aim was justified." This book was later reprinted as *The Life of the Buddha*.

Beck notes (in 1928 from Ceylon) that in writing *The Story of Oriental Philosophy* on the thought and thinkers of Asia, "my aim has been to convey what I have to tell in as clear and simple a manner as possible to readers unaccustomed to oriental modes of expression." She continues that in addition to "my personal knowledge of the countries, peoples, faiths and philosophies of which I write, I must acknowledge my sincere gratitude to the writers of the many books that I have consulted and to the many oriental friends with whom I have discussed these subjects." She ends her preface (almost as before), "If any scholars should look into this book I ask them to remember the enormous difficulty of clarifying Asiatic thought for the general reader. They will realize obstacles which none can know who have not faced them."

In the preface to *The Way of Power*, whose motto is "The Occult of Today Is the Science of Tomorrow," Beck acknowledges her debt to the great Indian thinkers of the past three millennia; her book seeks to clarify their writings, which use Sanskrit terms difficult to interpret. She describes experiments and knowledge "which led me to see the reality of the true occult world lying like an almost uncharted country behind the thick jungle of fraud and charlatanry." The book includes many anecdotes, initially involving herself, which led her to "vast conclusions" about the importance and pervasiveness of the occult.

When publisher Farrar and Rinehart decided in 1933 to publish a book on yoga, it found after much consultation that this could best be done by gathering together writings from Lily Beck. The first part of *A Beginner's Book of Yoga* considers early manifestations which led Beck on her lifelong search for truth and knowledge in the field of occult philosophers; the rest is not a series of instructions about yoga but rather metaphors about psychic ability and the power of concentration and meditation. With them one can "realize the possibilities of the soul in solitude and silence" and overcome dull minds and heavy hearts. She ends with a truth: "In India the wisest have never talked of good and evil. They have talked of knowledge and ignorance."

Bibliography

•Beck, L. Adams. 1926. *The Splendor of Asia: The Story and Teaching of the Buddha*. New York: Dodd, Mead, 269 pp.

•_____. 1928. *The Story of Oriental Philosophy*. New York: Cosmopolitan Book, 429 pp.

•_____. 1928. *The Way of Power: Studies in the Occult*. New York: Cosmopolitan Book, 285 pp.

•_____. 1937. *A Beginner's Book of Yoga, from the Writings of L. Adams Beck*. Edited by David Merrill Bramble. New York: Farrar and Rinehart, 229 pp.

Bell, Caroline 1928-? Caroline Bell was an English girl who came to Canada as one of the first refugees from wartime Britain.

Thank You Twice recounts Bell's experience of being plucked from wartime Britain and sent by ship to Canada where she had to fit into her new surroundings. I personally remember that her book caused a sensation among the families in Toronto who had taken in refugees, particularly where Bell described her negative feelings on being given a supportive kiss by one of these well-meaning and hard-working Canadian wives.

Bibliography
•Bell, Caroline. 1941. *Thank You Twice*. Toronto: Macleod, 112 pp.

Bell, Fannie Chandler. Fannie Bell was almost certainly a resident of Shediac, New Brunswick; her text mentions people called Bell who were perhaps relatives.

A History of Old Shediac describes the past and present of the small port of Shediac in four parts: The First English Settlers, Old Shediac, The Church of St-Martin-in-the-Wood and Ship Building.

Bibliography
•Bell, Fannie Chandler. 1937. *A History of Old Shediac, New Brunswick*. Moncton: National Print, 63 pp.

Bemister, Margaret 1877-? Margaret Bemister was an author living in Winnipeg who wrote fiction as well as non-fiction, for example, *The Arrow Sash: A Novel of New France for Young Adults* (1965), which was adapted from an earlier published short story.

Bemister writes that most of the Native stories in her book *Thirty Indian Legends of Canada* are drawn from their original sources, some printed for the first time, but others adapted from well-known authorities. She thanks five men for their assistance in writing her book, only one of whom has a stated Indian connection—Okanagan chief Antowyne.

Bibliography
•Bemister, Margaret. 1973 [1912]. *Thirty Indian Legends of Canada*. Vancouver: J.J. Douglas, 153 pp.

Bignell, Effie Molt 1855-1933. Effie Bignell was an American author.

Bignell's book *Saint Anne of the Mountains* recounts a visit she and a companion made to this village, a twenty-four-hour steamer journey down river from Quebec City. She describes village life and celebrations such as that of the fête of St John the Baptist, "Canada's patron."

Bibliography
•Bignell, Effie. 1912. *Saint Anne of the Mountains: The Story of a Summer in a Canadian Pilgrimage Village*. Boston: Richard G. Badger, 215 pp.

Bingham, Helen E. 1810-1906. Helen Bingham (maiden name unknown) was a religious Methodist woman who grew up in Thornhill, Ontario, and devoted herself to mission work. For a time, the subject of her book, Ann Preston, lived with her family as an old woman, so that Bingham became interested enough in her to write her biography.

Methodist "Holy Ann," the subject of *An Irish Saint*, was born in Ireland and attended school for one week before being sent home as unable to learn. She worked instead for a nearby family at domestic chores, herding cattle and cutting turf. When she was older she was called by God to follow Him, which she immediately did, often speaking against widespread drunkenness. She worked for a doctor's family with whom she emigrated to Thornhill when she was about twenty. She continued to wrestle with her sins, mainly her hot temper, and learned to read the Bible by herself (but continued to be unable to read anything else). She was known to confer openly with her heavenly father. For the rest of her life she performed many miracles, such as having a hen come unbidden to lay eggs daily for her when she was sick and, by her prayer, having a dry well in Thornhill yield water. She died in 1906 at the age of ninety-six.

Bingham comments in her preface on the difficulty of publishing a book in 1907: at first she had thought her manuscript would never be published because she had little money. When it was finally presented to the Methodist Book Room, the publisher said that his press never assumed any financial responsibility for a book by an unknown author. After reading the manuscript, however, he agreed not only to publish it but also to pay royalties. Subsequently the book went into at least nineteen printings in English as well as printings in Danish, Chinese and Spanish. Bingham thinks its popularity relates to its theme:

> For if God could take hold of this poor ignorant Irish servant girl and transform her life, and then send forth the aroma of its sanctity to cheer and bless the very ends of the earth, and strengthen the faith of his own children in all parts of the world, then there is no life that need go unused or unfruitful if yielded to Christ.

Bibliography
•Bingham, Helen E. 1927 [1907]. *An Irish Saint: The Life Story of Ann Preston Known also as "Holy Ann."* Toronto: Evangelical Publishers, 155 pp.

Binnie-Clark, Georgina 1871-1947. Georgina Binnie-Clark was born in Dorset, England, to moderately wealthy parents, worked as a journalist in Britain, then came to Saskatchewan in 1905 with her sister. Story (1967, 586) writes that Binnie-Clark's books are "self-revealing accounts by an upper-class Englishwoman who came to the West to visit her brother, found that he and a friend were failing because they despised labour, conquered her own hauteur sufficiently to learn from pioneers of humbler backgrounds, bought a farm, and managed it successfully."

Binnie-Clark's *A Summer on the Canadian Prairies* is a breezy narrative of Canadian farm life which tries not to be too obviously an attempt to encourage immigration; a fellow author she meets notes that "The book-market is fed up with Canada" from that perspective. Following its publication, she joined the Canadian Women's Press Club. She continued to run a farm, largely with paid help, for much of the rest of her life, aided after the early 1920s by her sister Ethel. Although Georgina returned to England about 1936 and died there, her sister remained in Saskatchewan until her death in 1955.

Wheat and Women is a more general book about the prairies. Binnie-Clark was interested in all aspects of Canada, so that it is full of social history with comments on political and economic events. She was disadvantaged by law because Canada gave free farms to single men, but not to "bachelor" women. She also had to compensate for her class status and her nationality, these being alien and unpopular to most prairie farmers. She and her sister both worked for a proposed Union Jack Farm Settlement for British emigrants under the suggested sponsorship of King George V, but this never materialized.

Bibliography
•Binnie-Clark, Georgina. 1910. *A Summer on the Canadian Prairies*. London: Arnold, 311 pp.
•_____. 1979 [1914]. *Wheat and Woman*. Toronto: University of Toronto Press, 313 pp.

Bird, Isabella Lucy 1831-1904. Isabella Bird, the daughter of an Anglican minister and a Sunday school teacher, was born in England and educated at home. When she was seventeen she herself became a Sunday school teacher, then six years later began her career as a popular travel writer when she visited a cousin in Prince Edward Island; her father gave her one hundred pounds to spend, stipulating that she not return home until it was gone, which enabled her to make a seven-month grand tour of Canada and the United States, arriving back in England with five pounds. This adventure so delighted her that she subsequently visited Australia, New Zealand, China, Japan, Korea, Malaya, India, the Middle East and

Tibet, and wrote books about most of them. When she was fifty, Bird married a physician, Dr John Bishop. After he died five years later, she studied nursing, and with the support of the Church Missionary Society, founded small hospitals in India and China in memory of him and of her parents. In 1893 she was elected to the Royal Geographical Society as its first woman fellow, reflecting her extensive world travels.

The Englishwoman in America, her first book, describes her adventures during four-and-a-half months travelling with relatives in the United States and Canada. It is based "on letters and notes written for the amusement of her friends at home." She hopes that "my readers may receive one hundredth part of the pleasure from the perusal of this volume which I experienced among the scenes and people of which it is too imperfect a record." Some of her royalties were given to poor Scottish fishermen she had seen during early holidays in Scotland.

Bibliography
•Bird, Isabella Lucy. 1966 [1856]. *The Englishwoman in America*. Toronto: University of Toronto Press, 497 pp.

Bishop, Lillian.   Lillian Bishop was a teacher in Connaught Practice School in Calgary.

Bishop, together with normal school teacher Joseph Scott, wrote *Our Story of Travel and Transport* for school children. It begins with a chapter on how Native peoples of Canada travelled from place to place before the arrival of Europeans, carries on with later travel on land and water (including chapters on ocean vessels, trains, buses, and cars), and ends with "To and Fro in Toronto." The date of publication (1941) is reflected in the text: "Some of our best motor highways . . . are so wide that there is room for two lines of automobiles to travel in each direction. On these highways cars must travel in lanes divided by lines that have been painted on the concrete" (p. 204). The authors also describe the R-100 "airship," or dirigible, packed nearly full of hydrogen bags, which visited Montreal in 1930. It was as long as "a train of an engine and seven cars." Inside was a large area with three floors; the crew of forty-three lived on the bottom floor, the passengers on the middle floor, while the top floor, with large windows, served as a promenade or dance area (p. 224).

Bibliography
•Scott, Joseph M. assisted by Lillian Bishop. 1941. *Our Story of Travel and Transport*. Toronto: Ryerson, 275 pp.

Black, Martha Louise Munger Purdy OBE 1866-1957. Martha Munger was born in Chicago and educated at St Mary's College in Indiana, where she relished elocution and botany. She married, but left her husband and three children after ten years to go with her brother in 1898 to the Klondike Gold Rush, travelling with thousands of others up the Chilkoot Pass from Skagway. Her home base became the Yukon, where she worked her own gold claim, managed a sawmill and in 1904 married lawyer George Black. During the First World War she and her husband worked for the war effort in Britain, where she was elected a Fellow of the Royal Geographical Society (London). Her husband represented the Yukon in the House of Commons for twenty-three years while she served as an Ottawa hostess; when he became unwell for a term, she was elected in 1935 in her own right as a Member of Parliament for Yukon. She was the second woman to sit in the House of Commons.

Black's *Yukon Wild Flowers* is a small field guide to common flowers of the Yukon, with one page devoted to each species, which has a photo (taken by her husband in black and white), a common and a scientific name and a short description. She provides personal comments such as who first showed her a plant, or how it tastes in a salad. She confesses that she is not a botanist, but certainly a lover of flowers. She and her husband published their book jointly "so that our friends and others may share with us some of the gorgeous glory of the myriads of Yukon wild flowers."

Black's 1938 "autobiography" *My Seventy Years* was ghostwritten by Elizabeth Bailey Price. Two decades later, it was edited and updated by Whitehorse journalist Florence Whyard, who was elected an MLA in Yukon in 1958 and became mayor of Whitehorse from 1981-83.

Bibliography
Martin, Carol. 1996. *Martha Black: Gold Rush Pioneer.* Vancouver: Douglas and McIntyre.
•Black, Mrs George, FRGS. 1936. *Yukon Wild Flowers.* Vancouver: Peate, Templeton Syndicate, 95 pp.
•_____. 1958 [1938]. *My Seventy Years.* London: Nelson, 317 pp.
•Black, Martha Louise. 1976. *My Ninety Years.* Edited and updated by Florence Whyard. Anchorage, AK: Alaska Northwest Publishing, 166 pp.

Blakey, Dorothy BA MA PhD 1899-? Dorothy Blakey attended the University of British Columbia, where she earned a BA and Governor General's Medal in 1921 and an MA in 1922; her PhD was awarded by the University of London in 1933. She became an associate professor of English at the University of British Columbia where she was well-known among students as author of *The Preparation of Term Essays.* Later she served as assistant archivist of the Provincial Archives of British Columbia. Her married name was Dorothy Blakey Smith.

Blakey collected material for *The Minerva Press*, the subject of her PhD thesis, while holding the 1931 Travelling Scholarship of the Canadian Federation of University Women. Minerva Press was on Leadenhall Street in London, England; "in the years between the death of Smollett and the rise of Scott [Minerva Press] was the chief purveyor of the circulating-library novel," otherwise known as "cheap fiction." Her book is thoroughly academic, complete with extensive footnotes and a long list of books published over the years by the press.

Bibliography

•Blakey, Dorothy, PhD. 1939. *The Minerva Press 1790-1820*. London: Bibliographical Society at the University Press, Oxford, 339 pp.

Bompas, Charlotte Selina Cox 1830-1917. Charlotte Cox was the daughter of a London physician and his wife. The first part of her adult life was spent largely in Italy, where she attended many parties and revelled in music. Her circumstances changed completely in 1874 when she married her cousin, the newly consecrated Bishop of Athabaska. She lived with her husband in the Canadian northwest for the next thirty-two years as he served as Bishop of Mackenzie River and Bishop of Selkirk. They retired to the Yukon in 1891. After her husband's death in 1906, she spent the rest of her life in Quebec.

In *Owindia* she describes Indians of the Mackenzie River area and how she came to look after and raise a motherless Indian child. Bompas was torn between patronizing and admiring the Natives among whom she lived. She felt on the one hand that white women who settled in the north (for example over one hundred Anglicans between 1860 and 1945) should set a standard for Native women: "In your Christian households, in your modest demeanour, in your fair dealings with all let them see what they should seek to copy more than the jewels and costly attire which in their eyes are all that is needed to constitute a lady" (Rutherdale 1994, 45). Yet she also noted:

> It should not need many hours of argument to convince you that an Indian baby in a moss bag is a far happier and warmer creature than a poor little white baby with its whole outfit of cotton and wool etc. for the little Indian's moss is the cleanest, softest, most absorbent of substances and needs only occasional change to keep the baby as tidy and sweet as the baby should be.

During these northern years she sometimes lived "in isolated regions, among primitive and degraded Indians," the preface of *Heroine of the North* states. Sometimes she survived only by snaring rabbits and netting fish to eat. Always she wrote in letters and journals about her experiences, which were edited into this book by her niece after her death.

Bibliography
•Rutherdale, Myra. 1994. Models of G/race and Boundaries of Gender: Anglican Women Missionaries in Canada's North 1860-1945. *Canadian Woman Studies* 14, 4: 44-47.
•C.S.B. [on final page]. 1886. *Owindia: A True Tale of the Mackenzie River Indians, North-West America.* London: Wells Gardner, Darton, 60 pp.
•Bompas, Charlotte Selina. 1929. *Heroine of the North: Memoirs of Wife of the First Bishop of Selkirk (Yukon) with Extracts from Her Journal and Letters.* Compiled by S.A. Archer. Toronto: Macmillan, 187 pp.

Bonner, Mary Graham 1890-1974. Mary Bonner, the daughter of a bank manager and his wife, attended Halifax Ladies' College and Halifax Conservatory of Music. She then moved to New York City where she became an American author of many articles, stories, reviews and children's books, such as *Danger on the Coast: A Story of Nova Scotia* (1941). She listed her interests as an adult as basketball, hockey, rounders, swimming, high diving, iceboating and camping.

Canada and Her Story, her book on Canadian history aimed at an American audience, won an award from the Women's National Book Association. It is written in simple language, and sanguine equally about the Royal Canadian Mounted Police, the Canadian treatment of Indians and of wildlife, and the relationship between the French and the English. She states about the English victory of 1759 that "It was not long before the conquered people rejoiced that now the battle was over, they could settle down to peacetime pursuits. They danced and sang with their conquerors" (p. 93).

Made in Canada, as the title indicates, is the story, aimed at a young audience, of arts and handicrafts manufactured in Canada. Native artifacts, clay figures, songs and legends are all discussed. Bonner makes some sweeping statements, such as (p. 94), "Canada, a land of singing people, is such a vast and sparsely settled country, that each section knows only its own songs."

Bibliography
•Bonner, Mary Graham. 1942. *Canada and Her Story.* New York: Knopf, 187 pp.
•_____. 1943. *Made in Canada.* New York: Knopf, 116 pp.

Bosanquet, Mary 1913-? Mary Bosanquet, who grew up in England, loved to ride horses and yearned for adventure. She decided in 1938 that because she wanted to see Canada, she would ride a horse across it. She did so beginning in Vancouver the following year, arriving in Montreal a year and a half later without undue trouble. Bosanquet went on to become an author, writing among other books a biography of Dietrich Bonhoeffer (1968).

Bosanquet's *Saddlebags for Suitcases* (called *Canada Ride: Across Canada on Horseback* in the 1944 London edition) includes, besides her own experiences, impressions of life in Canada; for example, although she had often ridden to the hunt in England, she deplored the trapping of fur-bearing animals in Canada. After the war, her book in translation sold well in Germany.

Bibliography

• Bosanquet, Mary. 1942. *Saddlebags for Suitcases*. Toronto: McClelland and Stewart, 247 pp.

Boswell, Hazel 1882-1979. Hazel Boswell, born in Quebec City and descended from one of the original seigneurs of New France, became interested in the folklore of French Canada when, as a girl, she spent most of her summers on her grandfather's seigneury. Some years after her death, the book *Town House, Country House: Reflections of a Quebec Childhood* (1990) was edited from her writings.

French Canada: Pictures and Stories of Old Quebec has twenty-three chapters, each dealing factually with an item considered typical of early Quebec—dog derby, the curé, Sunday, eel fisheries, spinning. It was popular enough to be reprinted in 1967 to Boswell's pleasure; she comments: "it seemed especially important to call to the attention of a new generation of readers the charm of the old customs and ways of life which they may never have the opportunity of experiencing at first hand." Boswell published other books on Quebec history after 1945.

Bibliography

• Boswell, Hazel. 1967 [1938]. *French Canada: Pictures and Stories of Old Quebec*. Toronto: McClelland and Stewart, 76 pp.

Bott, Helen McMurchie BA MA 1886-? Helen Bott, who earned a master's degree in psychology, was married to Edward Bott, the head of the psychology department at the University of Toronto from 1922 to 1956, with whom she had three daughters. They were both intimately involved with William Blatz's famous Institute of Child Study at the University of Toronto, which pioneered the discipline of child development. Their research investigated the impact on children of rejection, dominance and hostility that had previously been seen as not necessarily a bad thing. Helen Bott was put in charge of Parent Education when the centre was founded in 1925. There was to be continual feedback between the parents and the school, with the parents giving the school information on their children's development (one student was Bott's daughter Elizabeth) and the school teaching the parents how to be better parents. Bott published two influential books with Blatz as well as smaller manuals and research studies on her own. Later, Bott's interest in child psychology declined when she became involved with the Oxford Group. To Blatz's annoyance, she resigned from the Institute of Child Study in 1938.

In 1928, Bott and Blatz published *Parents and the Pre-School Child*, which outlined the St George's School for Child Study's approach to the training of children; it was a major contribution to parent education dealing with "normal" healthy children. In it, parents were counselled to begin toilet training when a child was three months old.

The authors then wrote a less theoretical companion volume, *The Management of Young Children*, "unashamedly a philosophy of child training rather than a scientific treatise" (Raymond 1991, 98), which went through five printings in the next eleven years. (The copy of this book at the University of Waterloo gives only Blatz's name on the spine.) Both of these books emphasized that parents needed the guidance of experts to do a good job raising their children.

Bott's 1933 and 1934 books were the first and second in the University of Toronto's Child Development Series, both arising from study at St George's School. *Method in Social Studies of Young Children* "was undertaken with a group of graduate students as part of an introductory course on the nature of social development in pre-school children." Their observational data are presented in an academic format with a comprehensive literature survey.

In the second more theoretical book, *Personality Development in Young Children*, Bott thanks both Dr Blatz, and her husband, psychology head E.A. Bott, for their help and support. It focuses on the social adjustment of children, noting that this can be studied comparatively between individual children, or longitudinally as a particular student grows and develops.

Bibliography
•Blatz, William E. MB, PhD and Helen McM. Bott, MA. 1928. *Parents and the Pre-School Child*. Toronto: Dent, 306 pp.
•Blatz, William E., MB, PhD and Helen Bott, MA. 1930. *The Management of Young Children*. Toronto: McClelland and Stewart, 354 pp.
Bott, E.A., W.E. Blatz, Nellie Chant and Helen Bott. 1928. *Observations and Training of Fundamental Habits in Young Children from the St. George's School for Child Study at the University of Toronto*. Worcester, MA: Clark University.
Bott, Helen. 1930. *Aims and Methods in Parent Education*. New York: n.p., 53 pp.
•Bott, Helen McM. 1933. *Method in Social Studies of Young Children*. Toronto: University of Toronto Press, 110 pp.
•_____. 1934. *Personality Development in Young Children*. Toronto: University of Toronto Press, 139 pp.

Bradley, Mary Coy Morris 1771-1859. Mary Coy was born in Gage-town, New Brunswick, the eighth of eleven children. She had only a few months of schooling, but even so taught herself to write in her diary about her religious experiences. Religion was so important to her that she tried to speak out in church about her beliefs, but she was always reprimanded by male elders. When she married her first husband, her life was hard. She made the milk from her two cows into butter and cheese, and obtained items she needed by bartering cloth that she wove herself. By 1805, she and her husband had saved enough to be able to move into St John where they kept a grocery store and rented out part of their house. Her husband was overbearing, but she found solace in religion. After he died in 1817, she married a man who suited her better. She never had children.

In the Dedication to *A Narrative of the Life and Christian Experience of Mrs Mary Bradley of St John, New Brunswick*, Bradley explains why one "so little known to the community" has written a book comprising extracts from her diary and correspondence during sixty years. "I have only to say, that my sole object in giving to the world this hitherto private account of my Christian life, is to endeavor to promote the glory of God and the good of the fellow creatures." It is arranged chronologically, with considerable comment about how religion had affected her life and what sermons she had heard. She narrates how she was able to overcome, through prayer, a fear of bears that had developed when she had had to go to the fields to round up the family cows. In her will she left most of her money to reli-gious causes.

Bibliography
•Fellows, Jo-Ann Carr. 1985. Mary Coy (Morris Bradley). *Dictionary of Cana-dian Biography*, s.v. Coy, Mary (Morris; Bradley).
•Bradley, Mary. 1849. *A Narrative of the Life and Christian Experience of Mrs. Mary Bradley of St John, New Brunswick*. Boston: Strong and Brodhead, 375 pp.

Brinley, Kathrine Gordon Sanger d.1966. Kathrine (alias Gordon) Brin-ley was an American author living in Massachusetts who, with her husband Putnam, visited four areas of Canada in four successive summers to write lively books of their adventures illustrated with drawings by her husband. She chose to publish these travel books under her second name, making her seem to be a man.

Away to the Gaspé is a light travelogue with much sprightly conversa-tion between two main protagonists, Dan and the Duchess. The couple drive in their car, Sally, from the United States to the southeast shore of the St Lawrence River, visiting various regions of the Gaspé, Quebec, over a two-month period.

In *Away to Cape Breton*, the main characters are again Dan, the Duchess and their car, Sally. This time they drive to Cape Breton, then slowly tour this island, visiting sites such as the grave of Alexander Graham Bell (in memory of whom she dedicates this book), the Cabot Trail, Neil Harbour, Cape Breton National Park and Louisburg, where excavations were in the preliminary stages. The book ends with information on fishing regulations and ferry and railway services.

In *Away to Quebec*, the Brinleys visit among other places St Joseph's Oratorio in Montreal, the Seigniory Club nearby where they wore evening dress, balouga [*sic*] whales near Manoir Richelieu, an Indian Chapel at Tadoussac, the Saguenay River and the area around Quebec City; on the Isle of Orleans they called on the famous painter Horatio Walker. An appendix offers information of interest to tourists.

In *Away to the Canadian Rockies and British Columbia*, Brinley and her husband travel west by train from Montreal, visiting the Calgary stampede and many tourist areas of the Rocky Mountains and southern British Columbia before arriving in Vancouver and Victoria. An appendix provides information on train times and mileage, rivers, Native tribes, flowers, trees, and tourist sites and activities. She intended this book, like her others, to be for ordinary travellers, because in a preface she warns archaeologists, botanists, engineers, ethnographers, ethnologists, geographers, geologists, historians, meteorologists, naturalists and mountain climbers to "PASS AT YOUR OWN RISK."

Bibliography
- Brinley, Gordon. 1935. *Away to the Gaspé*. Toronto: McClelland and Stewart, 200 pp.
- _____. 1936. *Away to Cape Breton*. Toronto: McClelland and Stewart, 266 pp.
- _____. 1937. *Away to Quebec: A Gay Journey to the Province*. Toronto: McClelland and Stewart, 286 pp.
- _____. 1938. *Away to the Canadian Rockies and British Columbia*. Toronto: McClelland and Stewart, 301 pp.

Broadus, Eleanor Hammond. Eleanor Broadus was married to a professor of English at the University of Alberta, Edmund Broadus, with whom she would compile and edit in 1925 an anthology of Canadian prose and verse. She was fluent in Italian, translating with a friend a book on Dante from Italian into English.

Although the contents of her 1910 gilded *A Book of the Christ Child* include conversation and seem fictional, they are in fact legends "which had their inception in the religious fervor of early Christianity, [and] are recorded mainly in the *Apocrypha*, in mediaeval saints' lives, in mediaeval art, and in popular tradition. The writer has used the outline of the stories

as they exist in the old records, but has treated the details with freedom."
Even so, she has "tried to remain faithful to the spirit of reverence and ide-
ality which was the mainspring of the original legends." Some of the stories about Jesus' youth are similar to those in the Bible.

Bibliography
•Broadus, Eleanor Hammond. 1910. *A Book of the Christ Child.* New York:
   D. Appleton, 158 pp.

Brown, Audrey Alexandra OC 1904-1998. Audrey Brown was born and
grew up in Nanaimo. She became a renowned poet for such works as *Dryad
in Nanaimo* (1931), receiving medals from the Canadian Women's Press
Club (1936) and the Royal Society of Canada (1948) for her distinguished
contributions to Canadian literature. After she published her first book of
poetry and while still a young woman, she contracted rheumatic fever and
arthritis, from which she suffered for many years.

Her diary/book *The Log of a Lame Duck* describes her illness and ten-
month stay with nursing care in The House of Good Hope on Vancouver
Island. She was bedridden and in pain for three years; for the next eight
years she was so crippled that she spent six of them in a wheelchair. Eventually she returned almost to full health and was able to walk for short periods without crutches.

Bibliography
•Brown, Audrey. 1938. *The Log of a Lame Duck.* Toronto: Macmillan, 292 pp.

Brown, Marguerite W. Marguerite Brown travelled widely with her husband, living first as a missionary in China for four years, and later in
Chatham, Ontario, Ithaca, NY, Washington, DC, and Toronto. In Toronto,
as a mother of three children, she took courses on parent education at the
Institute of Child Study and the following year, in 1949, joined the staff of
the Institute. In 1953 she published *It Takes Time to Grow*, a book on raising children to live a Christian life, in which she thanks **Dorothy Millichamp** and **Mary Northway** for their help.

The Woman's Missionary Society asked her to write *Towards a Friendly
World* for the use of Baby Bands, or rather the mothers of children in the
United Church. The aim was "to develop children who, carrying with them
the heritage of the past, will be enabled to fulfil themselves in accordance
with the best that is in them." Brown found that mothers often attended Child
Study groups "to learn how to train their children, but what they actually
learned was to control themselves." Chapters describe at length how children
can be educated to be good neighbours, and what they should be taught about
God, prayer, giving and religion and the church. Brown uses anecdotes and

logic to make her points. She concludes that the church can provide a meeting place for children of different nationalities and social classes; induce a feeling of Christian community; acquaint the child with the history of the religion to which he [*sic*] belongs; undertake projects of the nursery school type; assist the parents through study groups and aid the child by helping him [*sic*] evolve a satisfactory philosophy of life.

Bibliography

•Brown, Marguerite W. 1938. *Towards a Friendly World*. Toronto: Woman's Missionary Society, United Church of Canada, 61 pp.

Bruce, Constance. Constance Bruce was a trained nurse who sailed from Canada to London shortly after the outbreak of the First World War to offer her services to the men wounded in war.

In *Humour in Tragedy*, she describes her trip to England and the wartime adventures of fellow nurses and herself successively in No. 1 Canadian Stationary Hospital in France, in Lemnos, in Cairo and in Salonica. After three weeks in London, the nurses embarked for immediate medical duty in France. Despite the horror of caring for wounded and dying men, the author tries to keep her descriptions upbeat with sixty-four of her own humorous illustrations and with amusing anecdotes. She urges that after the war her readers remember that each soldier "marched bravely away one morning, prepared to die, that you, at home, might live." She asks that they try by their actions to "efface a part of the stupendous debt that you owe him."

Bibliography

•Bruce, Constance. n.d. [about 1919]. *Humour in Tragedy: Hospital Life behind Three Fronts by a Canadian Nursing Sister*. London: Skeffington, 67 pp.

Buchan, Anna 1878?-1948.   Anna Buchan lived in Scotland where she attended private schools while growing up. Her large family was a close-knit one, with her father a minister of the Free Church of Scotland and her mother a homemaker. Buchan served in Scotland as a Justice of the Peace, but her life was mostly devoted to writing many successful novels such as *Priorsford* (1935). She used a pseudonym, O. Douglas, because she did not want to compete openly with her brother, the novelist and biographer John Buchan; as Lord Tweedsmuir, he was the Governor General of Canada from 1935 to 1940.

Buchan's biography of this beloved brother, *Unforgettable, Unforgotten*, written after he died, includes many details of his life while in Canada. In her preface she notes that "It was written [during the war] in an effort to lighten dark days by remembering happier ones. My brother John used to say that when he wrote stories he invented, but that I in my books was always remembering. Here in this chronicle is the fount of all my memories."

Bibliography

•Buchan, Anna (O. Douglas). 1945. *Unforgettable, Unforgotten*. London: Hodder and Stoughton, 247 pp.

Buckley, Joan. Joan Buckley was a poet who grew up in Armstrong, British Columbia, and published several books of poetry.

Buckley begins *The Technique of Poetry* as follows: "It is proposed in these pages to furnish some pointers on technique so that versifiers may know more about the art which gives them pleasure to pursue. It is no slur (rather the opposite) on the ability of the apprentice, to correct, prune and polish his [*sic*] work. The more finished the craftsman, the more careful he is to see that there is no fault which he can remedy in the final copy of his poem." She discusses the mechanics of poems in three sections: accents, metre, anapests and scansion, etc.; form (ballad, sonnet, rondeau, triolet, etc.); and craftsmanship (sounds, synonyms, rhymes, grammar, etc.). Her advice is useful: "When composing free verse, never approach anything resembling metre, and also studiously avoid rhyme, or near-rhyme. If one rhyme is used, the reader expects another" (p. 52). Or, in free verse "Always present an image" and "Strive to produce poetry that is hard and clear, never blurred and indefinite." Her admonitions are accompanied by examples that make her points obvious.

Bibliography

•Buckley, Joan. 1944. *The Technique of Poetry: Hints on Verse-Writing*. Langley, BC: self-published, 63 pp.

Bugeia, Julia Henrietta S. 1843-1926. Julia Bugeia was a Quebecer devoted to Stanbridge Academy.

Bugeia's and Theodora Moore's book *The Old Missisquoi* focuses on the eastern townships of Quebec bordering the Vermont border, and on the non-sectarian Stanbridge Academy for boys and girls which was founded there in 1854. The Foreword, by the long-time director of the academy, describes the information the authors "have reverently sought to gather up into this little book [211 pp.!], for the years to come, the quintessential spirit and life of this Our Academy."

Bibliography

•Bugeia, Julia H.S. and Theodora Cornell Moore. 1910. *The Old Missisquoi, with History and Reminiscences of Stanbridge Academy*. Montreal: John Lovell, 211 pp.

Bulloch, Ellen Guthrie. Ellen Bulloch grew up and lived as a pioneer in the Reston area of southwest Manitoba.

In *Pioneers of the Pipestone* Bulloch describes the history of this area. The first settlers arrived in 1881 when the land was without trees because of frequent fires set by the Indians. After the land was "broken" and fires prevented, poplar bluffs became common. The story she relates (up to 1893, when the railway from Winnipeg had reached Reston) is bound up with the individuals (usually male) who farmed there—where they came from, where they settled, what they grew and whom they married; pioneers listed include four Guthrie men and four Bulloch men. (She does describe the killing of a wolf by Mrs Peter Guthrie with her shovel, however). The second half of the book describes such things as domestic life, early excitements, the church, building the school house and "interesting personalities." There is an appendix of the names of 174 early pioneers and their holdings, all male except two. Bulloch dedicates her "little booklet" to the Pioneers of the Pipestone who developed their new home in Manitoba and to the Women's Institutes of Reston and Pipestone. Her name is not given on the title page, but is used to sign the Preface.

Bibliography
•[Bulloch, Ellen G.]. 1929. *Pioneers of the Pipestone*. N.p., 63 pp.

Burgess, Nellie V. See Isabel Griffiths entry.

Burkholder, Mabel Grace 1881-1973. Mabel Burkholder was born in Hamilton, Ontario, into a family of early German settlers. She obtained a teacher's first-class certificate and taught briefly before becoming an author (published from 1911 to 1968) of short stories, articles and poems as well as books, mostly of history. She, along with her friends **Kit Coleman** and **Ethel Raymond**, was a member of the Hamilton Branch of the Canadian Women's Press Club.

Before the White Man Came comprises ninety Indian legends chosen from hundreds belonging to tribes across Canada. She notes in her preface:

> these stories have been handed down through so many generations by word of mouth, rather than by writing, [which] accounts for the confused state in which they are found to-day. In many instances it is almost impossible to get at the pure legend in its original form. Each Indian narrator has added his impressions, and the story has lost nothing at the hands of the whites.

She states of the stories that "Many are fragmentary, and meaningless. Some are foolish and unimportant, merely relating the pranks of animals. Not a few are repulsive, bestial, hideous. In this book an effort has been made to collect the most attractive and important legends cherished among the Indians."

The Story of Hamilton is a thorough work, culled from early historical documents, old diaries, newspaper accounts and personal recollections. The Foreword states that "the author has answered an insistent call for such a work. The widespread interest aroused by the announcement of the book proved that it was long overdue." She writes confidently that "Such a book of reference should furnish an inexhaustible source of material for school work. It is also hailed with delight by historical and patriotic societies. It only remains for the general reader to give it his [*sic*] loyal support."

Bibliography
- Burkholder, Mabel. 1923. *Before the White Man Came: Indian Legends and Stories*. Toronto: McClelland and Stewart, 317 pp.
- _____. 1938. *The Story of Hamilton*. Hamilton: David-Lisson, 183 pp.

Burton, Jean 1905-1952.   Jean Burton was a Canadian author who excelled in writing biographies of famous Europeans, two of them women. Later she wrote *Lydia Pinkham Is Her Name* (1949).

Burton's book *Sir Richard Burton's Wife* (Isabel Arundell Burton [1831-96]) was one of the first focusing on the spouse of a famous person; the title omits her name, perhaps to emphasize the dependency of wives in the 1800s. When Isabel Arundell at age nineteen first met the romantic explorer/scholar/orientalist, she determined to marry him, and worked toward that end until she was successful ten years later. Richard Burton (1821-90) was the first European to see Lake Tanganyika and to visit in disguise forbidden Islamic cities.

According to the authors, *Elisabet Ney* (1833-1907) was a feminist and one of only two German career women in the nineteenth century, the other being Clara Schumann. Ney was not only a famous sculptor but also "a vibrant, beautiful, and unconventional woman [who] came to be the friend of philosophers and the delight and scandal of courts." She was the grand-niece of Napoleon's famous Marshal Ney. She studied art in Munich, then began a lifelong career, which included making a bust of Queen Victoria. She married in 1863 and had children, but this was never admitted publicly. The couple moved to the United States where for many years she worked from her studio in Austin, Texas. The book is rich with anecdotes and includes much conversation.

Jean Burton's book *Garibaldi*, aimed at children, was published in the Borzoi Books for Young People series. The story of this Italian patriot and soldier, who fought in civil wars in Brazil and Uruguay as well as in Italy, is told simply, advanced in large part by conversation.

Bibliography
•Burton, Jean. 1941. *Sir Richard Burton's Wife*. New York: Knopf, 391 pp.
•_____. 1945. *Garibaldi, Knight of Liberty*. New York: Knopf, 225 pp.
•Fortune, Jan and Jean Burton. 1943. *Elisabet Ney*. New York: Knopf, 305 pp.

Burton, Katherine Kurz BA DLitt 1890-1969. Katherine Kurz was born in Cleveland, OH, and educated at Case Western Reserve University. She married Harry Burton, an editor, when she was twenty and had three children. She also taught in a private school and was associate editor for *McCall's* and *Redbook* magazines as well as a freelance writer. She converted to Roman Catholicism when she was forty, and chose thereafter to write dozens of biographies about Catholics in the United States; she wanted to demonstrate that these individuals could be good Americans as well as good Catholics. The popular style employed by Burton annoyed some scholars, but she claimed it allowed her to appeal to a wide audience. She was awarded a DLitt in 1955 from St Mary of the Springs College.

Her book *Brother André of Mount Royal* details the life of Alfred Bessette (1845-1937), a pious man to whom many attributed miraculous healings. Shortly after his death, she visited St Joseph's Oratory in Montreal to soak up the atmosphere in which he had lived. As well as describing Brother André's life, Burton portrays people who were apparently healed by his prayers.

Bibliography
•Burton, Katherine. 1943. *Brother André of Mount Royal*. Notre Dame, IN: Ave Maria Press, 197 pp.

Butler, Elizabeth F., nun 1857-? Elizabeth Butler was a long-time member of the Congrégation de Notre-Dame in Montreal, founded by Marguerite Bourgeoys (1620-1700), the subject of her biography.

In *The Life of Venerable Marguerite Bourgeoys*, Butler invariably describes Bourgeoys in pious terms. Bourgeoys was a teacher and administrator for most of her life in Canada, where she arrived from France in 1657. In 1910, the Sacred Congregation of Rites proclaimed her to be heroic and arranged to examine four major miracles performed through her intercession; examples of such miracles are included in chapter twenty-three entitled "Intercessory Power." She was canonized in 1982. Butler's name does not appear on the title page of her book, but only in small letters under the date on the following page.

Bibliography

•[Butler, Elizabeth F.] 1932. *The Life of Venerable Marguerite Bourgeoys, Foundress of the Congrégation de Notre Dame of Montreal*. New York: P.J. Kennedy and Sons, 231 pp.

Byng, Viscountess Marie Evelyn Moreton 1870-1949. Evelyn Moreton was born in London to wealthy parents. When she was eight, she came to Canada for the first time as a child member of a royal entourage: her father was comptroller to Lord Lorne and her mother lady-in-waiting to Princess Louise. She wanted to write as she grew older, but her mother forbade this as being unsuitable; instead she was allowed to break and train horses. In 1902 she married Colonel Julian Byng, later Viscount Byng of Vimy. While living in India she had several miscarriages, which rendered her unable to have children. Viscount Byng led Canadian troops with distinction at the Battle of Vimy Ridge; according to the wish of many Canadians, he was made Governor General. The Viscountess returned to Canada while he served in this position from 1921 to 1926, travelling with him over much of the Dominion. Although she and her husband were mandated to be politically neutral, she loathed Prime Minister Mackenzie King. In 1922 she became first honorary president of the newly formed Canadian Authors Association, and in 1925, to honour a sport she loved, she donated the Lady Byng Trophy for sportsmanship and excellence for a player in the National Hockey League. She was also active in anti-cruelty to animal campaigns.

While on her fourth prolonged visit to Canada, after her husband's death, Lady Byng wrote her autobiography, *Up the Stream of Time*. In it, she describes among other things her dismay in volunteering at an Ottawa thrift shop during the Second World War, where buyers tried routinely to cheat the management (p. 246). She also wrote several novels.

Bibliography

•Byng of Vimy, Viscountess. 1945. *Up the Stream of Time*. Toronto: Macmillan, 274 pp.

Caldwell, Irene Annie. Irene Caldwell, who lived in Bristol, New Brunswick, was deeply interested in economics, belonging to a club whose purpose was to grapple with financial problems generated by the Great Depression.

An introductory note in *Money—What Is It?* indicates that I.A. Caldwell (never specified as female) wrote this book

> in collaboration with a prominent Canadian manufacturer; a merchant who ships Canadian products to all parts of the Dominion and to practi-

cally every country in the world; and a banker, with extensive banking experience in the handling of credits and all instruments of credit, called money, that have to do with Industry, Commerce and Finance. Furthermore, this volume gives expression to the school of thought on the subject of money, for which Mr Neil McLean of St John, New Brunswick, is responsible.

As the foreword states, "We believe that excessive interest is the criminal, the ingrate, who took the profits of our commerce to swell its opulent treasuries and then made money to be master in the house where it should have been the servant." They base their reasoning on Scriptures, which denounce usury, and on "economic laws founded on the eternal righteousness of the Universe," describing how economic activity evolved in history and how it could be rectified in the present.

Bibliography
•Caldwell, I.A. 1935. *Money—What Is It?* Toronto: Garden City Press Study Club, 181 pp.

Cameron, Agnes Deans 1863-1912. Agnes Cameron was born in Victoria to adventurous parents who had recently retired from the goldfields of California. At the age of eighteen she became the first woman high-school teacher in British Columbia, and in 1894 the first woman school principal in the province. In her spare time she biked and coached sports; was active in the women's suffrage movement, the YWCA and the Canadian Women's Press Club; and wrote for magazines and newspapers. Her licence to teach was revoked when she allowed her students to use rulers in an art class examination, so she moved to Chicago in 1906 to become a journalist and editor. Two years later, Cameron and her young niece Jessie Brown bought tickets to the Arctic from the Hudson's Bay Company. They travelled for nearly six months, either by stagecoach, scow or steamboat on the Athabaska, Slave and Mackenzie Rivers, lugging with them cameras and a typewriter to document and thus pay for the expedition. After Cameron's book about this trip was published in 1909, she lectured extensively about the golden opportunities in the Arctic; she was so enthusiastic that in Great Britain her lectures were supported financially by the Canadian government as part of its immigration effort. Her career ended tragically in 1912 when she died in Nanaimo, following an operation for appendicitis.

In *The New North*, Cameron kept special note of women they encountered, such as nuns from a Catholic convent, women printing books in Cree, a woman trader from Scotland and Inuit women. She says there are no unhappy marriages among the Inuit, because the couple separate if one member is displeased with the other (p. 219). She was well aware of racial prejudice, admitting at one point that she was glad to be white (p. 43) and at another giving her name to a Native baby girl who would otherwise have been declared illegitimate and therefore ineligible for treaty money (p. 250).

Bibliography

•Cameron, Agnes Deans. 1986 [1909]. *The New North: An Account of a Woman's 1908 Journey through Canada to the Arctic.* Saskatoon: Western Producer Prairie Books, 311 pp., rev. ed.

Cameron, Charlotte OBE, FRGS d. 1948. Before the First World War, Charlotte Cameron, who was British, toured Africa, including the German colonies, writing a book about these (as well as several other travel books) which enabled her later to give advice about German administrations to the Allied armies. She also lectured across America on Germany and its poor treatment of Africans. Following the war, she travelled "from Seattle via the Yukon—2,200 miles on the Yukon River, one of the four largest in the world—to Alaska, and back" and wrote a book about the trip.

A Cheechako in Alaska and Yukon notes that she made the acquaintance "of strange peoples—the Indians and Eskimoes— their manner of life, and became more familiar with this vast Northland, a place where the hospitalities are boundless." Like Vilhjalmur Stefansson, Cameron was incredibly optimistic about the future of the north, suggesting as early as 1930 that it might be enjoying a rebirth. "For men have but scratched the surface of this frozen zone, just as the unchanging Arab has merely scratched the soil of his homeland. What are the treasures of India as compared with the treasures of this limitless land of sunshine and snow?"

Bibliography

•Cameron, Charlotte OBE, FRGS. 1920. *A Cheechako in Alaska and Yukon.* London: Fisher, 292 pp.

Campbell, Elizabeth Louise Bethune. Elizabeth Campbell was the daughter of Lady Hamilton and James Bethune, a barrister of Toronto. Her father made many trips to Britain to bring appeals before the Privy Council on behalf of Canadian clients, so Campbell decided in 1939 to take her own 1928 case before the Judicial Committee of the Privy Council in London.

In her book *Where Angels Fear to Tread*, Campbell describes her decision to fight the ruling of the Supreme Court of Ontario regarding the handling of her mother's estate by the trustees. She won her legal action, and was the first woman to appeal in person to the Judicial Committee.

Bibliography
•Campbell, Elizabeth Bethune. 1940. *Where Angels Fear to Tread*. Boston: St John's Rectory, 222 pp.

Campbell, Isabella 1830-1887. Isabella Campbell left Quebec in 1852 to travel to the goldfields of Australia. She stayed there for five months, then returned to Quebec two years later, having sailed around the world.

In *Rough and Smooth*, Campbell describes this adventuresome trip in detail. She originally wrote up her travels for the amusement of her children, but was urged to publish her adventures so other children could also enjoy them. The style and subject matter of her book make it of interest to adults as well as children.

Bibliography
•Campbell, Isabella. 1865. *Rough and Smooth, or, Ho! for an Australian Gold Field*. Quebec: Hunter-Rose, 138 pp.

Campbell, Jessie Buchanan d. 1900. Jessie Buchanan grew up in Scotland and came with her birth family to Canada in 1822 when her father, George Buchanan (1761-1834), answered a call to a new church at Beckwith, near Ottawa. Her father, who was both a doctor and a minister, was then sixty, and her nine brothers and sisters all adults. She married Duncan Campbell in 1841, setting up house in Rideau Ferry, near Perth, Ontario. He died in 1898, following fifty-seven years of marriage, after which Campbell moved to Toronto.

In her biography of her father, *The Pioneer Pastor*, Campbell writes, "This sketch, designed as an humble tribute to the Beckwith pioneers and their first minister, is published in response to numerous requests." She praises the pioneers of the country: "Heroes without epaulettes, they performed their duty nobly, bearing a heavy burden for the sake of those who should come after them. Although the snows of many winters have drifted over their graves, let not their memory be forgotten."

Bibliography
•Campbell, Jessie Buchanan, his only surviving daughter. 1900. *The Pioneer Pastor: Some Reminiscences of the Life and Labors of the Rev. Geo. Buchanan, MD, First Presbyterian Minister of Beckwith, Lanark County, Upper Canada*. Toronto: Author, 56 pp.

Campbell, Marjorie Elliott Wilkins CM OC 1901-1975. Marjorie Wilkins, born in England, immigrated in 1904 with her family to the Qu'Appelle Valley in Saskatchewan where their first home was a sod hut. She later married and moved to Toronto where she was a full-time writer, receiving a Governor General's Award for non-fiction for her history book

The Saskatchewan (1950). She became a Member of the Order of Canada in 1978.

Campbell writes in the preface of *The Soil Is Not Enough* that "Occasionally a story becomes so insistent that it must be written to purge the host of its presence. This chronicle of seven years of my father is like that." She describes, writing in her father's voice and using some fictional characters, how their family became pioneer farmers. William H. Wilkins was inexperienced in farming, but "pitted his trained intelligence against the forces of nature." As the title indicates, at the time "the soil was not enough, when we were dependent solely upon the methods of trial and error for the proper seed to sow and the time of year for seeding, and upon our own ways of combating the farmer's natural enemies."

Bibliography
•Campbell, Marjorie Wilkins. 1938. *The Soil Is Not Enough*. Toronto: Macmillan, 285 pp.

Campbell, Sara Leitch.   Sara Campbell, whose birth name is unknown, was a member of the Brooke Women's Institute who undertook the task of compiling a history of Brooke Township, Lambton County, in Ontario.

Campbell's book was conceived when the Ontario Provincial Department of Agriculture suggested in 1931 that Women's Institutes undertake research into the history of their communities. *Brooke Township History*, dedicated to "Our Mothers and Grandmothers," was completed in 1934 and published two years later to great local interest. The University of Waterloo copy was presented to the Historian's Office of the Church of Jesus Christ of Latter-day Saints in Salt Lake City, Utah, from where it found its way to Waterloo.

Bibliography
•Campbell, Sara L. 1936. *Brooke Township History 1833-1933*. N.p.: Brooke Women's Institute, 171 pp.

Cannell, Kathleen Biggar Eaton BA 1891-1974.   Cannell's mother, born in Picton, Ontario, of United Empire Loyalist stock, married an American and settled in New York state where their family of four was born. When Cannell was seven, she moved with her mother and siblings to Port Hope, Ontario, for the next ten years. She then attended both the University of Toronto and the Sorbonne before settling in Paris in 1931 as a reporter and fashion editor for the *New York Times*. Following her divorce, she fell in love with Harold Loeb; her circle of American friends in Paris included Ernest Hemingway, who parodied their affair in his book *The Sun Also Rises*. She remained a journalist until 1964.

Cannell wrote *Jam Yesterday* after existing for nearly four years in German-occupied France and being arrested twice. By concentrating on her happy youth she hoped for "an escape from the cold, hunger, dirt, restrictions, depression, bombardments and boredom—above all, from the uncertainty—which characterize the French state of being still *of* rather than *in* the war." Her book includes stories of "our jubilant early life under two free flags" early in the century.

Bibliography

•Cannell, Kathleen. 1945. *Jam Yesterday*. New York: Morrow, 238 pp.

Carnochan, Janet 1839-1926. Janet Carnochan was born in Stamford, Ontario, but lived for most of her life in Niagara, where she was for twenty-three years a high-school teacher of history, literature and mathematics. When she retired, she devoted herself to the work of the Niagara Historical Society, of which she was a president.

Her name is not on the title page of her first book about a Niagara church, *Centennial St Mark's Church*, but she is acknowledged in the preface by three church officials: "The work of compilation and writing was committed to one of our best local historical writers, and all will concede that Miss Janet Carnochan has faithfully performed her part, and we would add has done so gratuitously." She ends her short book on a historical note, quoting a worshipper: "I would far rather, when I may, worship in an old church whose very stones are a history of how men strove to realize the infinite, compelling even the powers of nature into the task."

Carnochan also revered the history of her own church, about which she wrote her second book, *Centennial St Andrew's*. This time she is less reticent, having her name on the title page and writing in the preface, "The favor with which the first volume has been received encourages the issuing of the present, hoping that it may be kindly treated and its faults pardoned." At the end she again quotes the same worshipper: "I thought how many witnesses to the truth had sat in these pews. I honored the place; I rejoiced in its history; it soothed me, tuned me to a holy mood."

For her *History of Niagara (in Part)* about Niagara-on-the-Lake, "mine own romantic town," Carnochan collected over many years relevant items from books of travel, old papers, original documents and oral histories. She knew that more could be written, however, and so added "in Part" to her title. An admirer writes in the foreword:

> If anyone doubted the genius for research in the historical field which Miss Janet Carnochan possesses, the following pages would dispel the doubt. The work is an example of elaborate and untiring investigation. . . . Miss Carnochan has long been famous for devotion to tasks of this kind. The

transactions of the Niagara Historical Society bear evidence to her zeal in the cause of original research. The establishment of the unique Historical Museum in the town is due to her indomitable enterprise and owes much to her generosity and unselfishness.

Bibliography

• Anonymous. 1892. *Centennial St Mark's Church, Niagara*. Toronto: James Bain, 56 pp.
• Carnochan, Janet. 1895. *Centennial St Andrew's, Niagara 1794-1894*. Toronto: Briggs, 70 pp.
• _____. 1914. *History of Niagara (in Part)*. Toronto: Briggs, 333 pp.

Carr, Emily 1871-1945.   Emily Carr was born in Victoria, British Columbia, to a successful businessman and his wife. In her ambition to become an artist, she studied art for many years in California and in England and France, then painted Western scenery and Native sites in British Columbia, preserving on canvas Native towns and totem poles which have since fallen into disrepair. Her work gained national attention only after 1927, when it became widely known and so acclaimed by the Group of Seven and other artists that the National Gallery bought seventeen of her canvasses. Her final book of autobiography, *Growing Pains*, was published the year after her death, followed by *Pause* (1953) and *Hundreds and Thousands: The Journals of Emily Carr* (1966). Recently the Emily Carr Institute of Art and Design in Vancouver was named in her honour.

After a heart attack in 1937, when she could no longer paint, Carr devoted her time largely to writing, publishing her first book, *Klee Wyck*, when she was seventy. Despite such a late start,

> she wrote immediately with the kind of ease that usually comes from years of practice, and she applied to her new art all the clarity of observation and vividness of presentation she had developed in her painting. But she added also a sense of comedy that finds little scope for expression in her visual art, and a sharp perception of the frailties of human beings and the virtues of animals, whom—as she looked out of the heart of her irremediable loneliness—she preferred. (Woodcock 1988)

Carr won a Governor General's Award for *Klee Wyck*, which comprised vignettes written at various times from her trips along the British Columbia coast and the Queen Charlotte Islands. The title, meaning "Laughing One," was given to her by Natives of Ucluelet, where in 1898 she visited missionaries and sketched. She dedicated this book to Sophie, a Native friend of forty years. In *Klee Wyck* Carr is "true to facts and details so that the Indian way of living is never idealized, yet the Indians themselves are described entirely without patronage as self-sufficient people living differently from white men" (Woodcock 1988). It is hard, then, that her reputation has recently been challenged because of her alleged appropriation of Indian "voice" (Crosby 1991).

The Book of Small is Carr's impression of herself growing up, paralleling the growth of her home town, Victoria. As a child she already had an observant eye, judging by her depiction of life in a small colonial city, and a tendency to like being alone.

The House of All Sorts was built by Carr in 1913 so she could support herself by renting rooms; the scheme worked out so badly that for many years she had little time or energy for painting. This book describes in brief sketches her unhappy career as a landlady.

Bibliography

•Blanchard, Paula. 1987. *The Life of Emily Carr*. Seattle: University of Washington Press.

•Crean, Susan. 2001. *The Laughing One: A Journey to Emily Carr*. Toronto: HarperFlamingo Canada.

•Crosby, Marcia. 1991. Construction of the Imaginary Indian. In Stan Douglas, ed. *Vancouver Anthology*. Vancouver: Talonbooks.

Hembroff-Schleicher, Edythe. 1969. *m.e.: A Portrayal of Emily Carr*. Toronto: Clarke, Irwin.

————. 1978. *Emily Carr: The Untold Story*. Saanichton, BC: Hancock Press.

Pearson, Carol. 1954. *Emily Carr as I Knew Her*. Toronto: Clarke, Irwin.

Shadbolt, Doris. 1990. *Emily Carr*. Vancouver: Douglas and McIntyre.

•Tippett, Maria. 1979. *Emily Carr: A Biography*. Toronto: Oxford University Press.

•Walker, Stephanie Kirkwood. 1996. *This Woman in Particular: Contexts for the Biographical Image of Emily Carr*. Waterloo, ON: Wilfrid Laurier University Press.

•Woodcock, George. 1988. Emily Carr. *Dictionary of Literary Biography: Canadian Writers, 1920-1959*, s.v. Carr, Emily.

•Carr, Emily. 1941. *Klee Wyck*. Toronto: Oxford University Press, 155 pp.

•————. 1943. *The Book of Small*. Toronto: Oxford University Press, 164 pp.

•————. 1967 [1944]. *The House of All Sorts*. Toronto: Irwin Publishing, 166 pp.

•————. 1946. *Growing Pains: The Autobiography of Emily Carr*. Toronto: Oxford University Press, 381 pp.

•————. 1953. *Pause: A Sketch Book*. Toronto: Clarke, Irwin, 148 pp.

•————. 1966. *Hundreds and Thousands: The Journals of Emily Carr*. Toronto: Clarke, Irwin, 332 pp.

Carr-Harris, Bertha Hannah Wright 1863-1949.   Bertha Wright was born in Ottawa where she carried out religious work as described in her first book; this included organizing a centre called The Home for Friendless Women which has a dispiriting ring. When she married Robert Carr-Harris, a professor at the Royal Military College, they lived in Kingston for many years. After he died, she moved to Toronto.

Lights and Shades of Mission Work, attributable to her only by her initials, was published under the auspices of the Young Women's Christian Institute. It begins, with an odd mixture of humility and insouciance:

> To write the story of the past seven years of service for the Master as it ought to be written is a task beyond the ability of the author. All that is offered therefore is a series of rapid sketches portraying the main features of the work rather than giving a connected historic narrative. That, written as it has been, amid the rush and whirl of a busy life, it is not free from blemishes which a careful revision would have removed, will be apparent to the reader.

Her self-appointed mission in Ottawa, in which she was joined by her friend **Henrietta Edwards**, was to bring the word of God to working young women, prostitutes, alcoholics and female prisoners. She describes the founding of the Institute and its early history using conversation and anecdotes. When representatives of YWCAs across Canada met in 1893 to form a National Council, she was elected its first president.

The Five A's . . . is a religious tract written to counteract "the infamous propaganda" of the American Association for the Advancement of Atheism (the four As) in Canadian and American schools and colleges; she claimed that this group was backed by a donation of fifty million dollars (which is difficult to believe). The five As of her title refers to the same association with the addition of "Anti" before "Atheism." Her book contains many sections, among them four entitled "Godless Evolution," "Improper Literature," "Cannibalism" and "Insane Sex Ideas."

In 1863, Frances Rolleston published in England a book called *Mazzaroth*. She studied "rabbinical and ancient Arabic lexicons, from Egyptian, Syriac, Coptic, Chaldean, Persian, Sanskrit, Chinese, Greek and Latin works," and read books by Ulugh Beigh, Aben Ezra, Eudoxus, Albumazer, Aratus, Josephus, Ptolemy, Cicero, Virgil, Hesiod and Homer, among others. She found that many roots of the original language in which Adam had conversed with Eve "had survived time and change, and appeared in various dialects, ancient and modern, to attest a common source." These primitive and widely diffused roots were preserved in the heavens; the names of over one hundred stars, when traced back to their original root, enabled Rolleston "to tell out the whole story of redemption of a fallen race from all the power of the enemy." Carr-Harris wrote *The Hieroglyphics of the Heavens* to make Rolleston's work more readily understandable. She beseeches, "Would that through the meaning of the constellations as well as through the written Word the pathetic appeal of our long-suffering God might be broadcast to every tribe and nation. 'O earth! earth!! earth!!! Hear the word of the Lord.' "

Bibliography
•B.H.W. 1892. *Lights and Shades of Mission Work: Or Leaves from a Worker's Note Book Being Reminiscences of Seven Years' Service at the Capital 1885-1892*. Ottawa: Free Press Publishing, 103 pp.
•Carr-Harris, Bertha. 1928. *The Five A's vs the Four A's*. Kingston, ON: Hanson and Edgar, 82 pp.
•Carr-Harris, Mrs. 1933. *The Hieroglyphics of the Heavens, or the Enigma of the Ages*. Toronto: Armac Press, 101 pp.

Carter, Mary Duncan 1896-?   Mary Carter was an economist whose maiden name is unknown.

Carter's *The Story of Money* is aimed at children, although it should also be of interest to adults. Stephen Leacock, in his male-biased Preface for Grown-ups, suggests that any perplexed businessman "should read the book aloud to his little boys as a generous assistance to their education. He can do this without loss of dignity under the pleasant pretence that he knows all about it himself. When he finishes the book he will find that he knows quite a lot." She describes why we need money, why money is gold or paper, and how we earn, use, save and make fortunes of money. The book was published during the Great Depression, when financial concerns were paramount. She ends her book: "If we try to understand the proper uses of money, we shall be able to help put money where it belongs in the general scheme of things, and to make the world a better place in which to live."

Bibliography
•Carter, Mary Duncan. 1932. *The Story of Money*. New York: Farrar and Rinehart, 71 pp.

Cary, Elizabeth Marguerite Pseudonym of Bessie (Mrs V.L.) Miller. Elizabeth Carey grew up in Isaacs Harbour, Nova Scotia. Items from her books indicate that she was married and had three doctors among her relatives.

The title *A Jumble Jar* refers to the jumble of anecdotes, mostly from Isaacs Harbour, that make up this collection of Cary's childhood memories. She writes that she uses real names in her work: "Every name is too dear to cloud, even temporarily, with another that might make you unrecognizable to your friends." However, she has a double standard because she does use pseudonyms for the immediate family and for herself: "They are but the curtain drawn to protect from publicity. For those who are interested and those who know, the curtain rises." Because of these pseudonyms it is difficult to know what is going on in her book. Much of it comprises letters written in 1927 and 1928 by the author to close family members recalling domestic events. It was undoubtedly privately printed.

Bibliography
•Cary, E. Marguerite. 1928. *A Jumble Jar*. N.p., 236 pp.
?_____. 1945. *My String of Pearls*.

Cash, Gwen Goldsmid 1891-? Gwen Goldsmid was born in England to a Jewish editor and his wife. After her father died young, her mother taught French in Birmingham, where her daughter was also educated before attending Stockwell Teachers Training College. She taught school for a few years, as well as entertaining hospitalized soldiers in the evenings. In 1917 she emigrated to Vancouver where she became a reporter on the *Daily Province*, the start of a journalistic career which would last on and off for sixty-five years. She married within the year and soon had a son. She and her family lived in a variety of places before settling down in 1938 to build a house behind Esquimalt Harbour on Vancouver Island. At the time, she was press representative for the Empress Hotel in Victoria. In the introduction to her 1977 autobiography *Off the Record*, she notes that "Much of [my] writing has been hack work, a desperate attempt to keep a jump ahead of the sheriff; a little of it has been deathless prose; only occasionally have I reaped the rewards of the ecstasy and anguish of writing. All of it has been fun." Her first book of poetry, *Unicorns* (1980), was published when she was eighty-nine.

During her first twenty years in British Columbia, Cash lived in an internment camp for alien Germans, on an Okanagan apple orchard, and in Squamish, Vancouver and Victoria. The title of her book, *I Like British Columbia*, reflects her satisfaction with the province, although she relates some negative events: the mosquitoes in the Fraser Valley were appalling when she picked berries there (p. 6); she found the clearcutting around Cowichan Lake sickening, even though she was told that "if a seed tree was left every so many square miles, there would be a natural reforestation in a very few years" (p. 165); and she was nearly arrested for playing craps with dice, not knowing that gambling in the province was illegal (p. 29). This book was illustrated by **Jean Middleton Donald**, the Quebec author and artist.

Cash published *A Million Miles from Ottawa* in 1942, when she feared that the Japanese would attack Vancouver Island, bombing Esquimalt Harbour and their home. From February to April she used a diary format to describe the general atmosphere of dread on the Island and the community anger that Ottawa wasn't planning for an evacuation of citizens, unlike Washington State (although Canada was sending valuable records and books east for safety); she also wanted increased repression of residents of Japanese origin, writing (p. 9):

why should any Jap feel any particular allegiance to Canada? We have denied them voting rights. It's just foolishness to kid ourselves any of them like us particularly well. Disguise it as they do, I'm sure there is a smug, tittering satisfaction over our grief and horror about Singapore behind their inscrutable slant eyes. It would be queer if they didn't feel that way.

She buys Victory Bonds and urges increased war effort among Canadians, but inveighs against the government in Ottawa being "controlled by the French-speaking minority in Quebec" (p. 17).

Bibliography
•Cash, Gwen. 1938. *I Like British Columbia*. Toronto: Macmillan, 192 pp.
•_____. 1942. *A Million Miles from Ottawa*. Toronto: Macmillan, 152 pp.
•_____. 1977. *Off the Record*. Langley, BC: Stagecoach, 170 pp.

Cate, Alice E. Alice Cate was an American author.

Cate's short book *Henry Hudson* (with blank pages between each of the seventeen chapters) describes in flowery language the last few years of Henry Hudson, who explored with his men the coast of northern Europe, the Hudson River and Hudson Bay in Canada. She focuses on the mutiny of his crew on the final trip, "as atrocious a deed as ever blackened the murky chronicles of the sea" (p. 92). Following a terrible winter ice-bound in Hudson Bay, where all the men on the ship suffered from extreme hunger and cold, some of the crew put Hudson, his young son, and six feeble and sick crew members into a small boat and left them to die.

Bibliography
•Cate, Alice E. 1932. *Henry Hudson: The Romantic Story of an Unromantic Man*. Boston: Gorham Press, 121 pp.

Champion, Helen Jean 1910-? Helen Champion was an author who enjoyed Prince Edward Island.

Champion recounts in *Over on the Island* her visit just before the Second World War to Prince Edward Island, which she explored by foot and bicycle. She describes many historical episodes as well as whom she met and what she saw and experienced.

Bibliography
•Champion, Helen Jean. 1939. *Over on the Island*. Toronto: Ryerson, 262 pp.

Chant, Nellie Irene Cooper 1899-? See Bott, Helen entry. Nellie Chant worked at the St. George's School for Child Study at the University of Toronto.

Chase, Eliza Brown. Eliza Chase was one of a group of eight Americans, all interested in music, who discussed coming to Canada to visit Acadia and other parts of Nova Scotia. When they agreed to this expedition in the early 1880s, they were "surprised at the comparative ignorance shown regarding a region which, though seemingly distant, is in reality so accessible." After accumulating railway and steamer information, schedules, maps and excursion books, the group travelled to nine areas of the province, to each of which Chase devotes a chapter in *Over the Border*, recounting their minor adventures and adding historical notes of interest.

The success of this expedition led Chase to make others to Canada many years later and to write them up in other books. Most of Chase's *Transcontinental Sketches* describes conditions in eastern Canada that she experienced along with her friend Helen while travelling westward. She includes a number of poems and melodies in her text as well as Native legends.

Bibliography

•[Musical Notes for E, B and C]. 1884. *Over the Border: Acadia, the Home of "Evangeline."* Boston: James R. Osgood, 215 pp.
? Chase, Eliza Brown. 1902. *In Quest of the Quaint: New Brunswick and Quebec.* Philadelphia: Ferris and Leach, 253 pp.
•Chase, Eliza B. 1909. *Transcontinental Sketches: Legends, Lyrics and Romances Gleaned on Vacation Tours in Northeastern and Middle Canada and the Pacific States.* Philadelphia: John C. Winston, 344 pp.

Chipman, Eliza Ann 1807-1853. Eliza Chipman was born in Cornwallis Township, Nova Scotia, and raised in a religious family. In 1827 she married a cousin of the same name old enough to be her father; he had eight living children and together they had twelve more, eight of whom survived infancy. He soon became a Baptist minister, and head of a small congregation which necessitated their pioneering a small farm to make ends meet. As well as raising her large family, Eliza Chipman led women's prayer groups, taught Sunday school, established a day school in her home, and entertained ministers on circuit and lonely students from nearby colleges.

Chipman kept a secret spiritual diary for thirty years which she told her husband about a few days before her death. She wanted it published, "for she had enjoyed much comfort in reading christian Diaries, and therefore, if there could be a selection of gleanings from her own, which might be useful to others, she was willing that her friends and the public should have the benefit" (Gerson 1994, 21). *Memoir of Mrs Eliza Ann Chipman* is composed of hundreds of journal entries, each devoted to conversations with the Lord and/or observations about her state of spirituality. She begins her book: "July 20, 1823—This little book was made yesterday, for the purpose of penning down a few of the exercises of the mind. But filled as I am with a sense of my own weakness and insufficiency, I rejoice that the Lord is able to bless the weakest means for the good of his chosen."

Bibliography

•Janzen, Carol Anne. 1985. Eliza Ann Chipman. *Dictionary of Canadian Biography*, s.v. Chipman, Eliza Ann (Chipman).

•Chipman. 1855. *Memoir of Mrs Eliza Ann Chipman, Wife of the Rev. William Chipman, of Pleasant Valley, Cornwallis*. Sold by John Chase, Wolfville, 188 pp.

Chown, Alice Amelia BA 1866-1949.   Alice Chown grew up with six brothers in a prosperous Kingston family. She was an early graduate of Queen's University, where she studied political science and economics (BA 1887). As a dutiful daughter, she stayed at home until her deeply religious mother died when she was forty. From that time on she was free to do as she pleased, travelling extensively and exploring ways to improve society. She worked for female suffrage, women's trade unions and the League of Nations. During the First World War she was an ardent pacifist, which created tension in the women's movement in Canada and prompted her to move in 1917 to the United States. She lived there for the next ten years, teaching leaders at a trade union college. Her later varied activities included travelling to Europe and Russia to study trade unions, organizing teas for Jews and gentiles to foster racial understanding, writing a column for *The United Church Observer* and becoming honorary president in 1945 of the United Nations Society in Toronto.

The Stairway is the story of Chown's independent life from 1906 until after the First World War based on her diaries. She describes her various experiences in the context of a stairway, each step leading to greater freedom for herself and for others.

Bibliography

•Chown, Alice A. 1988 [1921]. *The Stairway*. Toronto: University of Toronto Press, 340 pp.

Churchill, Matilda Faulkner LLD 1840-1924.   Matilda Faulkner was raised in Nova Scotia where she attended normal school in Truro and taught for ten years. In her spare time she served as a volunteer Baptist missionary among the black population of Truro; she had wanted to be an overseas missionary, but single women were discouraged at that time. When she was thirty-one, she married George Churchill, a Baptist minister with whom she went to Siam and then India to spread God's word. While in Canada in 1884 on one of her few leaves, she spearheaded the formation of the Woman's Baptist Missionary Union.

Letters from My Home in India comprises extracts of Churchill's letters written between 1871 and 1916. They describe in detail the schools she ran, the place religion had in her everyday life, her discouragement in making few converts over the years and the "knarls and kinks of heathenism" in the older people with which she had to contend (p. 61). When she was in Nova Scotia in 1916 on furlough, now a widow both deaf and lame, she felt too sick to prepare her letters for publication; this was done by **Grace McLeod Rogers**, MA, so that they would inspire church women in Canada. Churchill arranged that every Baptist Sunday school have a copy. She returned permanently from India to Nova Scotia when she was eighty-one. Two years later, a year before her death, she received an honorary degree from Acadia University. Conrad et al. (1988, 118-33) write:

> [Churchill's] words convey the strong sense of purpose that she brought to her chosen career, the special relationship that she developed with the women among whom she worked, and the determination with which she carried on despite tragedy [three of her four children died in India and she was separated from her daughter in Canada], heartbreak and, finally, the infirmities of old age. Although Matilda's smug sense of superiority may seem misplaced, her pragmatic approach to missionary work yielded success in her own terms and enabled her to love her adopted India as much as her native Nova Scotia.

Bibliography
•Churchill, Matilda Faulkner. 1916. *Letters from My Home in India, Being the Correspondence of Mrs George Churchill (1871-1916)*. Toronto: McClelland, Goodchild and Stewart, 305 pp.

Clark, Mattie M.I. BA MA 1913?-1996. Mattie Clark graduated from the University of Toronto in 1934 and earned her master's degree two years later, writing her thesis on John Graves Simcoe. She became a teacher of English and history at several high schools in Ontario, notably at Monarch Park Collegiate in Toronto where she worked for twenty years; she retired as head of the guidance department there in the late 1970s. In retirement she helped foreign graduate students with their English, and gave tours to visitors of the University of Toronto campus.

The focus of *The Positive Side of John Graves Simcoe*, which evolved from Clark's master's thesis, was "to explain the economic point of view that lay behind Simcoe's work in Upper Canada. Discussions of Simcoe have in the past laid so much emphasis on the military and sentimental sides of his character that the practical side has received much less attention than it merits."

Bibliography
•Clark, Mattie M.I. 1943. *The Positive Side of John Graves Simcoe*. Toronto: Forward Publishing, 121 pp.

Clarke, Flora KIH d. 1961. Flora Clarke grew up in Nova Scotia, where
she trained to be a teacher. She taught in small schools for a few years
before sailing for India in 1901, backed by First Moncton United Baptist
Church. There she served as a missionary for thirty-five years under the
Canadian Baptist Foreign Mission Board, founding and managing four
schools and an institute for lepers. In addition, she led seventy women in
Sunday school classes, daily Bible meetings, weekly women's gatherings
and evangelistic rallies and campaigns. She was awarded the Kaisar-i-Hind
medal by King George V for her efforts.

After she retired, Clarke wrote *Sisters: Canada and India* to describe
her work in India, draw these two countries closer together and pay tribute
to scores of fellow church workers in India and Canada, including **Matilda
Churchill** and **Katherine McLaurin** and her mother.

Bibliography
•Clarke, Flora, KIH. 1939. *Sisters: Canada and India*. Moncton, NB: Maritime
  Press, 682 pp.

Clint, Mabel Brown, ARRC 1874-1939. Mabel Clint was a writer and
nurse who, with the declaration of war in 1914 when she was forty, joined
the war effort "for the duration," although no one knew how long that
would be. She was one of the first nurses to reach the front in France, and
later nursed also in Greece and Belgium.

Our Bit, based on her diary, recounts her war experiences. Despite her
considerable seasoning, she writes in a diffident manner; at one period she
is hospitalized for some time, but does not tell why. She recalls in 1915
hearing the strains of "O Canada" before it had official English words: "It
is time it should be sung as well as played, though it must of course remain
secondary to the 'The King,' the anthem of the British Empire (p. 51)."
Clint wrote the book because she believed there were no others that told the
story of the Canadian nurses' efforts. Its publication was made possible by
the Alumnae Association of the Royal Victoria Hospital in Montreal and by
other subscribers. Clint was also a novelist.

Bibliography
•Clint, M.B., ARRC. 1934. *Our Bit: Memories of War Service by a Canadian
  Nursing-Sister*. Montreal: Alumnae Association of the Royal Victoria Hospi-
  tal, 177 pp.

Coleman, Kathleen Blake Willis Watkins 1864-1915. Kathleen Blake was born in western Ireland and when sixteen wed George Willis in a marriage arranged by her father. When her husband died four years later, she came to Canada, worked briefly as a secretary, then married her boss, Edward Watkins. They moved to Winnipeg, where they had two children before he died of a heart attack in 1889. She returned to Toronto to become a journalist, with one of her first assignments in Cuba to cover the Spanish-American War (1898) and another the aftermath of the San Francisco earthquake (1906). She became editor of a weekly woman's page, "Woman's Kingdom," in the *Toronto Mail*, a position she held for twenty-one years. It was read and enjoyed by thousands, including the prime minister, Wilfrid Laurier, with whom she had shared a royal coach at Queen Victoria's Diamond Jubilee. Later her column was syndicated. When she was thirty-four, she married a doctor, Theobald Coleman, but continued her career even while living with him at Copper Cliff, Ontario. She was both emancipated and sexist, approving smoking and drinking by men, but not by women. She considered marriage a career, but felt it should not prevent other work. She wrote: "The man who stands in the path of the New Woman can be compared to an idiot attempting to force back a tidal wave with a cricket bat" (Ferguson 1978, 8). She was the first president of the Canadian Women's Press Club and a friend and supporter of **Pauline Johnson**, **Mabel Burkholder**, **Katherine Hale** and **Gertrude Balmer Watt.**

To London for the Jubilee is in the form of letters from her newspaper column, describing her visit to England in 1897 for Queen Victoria's Diamond Jubilee. She published it because she was "obeying the commands of certain shadows who ... have written over vague signatures asking that such letters be gathered together and presented in the form of a book." She did not edit the letters because they "were set down with a hot pen while the events related were yet happening."

Bibliography
- Ferguson, Ted. 1978. *Queen of Hearts*. Toronto: Doubleday.

Freeman, Barbara M. 1989. *Kit's Kingdom: The Journalism of Kathleen Blake Coleman 1889-1915*. Ottawa: Carleton University Press.
- Coleman, Kit. 1897. *To London for the Jubilee*. Toronto: Morang, 154 pp.

Collier, Della. Della Collier was an author who cherished her magnificent garden, Woodbine, which was surrounded by woods on the coast of British Columbia. It had belonged to pioneers Mary and David (no last name given) from England, who first planted it in the nineteenth century.

In *Echoes from an Old Garden*, Collier devotes short chapters to different aspects of the garden, such as the owners, seeds, paths, scent, vegetables, lawn, bees and herbs. The last chapter, "Floweralities," discusses some of the plants grown, along with recipes and anecdotes. She describes the European plant Bouncing Bet, for example, as "a healthy, lively, buxom, wandering adventuress." Although the tone of the book is nostalgic, she ends it on an up-to-date pragmatic note, correlating gardening with war. She writes, "A few trials and hardships have taught men to be ready for the predatory Japanese beetles, Nazi and Fascist greedy bugs that creep in unawares, and it will, I am sure, promote a pleasant feeling in our fighting men as they drop a destructive, yellow, slant-eyed beetle, a greedy, black-shirted, scaly-scab, or a spotted, sallow Nazi worm with a shot of spray."

Bibliography
•Collier, Della. 1944. *Echoes from an Old Garden.* New Westminster: Jackson Printing, 104 pp.

Concannon, Helena Walsh BA MA DLitt TD 1878-1952. Helena Concannon was born in Ireland, the daughter of a judge and his wife. She married in 1906 after receiving a good education which enabled her to become a noted historian, biographer, and poet. As an early feminist, ardent nationalist and Roman Catholic, she wrote several books about Catholic saints and *Women of 'Ninety-Eight* (1920), the story of mothers, wives and sisters who fought, died and grieved in the Irish battle for freedom of 1798. She was fluent in the Irish language, working to revive this and Irish culture from her home in Galway.

White Horsemen contains the stories of eight Jesuit Martyrs who died in North America; they appeared in serial form in the Catholic mission newsletter *Far East* the year the men were canonized as saints. Five of these men went to Canada to convert the Natives to Catholicism. Concannon devotes about a chapter to each, including the well-known missionaries Father Jean de Brébeuf and Father Gabriel Lalemant, who were tortured and killed by Iroquois Indians in 1649 near what is now Midland, Ontario. She calls their murders their "glorious triumph" when "these victims of the Indians' hatred of the Faith inspired in the hearts of their fellow-missioners and contemporaries the reverent devotion due to martyrs." The author gives a chronology of the process by which these men were sanctified, commending Canada for "her long fidelity, her warmth of devotion to the memory of her Martyrs" and the United States for "an energy of action and initiative, which expect and obtain speedy results."

Bibliography
•Concannon, Mrs Thomas, MA DLitt. 1930. *White Horsemen: The Story of the Jesuit Martyrs of North America.* London: Sands and Co., 125 pp.

Cook, Marjorie See Grant, Marjorie entry.

Copleston, Mrs Edward. Mrs Copleston and her husband, two small daughters and a nurse emigrated to Ontario from England in 1856 because "Painful circumstances, over which we had no control, have altered our fortunes at home." They spent their first winter in the bush outside Orillia, then turned to farming to make a living.

Copleston's book describes their early experiences, with chapters on the climate, on animal and plant life and on farming. She writes modestly in *Canada: Why We Live in It, and Why We Like It* that "These unpretending sketches of recent life in Canada were sent home under peculiar circumstances, and accompanied by an earnest injunction from the writer, that her name should not appear" in connection with them. However, the Archbishop of Dublin, who had access to the manuscript, advised that it should be published with normal credit to the author (although the author's first name is not given).

Bibliography
•Copleston, Mrs Edward. 1861. *Canada: Why We Live in It, and Why We Like It.* London: Parker, Son and Bourn, 121 pp.

Cowan, Helen I. BA MA, PhD. Helen Cowan was educated at the University of Toronto, Columbia University, Harvard University and the University of London. She taught briefly, then did historical research privately and for business and government. She was also involved in publishing historical periodicals, Canadian magazines and newspapers.

Cowan's important book, *British Emigration to British North America 1783-1837*, was first published in 1928, then republished in 1961 in a new, revised and enlarged edition. It was an adaptation of her thesis, written while she spent two years in postgraduate work at the Institute of Historical Research in London. She writes, "Every effort has been made to continue the specific detail of persons and places and of programmes and policies for emigration which was said to be a helpful feature of the first study." When she undertook her work, research in emigration was just beginning; its chief proponent was Prof **Lilian Knowles**, who taught at the London School of Economics.

Bibliography
•Cowan, Helen I. 1961 [1928]. *British Emigration to British North America 1783-1837.* Toronto: University of Toronto Press, 321 pp.

Cowan, Mary Edith. Mary Cowan was for many years a teacher for the Ottawa School Board, but she also took time off for a world trip in 1921 with her six-year-old adopted daughter.

Rainbow of Life comprises a series of vignettes based on her world trip; a section devoted to her career in education; and a potpourri of short excerpts, most with a religious context.

Bibliography
•Cowan, Mary Edith. 1945. *Rainbow of Life*. Ottawa: private, 52 pp.

Cramp, Mary 1834?-1913. Mary Cramp was a deeply religious woman devoted to the Baptist missionary movement.

The first Missionary Board in Canada, formed in 1870, was that of Baptists of the Maritime Provinces. The Woman's Baptist Missionary Union in the Maritimes, founded in part by **Matilda Churchill**, arose from this and, having "yielded fruit," was "thought worthy of a simple record." Cramp's *Retrospects* considers the state of mission work by these maritime women in five-year periods beginning in 1870. She quotes a fellow worker at the end of her book: "Every department of Christian effort feels the throb of a quickened life, and the sinning and suffering of every age, grade, and class, are being helped and rescued. Equipped as we are for work, and inspired as we should be by success, shall we not take fresh courage and put on new strength."

Bibliography
•Cramp, Mary. 1892. *Retrospects: A History of the Formation and Progress of the Women's Missionary Aid Societies of the Maritime Provinces*. Halifax: Holloway Bros, 49 pp.

Cramp, Mary. Mary Cramp may or may not be related to the older Mary Cramp noted in the previous entry. This second Mary Cramp spent many years as a school teacher and administrator with her friend Maud Edgar; together they founded Miss Edgar's and Miss Cramp's School, which is still functioning in Montreal.

Eternal Youth, which comprises the authors' addresses to their school students (by Cramp) and graduating class (by Edgar), deals "with the problems of youth, which, with superficial variation due to time, place and circumstances, remain ever essentially the same." They resemble sermons, with each focused on a worthwhile theme (friendship, courage, thrift, loyalty, standards, education) and offering uplifting thoughts. In the hope that their book will be "of some interest to others [besides schoolgirls] with similar problems to solve, [the authors] venture to commit to print words first spoken to a small, but sympathetic and indulgent audience." The final paragraph in the book, addressed to a graduating class, reads, "But happily the voyage of life, although it may have its occasional storms, has also long spells of calm waters, blue skies and smiling sunshine. So if I cannot *promise* you, let me, at least, join with Prospero in *wishing* you Calm seas, propitious gales and sail so expeditious as may bring you, after a happy voyage, to the Islands of the Blessed."

Bibliography

•Cramp, Mary and Maud C. Edgar, BA. Headmistresses of Miss Edgar's and Miss Cramp's School Inc, Montreal, Canada. 1931. *Eternal Youth: Addresses to Girls, 1913-1930*. Toronto: Macmillan, 262 pp.

Cran, Marion 1879-1942. Marion Cran was a noted British gardener who wrote many books about gardens, for example, those in America and South Africa, as well as about her own gardens in Surrey and Kent, *I Know a Garden* (1933). She was given travelling expenses by the Canadian government and by Canadian railways to visit Canada twice for a period of six-and-a-half months in the hope that she might by her writing persuade British people to emigrate there. She received no pay, so felt that she was not constrained from telling the truth about the country as she saw it. Five newspapers printed her articles before her book was published.

Cran saw *A Woman in Canada* (1908) not as a travel book, but rather "a series of snapshots, offered with ragged edges— unglazed, unmounted, unframed, rapid, disconnected reproductions of this picture and of that which burned into the memory." She considers especially the possibilities Canada has for women who might want to immigrate on their own, and for people heading for the prairies and for British Columbia. She advises against settling in central and Eastern Canada where the cities are over-full and farms are already in production. She found Canada to be fascinating, primitive and in need of manual labour.

Bibliography

•Cran, Mrs George. 1908. *A Woman in Canada*. Toronto: Musson, 283 pp.

Creswicke, May Spry 1870-? May Creswicke's life, like that of her family and forebears, centred around her church in Barrie, Ontario. She headed the Woman's Auxiliary, led a girl's Bible class, and served on the Building Committee struck to oversee the rebuilding of the church after fire destroyed its interior in 1934, just as her husband had been involved in 1907 in an earlier renovation project. One daughter was organist from 1921-26 and another from 1928-32. The church has a 1930 stained glass window in honour of her husband, a 1930 bronze plaque in memory of a son, and a 1934 Chapel Aisle Lamp to commemorate a daughter.

The History of Trinity Church, Barrie, which was written for its centenary, contains descriptions of the church and its activities under succeeding
rectors. Creswicke ends it: "God planted His Church in Barrie. It has been
faithfully kept alive and handed on to us. It is for us to hand on the torch in
unbroken continuity."

Bibliography

•Creswicke, Mrs A.E.H. (May Spry). 1935. *The History of Trinity Church, Barrie, Ontario, Canada 1835-1935*. Barrie: author, 60 pp.

Cruickshank, Julia E. Kennedy d. 1921.   In 1904, Julia Cruickshank
received from E., presumably her husband, an acre of land surrounded by
deep, inaccessible ravines opposite the whirlpool on the Canadian side of the
Niagara River. They tented on their land during that summer and the next
summer lived in their newly built barn. Unfortunately, by then she realized
that "The Dream House will always be a dream," because E. accepted a
position at the Public Archives. They moved in 1905 to Ottawa, planning to
visit their property for a few weeks each summer.

Whirlpool Heights, the name of her book as well as of the property, is
composed of irregular diary entries ostensibly about "the making of a
home" by her and E., but often describes instead more mundane activities
such as ruminations on books she is reading or comments about nature and
the weather.

Bibliography

•Cruickshank, Julia. 1915. *Whirlpool Heights: The Dream-House on the Niagara
River*. London: Allen and Unwin, 254 pp.

Cummings, Emily Ann McCausland Shortt Willoughby, DCL
1851-1930.   Emily Shortt from Port Hope, Ontario, the daughter of a minister and his wife, married the barrister Willoughby Cummings in 1871.
She was always religious, helping in 1885 to found the Woman's Auxiliary
to the Missionary Society of the Anglican Church in Canada. After her
husband's death in 1892 she became a journalist, working on the editorial
staff of the Toronto *Globe* from 1893 to 1903. She then entered the civil
service in Ottawa. When the National Council of Women was founded in
1893, Cummings became Corresponding Secretary, a position she retained
until 1910. In 1910 she was given an honorary degree of DCL from King's
College, Windsor, in recognition of her active involvement in work for
women and children. The oration in Latin praised her as a woman, and continued "but truth compels me to state that there are others, the militant suf-
fragettes, who smash windows and go on disagreeable hunger strikes. It is
not such a one I now present to you for this honour, but rather. . . . "

Cummings was the ideal person to write *Our Story*, a history of the Woman's Auxiliary which she had helped found, because for twenty-five years she was the editor of its official magazine, *The Living Message*. From its establishment in 1885 with seven members, it was so successful that it soon became less an auxiliary than an independent body; by 1928 it had 94,256 members, supporting thirty-four overseas missionaries.

Bibliography

•Cummings, Mrs Willoughby, DCL. 1928. *Our Story: Some Pages from the History of the Woman's Auxiliary of the Missionary Society of the Church of England in Canada 1885-1928*. Toronto: Garden City Press, 148 pp.

Currie, Emma Augusta Harvey 1828?-1913. Emma Harvey, who came of United Empire stock, was born in Niagara, Ontario, educated in New York state and married the Hon. J.G. Currie MLC in 1865. She was a reformer who believed that Canadian women had earned the right of political equality with men. When Currie acquired a newspaper clipping about how, in 1813, Laura Secord had walked thirty km from Queenston to Beaver Dams (but almost certainly not with a cow) to warn the British of an impending American attack, she prepared a paper on her to present to the newly formed Women's Literary Club of St Catharines, where she lived. Her interest in Secord lasted her whole life; in 1911, when she was in her eighties, Currie was instrumental in securing a grant from the government to erect a memorial to Laura Secord at Queenston Heights.

Currie wrote her book, *The Story of Laura Secord*, because she felt that not enough was known about this heroine; after the War of 1812, Secord had lived with her husband's relations, virtually unknown, for twenty-five years. To obtain material for the book, Currie contacted Secord's relatives in Great Barrington, MA, where Secord was born, as well as other relatives elsewhere.

Bibliography

•Currie, Emma. 1900. *The Story of Laura Secord and Canadian Reminiscences*. Toronto: Briggs, 254 pp.

Currie, Margaret. Margaret Currie was the pseudonym of Irene Currie Love, later Mrs Elfred Archibald of Montreal, a popular columnist for a Montreal newspaper. When she was a school girl in 1904, she won a writing competition whose prize was a trip to the World's Fair in St Louis. She went with fifteen Canadian women journalists who, on the train trip home, decided to found the Canadian Women's Press Club, of which **Kit Coleman** was first president (Rex 1995).

Currie dedicates *Margaret Currie, Her Book*, "To my correspondents— to you who have made 'Margaret Currie' possible by your encouragement,

your co-operation and your continued support during the ten years I have conducted my page on the *Montreal Star*—this little [*sic*] book is dedicated in all
humility. Many of you have been good enough to say you would like to have
some of my pages in book form and it is because of these requests that this
book has been compiled." The entries cover personal ruminations plus comments on relationships, clothes, games, beauty, household hints and especially
food. In her chapter "Street Car Manners" (pp. 24-27), she urges mothers in
a crowded car not to put their child onto a seat offered by a gentleman who
has given up his; if she continued standing, this would necessitate the next
man getting up too; she also observes that nothing makes men "rage so furi-
ously as to see a woman standing at the back when there are vacant seats up
front." She writes, "Girls, don't cross your limbs on the car—it isn't lady-
like, and it's positively shocking if you wear white stockings." Her last admo-
nition is: "When conversing on the car, do it in an undertone. Loud talking is
bad form; and don't laugh out loud—it draws attention."

Bibliography
•Currie, Margaret. 1924. *Margaret Currie, Her Book*. Toronto: Hunter-Rose, 352 pp.

Davidson, Laura Lee.   Laura Davidson was an author who lived in
Toronto.

In *A Winter of Content* Davidson spends a winter alone at the start of
the First World War in the cottage on a rocky island in Frontenac County
which served as a summer retreat away from Toronto for her birth family.
She writes often amusingly about nature all around her and about the activities of her neighbours who are long-time residents. She asks them not to
hunt or let their dogs chase snowshoe hares on her island so that they and
she can enjoy the solitude.

In *Isles of Eden* she describes her return to the island three years later to
spend a summer, this time with a friend, Patricia. The book is in diary format, describing the plants and animals around her and again chronicles her
neighbours' doings.

Bibliography
•Davidson, Laura Lee. 1922. *A Winter of Content*. New York: Abingdon, 217 pp.
•_____. 1924. *Isles of Eden*. New York: Minton, Balch, 200 pp.

Davies, Blodwen 1897-1966.   Blodwen Davies was born in Longueuil,
Quebec, and would eventually write a number of books about her native
province, although she lived most of her life in Markham, near Toronto. In
the early 1930s, when she was a struggling freelance writer, she fell in love
with Frederick Banting who also attended functions of the Arts and Letters
Club in Toronto; at the time she wanted medical advice for the book she

was writing about Tom Thomson and he wanted help in becoming a writer. She was shattered when, after the breakup of his marriage in 1932, he refused to marry her. Most of her books were "light but competent travel books that combine description, local history, and legend" (Story 1967, 202). Davies, an idealist, was active during the Second World War in the movement directed at making the government more responsive after the war to culture and the cultural community. Her last book, *A String of Amber: The Heritage of the Mennonites*, about the mass movement of Mennonites from Pennsylvania to Ontario, was published posthumously in 1973.

The Storied Streets of Quebec discusses early Quebec City buildings, its past inhabitants (especially Champlain and his wife Hélène, so lovely "that the Indians thought she was one of the angels the Recollets had taught them of") and the 1759 Battle of the Plains. She ends with a memorial to Wolfe and Montcalm which reads: "History gave them a common fame, destiny a common death, and posterity a common monument."

In *Ruffles and Rapiers* Davies describes eight historical romances with a Canadian connection. Among these stories are those of Champlain's wooing of a "Huguenot maid" considered socially beneath him; Count de Frontenac's relations with his wife Anne (after his death in Quebec his heart was sent back to Anne in Paris in a silver box, but she refused to accept it); James Wolfe and the two English women he might have married; and the morganatic marriage of Mde Julie de St Laurent and the Duke of Kent, the fourth son of King George III, who lived together for eight years in Canada. (When England needed a future sovereign, he had to leave his wife and marry a royal princess who would produce Princess Victoria.)

Saguenay, about the Saguenay River in Quebec, was commissioned by the Canada Steamship Lines, which ran trips up and down this river. It gives information on the surroundings and their history and would presumably be sold on these excursions to tourists.

Storied York begins with a general history of Toronto, then discusses in detail the various old buildings and areas in the downtown area. There are short chapters devoted to Old Fort York, Osgoode Hall, Queen's Park, University of Toronto and the Toronto Exhibition. She mentions in a section devoted to the Art Gallery of Ontario that it does not own sculptures by the talented Elizabeth Wyn Wood but had acquired a bust of her done by her husband, also a sculptor.

Romantic Quebec covers not only Quebec City, but also the history of inhabited areas of the province that lie mostly along the St Lawrence River. She writes, "Like the traveller of many generations ago, we go to Quebec bent on 'health, pleasure, and the pursuit of a reasonable curiosity,'—and our desires will almost certainly be satisfied."

The Charm of Ottawa describes this city and gives historical accounts of its various regions and prominent inhabitants. Davies describes the terrible death from hydrophobia of the Duke of Richmond while he was on a canoe trip, after being bitten weeks before by a pet fox with rabies. The town of Richmond near Ottawa was named for him.

Davies set up in type herself, with the help of artist Frank Carmichael, her book *Tom Thomson* and published one hundred copies, charging $5.00 each, which seemed expensive in the 1930s. Before she died, she asked the artist A.Y. Jackson to have the book republished and updated, which he did in a handsome memorial edition. Thomson (1877-1917) was an artist who devoted the last few years of his life to painting in northern Ontario.

Planetary Democracy, which Davies co-authored, reflects the ideas of a small group of scientific humanists who were planning a democratic future for the world. They espoused the Chinese way of life of "practical idealism," since the Chinese were "in search of qualities which guarantee the humanity · of man, individual courage, individual initiative, individual adaptability, and individual discrimination." The group recognized the need, because the airplane, radio and television had in effect shrunk the world, to "formulate a new set of global concepts: planetary ideas about trade, ethical responsibilities, money, tariff, debts, raw materials, techniques for doing things, and so on."

Bibliography
•Davies, Blodwen. 1929 [1927]. *The Storied Streets of Quebec*. Montreal: Louis Carrier, 94 pp.
•_____. 1930. *Ruffles and Rapiers, Being the Half-Forgotten Romances of the Gallant Women and Doughty Men in the Days of Colonial Adventure*. Toronto: Ryerson Press, 124 pp.
•_____. 1930. *Saguenay "Sâginawa": The River of Deep Waters*. Montreal: Canada Steamship Lines, 204 pp.
•_____. 1931. *Storied York: Toronto Old and New*. Toronto: Ryerson, 127 pp.
•_____. 1932. *Romantic Quebec*. New York: Dodd, Mead, 213 pp.
•_____. 1932. *The Charm of Ottawa*. Toronto: McClelland and Stewart, 250 pp.
•_____. 1967 [1935]. *Tom Thomson: The Story of a Man Who Looked for Beauty and for Truth in the Wilderness*. Vancouver: Mitchell Press, 102 pp.
•Reiser, Oliver L. and Blodwen Davies. 1944. *Planetary Democracy: An Introduction to Scientific Humanism and Applied Semantics*. New York: Creative Age Press, 242 pp.

Davis, Mary Lee Caldwell BA MA. Mary Lee Caldwell was born in New Jersey and attended Wellesley and Radcliffe Colleges. After her marriage in 1908, she lived for eight years in the interior of Alaska. She was likely an American imperialist, given the titles of some of her books about this territory (*Uncle Sam's Attic*, 1930; *Alaska: The Great Bear's Cub*, 1930 and *We Are Alaskans*, 1931), but she was also interested in the Yukon and its history.

One day, her doctor mentioned to her that not only had he been part of the goldrush up and over the Chilkoot Trail but that he had kept two journals of his adventures on the trail and in Dawson City. Davis questioned him at length on his memories which, jogged by his journal entries, form the basis of her book *Sourdough Gold.*

Bibliography
•Davis, Mary Lee. 1933. *Sourdough Gold: The Log of a Yukon Adventure.* Boston: Wilde, 351 pp.

Day, Catherine Matilda Townsend 1815-1899. Catherine Townsend was the fifth of six children of Samuel and Pamelia Townsend who were pioneer farmers near Brome, Quebec. The family soon moved to Vermont, where the father died of fever. When she was twenty-one, Townsend, a religious young woman, worked in a textile mill in Lowell, MA, earning one dollar a week. Three years later she was employed as a teacher in a private school in Quebec near Lake Champlain. In 1840 she married Henry Day, a mill worker, with whom she would have six children. After her husband's death fourteen years later, she continued her teaching, settling in Stukely, Quebec. In her little spare time she wrote a novel and began gathering information about pioneer families of the area, publishing her historical books in 1863 and 1869. She had some difficulty selling them, travelling by train, boat and foot between small towns and farms to do so, but they gradually became popular; both have recently been republished. Day retired in 1875, moving first to Iowa to live with her daughter and be near two sons, and then back to Stukely where she died. La Société Historique du Comté de Shefford, located at Vittie House in Granby, has dedicated a research room in their building to her memory.

In *Pioneers of the Eastern Townships*, Day describes in detail the European people who first homesteaded there. Her aim was "to bring to a more lively remembrance the hardships and privations suffered by the early settlers of these townships." She concludes her preface: "We, their children and grand-children, living in the daily enjoyment of what, though seemingly necessary to us, were luxuries to them, are quite too ready to forget the price at which our comforts were bought."

In her heftier companion volume, *History of the Eastern Townships*, Day mourns the lack of respect given to Canadian authors:

> The importance of encouraging and building up a literature decidedly Canadian, commends itself to the intelligent and patriotic, with all the strength of conviction. A national literature is an essential element in the formation of a national character; a fact confirmed by all history; for among the nations of antiquity, the fame of poet, philosopher, hero or

> statesman, belonged to the people: was celebrated by them in story and in song; was incorporated into the national heart, and became a strong bond of national unity. So also has it been in later ages of the world.

She blames a lack of Canadian literature on national prejudices, religious animosities, and lack of time for reading "in this [1860s] world of hurry and encroachment." However, she is hopeful for the future:

> there is a growing conviction in the minds of the observing and clear-thinking of our people, that the evils to which we are unavoidably subjected, should find counteraction in a patriotic literature based on loyal sentiment and intelligent appreciation. Were the truth properly kept before the minds of our people, accepted and adopted by them, that Canadians of all origins and creeds, should merge minor differences in a nationality where all might meet on common ground; and were the pulpit, press and schoolroom rightly enlisted in forming correct standards of thought and action on this subject, we should soon witness improvement in a matter that vitally concerns us as a people.

Bibliography

Phelps, Marion L. 1988. *Biography of Mrs C.M. Day*. Knowlton, QC: published by the author.
•Day, Mrs C.M. 1863. *Pioneers of the Eastern Townships: A Work Containing Official and Reliable Information Respecting the Formation of Settlements; with Incidents in Their Early History; and Details of Adventures, Perils and Deliverances*. Montreal: J. Lovell, 171 pp.
•_____. 1869. *History of the Eastern Townships, Province of Quebec, Dominion of Canada, Civil and Descriptive*. Montreal: J. Lovell, 475 pp.

Dean, Mary Morgan. Mary Dean was a Canadian author.

For her biography *The Lady with the Other Lamp*, Dean extracted details from the life of her friend **Blanche Read Johnston**, who had worked all her life in public service. Dean writes, "As all the reforms to which she gave these years of splendid service are subject of vital and public interest, we persuaded Mrs Johnston to permit her life story to be told in the present form." This format resulted in an unusual text. For example, the first page of the book reads " 'I loved, with fleet foot and merry laugh, to chase the sun-touched butterflies,' says Mrs Blanche Read Johnston of her childhood."

Bibliography

•Dean, Mary Morgan. 1919. *The Lady with the Other Lamp: The Story of Blanche Read Johnston*. As told to Mary Morgan Dean. Toronto: McClelland and Stewart, 282 pp.

Dease, Teresa, Rev. Mother See Member of the Community.

De Kiriline, Louise See Lawrence, Louise entry.

De la Roche, Mazo 1879-1961.   Mazo Roche (as a child she added the French prefix to her family name) was born in Newmarket, Ontario, to a carpenter and his wife. She grew up mostly in Toronto, where she became close friends with her cousin, Caroline Clement, who would live with her for seventy years. She attended the Ontario School of Art, but turned to writing to earn her living after her father died when she was thirty-six. She became internationally famous in 1927 when her fourth novel, *Jalna*, won a prestigious $10,000 prize offered by the *Atlantic Monthly* magazine. From 1929 to 1938, she and Clement lived in England, raising two orphaned children they had adopted.

De la Roche wrote twenty-three novels and over fifty stories and plays, often to great acclaim, but in the war years she also wrote one non-fiction book commissioned by Doubleday Press. *Quebec, Historic Seaport* is a readable and anecdotal history of Quebec City, a place she had always found romantic. "Exhilarated at the prospect of venturing into a new genre, she described the year's project as a cuckoo's egg deposited in 'the austere nest of the historians'" (Givner 1989, 194). De la Roche writes in her book's preface, "After having spent the greater part of my life in writing of imaginary characters it has been a novel experience to write an account of historical events, a strange experience to keep my very active imagination in leash. I have found great fascination in these characters of the past, even with their weight of cold dates, treaties, and acts." She ends her preface, "I hope I have written an interesting history of the Port of Quebec. But if my readers decide that I have not, I can promise them this—nothing of the sort will ever happen again!" The book is dedicated to fellow author **Katherine Hale**, "in friendship and in appreciation of her vivid sketches of the Canadian scene."

Bibliography

Bratton, Daniel. 1996. *Thirty-two Short Views of Mazo de la Roche*. Toronto: ECW Press.

•Daymond, D.M. 1988. Mazo de la Roche. *Dictionary of Literary Biography: Canadian Writers, 1920-1959*, s.v. de la Roche, Mazo.

•De la Roche, Mazo. 1944. *Quebec, Historic Seaport*. Garden City, NY: Doubleday, Doran, 212 pp.

Denison, Grace Elizabeth Sandys d. 1914. Grace Sandys, born in Chatham, Ontario, was the daughter of a venerable archdeacon and his wife. After being educated in New York and London, she married, but later separated from her husband and became a journalist. She was known as "Lady Gay" while social editor of *Saturday Night* and as such edited *The Canadian Family Cook Book* (1914 revised edition, 538 pp.) by "Prominent Canadian Ladies."

For her book *A Happy Holiday*, Denison set off by ship from New York to travel through Europe by herself, carrying all her clothes in a hand-made carry-all and keeping an extensive journal of her adventures. The book was apparently self-published, as she refers to "the dear five hundred friends who shall read my first edition." Denison makes no apology for the everyday incidents she describes: "is not the common-place too near to every one of us to be despised? And should the reading of their happenings give one hundredth part of the pleasure the living of them did, my temerity in laying them before you will be forgiven."

Bibliography
•Denison, Grace E. 1890. *A Happy Holiday*. Toronto: n.p., 255 pp.

Dennis, Clara Gertrude LittD 1877-1963. Clara Dennis, who was born and raised in Nova Scotia, was the daughter of Senator William Dennis and Agnes Dennis MA CBE, who was prominent in the Victorian Order of Nurses and in National Council of Women work. Clara Dennis was a life member of the Nova Scotia Historical Society and a member of the Canadian Women's Press Club. During the First World War she entertained thousands of soldiers in her home, and supported in any way she could prisoners of war and foreign troops passing through Halifax. She was awarded a LittD from Mount Allison University in 1938 in recognition of her contribution to Nova Scotian literature.

Dennis was so enamoured of her home province that she wrote three books about it, the first of which went into six printings in thirteen years. *Down in Nova Scotia*, with a complimentary foreword by former Prime Minister Robert Borden, was inspired by Dennis consulting a map of this province and deciding that she must visit the many unfamiliar places it named. She writes:

> I would travel over her highways and byways. I would know her cities, her towns, her villages. I would visit the remote and but little frequented islands of her coast. I would talk with the men, women and children I might meet. In their lives would be unfolded the soul of Nova Scotia. I would learn too, about those who had gone before, the pioneer men and

women who shaped the policies and moulded the destinies of Nova Scotia. I would pause in silent tribute at their pioneer graves.

And she did what she proposed, setting out by car for Windsor, then working her way east and south to Shelburne and Sable Island.

In her second book, *More about Nova Scotia*, Dennis resumes her quest to acquaint herself with her province, beginning in Shubenacadie and visiting the rest of the mainland. At Port Mouton she describes a game of golf in progress on a sandy beach with red golf balls; at Chester an old house with a secret staircase behind the fireplace for escape from an Indian or pirate raid; and near Springhill mines fossils of ferns and trees from a once-mighty forest that grew there.

In *Cape Breton Over*, which completes Dennis's tour of Nova Scotia, she continues to meet a variety of Nova Scotians and to delve into the history and diversity of each locality. She describes Alexander Graham Bell's association with the island, noting that one of his little-known projects, which lasted for thirty years, was raising multi-nippled sheep so that if a ewe gave birth to twins, she could feed them more expeditiously.

Bibliography
•Dennis, Clara. 1934. *Down in Nova Scotia*. Toronto: Ryerson, 411 pp.
•_____. 1937. *More about Nova Scotia*. Toronto: Ryerson, 412 pp.
•Dennis, Clara, LittD. 1942. *Cape Breton Over*. Toronto: Ryerson, 342 pp.

Derick, Carrie Matilda BA MA (PhD) 1862-1941. Carrie Derick was born in Clarenceville, Quebec, into a United Empire Loyalist family. She became a teacher, then studied botany at McGill University from 1887-90, graduating with the gold medal in natural science. She was appointed a demonstrator in botany at McGill in 1891, the first woman to serve on the faculty. After studying part-time she earned her master's degree there in 1896. Although she knew that because she was a woman she would not be awarded her PhD, she took time off from teaching to do the work for this degree at the University of Bonn, Germany. In 1904 she became an assistant professor at McGill and in 1912 was promoted to full professor, the first woman to be appointed to this rank at a Canadian university (Gillett 1990). Because of her extensive research publications, she became a Fellow of the Botanical Society of America and a member of the American Association for the Advancement of Science, the American Genetics Association and the Canadian Public Health Association at a time when such memberships were rare for women. "Her witty lectures on civic reform and botany kept her in demand as a speaker. As president of the Montreal Suffrage Association from 1913 to 1919, she urged that domestic service be given the status of a profession and wanted women to pursue careers in agriculture" (Bannerman 1977, 69). She was a lifelong member of the National Council of Women and a close friend of fellow-professor **Maude Abbott.**

Derick's *Flowers of the Field and Forest* lacks her name as author, but the preface notes that the articles, first printed in *The Star Weekly*, "are from the pen of a well known botanist of high standing and are accurate and trustworthy in every detail." She usually drew and described the many species from actual specimens. The descriptions are far more detailed than one would currently expect to find in a newspaper article: for example, the pussy willow catkin is "a cluster of very simple flowers, each of which, being destitute of calyx, corolla and pistil, consists of two slender stamens standing in front of a little hairy leaf called a bract." As well as describing individual flowering plants, she states which species flower during the different seasons of the year, where in Canada they can be found and interesting floral lore—"the essential problem is to understand the life of the plant, to comprehend its functions, to inquire what is the use to the plant of its root, stem, leaves, its flower and fruit." She ends her book:

> Though the last flower of the year will soon fade [in autumn], there will be much to delight a botanist in woodland walks. The delicate and characteristic tracery of naked branches against blue sky, the scattering of fruits and seeds, the protection of growing tips in buds, the habits and forms of evergreens—all afford subjects of study and objects of interest to the nature-lover, who finds no season unlovely or dull.

Bibliography
•Gillett, Margaret. 1990. Carrie Derick (1862-1941) and the Chair of Botany at McGill. M.G. Ainley, ed. *Despite the Odds*, 74-87. Montreal: Véhicule.
•D., C.M. 1901. *Flowers of the Field and Forest: Reprint of a Series of Articles which Appeared in the Family Herald and Weekly Star during the Summer of 1900*. N.p.: Family Herald and Weekly Star, 65 pp.

Dickie, Donalda James BA MA PhD LLD 1883-1972. Donalda Dickie, born in Hespeler, Ontario, was educated at Queen's (MA 1910), Oxford, Columbia and the University of Toronto (PhD 1929, LLD 1952). She taught in Alberta normal schools (Camrose, Calgary and Edmonton) from 1910 to 1945 when she retired to Vancouver. She wrote:

> Almost all the supplementary reading we have for children . . . has been written by English or American authors for English or American children. Canadians have as yet written scarcely anything for children. Yet few countries provide richer sources—romantic, historic, geographic, industrial. Moreover, writing for children pays—The need is great. The field is wide and almost virgin. It waits for you who will enter in and possess it. (Harrington 1981, 108)

Dickie took her own advice to heart, writing more than sixty books, many of them history readers and instructional works for teachers. She won the Governor General's Award for Juvenile Literature in 1951. Although this compendium does not in general include women who wrote only school readers or instructional manuals, an exception is made in the case of Dickie, who played such an important role in the education of Canadian schoolchildren. Four of her early books are here discussed briefly.

For one of her first books, *The Long Trail*, Dickie notes in the preface, "It is scarcely necessary to say that no original research has been done in preparing these stories, though the facts have been checked and rechecked by reference to as many writers as possible." (Even so, a note indicates that the Hudson's Bay Company found certain statements in the first edition "to be inaccurate, misleading and unfair to the Company" and that the publisher will amend future editions with the help of this company.) The eighty-one chapters each deal with a different person or incident, often by way of conversation and sometimes by means of a short play. (At Champlain's arrival, Indian Chief's only lines are: "(grunting). Great White Chief come home again. Great White Chief, Indian's brother. Indian glad. No prick. Indian sing. Indian dance."

In *When Canada Was Young*, Book 5 of Dent's Canadian History Readers, also first published in 1925, Dickie again makes the same disclaimer about the lack of original research for the book. She ends this reader after the final chapter on General Wolfe: "Thus the old Quebec became the new; and French and British join hands, inheriting the glory of the past and looking courageously toward the unknown future."

In *The Canadian West*, Book 7 of the Dent series, she writes about the Carrier Indians (p. 70) that the men were naked in summer until the white men came, when "a few adopted the breech-cloth which they wore one day about the loins, the next on their heads, and the third about their necks." She also notes that Carrier men "were very fond of their wives, and did all the hard work."

In Pioneer Days, about eastern and central Canada, has ninety-two chapters, some excerpted from other authors, including those on Grandma's bear, Old time lacrosse, Making soap, Writing a letter and a Pioneer library. There is a play about parliament, a fictional story and poems.

Bibliography

•Dickie, D.J. 1925. *When Canada Was Young*. Toronto: Dent, 224 pp.
• _____. 1927 [1925]. *The Long Trail*. Toronto: Dent, 175 pp.
• _____. 1926. *The Canadian West*. Toronto: Dent, 315 pp.
• _____. 1927 [1926] *In Pioneer Days*. Toronto: Dent, 287 pp.

Dimock, Celia C. d. 1959. Celia Dimock was an author who lived on Cape Breton Island.

Dimock notes in her preface that the stories about Cape Breton Island making up *Isle Royale* were mostly fireside tales handed down from one generation to the next; thus they may not be very accurate, "yet they are extremely interesting, with their associations of past days on this island." (This was before the island was joined by a causeway to the rest of Nova Scotia.) She also includes historical items from a variety of sources, and information on Micmac Indians, pioneers and missionaries.

Bibliography
•Dimock, Celia. 1929. *Isle Royale: The Front Door of Canada.* Halifax: Allen, 81 pp.

Donald, Jean Middleton. Jean Donald was a Quebec author and artist interested in her province.

Donald's *Quebec Patchwork* divides this province into twenty-eight geographical areas, each of which she equates with a kind of cloth—for example, tartan is the St Andrews area of the Ottawa River, buckskin a Native reserve area north of Quebec City, and watered silk the Saguenay River region. Each chapter discusses the character or history of one of these patches and the people who then lived in it. She illustrated the book herself with attractive black-and-white pictures.

Bibliography
•Donald, J.M. 1940. *Quebec Patchwork.* Toronto: Macmillan, 368 pp.

Dougall, Lily 858-1923 LLA. Lily Dougall was born in Montreal to Scottish immigrant parents; her father, John Dougall, was editor of a successful religious newspaper. She was the youngest of five children, all of whom were educated at private schools and deeply religious. However, although she was raised as an evangelical Presbyterian, she chose to be confirmed in the Episcopal church in her teen years (McMullen 1986). When she was twenty-two, Dougall moved to Scotland to be a companion to her aunt and to study at the Universities of Edinburgh and St Andrews in preparation for becoming an author. She graduated in 1887 from St Andrews with an LLA (Lady Licentiate in Arts), because women were not then allowed to receive an MA. She immediately began writing, publishing in all eight philosophical and theological works, short stories and articles as well as ten novels; her second novel, *What Necessity Knows* (1893), involves a diverse group of British immigrants living in a small town in eastern Quebec. Sometime after her first book of non-fiction was published in 1900, Dougall moved permanently from Canada to England, in part because England better suited her health. She settled near Oxford where she made her home into a centre for religious discussions and the publication of essays emanating from them.

In her 1900 book *Pro Christo et Ecclesia*, Dougall "develops the religious ideas she dramatized in her fiction, criticizing sectarianism and urging Christians to accept and adapt to new knowledge. Dougall stresses love—of God and neighbor—and voices objections to those denominations that reject art" (McMullen 1990). She wanted religion to be an integral part of everyday life, a part of drama, novels, songs and dance, rather than just a Sunday exercise. *Pro Christo et Ecclesia* was published anonymously and praised as a "work of great power" because it was assumed to be by an eminent (male) minister (McMullen 1990).

Bibliography

•McMullen, Lorraine. 1986. "Lily Dougall's vision of Canada." In *A Mazing Space: Writing Canadian Women Writing*, edited by Shirley Neuman and Smaro Kamboureli, pp 137-47. Toronto: Longspoon/NeWest Press.
•_____. 1990. Lily Dougall. *Dictionary of Literary Biography: Canadian Writers, 1890-1920*, s.v. Dougall, Lily.
•Anonymous. 1900. *Pro Christo et Ecclesia*. London: Macmillan, 189 pp.

Douglas, Frances Mary d. 1963. Frances Mary Douglas was born in Winnipeg to a doctor and his wife. After graduating from Bishop Strachan School in Toronto, she worked in New York before enlisting in the first group of the Royal Canadian Air Force Women's Division in 1941, serving overseas until 1945 as a flight officer and in public relations. She was then employed by the T. Eaton Co. as editor of the company's staff magazine, and by the Royal Conservatory of Music in Toronto in public relations.

The popular *Britannia Waives the Rules* was written by Douglas before she had been overseas and by her friend Thelma Lecocq. It is dedicated to "hit and run writers from England, but for whose charming inaccuracies on Canada we would not have dared—to Queen Mary of Scots, Joan of Arc, and other ladies who have misjudged the English—and to the Atlantic Ocean, which keeps us apart." It is a guidebook to England and the English that makes fun of their (to Canadians) peculiarities, reminiscent of similar books on Canada written by British travellers who had spent little time there. They discuss flippantly odd English words and pronunciations, sports, clothing, food, theatre, tourist sights, the countryside and the class system.

Bibliography

•Douglas, Frances (Who has never been there) and Thelma Lecocq (Who has). 1934. *Britannia Waives the Rules: A Confidential Guide to the Customs, Manners and Habits of "The Nation of Shop-keepers."* Toronto: Dent. 112 pp.

Doyle, Sister St Ignatius, CND, nun. The Reverend Mother Ignatius was a nun and teacher of the Congrégation de Notre-Dame in Montreal, whose founder was the subject of her biography.

Marguerite Bourgeoys and Her Congregation depicts the life of Bourgeoys with conversation and description so that it will appeal to and inspire young girls. Biographies of this same woman were written earlier by **Elizabeth Butler** and **Margaret Mary Drummond**, also nuns.

Bibliography
- Doyle, Sister St Ignatius. 1940. *Marguerite Bourgeoys and Her Congregation.* Gardenville, QC: Garden City Press, 318 pp.

Dressler, Marie 1869 or 1873-1934. Marie Dressler was born Leila Koerber in Cobourg, Ontario, (where she is still memorialized) and grew up with a desire to act. She appeared in Broadway theatres from 1896 on, and made her first film, "Tillie's Punctured Romance," in 1914. She was not pretty in the usual sense, but superb in physical comedy, exploiting her majestic ninety-kilogram size. During this time she was active in the suffragette movement, canvassing for votes for women. Her prominence faded in the 1920s, but resurged with the advent of talking movies. In the early 1930s she was the most famous film star in the United States, and the first actor whose face appeared on the cover of *Time* magazine. Between 1930 and her death in 1934 she played in twenty-four movies as a comedienne or dramatic actor. Today her most remembered films are those with the Marx Brothers. In a review of her 1997 biography by Betty Lee, David Weaver wonders "how an overweight, homely, less than charismatic woman could, at the advanced age of sixty, capture and hold the attention of Depression-era filmgoers so unwaveringly" (*Globe and Mail* October 4, 1997).

Dressler's autobiography, *The Eminent American Comedienne Marie Dressler*, describes her life before the advent of talking movies.

Bibliography
Lee, Betty. 1997. *Marie Dressler: The Unlikeliest Star.* Lexington, KY: University of Kentucky Press.
- Dressler, Marie. 1924. *The Eminent American Comedienne Marie Dressler in the Life Story of an Ugly Duckling: An Autobiographical Fragment in Seven Parts.* New York: McBride, 234 pp.

Drummond, Margaret Mary, CND nun 1882-? Margaret Drummond was a member of the Congrégation de Notre-Dame of Montreal.

Drummond's book *The Life and Times of Margaret Bourgeoys*, about the first teacher of Ville-Marie (Montreal) and the founder of Drummond's order of nuns, was written for its "pupils past and present." The Archbishop of Montreal, who worked for the sanctification of Bourgeoys, notes in the preface:

> The gifted authoress of this life of your Foundress has conferred a favor upon our Catholic people by producing this truly admirable book. The remarkable skill with which she has interwoven with the life of her heroine the most beautiful and thrilling incidents of the history of this city of Mary, gives additional value to her work. I hope this charming book will be extensively read, especially by our young people, who will find in it a glorious record of the sterling virtues of their ancestors and an antidote to the baneful literature of the day."

Other biographies of Bourgeoys would be written by nun **Elizabeth Butler** twenty-five years later, and by nun **Sister Doyle** thirty-three years later.

Bibliography

•Drummond, Margaret Mary. 1907. *The Life and Times of Margaret Bourgeoys (the Venerable)*. Boston: Angel Guardian Press, 275 pp.

Drummond, May Isabel Harvey, 1870?-1939. May Harvey, who was raised in Jamaica, met her future husband, William Henry Drummond, during a visit to Montreal. After their marriage in 1894 they settled in Montreal, where they had four children, although two sons died young. She died after a long illness in the small town of Ivry North, north of Montreal.

After her husband's death, Drummond wrote his biography, which was published posthumously in *The Great Fight* (1908). William Drummond (1854-1907) was born in Ireland, immigrating to Canada when he was ten. He became a doctor in the Montreal and Brome County areas, but was far more famous for his narrative verse in the rough dialect of French Canadian farmers.

As a friend and admirer of Thomas Chapman (1823-1912), the influential Rector of St Paul's Church in Marbleton, Eastern Townships of Quebec, Drummond collected, organized and published his memoirs. She arranged for *The Grand Old Man of Dudswell* to be sold largely by subscription; if there were a profit, this would go to Chapman's two daughters.

Bibliography

•Drummond, MD, Henry. 1908. *The Great Fight: Poems, Sketches*. Edited and with a biographical sketch by May Harvey Drummond. Toronto: Musson, 158 pp.
•Drummond, May Harvey. 1916. *The Grand Old Man of Dudswell Being the Memoirs of the Rev. Thos. Shaw Chapman, MA*. Quebec: Telegraph Printing, 182 pp.

Duff, Dorothy James. Dorothy (Annis) Duff loved books so much as a child that she became a librarian and bookseller. After she married, she raised her two children to love books too; when the girl was ten and the boy four, she wrote a book in turn describing how she did this. In 1953, Duff published a second book, *Longer Flight*, on the same theme, but focused on books for older children. The family spent summers at their cottage on Georgian Bay where they continued to enjoy literature.

The Duff family began reading aloud together when their first child was one and a half years old, following the earlier recitation of poetry and the singing of nursery rhymes—"good 'conversation' for a solemn small person who lies on a bath-table and listens with gratifying attention." They continued to read to her and to her younger brother as they grew older. In *"Bequest of Wings,"* Dorothy Duff analyzes many children's books at length; includes chapters on poetry, fairy tales, picture books and children's music; and discusses many other relevant topics using anecdotes and personal philosophy.

Bibliography
•Duff, Annis. 1944. *"Bequest of Wings": A Family's Pleasures with Books*. New York: Viking, 204 pp.

Dufferin and Ava, Hariot Georgina Rowan Hamilton, Countess of, 1843-1936. Hariot Hamilton was born in a castle in Northern Ireland and married a neighbour, who would become Lord Dufferin, in 1862. They lived in Ireland for ten years before coming with their five children to Canada where her husband had been appointed Governor General. While there she wrote about their experiences in weekly letters home to her mother, which were later fashioned into a book. Other published journal/diaries of Lady Dufferin were *Our Viceregal Life in India* (1890) and *My Russian and Turkish Journals* (1917).

My Canadian Journal 1872-1878 recounts the activities of her family, including the arrival of two more babies, and mentions various people they met, but does not deal with political matters. She seems very much a stereotypical lady and a homebody, with little intellectual curiosity. When she visited a suspension bridge under construction at Niagara, she reports "We saw the whole plan,—but I will not attempt to describe anything so scientific" (Fowler 1982, 191). Her nephew was the author Harold Nicolson.

Bibliography
•Dufferin, Lady. 1969 [1891]. *My Canadian Journal 1872-1878*. Edited and Annotated by Gladys Chantler Walker. Don Mills, ON: Longmans, 325 pp.

Duffin, Mother Mary Gertrude, nun, 1863-? Mother Mary Duffin was a Grey Nun of Montreal, especially renowned because she was asked to write for the bicentennial anniversary of the Institute of Grey Nuns, Sisters of Charity, the story of its founder and of the Institute.

A Heroine of Charity: Venerable Mother d'Youville describes the life of the "Foundress" (1701-1777) who was born in Varennes, Quebec, and educated at the Ursuline convent in Quebec City. She married M. d'Youville who beat her and proved unable or unwilling to support her and their five children. When he died after eight years of marriage, d'Youville and three friends increased their religious and charitable work for the sick, the poor and the battered, setting up in 1738 a house and later institutions for them, including a hospital; they were Canada's first religious community. The preface notes that "A Divine Providence endowed her not only with personal sanctity but also with wide social vision so that she became a fit instrument in the hand of God for the development of great virtue in others and untold good to her fellow-men" [*sic*]. Duffin includes in her book summaries of the lives of some of Rev. Mother d'Youville's successors and the current status of the Grey Nuns; by 1938, sixty-seven missions had been founded and 1,435 nuns had taken vows.

Bibliography

•Duffin, Mother Mary G. 1938. *A Heroine of Charity: Venerable Mother d'Youville*. New York: Benziger Brothers, 197 pp.

Duncan, Dorothy BSc 1903-1957. Dorothy Duncan was born in New Jersey and raised in Chicago, obtaining a BSc from Northwestern University in 1925. When she married the novelist Hugh MacLennan in 1936 she moved to Canada, but continued to use her maiden name on her books. She died prematurely of cancer.

Written for an American audience, *Here's to Canada!* has a chapter devoted to each province and one for the northern territories. For the provinces she provides a description, anecdotes and factual information provided by each government. Her husband wrote of her that "It was she who helped me to discover Canada, so that I could put some of it into words; for she, in her own way, found another framework of differences when she came to live in my country" (Cockburn 1969, 17). Duncan hoped that her book would persuade Americans to visit their northern neighbour after the war.

Duncan's *Bluenose* was also aimed at American readers; it is a portrait, but not a photograph, of Nova Scotia. She set out

> to depict the personality of a place and a people in much the same way
> that a novelist draws the personality of a character. . . . Everything here

written has previously passed through the lens of my own mind, colored by my background and temperament. Inevitably it has emerged with distortions. What the reader sees in the pages of the book will, in turn, be distorted by his [sic] mind.

Duncan's biography of Jan Rieger, *Partner in Three Worlds*, won the Governor General's Award for non-fiction in 1944. He was a Czech of international stature whom she and her husband befriended by chance in Montreal early in the war.

Bibliography

• Cockburn, Robert H. 1969. *The Novels of Hugh MacLennan*. Montreal: Harvest House, 163 pp.

• Duncan, Dorothy. 1941. *Here's to Canada!* New York: Harper, 334 pp.

• _____. 1942. *Bluenose: A Portrait of Nova Scotia*. New York: Harper, 273 pp.

• _____. 1944. *Partner in Three Worlds*. New York: Harper, 340 pp.

Duncan, Jessie 1866-1952. Jessie Duncan was born in Port Hope, Ontario, but moved with her family to Stratford when she was six. Because of her religious upbringing, she felt her life's duty lay with helping people in foreign lands. She prepared for this mission by studying in Stratford, at normal school in Toronto and in Chicago. She was a schoolteacher and principal before being sent to India in 1892 under the auspices of the Stratford Presbytery. During her forty years there she worked in day schools and orphanages before becoming principal of the Canadian Mission Girls' School at Indore for twenty-eight years. She campaigned among her students against caste rules and the seclusion of purdah, and for their education and their independence so they could help their less privileged sisters.

In *Life in India*, Duncan planned to describe "some of the outstanding facts I learned regarding [India], and to give a picture of some of the beautiful places it was my privilege to visit. But above all I would like to tell of the varied experiences I have had among the people which furnish the reason for my long sojourn in that land." As well as places and people, her book describes some animals and Indian culture and customs. She ends with a plea for more missions, for greater literacy so that the people can read the Bible, and for the emancipation of Indian women.

Bibliography

• Duncan, Jessie. 1944. *Life in India*. Toronto: Ryerson, 156 pp.

Dunham, Aileen BA MA PhD 1897-? Aileen Dunham earned a BA (1920) from the University of Alberta, an MA (1921) from the University of Toronto, and a PhD (1924) from the University of London. From 1924, Dunham taught history at the College of Wooster in Ohio, doing research in international relations and in modern European history.

Political Unrest in Upper Canada, based on Dunham's doctoral thesis, was selected as the first volume in the Imperial Studies series sponsored by the Royal Empire Society (now the Royal Commonwealth Society). The preface to the 1969 edition states that it

> revolutionized the history of Upper Canada prior to the so-called Rebellion of 1837, and it has not been superseded. Before Miss Dunham's book appeared a great deal had been written on the subject, but most of it was so distorted by partizan prejudice, on both sides, that it was almost worthless. It was necessary for her to begin *de novo* with a thorough examination of the documents such as had never been undertaken. The result was striking. For the first time conflicting issues were presented with an admirable impartiality and clarity, and placed in a much broader perspective than that of local petty politics.

Berger (1970, 271) states that her thesis "reduced the importance of the radicals and contended that the Rebellion was an anti-climax, and out of harmony with the real sentiments of Upper Canadians."

Bibliography
•Dunham, Aileen. 1969 [1927]. *Political Unrest in Upper Canada 1815-1836.* Toronto: McClelland and Stewart, 204 pp.

Dunham, Bertha Mabel BA DLitt 1881-1957. Bertha Mabel Dunham was born near Harriston, Ontario, and educated in Berlin (Kitchener) and at Toronto Normal School. She taught school for six years before entering the University of Toronto, earning her BA in 1908. She was librarian at the Kitchener Public Library from 1908 to 1944 where she established a model children's department and instituted the first picture collection in an Ontario library. She also lectured on library science at Waterloo College of Arts (now Wilfrid Laurier University) and wrote novels such as the popular *The Trail of the Conestoga* (1924). Dunham was given an honorary Doctor of Literature degree in 1947 from the University of Western Ontario, the first woman librarian to be so honoured.

Dunham's *Grand River*, a history of the river that flows through Kitchener, is divided into three main sections. The first, People of the Longhouse, deals with the Native people who lived along the Grand River and their interaction with newly arriving Europeans. People of the Settlements discusses settlers in the Grand Valley, among them Mennonites from Pennsylvania, Germans, Britons and Natives from the Six Nations Reserve. The final section deals with development along the river of agriculture, industry, government, transportation, communication and river control.

Bibliography
•Dunham, Mabel. 1945. *Grand River.* Toronto: McClelland and Stewart, 299 pp.

Dunlop, Florence Sara BA MA PhD 1896-1963. Florence Dunlop was born in Rideau View, Ontario, and attended normal school in Ottawa. She taught in nearby rural areas before attending university, receiving a BA (1924) from Queen's University and an MA (1931) and PhD (1935) in psychology from Columbia University, where she later taught for fifteen summers. From 1927 on she was supervisor of special classes in the public school system of Ottawa and later school psychologist. She helped found Carleton University in Ottawa, where she lectured from 1942 to 1945. As a psychological consultant she advised the office of education in Washington and visited countries around the world to study educational systems. She retired in 1962 as a professor of special education at San Francisco State College.

Dunlop's book *Subsequent Careers of Non-Academic Boys*, adapted from her PhD thesis, described research into the schooling and succeeding years of Canadian boys with an I.Q. range of fifty to seventy-five, about 2 percent of the school population. By writing up and publishing her results, she hoped to find ways in which the lives of these boys could be improved so that they would become "good citizens." She would later study gifted children from the other end of the I.Q. scale.

Bibliography
•Dunlop, Florence S. MA, PhD. 1935. *Subsequent Careers of Non-Academic Boys.* Ottawa: n.p., 93 pp.

Edgar, Helen Madeline Boulton d. 1933. In 1893, Helen Boulton married her first cousin, Pelham Edgar, son of **Matilda Edgar**, who would become a renowned professor of literature at Victoria College in Toronto. The couple, who had no children, enjoyed exotic travel.

Edgar's book *Dahabeah Days* refers to a three-month holiday in Egypt spent on "an animated house-boat," a two-deck structure similar to those used by pharoahs, which housed a crew and galley on the bottom deck with tourist quarters above. The author and her husband joined another couple of which the man, Professor C, was described as the curator of a well-known Canadian museum looking for new acquisitions for his collections. (Professor C was Charles Currelly, who collected archaeological material for the Royal Ontario Museum, as he related in *I Brought The Ages Home*

[1956].) In Cairo the group hired and provisioned the boat themselves to save money, then sailed in late January south on the Nile, having three minor collisions in the first four days. They reached and toured the Valley of the Kings in early March, at a time when the opening of Tutankhamen's tomb was providing great excitement in the press. Edgar tells the story of their daily adventures with verve and humour.

Bibliography
•Edgar, Helen M. 1923. *Dahabeah Days: An Egyptian Winter Holiday*. Toronto: Ryerson, 85 pp.

Edgar, Matilda Ridout, Lady 1844-1910. Matilda Ridout was the fifth of eleven children, born into a wealthy and prominent Toronto family. Her father was manager of the Bank of Upper Canada and deeply involved in politics, as James Edgar, whom she married in 1865, would also be. They had eight children, who kept her busy even though she had domestic help; one son was Pelham Edgar who would become a professor and marry **Helen Boulton**, subject of the previous entry. If her husband was away, she wrote him a letter every day, which he as frequently answered. Edgar was interested in history, but found time to write books on the subject only in her forties, after she had weaned her last child. She later involved herself outside her family in connection with her husband's political career in Ottawa. When he was chosen speaker of the Dominion House of Commons in 1896 and knighted two years later (so that she was Lady Edgar), she became associated with various worthy causes: a volunteer with the Infants' Home in Toronto, Vice-president of the United Empire Loyalist Association, President of the Women's Art Association, President of the International Women's Council, and President of the Women's Canadian Historical Association.

After her husband died in 1899, she turned in grief to spiritualism. During seances, she received guidance and good wishes from his spirit; these messages were written down by one of her children and helped to comfort her. Later, she worked for feminist causes through the National Council of Women, of which she was president in 1909. Among her friends she counted authors **Lady Aberdeen**, **Mary Agnes Bernard Fitzgibbon** and **Emily Cummings.** She was at Windsor Castle, in England, researching material for a book about her husband's Scottish ancestors, when she collapsed and died from a heart attack.

Edgar's books belonged to the "nationalist school of historical writing wherein the historian's objective was to celebrate Canada's achievements, such as winning the War of 1812, in order to further national consolidation" (Breault 1994). *Ten Years of Upper Canada in Peace and War,*

1805-1815 was based on letters of her father Thomas G. Ridout (who had been captured by Shawanese Indians in 1788 and later [1810-29] was Surveyor-General of Upper Canada) among which she weaves her annotations and text. She notes: "It has been a labour of love to collect these memorials of an honoured father. Perhaps their publication may lead other descendants of the pioneers of this country to search in dusty boxes, and ancient desks, for other records of these 'days that are no more.'" The reviews for this book were all favourable, although one noted that the "natural sympathy and tenderness" of women "militate against [their] excellence as historians" (McLean and Stamp 1998, 162).

General Brock was part of the prestigious "Makers of Canada" series. Edgar was a great admirer of this general (1769-1812) who came to Canada in 1802 to spend the last ten years of his life. In the War of 1812,

> he entered upon the defence of the country entrusted to his charge with an indomitable spirit. . . . He taught the youth of the country a lesson in courage and patriotism, and with infinite patience, tact, and judgment, he led them through their first days of trial. By his contemporaries Sir Isaac Brock was looked upon as the saviour of Canada and time has not tarnished the lustre of his fame.

A Colonial Governor in Maryland, Edgar's book about Horatio Sharpe who was Governor of Maryland before the American Revolution, was based in part on documents and letters from his young secretary, John Ridout, who was one of her ancestors. It was published two years after her death.

Bibliography
•Breault, Erin. 1994. Matilda Ridout Edgar. *Dictionary of Canadian Biography*, s.v. Ridout, Matilda (Edgar, Lady Edgar).

McLean, Maud J. and Robert M. Stamp. 1998. *My Dearest Wife: The Private and Public Lives of James David Edgar and Matilda Ridout Edgar*. Toronto: Natural Heritage/Natural History Inc.

•Edgar, Matilda. 1890. *Ten Years of Upper Canada in Peace and War, 1805-1815; Being the Ridout Letters with Annotations*. Toronto: Briggs, 389 pp.

•Edgar, Lady. 1906 [1904]. *General Brock*. Toronto: Morang, 322 pp.

•_____. 1912. *A Colonial Governor in Maryland: Horatio Sharpe and His Times 1753-1773*. London: Longmans, Green, 311 pp.

Edgar, Maud Caroline BA d. 1960.   Maud Edgar, the daughter of Sir Edgar and **Lady Matilda Edgar** of Toronto, earned a BA and medal in modern languages from the University of Toronto in 1896. She taught at Havergal College in Toronto from 1899, then co-founded in 1909 a ladies' school in Montreal which she ran with her friend **Mary Cramp.** (See Mary Cramp entry.)

Edwards, Henrietta Louise Muir 1849-1931. Henrietta Muir, born and educated in Montreal, was always interested in the problems of women. In 1875, a year before her marriage, she helped finance the Working Girls' Association, which provided vocational training for young women, by selling her art, including a miniature painting of Sir Wilfrid Laurier. For years she and her sister edited the journal *Woman's Work in Canada*, and she also helped Bertha Wright (later **Bertha Carr-Harris**) with her mission work in Ottawa. After marriage and three children, Edwards moved with her family to Edmonton, where she became immersed in further social issues. She was one of five women involved in the 1929 appeal from the Supreme Court of Canada to His Majesty's Privy Council in England on whether women were "persons" under the terms of the BNA ACT and therefore eligible for appointment to Canada's Senate; her knowledge of law in this case was invaluable. This law case, organized by **Emily Murphy**, also included **Nellie McClung**; all five women are honoured by a monument on display in Calgary and in Ottawa.

Edwards was First Convenor of the Nation Council of Women's Standing Committee on Laws Affecting Women and Children, a position she held for thirty-five years. She noted in the preface of *Legal Status of Canadian Women*:

> The question, "What is the law?" on this or that subject, was so frequently asked in our Council [National Council of Women of Canada] meetings when discussing various topics that related to women, and so much delay was incurred in coming to any conclusion till the question could be answered, that I thought it advisable to prepare a brief synopsis of such laws as especially affect women.

She gave the laws of each province relating to women and their activities, and updated this small book regularly.

In 1916 she published a similar work for her home province, *Legal Status of Women in Alberta*, which pointed out that these women "except in dower rights, are more favoured in regard to legal status than are those of any other Province of Canada." She supported divorce on equal grounds for men and women, prison reform and mothers' allowance.

Bibliography

•Edwards, Henrietta Muir. 1908. *Legal Status of Canadian Women as Shown by Extracts from Dominion and Provincial Laws Relating to Marriage, Property, Dower, Divorce, Descent of Land, Franchise, Crime and Other Subjects.* Ottawa: National Council of Women, 61 pp.

•_____. 1921 [1916]. *Legal Status of Women in Alberta as Shown by Extracts from Dominion and Provincial Laws.* Fort MacLeod: n.p., 80 pp., 2nd edition.

Eliot, Elinor Marsden. Elinor Eliot became so interested in Canada when a Canadian couple visited her family in England that she decided when she was twenty-five to go there. She lived mainly in Manitoba and Alberta, keeping a diary about her year's experiences.

Eliot's book *My Canada*, based on this diary, describes many people and gives lively anecdotes, admitting that the text is "an inextricable tangle of fact and fiction." She hopes her stories will "contribute to a better understanding between Canada and the Motherland."

Bibliography
•Eliot, Elinor Marsden. 1915. *My Canada*. London: Hodder and Stoughton, 269 pp.

Elliott, Sophy L. Sophy Elliott was an author interested in women and in history.

Elliott wrote *The Women Pioneers of North America*, describing the history of early immigrant French women because of the lack of such books, especially in English. She "studied the brilliant records of our women pioneers, endeavoring to set them up in more or less compact form, so that the reader may not be deluged with dates of battles, along with too much detail relative to politics, losing at the same time the real human aspect of the picture" (p. ix). The introduction notes that the book was inspired by the special message of Queen Elizabeth who visited Canada in 1939; she had urged French and English Canadians "to use every effort possible to cement friendship and understanding between the two races." The copyright is held by Elliott and her friend Cecile Ena Bouchard, "whose splendid counsel and encouragement were largely responsible for" its publication. To illustrate her work, she learned to paint well enough that her original watercolours are held in the National Archives.

Bibliography
•Elliott, Sophy L. 1941. *The Women Pioneers of North America*. Gardenvale, QC: Garden City Press, 302 pp.

Emigrant Lady. The author, whose identity is unknown, joined her son in the early 1870s living on "free-grant lands" of Muskoka because she had had various personal setbacks and was too poor to survive in Europe. However, she was to find that farming in Muskoka was also difficult.

Letters from Muskoka describes with feeling the adventures and setbacks of the author and her relatives. After four years, they knew only too well that "the capabilities of [Muskoka's] soil for agricultural purposes have been greatly exaggerated" (p. 156). Her final chapter, "A plea for poor emigrants," discusses ways in which their problems of finding land and settling down might be ameliorated.

Bibliography
•Emigrant Lady, An. 1878. *Letters from Muskoka*. London: Richard Bentley, 289 pp.

Fairchild, Queenie 1880-1925.   Queenie Fairchild lived in the United States for many years before returning to Canada to settle in Quebec along the St Lawrence River.

In *My French Canadian Neighbours and Other Sketches*, Fairchild describes learning about French-Canadian people and customs through her three permanent servants and other more ephemeral employees. She also depicts village characters, local happenings and historical events. She writes, "The sudden change from the common place American life to that of this quaint old French Province, was like dropping back a hundred years."

Bibliography
•Fairchild, Queenie. 1916. *My French Canadian Neighbours and Other Sketches*. Quebec: Telegraph Print, 121 pp.

Farncomb, Dora 1863-1938.   Dora Farncomb was the Toronto author of a weekly religious column called "Hope's Quiet House" in *The Farmer's Advocate*; her column essays comprise most of her two books.

Farncomb wrote the material collected in *The Vision of his Face*, she says in its preface, because she could not help it:

> On the Resurrection Day, the women who had seen their Risen Master received from Him this command: 'Go tell My brethren that they go into Galilee, and there shall they see Me.' Surely this command was also a permission to tell the wonderful news which they could not have kept to themselves if they had tried. . . . But the gracious permission was also a command.

She has obeyed this command in eighteen chapters dealing with the various aspects of her vision of Christ and of God. She dedicates the book to her "true and loyal friend, Mary Weld," to whose encouragement she is indebted and perhaps also her appearance in print, given the name of her publisher.

Farncomb writes in the preface of *In the Garden with Him*, "I know that this book is very faulty and that my metaphors are often mixed; but I have faithfully tried to deliver the message committed to me—the glad tidings that the Owner of the Garden never leaves it for a moment, and never trusts His precious plants in any hands less tender than His own." Each of the twelve chapters is an essay dealing with some aspect of Christianity and based on one or more biblical verses connected with gardens.

Bibliography
•Farncomb, Dora. 1909. *The Vision of His Face*. London, ON: Wm. Weld, 224 pp.
•_____. 1914. *In the Garden with Him*. London, ON: Wm. Weld, 135 pp.

Field, Edith Coventry 1864-? Edith Coventry was born on a farm near Woodstock, Ontario, to homesteaders who had emigrated from Scotland about 1833, when the land was entirely forested. Her family kept horses, oxen, cattle, sheep, pigs, geese and hens. They and their neighbours took turns killing cattle so they could share the meat before it turned bad. The author married and lived the last part of her life in Detroit.

Field wrote *The Good Old Days* because "some of our grandchildren might like to know 'first hand' how their forefathers lived when they came to this 'new' continent in the early eighteenth century and settled in the Wilds of America." She describes the farm life she knew as a child, including the building of a brick house to replace the original log one, the replacement of stump fences with rail fences, and the making of corduroy roads.

Bibliography
•Field, Edith Coventry. 1938. *The Good Old Days: A True Record of Pioneer Life on the North American Continent*. Detroit: Duo-Art Press, 96 pp.

FitzGibbon, Mary Agnes 1851-1915. Mary Agnes FitzGibbon, daughter of Agnes Moodie Fitzgibbon and granddaughter of **Susanna Moodie**, was born in Belleville, Ontario, but spent most of her life in Toronto where she founded the Women's Historical Society of Toronto.

Her first book, *A Trip to Manitoba*, recounts a trip she took from Toronto to Manitoba and back, partly by steamer and partly by train. She describes the countryside, the vagaries of travel and the people she met.

Years later, the editor of a magazine, *Dominion Illustrated*, suggested to the author that she write the biography of her grandfather, James FitzGibbon (1780-1863). She began *A Veteran of 1812* with a few private letters, a brief description of his wartime service in Upper Canada, and recollections of childhood stories, to which she added archival information. She writes: "I have had the book published in Canada rather than in England, preferring it should first see the light in the city [Toronto] whose loyalty and homes he had guarded with so jealous an arm in life, and to which his last conscious thoughts turned in the hour of death."

Bibliography
•FitzGibbon, Mary Agnes. 1880. *A Trip to Manitoba*. Toronto: Rose-Belford, 248 pp.
•_____. 1894. *A Veteran of 1812: The Life of James FitzGibbon*. Toronto: Briggs, 348 pp.

FitzGibbon, Mary Agnes Bernard 1862-1933.   Mary Agnes Bernard, born in Barrie, Ontario, was the niece of the Baroness Macdonald of Earnscliffe, the first prime minister's wife. She lived abroad for fourteen years following her marriage to Clare FitzGibbon, then in 1896 returned to Canada to live with her stepfather, a Toronto lawyer and politician. She later became a journalist for *The Globe* newspaper in Toronto before moving in 1907 to Victoria, British Columbia. She sometimes wrote under the name Lally Bernard, Lally being her mother's maiden name.

Her book *The Doukhobor Settlements* comprises a series of informative letters written for *The Globe*. They describe the author's visit to prairie settlements where she found the "Doukhobortsi" living under very hard conditions; unlike most farmers, they were vegetarians with a repugnance for killing animals.

Bibliography
•FitzGibbon, Mary Agnes Bernard. 1899. *The Doukhobor Settlements*. Toronto: Briggs, 68 pp.

Fitzroy, Yvonne Alice Gertrude 1891-?   Yvonne Fitzroy was an English writer who in early books described the experiences of Scottish nurses working in Romania during the First World War, and about her attendance on the viceroy and his wife on viceregal tours in India from 1921 to 1924. Subsequently she travelled by car across Canada.

Fitzroy describes *A Canadian Panorama*, documenting her drive from Cape Breton to Vancouver Island, as a "mild spinster setting out upon a voyage of discovery." She focuses on such disparate topics as the steel works of Cape Breton and the Doukhobors of British Columbia. Because she was British, she was conscious of her perspective, and of Canadian/British relations.

Bibliography
•Fitzroy, Yvonne. 1929. *A Canadian Panorama*. London: Methuen, 204 pp.

Fleming, Ann Cuthbert Rae Knight 1788-1860.   Ann Rae, born in Scotland to a merchant and his wife, was educated privately. She married James Knight in 1810 and emigrated with him and their son to Montreal in 1815, leaving behind a year-old daughter. She opened a school for girls there, which enabled her to earn a living after her husband died the next year. In 1820 she married James Fleming, a merchant. In the 1830s she was teaching again, trying out new theories on her pupils and her own two children. She consulted with many well-known men to gain acceptance for her work, travelling in 1843 to Kingston and Hamilton "to display her methods by teaching recalcitrant eight-year-old boys the delights of English grammar for a period of six weeks" (Trofimenkoff 1985).

The preface of *The Prompter* notes that "the design of the author is to communicate to teachers, and to all who feel an interest in the advancement of learning, a method of teaching English Grammar, which she has practised with success." The method involved leading children "by a series of suitable questions, to examine and to reflect on every subject which is in succession brought under their notice, and from its calling forth, and assisting them to arrange, and to bring into practical use, that knowledge of their mother tongue which they have unconsciously acquired." The lessons would be suitable for computer format, although the content far exceeds that taught even in university today. The final section of her book comprises fourteen opinions she sought "respecting the system developed in this work" from ministers, teachers, a professor, the Bishop of Toronto and others.

Bibliography

•Trofimenkoff, Susan Mann. 1985. Ann Cuthbert Rae (Fleming). *Dictionary of Canadian Biography*, s.v. Rae, Ann Cuthbert (Knight; Fleming).
•Fleming, Mrs. 1844. *The Prompter, Containing Principles of the English Language and Suggestions to Teachers with an Appendix in Which Are Stated the Opinions of Different Grammarians on Disputed Points*. Montreal: Lovell and Gibson, 214 pp.

Fletcher, Margaret Isabel BA 1897-1981. Margaret Fletcher, the daughter of Professor Fletcher and his wife, graduated from Bishop Strachan School in 1914 and studied psychology at the University of Toronto. She first met Dr William Blatz as one of his students being trained in 1917 to rehabilitate the First World War veterans (Raymond 1991). In 1927 she joined Dr Blatz's Institute for Child Study at the University of Toronto, where she worked closely with him for many years; as supervisor of the Nursery School (1932-65) she taught nursery school teachers, publishing in 1958 *The Adult and the Nursery School Child* which synthesized what she had learned and taught over thirty years. She was also involved in several major psychological projects, one to organize the lives of the Dionne quintuplets and another during the war to establish in Birmingham a training centre for daycare supervisors who would then be able to set up day nurseries around England to look after the children of war workers. She retired as assistant professor from the University of Toronto in 1965, and was honoured by this university when it opened the Margaret Fletcher Day Care Centre in the early 1970s. See **Millichamp, Dorothy** entry.

Flock, Elizabeth Burnett 1897-?   Elizabeth Flock was a botanist who lived on the prairies.

Flock wrote *Wild Flowers of the Prairie Provinces* "for flower lovers who wish to become familiar with some of the more common plants." Although two thousand varieties of plants grow in the area between Winnipeg and Calgary, she dealt with only two hundred common and representative species. The flowers are listed alphabetically, three on a page; each, sketched with a line drawing, has a common and a scientific name, its family name and a brief description. These pages are interspersed with more general topics such as plant parts and various habitats. The author concludes by noting that after readers have learned the plants in their own area, they can turn to other regions, and then to non-flowering plants such as algae, mosses, lichens, fungi and ferns. They can research legends about plants, and their medicinal uses. "One branch of plant study naturally leads to another, which proves what a very fascinating hobby it can become. A single lifetime is not enough to exhaust it."

Bibliography
•Flock, Elizabeth Burnett. 1942. *Wild Flowers of the Prairie Provinces*. Regina: School Aids and Text Book Publishing, 112 pp.

Forsyth Grant, Minnie Robinson d. 1923. Minna Robinson was born in Toronto to the Chief Justice of Upper Canada and his wife. She married Forsyth Grant in 1881, then accompanied him on a missionary trip to Hawaii. They sailed from San Francisco along with King Kalakua of the Hawaiian Islands, who was returning to his homeland. She eventually returned to Toronto to live where she was active in the Woman's Auxiliary to the Missionary Society of the Church of England.

In *Life in the Sandwich Islands* Forsyth Grant reports on their adventures in Honolulu and while travelling around Kauai Island. She writes in the preface:

> As I have been induced by kind friends to give publicity in this form to my notes and observations while on my journey to Hawaii and stay there, I must ask them and others who may care to read them, to be lenient in criticism, and to remember my only wish is to interest by telling them a little of this small Kingdom in the Pacific, generally known only as the most encouraging exemplification of the noble efforts of missionaries to civilize and christianize a savage and voluptuous race.

Bibliography
•Forsyth Grant, M. 1888. *Life in the Sandwich Islands*. Toronto: Hart and Co., 203 pp.

Foster, Annie Harvie Ross BA MA 1875-? Annie Ross, born in Woodstock, New Brunswick, graduated in English from the University of New Brunswick with a BA (1896) and an MA. She then trained for and became both a teacher and a nurse. After marrying Garland Foster in 1914, she worked during the war for the Red Cross in an English military hospital. After her husband's death in 1918, she was invalided back to Canada to settle in Nelson, British Columbia, where she served as a city alderman. In 1924 she moved to Vancouver, in 1945 marrying Patrick Hanley.

Foster was a fierce admirer of **Pauline Johnson**, the subject of her biography *The Mohawk Princess* (see Johnson entry). In the foreword she writes:

> Tekahion-wake, 'tis true, was not a princess in the ordinary acception of the term, but this is the only term that accurately describes what she really meant to the country she loved. The regal manner in which she carried herself through doubt, discouragement, illness, criticism and misunderstanding, must persuade anyone not troubled by contemporary astigmatism, that she was in her art, in her genius, in her patriotism, just a little above the rank and file of us. It is for this reason that she is here called a Princess.

Foster's and Grierson's reference book *High Days and Holidays in Canada* gives short descriptions of sixty-four "special" days that children should know. Most of these are religious, such as saints' days and Jewish holidays, but also included are April Fool's Day, Arbor Day, Empire Day and Labour Day. The authors tell why each day came to be named and who celebrates it where and how.

Bibliography

•Foster, Mrs W. Garland. 1931. *The Mohawk Princess, Being Some Account of the Life of Tekahion-wake (E. Pauline Johnson)*. Vancouver: Lions' Gate Publishing, 216 pp.

Foster, Annie H. MA and Anne Grierson BA. 1970 [1938]. *High Days and Holidays in Canada: A Collection of Holiday Facts for Canadian Schools*. Toronto: Ryerson, 95 pp.

Foster, Kate Adele Pattullo 1878-1959. Kate Pattullo was born and raised in Woodstock, Ontario, where her father was editor of the local paper. She became Mrs Percival on marriage, but when her husband died several years later she reverted to her maiden name and began a fifty-year career in social work, often associated with the Young Women's Christian Association of Canada for which she worked for many years as field secretary. During the First World War she created hostess centres for servicemen in Toronto and Beamsville, and in the Second World War she organized the Women's Farm Service Corps for the Ontario government.

Foster's book *Our Canadian Mosaic*, sponsored by the YWCA, was written for two reasons: to make available accurate information about Canada for immigrants, and to discuss immigration policy of Canada. The President of the Royal Society of Canada notes in a foreword that there seemed to be a general consensus that only readily assimilable races should be admitted to Canada, namely people of Anglo-Saxon, Teutonic, Scandinavian and northern Celtic stock. Foster gives the history of various races in Canada and describes what various institutions and the provinces were doing to help newcomers settle down. She founded the Council of Friendship to foster arts and cultures of ethnic groups and was active in this organization for twenty years.

Bibliography
•Foster, Kate. 1926. *Our Canadian Mosaic*. Toronto: Young Women's Christian Associations, 150 pp.

Fox, Genevieve May. Fox was a writer who married Raymond Fuller in 1932 although she wrote under her maiden name.

Fox's biography *Sir Wilfred Grenfell* is written in readable style with much conversation and many anecdotes. Grenfell (1865-1940), a medical missionary from England, practised among the fishing colonies of Labrador and in 1899 founded a hospital which he headed at St Anthony, Newfoundland.

Bibliography
•Fox, Genevieve May. 1941. *Sir Wilfred Grenfell*. New York: Crowell, 207 pp.

Frame, Elizabeth Murdoch 1820-1904. Elizabeth Frame, born in Shubenacadie into a prominent Nova Scotian family, was the eldest of ten children. She had a protracted education at Truro Academy (in her twenties) and normal school (in her thirties), taught school in small Nova Scotian towns for thirty years and wrote in her spare time. As well as two books (one a novel called *The Twilight of Faith* [1871]), she wrote many articles of religion, local history and biography, focusing on her family, the community, Micmac Indians and Canadian women pioneers. She was an active Presbyterian, teaching Sunday school and supporting foreign missionary work.

In *Descriptive Sketches of Nova Scotia*, Frame visits various places and discusses them and other topics with her friend Mr Andrew Urban, although nowhere in the book is her own identity divulged; she even had a pseudonym on the title page, apparently reluctant to use her own name because of her sex. In her preface, Frame notes, "The present work is neither a history of Nova Scotia nor an examination of its geological structures; it is a picture in part of Nova Scotia, sketched from Nature, interspersed with some historical and personal allusions connected with the localities." Reflecting her profession as a teacher, she addresses it to "the *Youth* of Nova Scotia; Not unconscious of many defects in her work, a daughter of Acadia offers it to the public as an effort on her part to direct the attention of our youths to the value of home."

Bibliography

•Nova Scotian, A. 1864. *Descriptive Sketches of Nova Scotia in Prose and Verse.* Halifax: A. and W. MacKinlay, 245 pp.

Fraser, Mary L. 1883-?, nun. Mary Fraser was a Sister of St Thomas of the Angels based in eastern Nova Scotia and a collector of old stories and legends.

Fraser wrote *Folklore of Nova Scotia* for an academic study supervised by a professor from Fordham University, New York. Her book notes that people expressed so much interest in these tales which she gathered locally that she decided to have them published. The folklore reflects a Celtic tradition from Ireland and Scotland with a mixture of Acadian French and Micmac Native cultures added in.

Bibliography

•Fraser, Mary L. 1931. *Folklore of Nova Scotia.* Toronto: Catholic Truth Society of Canada, 115 pp.

Führer, Charlotte H. 1834-1907.   Charlotte Führer was born Johanne Louise Charlotte Heise in Hanover, Germany, the daughter of Evangelical Lutheran parents. She entered domestic service when she was seventeen, then married the merchant Ferdinand Führer two years later. They soon emigrated to America, where they remained only a few years. On their return to Hamburg, she trained to be a midwife between 1856 and 1859, feeling that it was immodest for men to deliver babies as her two had been in the United States. With three children, the couple emigrated to Montreal in 1859, where she practised midwifery until shortly before her death.

Führer wrote *Mysteries of Montreal* to satisfy the curious about her practice, although she camouflaged the identity of the people she mentions so it is impossible to trace them. There are also discrepancies in the personal and family information she offers in the first chapter. It seems that she published the book herself—there is no record of the number printed or sold, nor was the book reviewed. However, it is important because it describes the lives of working-class people in mid-Victorian Canada. The editor Peter Ward writes, "She was not a social critic with a vision of reform but a moralist who called for greater personal virtue." She did so in a context of titillating stories about sexual misadventures.

Bibliography

Führer, Charlotte. 1984 [1881]. *The Mysteries of Montreal: Memoirs of a Midwife*. Edited by W. Peter Ward. Vancouver: University of British Columbia Press, 170 pp.

Gahagan, Alvine Cyr 1910-?   Alvine Cyr was born in Edmonton and grew up as a Roman Catholic on a wheat farm near Chauvin. She trained to be a nurse at the Edmonton General Hospital, then began public health nursing in 1933 in rural areas of central and northern Alberta. When she married Harry Gahagan she gave up this work and settled with him in the United States where they raised their daughter, Yvonne. The marriage lasted for over forty years.

Gahagan's book *Yes Father: Pioneer Nursing in Alberta* describes her nursing experiences carried out, as her book title indicates, in association with Catholic priests.

Bibliography

•Gahagan, Alvine Cyr. 1979 [1941]. *Yes Father: Pioneer Nursing in Alberta*. Manchester, NH: Hammer Publications, 186 pp.

Galloway, Margaret Agnes.   Margaret Galloway grew up in Paradise, Manitoba, founded in 1871, where her father opened the first general store ten years later. After describing her childhood years in *I Lived in Paradise*, she published another book in 1947, *A Song in My Heart: The Story of a Holiday in Europe*, detailing her enjoyable experiences on an overseas vacation.

Galloway states in her book *I Lived in Paradise*: "In abiding remembrance and in love so often—too, too often—voiceless, this little book of memories is dedicated to my Father and my Mother." She recounts what happened to her and to her family and acquaintances during her youth, and what the town was like to live in.

Bibliography

•Galloway, Margaret A. 1942. *I Lived in Paradise*. Winnipeg: Bulman Bros, 257 pp.

Garland, Bessie Ford.   Ford, born in Ireland, had little education and few expectations, so she decided as a young woman to come to Canada where she settled in Montreal. She married a man much older than herself and lived with him for over twenty-two years, until his death, at which time she became active in church work.

Garland's *The Old Man's Darling* is full of amusing anecdotes about people and places in many parts of Canada. One event was marrying a man of forty-three when she was much younger, so that she became an "Old

Man's Darling." She wonders (p. 90) "Why gentlemen, getting up in years, always want to marry persons younger than themselves."

Bibliography

•Garland, Bessie. 1881. *The Old Man's Darling: A Series of Character Sketches.* Toronto: self-published, 157 pp.

Geddie, Charlotte Lenora McDonald 1822-1916 and **Charlotte Anne Geddie Harrington** c.1840-1906. Charlotte McDonald, the daughter of Dr and Mrs Alexander McDonald of Antigonish, Nova Scotia, married the Rev. John Geddie in 1839. In 1848, under the auspices of the Presbyterian Church of Canada, the Geddies went as the first foreign missionaries to New Hebrides in the South Seas, which was then considered a heathen nation "sunken in utter darkness." Charlotte Geddie was especially supportive of the Native women and girls, teaching boarding-school girls, Sunday school classes and sewing classes. She also dispensed medicine. After her husband's death, she retired to Melbourne, where she founded a Presbyterian Woman's Missionary Society.

The Geddies's daughter, also called Charlotte, was born in Prince Edward Island, but was sent to school in England when her parents became missionaries. She joined them when she was seventeen, not recognizing them at first after an absence of eight years; she taught her younger brother and sister there, and probably Native women too. After two years she took her siblings to Nova Scotia, where her parents joined them while on furlough five years later. She married William Harrington, a Halifax merchant, in 1865, and settled with him in Halifax. Their four children became the centre of her life although she continued her interest in mission work as an active and lifelong member of the Woman's Foreign Missionary Society. In 1895 she became editor of its monthly magazine, the *Message*, expanding its size and distribution so substantially that eventually she was paid for her work.

The selected letters in *Letters of . . .* , published after the death of the two women, describe the mission work of Charlotte Geddie senior, and her daughter's life in the Maritimes as well as her visit when young to Samoa.

Bibliography

•Huskins, Bonnie. 1994. Charlotte Anne Geddie Harrington. *Dictionary of Canadian Biography*, s.v. Harrington, Charlotte Anne Geddie.
•Geddie, Charlotte and Charlotte Geddie Harrington. 1908. *Letters of Charlotte Geddie and Charlotte Geddie Harrington.* Truro: News Publishing, 64 pp.

Gellatly, Dorothy Hewlett. In 1912, Dorothy Hewlett married David Gellatly, the son of D.E. Gellatly, sometimes called "the father of the produce business in the Okanagan"—his first export was a train-car load of new potatoes sent to the mining towns of Kootenay in 1897 (p. 64). They settled in Westbank in the Okanagan Valley, British Columbia, where Gellatly gathered information about the early days. In 1951 she was awarded a trophy "in recognition of her tireless efforts over a period of many years, in the furtherance of community betterment" (p. 114).

Gellatly's *A Bit of Okanagan History* is the story of the Westbank area. As the foreword states, "Too often the little things, the personal and sometimes significant things which make history are lost in the welter of dates and more important events. In this book Dorothy Gellatly has gathered together some of these little things; some fact, some folklore and some legend." She recounts the history of the area, and information about early and later settlers.

Bibliography
•Gellatly, Dorothy Hewlett. 1958 [1932]. *A Bit of Okanagan History*. Kelowna, BC: Orchard City Press, 133 pp.

Gettys, Cora Luella BA PhD 1898-? Cora Gettys was an American social science scholar based in Washington.

Gettys's *The Administration of Canadian Conditional Grants* is one of three studies of the administration of grants-in-aid under the auspices of the Committee on Public Administration of the Social Science Research Council. In the first-ever such research she "reviews the history of each of the conditional grants which have been made to the provinces by the Dominion, and analyzes the experience under each."

Bibliography
•Gettys, Luella. 1938. *The Administration of Canadian Conditional Grants: A Study in Dominion-Provincial Relationships*. Chicago: Public Administration Service, 193 pp.

Gibson, Jean. Jean Gibson was a Canadian schoolteacher.

The authors' school text *Indians of Canada and Prairie Pioneers* has sections on the Indians of Eastern Canada, of the Prairies and of British Columbia, describing the way they live and their customs and beliefs. The final two sections discuss the explorers and early settlers of the Prairies. Each section lists "Things to Do," such as "Write five or six sentences about making a tomahawk" or "Make a canoe and paddle." Sex roles are portrayed as clearly delineated: "Among the Indians, if a boy, as he grew up, did not wish to become a warrior or a hunter he was looked down upon by everyone. He was dressed up as a squaw and sent among the women to help work about the camp" (p. 25). ("Draw a picture of the Indian boy dressed as a girl. Make him out of clay or plasticine and dress him up.")

Bibliography
•Scarrow, C.A. and Jean Gibson. 1943 [1936]. *Indians of Canada and Prairie Pioneers*. Regina: School Aids and Text Book Publishing, 156 pp.

Glynn-Ward, Hilda 1887-1966. Hilda Williams was the daughter of a classical scholar, W. Glynn Williams, and his wife. She was born and educated in Wales, then travelled extensively before coming to Canada in 1910 to settle down. She was a successful poet and novelist, writing after her marriage not under her married name, Hilda Glynn Howard, but under the pseudonym Hilda Glynn-Ward. She became especially well-known in 1921 as author of the racist novel *The Writing on the Wall*, a vicious propagandist tract against Chinese and Japanese people living in British Columbia.

Glynn-Ward wrote *The Glamour of British Columbia* for tourists and others (but presumably not Chinese or Japanese) whom she felt should know more about British Columbia. She notes that

> Southern B.C. is but sparsely settled; Central B.C. is comparatively unknown; Northern B.C. . . . is scarcely mapped with any accuracy and is entirely unpeopled. If, therefore, the following account of travels in the province serves to enlighten the reader as to the size and possibilities of this unknown West, it will not have been written in vain.

Bibliography
•Glynn-Ward, H. 1932 [1926]. *The Glamour of British Columbia*. Toronto: Doubleday, Doran and Gundy, 238 pp.

Godfrey, L.M. L.M. Godfrey was an early author and spinster living in Nova Scotia.

The title of her self-published book, *Indirect Domestic Influence, or Nova Scotia as it Was, as it Is, and as it May Be*, indicates supreme assurance on the part of the author, yet it lacks her name as author. She writes "Having been by untoward circumstances rebelliously drawn inkward, it becomes requisite in trespassing upon the 'indulgent public,' to state this fact in exculpation of the crime of inflicting upon the satiated reading community another book." The text is sprinkled with literary allusions and has decided opinions on such things as religious local intrigue, politics, commerce, literature, human nature and society in general.

Bibliography

•By a Provincial. 1855. *Indirect Domestic Influence, or Nova Scotia as it Was, as it Is, and as it May Be comprising a glance at a new page in the history of the British American Provinces, and combining sketches of provincial character as connected with their social aspect among the first and early settlers to the present time, with descriptions of scenery and local incident.* Boston: Godfrey, 64 pp.

Goforth, Rosalind Bell-Smith 1864-1942. Rosalind Bell-Smith grew up in a large religious family near Montreal, and then in Hamilton and Toronto where she attended art school. While doing good works in Toronto slums, she met and in 1887 married the Rev. Jonathan Goforth. They became life-long missionaries to China the following year. During her mission years she raised five children and watched three others die, as well as preaching to Chinese women and to Canadians back home.

Rosalind Goforth's first book, *Chinese Diamonds*, written after she had lived and worked in China for many years, comprises sketches of Chinese individuals that are "as photographically true as my knowledge of Chinese life and people can make them." She wanted to show that "missions do pay," and that there really were true Christian converts in China. She wrote in this vignette format rather than in the usual missionary-letters-home style because she felt some people found such letters too dry.

In the preface to *How I Know God Answers Prayer*, Goforth writes that she told acquaintances about how she knew God answered prayer during her first furloughs from China in Canada, but she found them unconvinced. Maybe solutions would have come even without prayer? She thought, "If they will not believe one, two, or a dozen testimonies, will they believe the combined testimonies of one whole life?" She decided in 1910 to document her prayers and their results "in meeting the everyday crises of my life." She admits that sometimes God didn't grant her petitions, but she found out later that this was a better solution anyway. And sometimes He didn't "because of some sin harbored in the life, or because of unbelief, or of failure to meet some other Bible-recorded condition governing prevailing prayer."

The Goforths wanted to continue the record "of God's miraculous power in the conversion of men [*sic*] as we have seen it in our Mission work in China." They had an opportunity to write *Miracle Lives of China* during a furlough in Canada, when her husband was forced to lie blindfolded following an eye operation. Rosalind wrote four of the chapters while he dictated the rest. They include "brief pen-pictures" of individuals, but state that many more Chinese people also led "miracle lives that have not been touched on, but which remain with us as precious memories."

Rosalind Goforth describes taking her small daughter Mary to a town where she and some converts preached. They spoke for hours with crowds of women, but what the "heathen women" remembered most, and what removed much of their opposition to the Christian message, was the little girl with her auburn hair.

A few days after her husband Jonathan Goforth (1859-1936) died, Goforth writes that "the conviction came to me that I had survived him for the writing of his lifestory" which became *Goforth of China.* Her work was facilitated by God, she thought, by way of a friend who gave her a home to work in and another who volunteered to be her stenographer. The author requested that royalties from the sale of her book be used for the support of Native evangelists. Goforth wrote her autobiography, *Climbing,* which ends with the death of her husband, at the insistence of friends and again, she thought, at the will of God. She ends her preface, "I am too old to rewrite, so, such as it is, the story is now sent forth with the hope that He who has sustained in the writing will use it to help other climbers up life's hillside." The many religious messages in her book are enlivened by personal anecdotes.

Bibliography

•Goforth, Rosalind (Mrs Jonathan Goforth). 1945 [1920]. *Chinese Diamonds for the King of Kings.* Toronto: Evangelical Press, 123 pp.
•_____. Missionary in China since 1888. 1921. *How I Know God Answers Prayer: The Personal Testimony of One Life-Time.* Philadelphia: Sunday School Times, 142 pp.
•Goforth, Jonathan and Rosalind. c1930. *Miracle Lives of China.* Toronto: Evangelical Publishers, 254 pp.
•Goforth, Rosalind. 1937. *Goforth of China.* Toronto: McClelland and Stewart, 364 pp.
•Goforth, Mrs Jonathan (Rosalind). 1940. *Climbing: Memories of a Missionary's Wife.* Toronto: Evangelical Publishers, 216 pp.

Gordon, Wilhelmina BA MA LLD 1886-? Wilhelmina Gordon was born in Winnipeg and educated at Halifax Ladies' College and Dalhousie University (1900-1903). She earned her MA in 1905 from Queen's University (and an LLD in 1950) and attended Bryn Mawr College and Oxford University before becoming a tutor and then professor at Queen's University, where her father was principal. She lectured in English, coached the girls' hockey team, and took many young women camping, among them her close friend **Charlotte Whitton.** From 1923 to 1937, she headed the National Educational Department of the Imperial Order Daughters of the Empire.

Daniel M. Gordon was Gordon's biography of her father, who was principal of Queen's College/University in Kingston from 1902-1915. She notes in her book: "In the Preface to the *Life of Principal Grant* [Gordon's predecessor at Queen's] his son quoted a criticism that a biography written by a son is only one degree less contemptible than one written by a daughter." She answers this charge by stating that although she draws on happy memories of her father, she also consulted many other sources, including her father's reminiscences written for his family. She was given leave of absence from her job to do the research and writing.

Bibliography
•Gordon, Wilhelmina. 1941. *Daniel M. Gordon: His Life*. Toronto: Ryerson, 313 pp.

Götsch-Trevelyan, Katharine 1908-? Katharine Trevelyan grew up in England, the daughter of Sir Charles Trevelyan, a Labour Minister of Education and his wife, and the niece of the explorer Gertrude Bell. She decided, after failing Latin at Oxford University, that rather than try again she would travel across Canada with a backpack and almost no money. She debarked at Montreal in 1931 and headed for Ottawa, sleeping on the ground at night in her tiny homemade tent. There, she was entertained by the Governor General, who knew her family. She hitchhiked to Toronto, meeting a variety of people on the road, and then travelled by boat and train and further hitchhiking to the West Coast. She had hoped to tour unnoticed, but was frequently bothered by reporters. On her return to England, Trevelyan married a German, Georg Götsch, and settled down with him in Frankfurt to live in Nazi Germany. This was so repugnant to her that she returned to England with her two daughters in 1936 and sued for divorce. She soon had another daughter, a nervous breakdown and a religious rebirth, as delineated in her memoir *Fool in Love* (1962).

Unharboured Heaths was published three years after her trip, with material taken from her letters and journals. It was a quick success, going through four printings in the first three months.

Bibliography
•Götsch-Trevelyan, Katharine. 1934. *Unharboured Heaths*. London: Selwyn and Blount, 222 pp.
•Trevelyan, Katharine. 1962. *Fool in Love*. London: Gollancz.

Gould, Margaret BA Sarah Gold 1889?-1981. Sarah Gold, born into a large family in Odessa, moved when she was four years old with her family to Canada and to a new name. After Margaret Gould graduated from the University of Toronto, she became one of the left-wing *New Frontier* group in the 1920s and an organizer in the needle trades. She worked as a researcher for the union movement before turning to professional social work, becoming Executive Secretary of the Welfare Council of Toronto as well as a special lecturer at the University of Toronto and an officer of the Toronto Local Council of Women. Her position as a radical with professional status gave her good access to the media. In 1936, she toured England, the Scandinavian countries and Russia with two other social work professionals, studying social institutions and systems and sending back reports that were published in the *Toronto Star*; her background was helpful in that she had family connections in Russia and a knowledge of the language. She was then hired full-time as a reporter by the *Toronto Star*, focusing on social injustice and welfare reform issues for twenty years until she retired in 1957. She married Jack Wechsler in 1953.

Gould describes her Russian experiences in detail in *I Visit the Soviets*, and generalizes about education, recreation, nutrition, housing, the family and religion. She is mostly positive about what she sees, comparing it often to earlier and inferior conditions under the tsars. She ends her book sarcastically: "Those poor Russians! They have hitched their wagon to a star." Joan Sangster (1989, 157) writes that Gould believed economic freedom was the basis of all freedom:

> In *New Frontier* she concluded that Canadian women did not need any "special legislation" but rather a "better understanding of the economic conditions which produced women's inequality." Although her analysis seemed primarily to echo well-known Marxist "truths," she also wrote with sensitivity about the problems of working women, defended the right of married women to work and to birth control, and spoke of the need to totally "emancipate women's personality and capabilities"— all indications that she was one of the CPC's [Communist Party of Canada's] more thoughtful exponents on the woman question.

Bibliography
•Gould, Margaret. 1937. *I Visit the Soviets*. Toronto: Francis White, 166 pp.

Graham, Clara 1888-? Clara Graham was an amateur historian who lived in the Kootenay region of British Columbia.

Graham was encouraged by her husband to write *Fur and Gold in the Kootenays*. It begins with descriptions of the Native inhabitants of the Kootenay area, then discusses early explorers, fur traders and missionaries (1807-58), and ends with early gold mining and other events (1856-88). Graham found that this first book "barely scratched the surface of the subject," so she produced a sequel in 1963, *This Was the Kootenay*, which elaborates on the history.

Bibliography
•Graham, Clara. 1945. *Fur and Gold in the Kootenays*. Vancouver: Wrigley Printing, 206 pp.

Graham, Ellen Maud 1876-? Ellen Maud Graham, from Owen Sound, Ontario, was one of forty women teachers, chosen from over a thousand who applied, sent in 1902 from Canada to South Africa to teach children in the refugee/concentration camps set up by the British for the enemy during the Boer War. They were later joined by teachers from New Zealand and Australia.

A Canadian Girl in South Africa recounts Graham's experiences during her twenty-five months in the Orange River Colony, and gives her opinion of various social issues such as "kafirs" and labour, repatriation and compensation, government relief, education and farming.

Bibliography
•Graham, E. Maud. 1905. *A Canadian Girl in South Africa*. Toronto: Briggs, 192 pp.

Graham, Emma Jeffers, d. 1922. Emma Jeffers was born in Wilton, Ontario, the daughter of a minister and his wife. When she was young, she contributed to the *Christian Guardian*, of which her father was editor; later she wrote for the Toronto *Globe*. She married a minister, with whom she lived in a number of parishes, and had six children.

Etchings from a Parsonage Veranda contains lighthearted vignettes of people and commonplace events in the life of a parson's wife such as herself, whom she calls Catherine Wiseacre. She writes that such a wife shares her husband's labours: "It is her delight to be his helper, to hold up his hands, to make his home bright." She describes only pleasant incidents, although she admits that parsonage life has darker experiences: "There is so much that is bright and beautiful that I have preferred to write in the sunshine, under God's smile."

Bibliography
•Graham, Mrs. E. Jeffers. 1895. *Etchings from a Parsonage Veranda*. Toronto: Briggs, 187 pp.

Grant, Jeannette A. Jeannette Grant was an author who travelled widely in Nova Scotia in researching her book. She sailed first to Yarmouth to visit with present-day Acadians (though she spoke French haltingly), then journeyed by train and horse carriage to Annapolis Royal and the Grand Pré area.

Grant's book *Through Evangeline's Country* focuses on Acadia in Nova Scotia (but not on Evangeline, who was a creation of Henry Longfellow and not a real person). Its four parts describe the history of the expelled French-speaking Acadians, Acadia as it existed when Jeannette Grant wrote her book, the old Acadia of the Annapolis area, and the "poet's" Acadia of the Cornwallis Valley and Grand Pré. Of the three thousand French settlers driven from Acadia in 1755, about two-thirds returned to Nova Scotia even though their houses and farms had been taken over by the British and they had to find new homes for themselves.

Bibliography
•Grant, Jeannette A. 1894. *Through Evangeline's Country*. Boston: Joseph Knight, 100 pp.

Grant, Marjorie. Marjorie Grant was a Canadian who sailed for Europe in 1916 to do what she could for the war effort. She lived for some months in Paris, wearing a white apron and a long navy-blue veil while working at a refuge/canteen for those fleeing the Germans. Then she joined the Alliances des Dames Françaises to help at a hospital. After the war she married, becoming Marjorie Cook, under which name she wrote seven novels.

Grant wrote *Verdun Days in Paris* in a diary-entry format, describing her experiences in France in 1916 during the Verdun battle, the longest and bloodiest of the war. She used fictitious names for the people she met. She ends her book back in London that same year, noting: "Living in France these agonising months of Verdun, I felt always tragically pitiful for the French, and sometimes uncertain as to what the end of the war would show. Now in England there is no uncertainty. These people cannot be beaten."

Bibliography
•Grant, Marjorie. 1918. Verdun Days in Paris. London: Collins, 239 pp.

Grant, Ruth Allison Fulton BA MA. Ruth Fulton was a native of Nova Scotia who graduated from Dalhousie University and obtained her master's degree from the University of Toronto in 1933, her thesis becoming the subject of her book. Upon marriage, she became Ruth Grant.

Grant was encouraged by the Maritime Trade Association to undertake research on fisheries for her graduate work. Harold Innis, the editor of her book *The Canadian Atlantic Fishery*, notes that, "In the breadth of her approach, historically and geographically, she has made an important contribution to the study of the fishing industry."

Bibliography
•Grant, Ruth Fulton. 1934. *The Canadian Atlantic Fishery*. Toronto: Ryerson, 147 pp.

Greaves, Ida Cecil BA MA PhD 1907-? Ida Greaves was a master's student at McGill University, researching the status of blacks in Canada. In her later career she became a professional economist, writing on international affairs and the balance of sterling economies.

The Negro in Canada, published in the McGill University Economic Studies series, is written in an academic format, complete with many footnotes. It discusses whether blacks can thrive in a cold country; early slavery; black settlers in the Maritimes; fugitive slaves in Canada; public policy toward blacks; distribution, assimilation and migration of blacks after 1865; employment; and the status of blacks. Greaves concludes that "Undoubtedly prejudice and discrimination against the Negro are deep-rooted and widespread in Canada," but that there has been little friction because they are excluded from nearly all jobs. By being prevented from being socially conspicuous or assertive, "for practical purposes financial disabilities have been substituted for legal."

Bibliography
•Greaves, Ida Cecil. 1930. *The Negro in Canada*. Montreal: Department of Economics and Political Science, McGill University, 79 pp.

Greeley, Floretta Elmore. Floretta Elmore married Dr Hugh Greeley in 1911 and set off with him on their honeymoon to St John's, Newfoundland, en route to the village of Pilleys Island. This was a fishing centre where Dr Greeley served as a physician and helped set up a clinic and hospital affiliated with the Grenfell Mission. Their son was born at the Mission during their first year there.

Work and Play in the Grenfell Mission describes their early experiences at Pilleys Island, when they travelled from place to place by snowshoe and dog team.

Bibliography
•Greeley, Hugh Payne MD and Floretta Elmore Greeley. 1920. *Work and Play in the Grenfell Mission*. New York: Fleming H. Revell, 191 pp.

Green, E. Eda. Eda Green was the secretary in Britain of the Algoma Association (in England) for Prayer and Work.

Green's first book, *By Lake and Forest: The Story of Algoma*, written with Frances Awdry, focuses on Algoma, which extends north from the shores of Lake Superior and Lake Huron and therefore separated eastern Canada from the new North West. It was of interest to Anglicans because of its large size and scattered inhabitants, which made mission work especially difficult. The preface urges readers to "think imperially" so they can "see in the material and spiritual struggles of a colony the shaping of a nation and the growth of the Kingdom of God." The text deals with the physical attributes of the district, the Natives living there, their reserves and schools, the coming of Christianity, Anglican bishops and archdeacons, missionary work, development and present conditions.

Our Opportunity in Canada, "intended primarily for the use of Missionary Study Circles," dealt chiefly with the work of the Anglican Church in Canada. Its text, describing the history and conditions of Canada as well as Anglican accomplishment, was vetted by a committee whose members "had experience in the conduct of Study Circles" and who represented the society that published it.

Pioneer Work in Algoma is an update of the earlier work about Algoma, which had had two editions. Green describes again the Ojibway Indians living in the Algoma area, the coming of Europeans in the early 1800s followed by mining and lumbering and the arrival of the church, beginning about 1832 in the Sault Ste Marie area. She states: "Let us never forget that the soul of Imperialism is the religion of Jesus Christ." Her last chapter discusses the religious status of people in Algoma at the start of the First World War.

Bibliography
• Awdry, Frances and Eda Green. 1905. *By Lake and Forest: The Story of Algoma*. Kensington: authors, 100 pp.
• Green, Eda. 1912. *Our Opportunity in Canada*. London: Society for the Propagation of the Gospel in Foreign Parts, 93 pp.
• _____. 1915. *Pioneer Work in Algoma*. London: Society for the Propagation of the Gospel in Foreign Parts, 93 pp.

Grierson, Anne Irene See Foster, Annie entry.

Griffith, Margaret R. Margaret Griffith was an Canadian author interested in foreign mission work.

Jean Dow (1870-1927), the subject of her book *Jean Dow, MD*, was born near Fergus, Ontario, and raised in a Presbyterian family. She was a regular teacher as well as a Sunday school teacher in Hespeler before enrolling as a medical student in Toronto. She was designated a medical missionary in 1895, one of the first such women in Canada, then sailed for China where she spent the rest of her life in Honan tending to the sick and to non-Christians. Her Christian faith was very strong; she once remarked, "If I could not myself give the gospel message to the patients, nothing would induce me to remain in China." She died in the field.

Bibliography
•Griffith, Margaret R. 1931. *Jean Dow, MD: A Beloved Physician.* Toronto: Woman's Missionary Society of the United Church of Canada, 63 pp.

Griffiths, Isabel S. Isabel Griffiths was a Canadian author devoted to the religious education of young people.

Griffith's *Landing Fields* has seven sections, each dealing with a different placement of United Church missionaries—Canada, Japan, Korea, China, India, Africa and Trinidad—and including Fact Sheets giving population, missionary activity, church membership and church work. It is aimed at young readers, with interesting descriptions relating to Canadian missions, and sometimes letters, or conversations to be acted out. In the section on China, Griffiths gives five brief scenes from the life of missionary Dr Bob McClure, beginning when he was a boy in China and ending with him as an established missionary doctor there.

The foreword of *Good Neighbours*, also a church study guide, begins:

> "Good Neighbours." Don't you like to live beside them? How appreciative they are when we share things with them, and how quickly they come to our aid when sickness, disaster or trouble threatens. If everyone in Canada would be a good neighbour, with active good will in his [*sic*] heart toward others, how different things might be!

The text gives examples for the various provinces of church programs for two age groups of children which elaborate on what good neighbours are and how members can become good neighbours. In addition, there are sections on making gifts, various games to play and missionary facts about Canada and its provinces.

Bibliography
•Griffiths, Isabel. 1937. *Landing Fields: Sketches of the United Church of Canada and Young People around the World.* Toronto: Board of Christian Education, Committee of Missionary Education, and Woman's Missionary Society of the United Church, 121 pp.
•Burgess, Nellie V. and Isabel Griffiths. 1938. *Good Neighbours.* Toronto: Woman's Missionary Society, United Church, 80 pp.

Gruchy, Lydia BA BTh DD 1894-1992. Lydia Gruchy was born of English parents near Paris, France, one of ten children. When she was eighteen, the family immigrated to Western Canada. She graduated from the University of Saskatchewan in 1920 with the Governor General's Gold Medal, and three years later graduated in theology from St Andrew's College in Saskatoon, heading her class. In 1926 she first requested ordination in the newly formed United Church of Canada; this request was finally granted ten years later, when she became the first female minister of this church. Before that she had successfully served the spiritual needs of three large rural Saskatchewan congregations, visiting church members on horseback and by buggy and car. From 1938 she was executive secretary of the committee to oversee the work of deaconesses and women volunteers, whom she felt were too often disregarded. In 1953 she was awarded the honorary degree of Doctor of Divinity from her alma mater, the first ever conferred on a Canadian woman. She retired in 1962.

After her graduation in theology, Gruchy worked among the Doukhobors, about whom she wrote *The Doukhobors in Canada*, describing their historical background, their move to Canada and the culture they shared in the west. She notes (p. 51): "The Doukhobors believe that Nationalism is at the root of war. Therefore, they do not wish to become citizens of any land." Gruchy ends her work: "To Canadians comes the challenge to make their contacts with the Doukhobors such that in friendliness and co-operation they may together help to build the Kingdom of God in our land."

Bibliography
•Gruchy, Lydia E. 1927. *The Doukhobors in Canada*. Toronto: United Church of Canada, 64 pp.

Guernsey, Isabel Russell.   Isabel Guernsey from Vancouver, whose maiden name is unknown, was one of seven Canadian women, strangers to each other, who sailed on an Egyptian ship from New York to Capetown during the Second World War; when their ship was torpedoed and sunk, they were captured at sea and reached Germany instead. The women spent three months at a women's internment camp, where they were joined by two other Canadian prisoners of war. The nine Canadians were held for further months in Berlin before being exchanged for other prisoners and returned to New York.

In *Free Trip to Berlin* Guernsey narrates the adventures of the Canadian women with verve.

Bibliography
•Guernsey, Isabel Russell. 1943. *Free Trip to Berlin*. Toronto: Macmillan, 230 pp.

Guillet, Mary Elizabeth Scott.   In 1925, Mary Scott of Brantford, Ontario, married Edwin Guillet, a noted Canadian historian and high-school teacher with whom she would have three children.

Together the Guillets wrote *The Pathfinders of North America*, a school history text presented in an ambitious way:

> In this book you will accompany the first sailors to our continent. You
> will march through Central America with Spanish soldiers, roam the

forests with French *coureurs de bois*, and shoot dangerous rapids in birch bark canoes; you will sail unknown seas with the most daring British navigators, and become familiar with the frozen Barrens of the far north.

Bibliography
•Guillet, Edwin and Mary. 1957 [1939]. *The Pathfinders of North America*. Toronto: Macmillan, 364 pp. Revised by Marian Prueter.

Haig, Kennethe Macmahon BA. Kennethe Haig was born on a farm near Brandon and educated in Manitoba, graduating with the Governor General's Medal in philosophy from the University of Manitoba. She was a colleague of **E. Cora Hind** on the *Winnipeg Free Press*, for which she wrote a column (both were feminists working for women's suffrage), and the first woman sent by the Canadian Press to a League of Nations' Conference. She was president of the Canadian Women's Press Club from 1923 to 1926.

Brave Harvest, a biography of Cora Hind, is written in a popular style, with conversation to carry along the story. (See **Hind** entry.) Haig describes Hind's interest in the Women's Christian Temperance Union and her admiration for farm women, quoting her: "if any change of outlook on the position of farming is needed, it must come from the women. When the last word is said women are the race, and it is their thought and their work and their actions which will mould the future race as they have in the past" (p. 169).

Bibliography
•Haig, Kennethe M. 1945. *Brave Harvest: The Life Story of E. Cora Hind, LLD*. Toronto: Allen, 275 pp.

Hale, Katherine, pseud. of Amelia Beers Warnock Garvin 1878-1956. Amelia Beers Warnock was born and educated in Galt, Ontario (now Cambridge), and Toronto; her father was a prominent Canadian manufacturer and her mother an American. In New York she studied singing and wrote poems, stories and articles; later, after touring as a soprano recitalist, she moved to Toronto to be literary editor for the Toronto *Mail and Empire*. In 1912 she married John Garvin, a leading editor and anthologist of Canadian literature. The rest of her life was devoted to literature: she was a public speaker and poet, she gave poetry readings set to music, she wrote nonfiction books about Canadian places and she was president of the Ontario branch of the Canadian Authors Association, of the Canadian Women's Press Club and of the Women's Canadian Club. She was admired by **Mazo de la Roche**, whom she described in a 1914 article as a poetess who kept chickens; this was well before de la Roche became world famous. Other literary friends included **Kit Coleman.**

Canadian Cities of Romance is said by her publishers to "give glimpses of a land where legend and romance still linger, and whose cities are characterized by a distinctly racial flavour, mingled with the vast resources and young virility of the North." She hoped that it would appeal to American readers.

Canadian Houses of Romance (revised and republished in 1952 as *Historic Houses of Romance*) describes famous and interesting houses across Canada, giving a brief history of each as well as descriptions of her visits to them.

For *This Is Ontario*, Hale drove around the province, beginning and ending in Windsor where the "bucolic charm" of Ontario contrasted with the "manic activity" she glimpsed in nearby Detroit. She discusses twelve areas, none in the north. Each had a distinct flavour of its own, she felt: "The shores of Lake Erie were as different from the Grand River Valley as the latter was different from the North Shore of Lake Superior, and the people were to some degree at any rate, shaped by their environment." She saw Ontario as having "a frontier still almost unexplored"—a land of promise. Her last book about her home city, *Toronto: Romance of a Great City*, was published the year of her death.

Bibliography
•Hale, Katherine (Mrs John Garvin). 1922. *Canadian Cities of Romance*. Toronto: McClelland and Stewart, 225 pp.
•_____. 1926. *Canadian Houses of Romance*. Toronto: Macmillan, 213.
•_____. 1946 [1937]. *This Is Ontario*. Toronto: Ryerson, 245 pp.

Hall, Mary Georgina Caroline. Mary Hall was an Englishwoman who visited North America in 1882, departing from Liverpool and touring New York, Washington, Chicago and St Paul en route to Winnipeg. She wrote many letters home while staying on her brother's farm in Manitoba during the summer, and during her fall visit to the western United States before returning in December to London.

Hall's correspondence was made into a book, *A Lady's Life on a Farm in Manitoba*, which states that "These letters were never intended for publication, and were only the details written to our family of an every-day life, and now put in the same shape and composition; not as a literary work, but in hopes that the various experiences we underwent may be useful to future colonists intending to emigrate and farm, either in Manitoba or Colorado."

Bibliography
•Hall, Mrs Cecil. 1884. *A Lady's Life on a Farm in Manitoba*. London: W.H. Allen, 171 pp.

Hallam, Lillian Gertrude Best BA MA d. 1939. Lillian Hallam was born in the Annapolis Valley and grew up in Nova Scotia. She graduated with honours in classics from Dalhousie University, obtained an MA, and then married the Rev. W.T. Hallam, who later became Bishop of Saskatoon. She was a leader, becoming president of church, civic and patriotic societies.

When You Are in Halifax gives a history of Halifax as well as maps of places of interest that would appeal to tourists. She obtained information largely from the Records' Office in London, newspaper files, old letters, and history books.

Bibliography
•Hallam, MA, Mrs W.T. 1937. *When You Are in Halifax: Sketches of Life in the First English Settlement in Canada*. Toronto: Church Book Room, 83 pp.

Hamer-Jackson, Celesta Grivot de Grandcourt. Celesta Hamer-Jackson is identified as "Officier d'Académie" on the title page of her book.

Hamer-Jackson wrote *Discoverers and Explorers of North America* for children, noting in the preface that "It is the aim and ambition of the writer to create a healthy curiosity to learn more about these pioneers, explorers, and discoverers who have blazed the trails through the wilderness for civilization to follow." These men and women were "heroes whose devotion to duty, and love of king and country, were equal only to their unwavering faith in God." The book ends with a chapter on Canada's transcontinental railways.

Bibliography
•Hamer-Jackson, Celesta. 1931. *Discoverers and Explorers of North America*. Toronto: Nelson, 319 pp.

Hardy, Mary McDowell, Lady Duffus 1825?-1891. Lady Duffus, a member of the English aristocracy, visited North America about 1880. Her party travelled through Quebec City, Montreal, Ottawa and Toronto by train and boat before heading for Niagara Falls and the United States.

The first fifty-eight pages of *Through Cities and Prairie Lands* describe the Canadian part of Lady Duffus's visit to North America. When for the first time she saw Native men and women, she noted after brief thought that:

> It is simply impossible to regard them as "men and brothers," and the more we study the nature, character, and capabilities of these people, the

more firmly we are convinced of that fact. Civilization, with its humanizing principles, may struggle with the difficulties, but it will never overcome the inborn blindness of the savage race. They have not the power to comprehend our codes, nor to feel as we feel. (p. 28)

She later notes (p. 40) that "The Canadians are the most loyal of all British subjects; . . . any criticism of [royalty] or their doings would be met with severe reprimand, if not positive maltreatment" despite the lack of "consideration or care it has received from the home government."

Bibliography
•Hardy, Lady Duffus. 1881. *Through Cities and Prairie Lands: Sketches of an American Tour*. New York: Worthington, 338 pp.

Harrington, Charlotte Geddie See Geddie, Charlotte.

Harrington, Rebie. Rebie Harrington felt herself while at home as a wife in Massachusetts to be doing "distasteful and menial" domestic tasks, so she decided to set off on an adventure. She took a train across Canada, sailed north from Vancouver, visited Alaska, then Yukon and finished again in Alaska.

In *Cinderella Takes a Holiday in the Northland*, Harrington describes her experiences travelling in the northwest and the people she met.

Bibliography
•Harrington, Rebie. 1937. *Cinderella Takes a Holiday in the Northland: Journeys in Alaska and Yukon Territory*. New York: Fleming H. Revell, 269 pp.

Harris, Leila Gott. Leila Gott, born in Canada, worked as a teacher in Fort William, Ontario, on the prairies, and in the Niagara area before marrying a distinguished Australian, Kilroy Harris.

In their jointly authored *Canadian Ways*, the Harrises note that the book tells "you [American boys and girls] something about Canadian people, their ways of living, playing, working, building homes, growing and finding food; their railways, waterways, highways and byways." The authors emphasize how alike Americans and Canadians are, and hope that the readers "will feel as friendly toward Canadians as they feel toward you." The ten chapters, dealing with various environments across the country, are illustrated with many photographs.

Bibliography
•Harris, Leila Gott and Kilroy Harris, DSO, FRGS. 1939. *Canadian Ways*. Bloomington, IL: McKnight and McKnight, 207 pp.

Harris, Martha Douglas 1854-1933. Martha Douglas was born in Victoria, British Columbia, the daughter of Sir James and Lady Douglas. She was educated in Victoria and England, then married Dennis Harris, an engineer, and settled with him in Victoria.

Harris writes that she translated the stories and myths contained in *Indian Legends* in order to preserve them and as a memento of British Columbia. There are twenty-one tales in all, beginning with "The Story of the First Man on Earth" and ending with "The Adventures of Hyas." All are written in a lively manner replete with conversation.

Bibliography
•Harris, Martha Douglas. 1901. *Indian Legends: History and Folklore of the Cowichan Indians*. Victoria: Colonist Printing and Publishing, 89 pp.

Harrison, Marjorie M. Marjorie Harrison was a British journalist who agreed to visit Canada with backing by the Canadian Pacific Railway and write a book that would appeal to potential Canadian immigrants. She spent most of her time in Toronto and points west, making notes on western immigration, prairie life, the Rocky Mountains and British Columbia.

In her book *Go West—Go Wise*, Harold Macmillan notes in a preface that "The study which she has made of conditions and prospects in the Dominion is both entertaining and valuable." Harrison concludes with four major impressions of Canada, all, she believes, shattering preconceived ideas:

1. Canada has great potential wealth and power in her mineral and forest resources;
2. Canada must somehow increase her population fast—"without resorting to a predomination of Continentals";
3. Canadian farming does not provide a satisfactory living and rural areas have inadequate medical services; and
4. Canada is slowly becoming Americanized.

She ends her book "Who will be [Canada's] inheritors? At present it looks as if an army of Slav peasants and American business men will share the honours. What will that mean? Canada, *quo vadis*?"

Bibliography
•Harrison, Marjorie. 1930. *Go West—Go Wise! A Canadian Revelation*. New York: Longmans, Green, 308 pp.

Hart, Margaret Janet 1867-1941. Hart was a great-great-granddaughter of Janet Fisher Archibald, an early pioneer of Nova Scotia.

Hart decided to celebrate Archibald's life with a biography. She based her account largely on rough notes of the memories of her mother, who had known Archibald for twelve years before she died. As Hart records, she is ashamed to say she never put her notes "into shape during her [mother's] lifetime. Now it is unfortunately too late to get the help I need. She and her generation are gone. I have set down some tales, fragmentary and no doubt sometimes incorrect, but perhaps better than none." The book contains many vignettes from New England and Nova Scotia, not only of family but of general social interest, such as sections on church and school, slaves in Truro, public roads and family life.

Bibliography

•Hart, Margaret Janet. 1934. *Janet Fisher Archibald, Wife of Matthew Archibald 1750-1843; Some Account of Her Ancestry, Environment and a Few of Her Descendants*. Victoria: Colonist Printing, 206 pp.

Hasell, Frances Hatton Eva MBE DD OC 1886-1974. Frances Hasell, from a wealthy family in Britain, had five years' experience there in Anglican religious education following training in London. She drove for the Red Cross during the First World War, nursed in a military hospital and took a mechanical course so that she could repair cars. She was therefore well prepared to bring religion to children in western Canada: "in the remote districts, 'the hungry sheep look up and are not fed.' Secular education alone does not satisfy. They are all longing for something higher." During four years in the 1920s her vans covered 15,000 miles, often under appalling road conditions. The Anglican Church in 1924 backed Hasell's religious work in areas "far removed from the Church's administrations." (It presumably did not want competition for its ordained ministers.) In the Depression years her van teams also distributed clothing to rural poor on the prairies, and she helped found a hospital in Fort St John. She received an honorary Doctorate of Divinity from the University of Saskatchewan in 1963.

In 1920, Hasell bought and equipped a Ford Sunday-school Mission van, rebuilt to her specifications, which with a friend she drove for four summer months in the rural areas of southern Saskatchewan. *Missionary on Wheels* describes their adventures bringing religion to homesteaders.

From 1922 on, she bought other vans and each year travelled with one, along with her sister or another woman. She also supervised the raising of funds for even more vans. At the end of a summer trip, each van was given to the Bishop of a diocese under the following conditions:

1. The van would be used each year for at least four months, and staffed by two women, one of whom had a religious education background. This "Sunday School expert" would visit homes, get new Sunday school members, give religious lessons, and organize Anglican services where there were none.

2. The non-expert would drive and repair the van, cook and wash, and if possible teach under the supervision of the expert.

3. The diocese should if possible raise money to support the van and the workers.

4. If a van was not used in the original diocese, it should be available for work in another diocese under the direction of Hasell, Organizer of Sunday-School Vans.

Through Western Canada in a Caravan focuses on the three missions Hasell undertook after her first one—in 1922 to the Calgary diocese, in 1923 to the Edmonton diocese and in 1924 to the Cariboo diocese.

Canyons, Cans and Caravans describes Hasell's further caravan adventures, to northern Manitoba in 1925, to the Kootenay diocese in 1926 and 1927 and to the Caledonia diocese, including the Peace River area, in 1928 and 1929. She ends it with a plea for money to support the vans and their Anglican mission.

Bibliography

•Fast, Vera. 1979. *Missionary on Wheels: Eva Hasell and the Sunday School Caravan Missions*. Toronto: Anglican Book Centre, 158 pp.

•Hasell, F.H. Eva. 1922. *Across the Prairie in a Motor Caravan: A 3,000 Mile Tour by Two Englishwomen on behalf of Religious Education*. London: Society for Promoting Christian Knowledge, 115 pp.

•_____. 1925. *Through Western Canada in a Caravan*. London: Society for the Propagation of the Gospel in Foreign Parts, 254 pp.

•_____. 1930. *Canyons, Cans and Caravans*. London: Society for Promoting Christian Knowledge, 320 pp.

Hathaway, Ann 1848-? Ann Hathaway was descended from the family of Shakespeare's wife. Her birth family emigrated from England to Canada in 1871, settling first in Toronto, where Hathaway worked in a store on Yonge Street for many years. When possible, Hathaway spent summer holidays in her beloved Muskoka. Eventually the entire family (except for one sister) moved to Muskoka, the author living in a house called Old Maid's Lodge because she never married.

Hathaway's *Muskoka Memories* is dedicated to the remembrance of her parents "who were amongst the earliest settlers of this district [Muskoka] the fruit of whose labors their children now enjoy." It describes the Muskoka area of about 1903, the history of the Hathaways in Ontario, and the activities of her extended family members who lived around her.

Bibliography

•Hathaway, Ann. 1904. *Muskoka Memories: Sketches from Real Life*. Toronto: Briggs, 227 pp.

Hayward, Victoria 1876-? Victoria Hayward was born in Bermuda and educated privately, becoming a journalist and author. She published articles in many Canadian magazines, although she lived in Connecticut. About 1922, she and her friend Edith S. Watson, a photographer, travelled across Canada documenting their observations in notes and by camera.

As a result of their journey, the two women wrote and illustrated their expensively produced *Romantic Canada*, which focuses on rural and "hinterland" people, especially those of different cultures who might seem "romantic" to urban Canadians—Scottish highlanders, Acadians, Doukhobors and Natives, for example.

Bibliography
•Hayward, Victoria. 1922. *Romantic Canada*. Toronto: Macmillan, 254 pp.

Henderson, Mary Gillespie 1840-1935. Mary Gillespie grew up on a Quebec farm, although her family were anglophones. Her father hired French-speaking farmhands with whom he had trouble communicating, so when she was eleven, his daughter was sent for a year to a French-Canadian school to learn French and be an intermediary. She became a teacher before marrying first a businessman who later died, and then a minister. She raised five children, whom she hoped would enjoy her book.

In *Memories of My Early Years* Henderson describes her upbringing on the family farm. She ends her book with information about her children, of whom she was proud: "I hope that those who read these memoirs will not accuse me of making out all my geese to be swans. But I can say that the different members of our large family have more than a modicum of good looks and ability, for which they may thank the ancestors who bravely started out on the great adventure of crossing the Atlantic to found a home in the New World" (p. 58).

Bibliography
•Henderson, Mary Gillespie. 1937. *Memories of My Early Years*. Montreal: Charters and Charters, 58 pp.

Hendrickson, Magda See Steen, Ragna entry.

Hendrie, Lilian Margaret BA 1870-1952. Lilian Hendrie was born and educated in Montreal, attending normal school and McGill University to become a teacher. She was Principal of Halifax Ladies' College from 1906-1911, then "Lady Principal, High School for Girls, Montreal," from 1911 to 1930.

Hendrie states that because her first book, *Junior History of Canada*, was intended for schoolchildren between the ages of ten and fourteen, she ignored the constitutional side of Canada's history and made it instead largely a series of biographies. She consulted original sources of information, such as diaries and letters of leading people, whenever possible. She concluded: "It looks to-day . . . as though Canada's future were indissolubly bound up with that of the British Empire. If it be so, it is a noble destiny, and one that would call for all that is best in the Canadian people."

Early Days in Montreal is a local history of Montreal. Hendrie writes: "The purpose of this little book is to give its readers some idea of the wealth of historic interest that attaches to Montreal itself and to the places more immediately surrounding it." She describes under the heading "Rambles" many historically interesting walks and drives that can be taken around the city.

Bibliography

•Hendrie, Lilian M. 1915. *Junior History of Canada*. Toronto: Educational Book Co, 311 pp.

•_____. 1932. *Early Days in Montreal and Rambles in the Neighbourhood*. Montreal: Mercury, 70 pp.

Hendry, Violet. Violet Hendry was deeply interested in the musical education of children.

Hendry's *Masters of Music* tells the stories of eleven great composers, from George Handel to Edward Grieg. All are men, although Clara Schuman, who married Robert Schuman and also composed wonderful music, is mentioned. The format includes fantasy and conversation to interest the child reader.

Bibliography

•Hendry, Violet. 1937. *Masters of Music: Stories of the World's Greatest Composers for Boys and Girls*. Toronto: Ryerson, 162 pp.

Heneker, Dorothy Alice BCL, LLB, ARCM. Dorothy Heneker was born in Montreal and educated at King's College, Nova Scotia, and at McGill University, studying music and law. She was the first woman to hold both Bachelor of Civil Law and Bachelor of Common Law degrees, but because Quebec regulations forbade women from practising law, she was forced to work as a subordinate in her father's law firm. In 1930, when she became the first president of the Canadian Federation of Business and Professional Women's Clubs, she agreed on behalf of the International Federation to tour fourteen European countries to organize new clubs. She was also active in the movement against cruelty to animals. On marriage, she became Mrs Cummins.

Heneker was supported in her research for *The Seignorial Regime in Canada* by the Quebec government; her subject was one of twelve listed and arranged "through the medium of 'The Canadian History Competition,' which has disclosed a field of absorbing interest in the history of those stirring years" in New France. She writes that "a study of that early system of government opens many doors to a more complete understanding of present day problems."

Bibliography
• Heneker, Dorothy A. 1980 [1927]. *The Seignorial Regime in Canada*. Philadelphia: Porcupine Press, 439 pp.

Henry, Mrs P.A. née Hayward. Mrs P.A. Henry (as the title page of her book calls her) was born to a minister and his wife, and on marriage became the daughter-in-law of Thomas Henry.

Her biography of her father-in-law, *Memoir of Rev. Thomas Henry* (1798-1879), describes his emigration from Ireland to Canada in 1811, his service in the War of 1812, and his activities as a preacher in Oshawa Christian Church and through Ontario for over forty years. Henry wrote her book because of the many people who wanted to know more about Thomas Henry—"old men and women, with dim eyes and trembling limbs . . . men and women, in the strength and fulness of life . . . and little children . . . because he was always pleasant and spoke to them." She concludes her work with extracts from his writings. As well, four poems "by the author are appended to this work by request."

Bibliography
• Henry, Mrs P.A., written and published by his daughter-in-law. 1880. *Memoir of Rev. Thomas Henry, Christian Minister, York Pioneer, and Soldier of 1812*. Toronto: Hill and Weir, 192 pp.

Henshaw, Julia Wilmotte Henderson 1869-1937. Julia Henderson was born in Durham, England, and educated by governesses and tutors who emphasized modern languages and art. She married Charles Henshaw of Montreal in 1887, with whom she then lived mostly in Vancouver. She was an active botanist in the Rocky Mountains, meeting **Mary Schäfer** there on similar business in 1905, as well as a mountaineer, journalist and novelist—her novels include *Hypnotized? or, The Experiment of Sir Hugh Galbraith, a Romance* (1898). Henshaw served overseas in the First World War on ambulance and recruitment duty, winning medals for her effort. She was a Fellow of the Royal Geographical Society for her exploration and mapping of the interior of Vancouver Island, and Honorary Secretary of the Alpine Club of Canada.

In *Mountain Wild Flowers of Canada*, Henshaw classifies each species according to flower colour so it appealed especially to the general public;

each species is also described in detail and given its scientific name. She knew people in high places: this book is dedicated to Sir Thomas Shaughnessy, and she thanks James Macoun and Professor John Macoun for their botanical help, including in the introduction a laudatory letter from the latter (who was by 1915 Dominion Naturalist). This book is still in use in at least one university (University of British Columbia).

The text of *Wild Flowers of the North American Mountains* overlaps to some extent with that of Henshaw's earlier book, although it describes many more species, including those from the United States. She dedicates this book to the Duke and Duchess of Connaught "in remembrance of days spent by their royal highnesses in the Rocky Mountains," and again thanks the Macoun brothers for their assistance. This book also is in use at the University of British Columbia.

Bibliography
•Henshaw, Julia W. 1906. *Mountain Wild Flowers of Canada*. Toronto: Briggs, 384 pp.
•_____. 1917. *Wild Flowers of the North American Mountains*. New York: Robert M. McBride, 383 pp.

Hensley, Sophie Margaretta Almon 1866-1946. Sophie Almon was born in Bridgetown, Nova Scotia, the daughter of a minister and his wife. After studying in England and in Paris, she returned to her family home in Windsor, Nova Scotia, where she wrote and published poetry. When she was twenty-three, she married barrister Hubert Hensley with whom she soon moved to New York City; here she continued her literary work as well as becoming a radical public speaker and an executive member of a number of feminist and child welfare causes. Her social conscience led her in 1907 to publish *Woman and the Race* (using a pseudonym) and, after moving with her husband to London to live, *Love and the Woman of Tomorrow*. Despite her travels, Hensley when possible returned each summer to her home in Barton, Nova Scotia, visualizing herself as "a Canadian in thought, feeling, and expression" (Davies 1990). She returned to Canada permanently during the Second World War when her home in the Channel Islands was taken over by the Germans.

Although Hensley was perceived as a feminist, and one who would become acquainted with Emmeline and Christabel Pankhurst while in England, her sentiments are with society and eugenics rather than with individual women. She dedicates *Woman and the Race* to the young women of America who, among other things, "recognize the bearing and rearing of children as their highest duty and their supreme joy" and thus will help perfect the race. She feels that "Women for the most part are content to be ignorant," and urges that both boys and girls be given information about sex and reproduction. Men are to remain pure: she cites the case of a baby born blind because of an early indiscretion of its father, whose wife then left him (p. 112). Women are not to be vain: she gives an example of a pregnant woman who laced herself so tightly in an effort to be fashionable that both she and her baby died (p. 148). She ends her book optimistically: "Let the women of the world be strong, be wise, be loving, and the world will throw open the doors of its empty jails and asylums and proclaim an era of universal health, wealth and peace."

Hensley's *Love and the Woman of Tomorrow* must have had a small printing, because the only two library copies now available for perusal (but not lending) are in the New York Public Library and the British Library in London.

Bibliography

•Davies, Gwendolyn. 1990. Sophie Almon Hensley. *Dictionary of Literary Biography*, s.v. Hensley, Sophie Almon.

•Hart, Gordon [Sophie Almon Hensley]. 1907. *Woman and the Race*. Westwood, MA: "Published at the Ariel Press," 264 pp.

Hensley, Sophie Almon. 1913. *Love and the Woman of Tomorrow*. London: Drane's.

Herring, Frances Elizabeth Clarke 1851-1916. Frances Clarke, who was born and educated in England, married A.M. Herring of New Westminster, British Columbia, in 1874; two years later she was the first woman to obtain a first class A teachers certificate by exam in British Columbia. During her life there she raised a family of at least one daughter (who became a doctor) and wrote books and articles about her province. Two of her avocations were urging the government to spend money on education rather than on jails and fostering closer relations between Canada and England.

It is difficult to know whether to consider *Canadian Camp Life* fiction or non-fiction; the author wrote some fiction and makes her texts highly readable, but the background is solidly based on fact. She describes life in backwoods British Columbia from personal experience after travelling to many areas of the province, describing her adventures and the various people she met.

In *Among the People of British Columbia*, Herring again fictionalizes somewhat the people she encounters, but this book is more factual than her first, according to the author's preface. The protagonist is an orphan, Agnes, whose sojourns involve "a Chinese funeral, Indian ceremonies and various other cultural and industrial sites" which are each described (Marni Stanley in Neuman and Kamboureli 1986, 54).

For *In the Pathless West* Herring follows the same formula, including conversation in the text, but dealing with historical events. For example, she quotes from actual issues of *The Soldiers Gazette and Cape Horn Chronicle*, published during the ship *Thames City*'s 1858-59 journey with 121 military men plus wives and children from England to British Columbia. She describes the inhabitants of British Columbia as they were at that time, the miners seeking gold in the Fraser Valley and overseen by the Royal Engineers and the Marines, the settlers struggling to make a living and strife among the Natives.

In *The Gold Miners*, Herring describes the opening up of British Columbia following the discovery of gold in the Fraser River basin in 1858. As in her earlier books, she recounts the adventures of fictional people in actual events, such as the trial and conviction of a man who murdered his travelling companion near Barkerville so that he could have his belongings.

Bibliography

•Herring, Frances E. 1900. *Canadian Camp Life*. London: Fisher Unwin, 247 pp.
•_____. 1903. *Among the People of British Columbia*. London: Fisher Unwin, 299 pp.
•_____. 1904. *In the Pathless West with Soldiers, Pioneers, Miners, and Savages*. London: Fisher Unwin, 240 pp.
•_____. 1914. *The Gold Miners: A Sequel to The Pathless West*. London: Francis Griffiths, 120 pp.

Hill, Vivian Wood 1900-? Vivian Hill was a mother who lived in a small town of Canada and wrote about her interests, both personal and national.

Cross Roads . . . Panorama seems to be addressed to Hill's daughter; the first page states that "The greatest Gift in the world was mine when they placed You in my arms . . . Little warm Bit of my Heart." It comprises a series of short ruminations, many sprinkled with religious thoughts, written from and about her village at a crossroads. They include commentary on the Royal Visit to Canada in 1939 of "a gallant King and a lovely Queen"; on quilting bees—hoping that the days will be fashioned as skilfully, neatly and beautifully as the quilts being made; and "our little sons" going off to war accompanied by "the spirits of mothers who march with their sons." She urges her compatriots to labour harder for our Empire—"For neither pain . . . nor sorrow . . . nor death . . . shall dim the shining spirit . . . or silence the singing heart of Britain." This book's historical value is reduced as the location of the crossroads' village is not given, nor are the dates of her observations.

Bibliography

•Hill, Vivian Wood. 1940. *Cross Roads . . . Panorama*. N.p., 55 pp.

Hind, Ella Cora LLD 1861-1942. Cora Hind was born in Toronto and raised in Orillia, Ontario, but worked all her life in Winnipeg. She was the first typist west of the Great Lakes, and in 1893 the first public stenographer. In 1901, she joined the editorial staff of the *Winnipeg Free Press* as a special writer on agricultural affairs, a field with which she had become familiar while acting as a secretary for farming organizations. She worked for the paper from then on, becoming world famous for her ability to predict the nation's crop yields each year after inspecting the standing crops. She was active for women's suffrage and in the Canadian Women's Press Club, whose constitution she drafted; her friends there downplayed her mannish clothes by praising her knitting and her cooking. In 1935 she was given an honorary degree by the University of Manitoba in recognition of her services to western agriculture in Canada. When she was seventy-three, Hind was asked to travel around the world for two years collecting information on agricultural conditions and publishing her accounts in letters to the *Winnipeg Free Press.*

From 1935 to 1937 Hind visited twenty-seven countries where wheat was grown, sending back reports not only on wheat but also on social conditions, historical associations and people she met. Selections of her letters were reprinted by popular demand in her book *Seeing for Myself.* She recommended that Canadian wheat acreage not be increased because of world competition, but that Canada should build up a strong marketing organization for selling the wheat it produced. She also wanted Canadian agricultural experts sent to wheat-growing countries around the world to keep track of the competition. This book was such a success that her publishers "conjured Dr Hind to search amongst her papers and find enough [material from her trip] for a second book."

About this second book, *My Travels and Findings*, her publisher writes: "Add to her genius for observation, her shrewdness in inference, and her judicial quality in summing up and you have as charming a combination of travel book and worldly wisdom as we have come across in a long time." Each brief chapter gives a vignette or anecdote from various stops on her journey, often by air, around the world. (See also Haig entry.)

Bibliography
•Hind, E. Cora. 1937. *Seeing for Myself: Agricultural Conditions around the World.* Toronto: Macmillan, 347 pp.
•_____. 1939. *My Travels and Findings.* Toronto: Macmillan, 185 pp.

Hitchcock, Mary Evelyn Martin The author, who was raised in a wealthy American family, married Commander Roswell D. Hitchcock of the United States Navy. After he died, she and her friend Edith Van Buren, grandniece of ex-U.S. President Van Buren, boarded a ship in 1898 in San Francisco bound for Alaska. From there they took a boat up the Yukon River to Dawson City, where they became Free Miners on application to the government. The two women lived first in a tent in Dawson City before quickly having a small house built. They visited gold mining camps in the Klondike at a time when gold was actually being discovered, watched the mining process, took part themselves and made a multitude of friends and acquaintances. They returned to civilization in September, travelling by steamship up the Yukon River and to Skagway.

In *Two Women in the Klondike*, Hitchcock describes in detail their adventures (although she uses only letters for many individuals' names which decreases the value of her account as history), finishing with their arrival in Seattle. The subtitle of Hitchcock's book was presumably intentionally incorrect to attract American readers. A friend notes in the preface that for two travellers "born and reared in luxury and refinement . . . " the narrative of their daily life is "not only a tribute to their own perseverance and determination, but to the character of intelligent and fearless Anglo-Saxon women, who, among all sorts and conditions of men, never fail to secure protection and respect."

Bibliography

•Hitchcock, Mary E. 1899. *Two Women in the Klondike: The Story of a Journey to the Gold-Fields of Alaska*. New York: Knickerbocker Press, 485 pp.

Hogner, Dorothy Childs BA. Dorothy Childs, born to a physician and his wife in New York City, attended several universities, graduating in 1936 from the University of New Mexico. She wrote mainly children's books, illustrated by her husband, an artist, whom she married in 1932. Eventually she operated a farm in the Berkshires from which she sold herb plants.

For her book *Summer Roads to Gaspé*, the author and her husband set out from Connecticut to vacation by driving around the Gaspé peninsula, tenting at night to save money. Later, they took a steamer through the Strait of Belle Isle for a glimpse of Labrador. The author describes the scenery they pass, the people they meet, and the incidents they take part in or observe.

Bibliography

•Hogner, Dorothy Childs. 1939. *Summer Roads to Gaspé*. New York: Dutton, 288 pp.

Holmes, Vera Lee Brown BA MA PhD 1890-1980. Vera Lee Brown Holmes, born and raised in Fredericton, New Brunswick, received her BA and MA from McGill University and her PhD in history from Bryn Mawr (1922); she had to write her doctoral thesis twice, because the first version was destroyed when her father's house burned down. Although her career was as a history professor at Smith University, she continued to spend time in Canada, dying in her ninetieth year in Halifax.

Studies in the History of Spain, Holmes's first book, led to her later primary research interest on the history of the Spanish in the Americas. Her most prestigious book was the two-volume *A History of the Americas* first published in 1950.

Bibliography

Holmes, Vera Lee Brown. 1929. *Studies in the History of Spain in the Second Half of the Eighteenth Century*. Northampton, MA: Department of History of Smith College, 92 pp.

Holt Gethings, Charlotte 1828-1890. Charlotte Holt Gethings was born in Quebec City, the daughter of the manager of the Bank of Quebec and his wife. She attended school for nine years at the nearby Ursuline Convent after her mother died, then became a teacher. When her father died in 1852, she left home to teach in various schools in the United States, Cuba and Peru. Holt had a number of trials in her life, including learning, on her return to Quebec from Peru in 1870, that the man to whom she had sent her earnings had lost them in "wildest speculations." Once back home she married Daniel Macpherson, a notary public, who died a year before she did. (See entry for Charlotte Macpherson.)

Holt's *An Autobiographical Sketch* was apparently undertaken so she could recoup some of her losses. In her preface she states:

> Written under the pressure of calamity . . . no one can be more sensible than myself of the many imperfections of this, my first essay in the field of literature, which ill health has also often compelled me to lay aside. Possibly under happier circumstances, it might have been worthy of perusal. As it is, I trust it to the indulgence of the reader.

Bibliography

•Holt, Miss. 1875. *An Autobiographical Sketch of a Teacher's Life including a Residence in the Northern and Southern States, California, Cuba and Peru*. Quebec: James Carrel, 104 pp.

Hoodless, Adelaide Sophia Hunter 1857-1910.   Adelaide Hunter was born on a farm in Brant County, Ontario, the last of a family of ten children whose father died before she was born. She attended the local school and then briefly a Ladies' College before marrying the businessman John Hoodless of Hamilton when she was twenty-four. They had four children in the next seven years, but the youngest died when fourteen months, apparently from drinking contaminated milk. From that time on, Hoodless was adamant about the need for domestic hygiene. Because she had servants to help with the household duties, she was able to do volunteer work—for the YWCA and the new National Council of Women (of which Hoodless became treasurer at its founding in 1893). Her association with the YWCA, both local and national, convinced her that girls and young women should learn in school how to run a house; that ideal, and her connection with the National Council, gave her a powerful network to enable her to work toward this goal. With her encouragement, the Hamilton YWCA set up domestic science classes for girls in 1894; these classes gave her the expertise to write two books on the subject. In 1897, Hoodless helped found the Women's Institute for women who lived on farms so they could gather together regularly to educate themselves and to socialize. Hoodless died of a heart attack in 1910 while giving a speech to raise money and support for the teaching of domestic science at university. It is ironic that Hoodless, to improve society, worked unceasingly so that all girls would learn household science at school, while in the 1970s many of us, also for the sake of an improved society, worked to liberate girls from this stereotyped activity.

Even though Hoodless had no formal training in domestic science, the Ontario government commissioned her to write a textbook published in 1898, titled *Public School Domestic Science* and often called "the little red book," which she dedicated "To the school-girls, and future housekeepers of Ontario." She wanted it "to assist the pupil in acquiring a knowledge of the fundamental principles of correct living." It is mostly composed of information about foods, with recipes and discussions of diet. She thanks a number of nutrition experts for their help.

The second edition in 1905, with a slightly different name, was co-authored with **Mary Urie Watson**, a university graduate in domestic science. *Public School Household Science* is addressed to students rather than primarily to teachers, who are now assumed to have some training in the subject. As an elementary text it does not discuss the chemistry or bacteriology which "would create confusion in the mind of the average school girl, and tend to cause dislike of the subject." It continues to set high standards—refrigerators should be cleaned thoroughly once a week, removing all food and ice and using boiling water; dishtowels should be washed and scalded once a day.

Bibliography
•MacDonald, Cheryl. 1986. *Adelaide Hoodless: Domestic Crusader*. Toronto:
  Dundurn Press, 183 pp.
•Hoodless, Mrs J., President, School of Domestic Science, Hamilton. 1898. *Public School Domestic Science*. Toronto: Copp, Clark, 196 pp.
•Hoodless, Mrs J. and Miss M.U. Watson. 1905. *Public School Household Science*. Toronto: Copp, Clark, 164 pp.

Hopper, Jane Agar d. 1922. Jane Hopper was raised in Canada as a Primitive Methodist.

Hopper wrote *Old-Time Primitive Methodism in Canada* in order to:

> rescue from oblivion the names of some of the men and women, their walks and ways, their talks and traits, whose lives have influenced our lives, whose record is one of personal faithfulness, undaunted perseverance, and heroic-self-sacrifice. They were ordinary people, but they made the world richer.

She also notes in her preface: "If anything humorous should appear in these pages, let me humbly apologize; it is hard to wholly suppress the writer's mental make-up." Her book describes the rise of Methodism in Canada from early itinerant preachers to established congregations. It includes memories of the author's childhood, and descriptions of individual churches and preachers, church revivals and other activities. The book ends with the union in 1884 of the four Methodist bodies in Canada into one.

Bibliography
•Hopper, Mrs R.P. 1904. *Old-Time Primitive Methodism in Canada (1829-1884)*.
  Toronto: Briggs, 336 pp.

Hoskin, Mary 1851?-1928. Mary Hoskin, educated in part at the Ursuline convent in Quebec City, later moved to central Toronto where she lived as a devout Catholic. Her writings included a history of her parish and *The Little Green Glove and Other Stories* (1920).

At the request of her parish priest, Hoskin wrote *History of St Basil's Parish*, despite the "absolute lack of records" of parish affairs; she had to look to other sources, such as interviews and correspondence, for information. The parish was run by Basilian Fathers, the first of whom came to Toronto from France in 1850; soon a Catholic college was founded that would become St Michael's College, now part of the University of Toronto. Hoskin lists both priests and sisters associated with the parish. Parish priest Father McBrady's doubtlessly well-meant foreword revealingly refers to her "little" book twice, and to her "pretty book" and her "charming record."

Bibliography
•Hoskin, Mary. 1912. *History of St Basil's Parish, St Joseph Street.* Toronto: Catholic Register and Canadian Extension, 172 pp.

Hotson, Zella M. 1893-1978. Zella Hotson was a Baptist woman living in Ontario.

In *Pioneer Baptist Work in Oxford County*, Hotson describes Baptist pioneer families and the gradual growth of church organizations in Oxford County, Ontario, using early church records. In 1817, this county had only 530 people, with no school, no church building and no jail. As the population increased with the years, she goes into more detail, although not to the level of describing the histories of individual churches. Hotson ends with the history of Woodstock College, an academy for "ladies as well as men" which began in 1860 and closed in 1926. It gave rise to McMaster University, which opened in 1890 in Toronto.

Bibliography
•Hotson, Zella M. 1939. *Pioneer Baptist Work in Oxford County.* Innerkip: author, 52 pp.

Howey, Florence Rozelgha Ward 1856?-1936. In 1883, Florence Howey's husband (whom she had married in 1878) was hired as doctor (trained at McGill University) for the men constructing the CPR railway; the couple moved to Sudbury so that he could take up his work. Howey realized the historical interest of the early years in Northern Ontario, but it was not until 1933, Sudbury's fiftieth anniversary, that she decided to tell their story so it would not be forgotten.

Howey's *Pioneering on the C.P.R.* chronicles her life in early Sudbury and the surrounding areas from 1883 to 1885, while the railway was being built westward. It was published two years after Howey's death.

Bibliography
•Howey, Florence R. 1938. *Pioneering on the C.P.R.* Ottawa: Mutual Press, 141 pp.

Hubbard, Mina Benson. Mina Benson was born and grew up near Cobourg, Ontario, before moving to New York City to train as a nurse. She married Leonidas Hubbard, a junior editor of *Outing* magazine based in New York, who died of starvation in 1903 while trying to paddle six hundred miles across Labrador from south to north along unmapped rivers. His friend Dillon Wallace and Cree-Scot guide, George Elson, also turned back part way along their route, but managed to survive. On learning of her husband's death, and partly blaming Wallace for it, his wife decided to retrace the same rivers to complete their exploration. She hired George Elson and other Natives to do the paddling, and successfully completed the route that had defeated her husband, along the way holding a memorial service at the place where he had died. Dillon Wallace, stung by Mina Hubbard's unfair accusation, also set out in 1905 to retrace the same route with another group of men. They were less successful than Hubbard, but two of them did reach George River Post in the north before freeze-up.

Hubbard's *A Woman's Way through Unknown Labrador*, describing her adventures during that summer, sold well, in part because the competition between her and Wallace was widely reported in the newspapers of their day. She married Harold Ellis in 1908.

Bibliography
•Davidson, James West and John Rugge. 1988. *Great Heart: The History of a Labrador Adventure*. New York: Viking, 385 pp.
•Hubbard, Mina Benson. 1908. *A Woman's Way through Unknown Labrador*. London: John Murray, 338 pp.

Hughes, Katherine BA d. 1925. Katherine Hughes was born in Prince Edward Island and educated at Prince of Wales College in Charlottetown. She became a journalist in Montreal in 1903 and a charter member of the Canadian Women's Press Club; she worked in Edmonton from 1906. In 1908 she was appointed provincial archivist for Alberta, which enabled her to collect information for her studies of history. In 1909 she toured the Peace River and Athabasca districts by herself, using stagecoach, canoe and riverboat in search of archival material.

Hughes writes in the foreword of her biography *Archbishop O'Brien* that "It is not the purpose of this book to chronicle in any great measure the works of Archbishop O'Brien [a priest (1843-1906) who was born and served in Prince Edward Island and in Nova Scotia]—with which indeed the people of Canada are already familiar; it aims rather to portray the inner life of the man, out of which these words proceeded." She may have chosen this approach because he seemed too good a man to have a very exciting life, reflecting "the popular sentiment that the lives of good men are necessarily rather uninteresting and colorless."

Hughes was a friend of Father Lacombe (1827-1916), the subject of her second biography, and interviewed him about his service to the Natives and Métis of Western Canada over a period of years. She can therefore state with authority in her book *Father Lacombe* that:

> where I repeat conversations in Père Lacombe's Life I am not making magnificent guesses at what these people likely would have said. I am repeating from the lips of participants what actually was said—or what I myself heard. This record is History—picturesque western History

caught for posterity before it had passed out of memory—and while many of its makers still walked with us.

Bibliography
•Hughes, Katherine. 1906. *Archbishop O'Brien: Man and Churchman.* Ottawa: Crain, 230 pp.
•_____. 1920 [1911]. *Father Lacombe, the Black-Robe Voyageur.* Toronto: McClelland and Stewart, 471 pp.

Humberston, Clara Speight See Speight-Humberston entry.

Hutchison, Isobel Wylie 1889-1982. Isobel Hutchison was a botanist and author of such fiction as *Original Companions* (1922). Later, because she was unmarried, she was free to travel several times to the Arctic and write books about her experiences. In 1933, she visited the Yukon and Alaska in part to collect plants for the Royal Herbarium of Kew; she sent specimens of 238 species back to London. She also collected forty-eight artifacts from Alaskan Natives for the University Museum of Ethnology in Cambridge.

North to the Rime-Ringed Sun describes her adventures to the Canadian Arctic in detail, including her trip from Skagway to Dawson City and beyond, and that along the north coast of Yukon. She spent several winter months in the Mackenzie River delta.

Bibliography
•Hutchison, Isobel Wylie. 1934. *North to the Rime-Ringed Sun, Being the Record of an Alaskan-Canadian Journey Made in 1933-34.* London: Blackie, 262 pp.

Innis, Mary Quayle AB LLD LLD 1899-1972. Mary Quayle was born in St Mary's, Ohio, to a telephone worker and his wife. She lived in a variety of small American towns before attending the University of Chicago. She graduated as an English major in 1919 and married her economics professor two years later. The Innises settled in Toronto, where Harold Adams Innis was a professor and later dean at the University of Toronto. As a widow, and when her four children were grown, Innis become Dean of Women at University College, University of Toronto (1956-64), and author or editor of many books of history. She also wrote short stories and a novel about family life, *Stand on a Rainbow* (1943). She was awarded honorary degrees for her academic and literary pursuits by Queen's University (1958) and the University of Waterloo (1965). Her literary friends included **Viola Pratt** and **Marion Royce.**

When Harold Innis needed a textbook on the economic history of Canada for the students who took his course on this subject, he asked his wife to write one. She did so, although at the time she had four young children and only undergraduate courses in economics. *An Economic History of Canada* received good reviews and sold well for the next twenty years. Despite the academic success of her textbook, as her daughter I know that Innis felt frustrated about the unwillingness of other academics to treat her seriously, probably because she was a woman and wife of one of their peers.

Bibliography

•Pell, Barbara. 1989. Mary Quayle Innis. *Dictionary of Literary Biography: Canadian Writers, 1920-1959*, s.v. Innis, Mary Quayle.

•Innis, Mary Quayle. 1936. *An Economic History of Canada*. Toronto: Ryerson, 384 pp.

Jack, Annie L. Hayr 1839-1912. Annie Hayr, born in England, came to New York State in 1852 where she was educated further and became a teacher. She married a fruit-grower and settled down near Châteauguay, Quebec, where she wrote poetry, several books of fiction, many articles on horticulture, a gardening column in the *Montreal Witness* and a practical and enthusiastic book on gardening.

The Canadian Garden begins:

> When the snow lingers on the ground in broken patches, and grass looks up fresh and green beneath as it slowly disappears, it still seems a far cry to spring flowers and seed sowing, for the alternate freezing and thawing is very trying to the gardening temperament, especially that of an impulsive, optimistic amateur.

She tells what to plant where, and when to plant it, with sections on the hotbed; kitchen, fruit and flower gardens; indoor plants; gardening techniques; and insects and diseases. She ends with reminders of what to do in each month of the year. For example, in January, "It is no use to cork up all the windows and keyholes and then wonder why the plants die. Open a door or window every day for half an hour, unless too stormy, and regulate the heat if possible."

Bibliography

•Jack, Mrs Annie L. 1903. *The Canadian Garden: A Pocket Help for the Amateur*. Toronto: Musson, 121 pp.

Jackson, Mary Evangeline Percy MD, LLD 1904-? Mary Percy was born and educated in England, graduating with top marks as a doctor in 1927. She was finishing her internship in Birmingham, England, in 1929, when she answered an ad from the Alberta government for a doctor's position in the province's north. Her passage would be paid by the Fellowship of the Maple Leaf, an Anglican organization interested in the colonies. She was hired to practise medicine in northern Alberta for at least a year, but continued to do so for forty-five years, unpaid by the government after she married Frank Jackson in 1931. He was a widower with three sons who had settled further north in Keg River. In 1976 she received an honorary Doctor of Laws degree from the University of Alberta, and in 1983 membership in the Alberta Order of Excellence. Recently a more comprehensive autobiography, *The Homemade Brass Plate* (1994), was published, as well as a collection of her early letters (1995).

On the Last Frontier comprises Jackson's letters written to her parents in Britain during her first year in Canada. She notes:

> They were intended for circulation amongst my friends, but were not written with any intention of publication. Many of the statements made are unjust in the light of further experience, but I have left them unaltered, as they are the first impressions of a new country seen through English eyes.

The letters give a vivid description of life in a pioneer settlement one hundred miles north of the nearest railway and town, Peace River. She visited her patients using dog sleds, horse sleighs and riding horses, as well as cars.

Bibliography

•Jackson, Mary Percy. 1933. *On the Last Frontier: Pioneering in the Peace River Block*. London: Sheldon Press, 118 pp.

•_____. 1994. *The Homemade Brass Plate: The Story of a Pioneer Doctor in Northern Alberta as Told to Cornelia Lehn*. Chilliwack, BC: Fraser Valley Custom Printers, 215 pp.

_____. 1995. *Suitable for the Wilds: Letters from Northern Alberta, 1929-1931*. Edited by Janice Dickin McGinnis. Toronto: University of Toronto Press.

Jameson, Anna Brownell Murphy 1794-1860. Anna Murphy, daughter of an artist and his wife, was born in Dublin. From the ages of sixteen to thirty-one she was governess to three wealthy families, with one of which she toured the continent and began an infatuation with travel, great art and writing professionally that lasted all her life. In 1825 she married barrister Robert Jameson, with whom she shared a love of books and of literary society. The marriage soon broke down, however; when her husband was appointed Attorney General of Upper Canada in 1833, she did not accompany him there, but instead visited him in Toronto three years later. Most of her books appealed especially to growing numbers of women readers: *The Loves of the Poets* (1829), *Memoirs of Celebrated Female Sovereigns* (1831), *Characteristics of Women* (1832) and *The Beauties of the Court of King Charles the Second* (1833). Her most notable work was the four-volume *Sacred and Legendary Art* (1848), which she illustrated with her own drawings and etchings and those of her niece. The money she earned as an author helped support her birth family and her travels.

Jameson remained in Canada for nine months before deciding to separate from her husband permanently. During her stay she wrote about the superficial life she perceived in Toronto and about a trip she took through southwestern Ontario by carriage, small boat and canoe, accompanied by French Canadian voyageurs. *Winter Studies and Summer Rambles in Canada* remains a classic about early Upper Canada. Thomas (1990) notes that it is

> distinguished by her vivacity and adaptability as an enthusiastic traveler who formed quick, warm relationships with all manner of people. The critical and popular success of the book in both England and the United States confirmed her reputation as a writer to be taken seriously, though her outspoken remarks on the pettiness and pretentiousness of colonial society won her no admirers among Upper Canada's social elite.

Bibliography
- Thomas, Clara. 1990. Anna Jameson. *Dictionary of Literary Biography: Canadian Writers Before 1890*, s.v. Jameson, Anna.
- Jameson, Anna Brownell. 1965 [1838]. *Winter Studies and Summer Rambles in Canada: Selections*. Toronto: McClelland and Stewart, 173 pp.

Jamieson, Annie Straith.   Annie Jamieson, whose maiden name is unknown, was a foreign missionary based in Montreal.

Jamieson was a relative of the subject of her biography *William King*, which she wrote

> Not for the desirable object of preserving as history facts that might otherwise disappear into the realm of the unknown. Not, assuredly, because imagining any production of hers might be worthy a place on the world's already overladen bookshelves. Not even for the purpose of tracing the stages of an earthly journey from which some back-borne torch might hearten other way-worn pilgrims. No! She spent hours over the chapters here offered to any who care to read them simply because it was her duty to do so."

This duty was imposed upon her by God, although she considers herself unworthy. She collected her information from King's own autobiography, from letters received from his friends and from talks with King himself. King (1812-95) emigrated from Ireland to settle as a missionary near Chatham, Ontario; he was most noted for the large number of slaves he rescued from the southern United States and helped establish near him as farmers.

Bibliography
•Jamieson, Annie Straith. 1969 [1925]. *William King: Friend and Champion of Slaves*. New York: Negro Universities Press, 209 pp.

Jaques, Florence Page 1890-1972. Florence Page was born in Illinois and studied at Millikin and Columbia universities. In 1927 she married Francis Jaques, an artist, whom she accompanied on their honeymoon to the Rainy Lake area of northwest Ontario. Later she joined him on expeditions for the American Museum of Natural History. She also travelled privately to collect information for her (often children's) books, which were largely about travel and nature, some illustrated by her husband. Her journeys made her eligible for the Women Geographers' Society, of which she was a member. Her interest in Canada continued over many years and included a book called *Canadian Spring* (1947), about springtime in western Canada, and *As Far as the Yukon* (1951), about a trip from Texas to the Yukon, dealing especially with plants and birds.

Jaques wrote *Snowshoe Country* (reprinted in 1979) based on her year near Rainy Lake, noting that it "is no account of struggle and hardship; rather, it is the story of a release from the tenseness of present-day life. Its aim is a simple one—to give a picture of what anyone might find, through the winter, in the border country of Minnesota and Canada." She gives day-by-day sketches of how they managed to survive in the wilderness. A fellowship from the University of Minnesota, given through their Regional Writing Program, made her book possible.

Bibliography
•Jaques, Florence Page. 1944. *Snowshoe Country*. Minneapolis: University of Minnesota Press, 110 pp.

Jeanneret, Ethel Mellan. In 1938 Ethel Mellan married Marcel Jeanneret, the director of Copp Clarke publishing company.

From Cartier to Champlain, which was written by the Jeannerets and published by his company, was designed as a children's reader in history. Its foreword states that "Every paragraph has been developed directly from the original sources" and that "brief extracts from the simpler passages of the original chronicles have been introduced from time to time." It describes early Canadian history in a straightforward manner, with chapters divided into subsections to provide easy study and ending with questions for discussion and review.

Bibliography
•Jeanneret, Marcel and Ethel Mellan Jeanneret. 1941. *From Cartier to Champlain: The Story of the Founding of Canada.* Toronto: Copp Clarke, 64 pp.

Jenness, Frances Eileen Bleakney. Eileen Jenness first met New Zealander Diamond Jenness (1886-1969) when she was a secretary working in Ottawa; he was an anthropologist writing up his field notes after a three-year stay with Canadian Inuit in the Arctic. During their life together she raised three sons and sometimes travelled with her husband to visit Native peoples.

In her *The Indian Tribes of Canada*, Jenness thanks, in the Acknowledgement, "the assistance of her husband, Diamond Jenness, from whose volume *The Indians of Canada* she has derived her material." Her book devotes a chapter to each of seven groups of Native peoples, then ends with a five-page chapter on the effect of civilization on them.

Bibliography
•Jenness, Eileen. 1966 [1933]. *The Indian Tribes of Canada.* Toronto: Ryerson, 123 pp.

Jephson, Lady Harriet Julia Campbell 1854-1930. Harriet Campbell was born near Quebec, but moved to London after she married Captain Jephson, RN, where she published essays, painted and exhibited her art. She became Lady Jephson when her husband was knighted.

After revisiting Canada, Jephson published *A Canadian Scrap-Book*, which comprises anecdotal essays and stories about Canada, some of which had appeared in current magazines. In her preface, she notes that several reviewers had objected to two comments she made in her article on Canadian society, one on the importance of English officers to Canadian city life, without whom a city would be "fatally injured," and the other to a dislike for the Canadian accent. She writes that "should I in any way have wounded the feelings of my compatriots, I ask them to forgive me if it has been my misfortune to have heard with other ears, and seen with other eyes, than theirs." Her chapters describe visits with various French Canadians, shooting rapids and winter in French Canada.

Bibliography
•Jephson, Lady. 1897. *A Canadian Scrap-Book.* London: Russell, 183 pp.

Johnson, Amelia B. d. 1888 and **Annie G. Johnson** 1848-1869. Amelia Johnson and her husband, the Canadian Commissioner of Customs, had six children with whom she shared in her letters her deep religious ideals and moral principles, among them always abstaining from alcohol. Her eldest daughter, Annie, died at the age of twenty-one, leaving behind her letters describing her life at Mt Holyoke Seminary, which she had attended with her sister.

From Life's School comprises letters about the Johnson family and their daily experiences, mostly by Annie Johnson but also by her mother, Amelia, and her brother. Annie had returned home for a vacation and was thought to have overtaxed her brain with school work, because she soon developed a fever: "Fragments of Latin, or troublesome mathematical problems repeated by her in her delirium, shewed the condition of the overwrought brain, and after an illness of less than one week she passed away" (p. 177).

Bibliography

•J., M.R. Compiler and editor. 1888. *From Life's School to the "Father's House": A Brief Memoir and Letters of Amelia, Annie, and Thomas Johnson, Wife, Daughter and Son of James Johnson, Commissioner of Customs, Canada.* Toronto: Hunter-Rose, 204 pp.

Johnson, Annie See Johnson, Amelia.

Johnson, Emily Pauline 1861-1913. Pauline Johnson was the youngest of four children of the head chief of the Six Nation Indians and his English wife. Johnson, whose Mohawk name was Tekahionwake, grew up on Chiefswood estate on the Native reserve near Brantford, Ontario, where she immersed herself in poetry. She herself was also a poet, her collections *White Wampum* (1895), *Canadian Born* (1903) and *Flint and Feather* (1912) becoming well known in Canada and beyond. As an adult, for nearly twenty years she gave public readings of her poetry across North America and in England, dressed in Native costume with fringed buckskin, headdress and beaded moccasins; during the 1893-94 season she gave a remarkable 125 recitals in fifty different places. Her friends included other authors such as **Nellie McClung**, **Kit Coleman**, **Isabel Ecclestone MacKay** and C.G.D. Roberts. Although **Annie Foster** (see her entry) is said to have described Johnson as a "saccharine and virtuous Indian maiden poetess" (Keller 1981, 2), Keller depicts her rather as "aggressive, manipulative, talented, and utterly charming" (p. 2); she feels that Foster's book was a romantic fairy tale needed by Depression readers. About 1907, when her health began to suffer from constant touring, Johnson settled in Vancouver, where she transcribed and published Indian legends. After her death, part of the proceeds from this book went toward buying a gun for Canadian soldiers overseas with her name, Tekahionwake, inscribed on its barrel (Keller 1981, 277).

During her travels, Johnson collected Indian legends, which she later wrote up for the Vancouver *Daily Province* newspaper; most of them had been supplied by Chief Capilano, who had told them to no other English-speaking person. In her book of the collected articles, *Legends of Vancouver*, she writes: "To the fact that I was able to greet [the Chief] in the Chinook tongue, while we were both many thousands of miles from home [in Buckingham Palace], I owe the friendship and the confidence which he so freely gave me when I came to reside on the Pacific coast." In the book's preface, Bernard McEvoy writes, "In the imaginative power that she has brought to these semi-historical sagas, and in the liquid flow of her rhythmical prose, she has shown herself to be a literary worker of whom we may well be proud: she has made a most estimable contribution to purely Canadian literature." In the legends she "stresses the same values of heroism and loyalty as she did in her early poems . . . while at the same time pointing out the sad truth that Indian ways were dying" (Precosky 1990).

Bibliography

•Johnston, Sheila M.F. 1997. *Buckskin and Broadcloth: A Celebration of E. Pauline Johnson—Tekahionwake 1861-1913*. Toronto: Natural Heritage.
•Keller, Betty. 1981. *Pauline: A Biography of Pauline Johnson*. Vancouver: Douglas and McIntyre.
•Precosky, Donald A. 1990. Pauline Johnson. *Dictionary of Literary Biography: Canadian Writers, 1890-1920*, s.v. Johnson, E. Pauline.
•Strong-Boag, Veronica and Carole Gerson. 2000. *Paddling Her Own Canoe: The Times and Texts of E. Pauline Johnson (Tekahionwake)*. Toronto: University of Toronto Press.
•Johnson, E. Pauline. 1911. (Tekahionwake). *Legends of Vancouver*. Toronto: McClelland and Stewart, 165 pp.

Johnston, Blanche Goodall Read 1866-?   Blanche Goodall's father worked for the Northern Railway, which entailed the family living in Orillia, Toronto and Guelph during her girlhood. She joined the Salvation Army after being exposed in Guelph to the passion of its religion and charity work, devoting her life to social causes, mostly in Toronto. Captain Goodall married first Major John Read of the Salvation Army, and after his death, N.B. Johnston of Barrie. As one of the first women to visit people in prison, she instituted prison reforms that were later taken over by the Salvation Army; she looked after children whose parents were unable to care for them before the formation of the Children's Aid Society; she worked for censorship "over plays of questionable character"; and she appealed to the government for protection for feeble-minded women.

Johnston told the story of her life to **Mary Morgan Dean** who wrote it down for *The Lady with the Other Lamp*. Dean notes: "She travelled thousands of miles, from Newfoundland to British Columbia; from Old Orchard, Maine, to Spokane, Washington; lecturing in theatres, churches, slums, casinos, drawing-rooms, music halls, and school houses." See also Read, Blanche entry.

Bibliography
•Johnston, Blanche Read. 1919. *The Lady with the Other Lamp: The Story of Blanche Read Johnston.* As told to Mary Morgan Dean. Toronto: McClelland and Stewart, 282 pp.

Johnston, Elizabeth Lichtenstein 1764-1848. Elizabeth Lichtenstein was born into a wealthy Tory family of Russian descent in the state of Georgia and educated at home. Her father was often absent, involved in the American Revolutionary War, and as a British loyalist he escaped to Nova Scotia in 1776. She married William Martin Johnston in 1779 with whom she would have ten children, although only three survived her. They were eventually forced to flee to Florida because of their British allegiance following the American Revolution. They sailed to Scotland where her husband trained to be a doctor, then settled in Jamaica where he practised medicine. In 1810, after his death, Johnston and her family moved permanently to Annapolis Royal, Nova Scotia, to be near her father and daughter; one son became leader of the Conservative Party of Nova Scotia, and another a member of the House of Assembly.

For the sake of her grandchildren, Johnston wrote *Recollections of a Georgia Loyalist* in 1836 when she was seventy-two years old. Although she lived through exciting times, her recollections are largely those concerned with her family; she writes in a puritanical tone, believing that her sorrows were punishment for her sins.

Bibliography
•Morris, Julie and Wendy L. Thorpe. 1988. Elizabeth Lichtenstein (Johnston). *Dictionary of Canadian Biography*, s.v. Lichtenstein, Elizabeth (Johnston).
•Johnston, Elizabeth Lichtenstein. 1901. [1836]. *Recollections of a Georgia Loyalist.* New York: Bankside Press, 224 pp.

Johnston, Mona Troop. Mona Johnston was a deeply religious woman and author.

Johnston's contribution to *Prophet, Presbyter, and Servant of Mankind* is a personal account of the life of her father, Canon Troop, written after his death. He was raised in the Annapolis Valley and after his ordination in 1877 became a curate, working for over fifty years in such places as Halifax and Montreal. The author writes in an extremely religious and sentimental way: of his death, she recounts that his family watched over him "until the Light had led Evangelist past the Sunset Bars, and he was 'absent from the body, at home with the Lord.' " The last part of the book comprises a selection of Troop's writings.

Bibliography

Hague, Rev. Canon Dyson. 1935. *Prophet, Presbyter, and Servant of Mankind: A Memoir of The Reverend Canon G. Osborne Troop, MA, containing "Intimate Recollections" by Mona Johnston and a Selection of His Writings.* No city or publisher given, 222 pp.

Johnstone, Catherine Laura 1838-1923. In the early 1890s, when the Englishwoman Catherine Johnstone (whose maiden name is unknown) was in her fifties, she took the train from Quebec to Qu'Appelle, then lived and travelled on the prairies during the winter, noting the geography, towns, weather and anything else that might interest possible immigrants. She planned to write a book to give a complete picture of settling in the west.

Johnstone explains in her introduction to *Winter and Summer Excursions in Canada* that although there are many optimistic pamphlets on the prospect of emigrating from Britain to Canada, there are none devoted to immigrant failures. "It is no business of [immigration agencies] to give the many heavy losses, their cause, and how to avoid them." She concludes that "If farming is hazardous and slow to bring a profit in England, it is far more hazardous and experimental in the most uncertain climate of the north-west." Her comments come from a middle-class perspective: "The husband ought to be able to keep a servant exclusively for his wife, unless he helps her in the house himself. Canadian boys are brought up to cook or do anything in domestic science; so it is not absolutely necessary for her to have a female servant, often very difficult to obtain" (p. 152).

Bibliography

•Johnstone, C.L. 1894. *Winter and Summer Excursions in Canada.* London: Digby, Long, 213 pp.

Joynes, Agnes. Agnes Joynes was a poet (her chapbook *The Shepherd of the Hills* was published in 1926) and scholar who worked in the Royal Ontario Museum in Toronto.

Joynes's publisher writes in the foreword of *Treasure Seeking*: "In a vivid and entertaining manner, Miss Joynes traces the origin and development of those simple things by means of which society has worked its way up out of barbarism." She begins with prehistoric axe heads and knives, and continues with chapters on first dwellings, boats, lamps, paper and ink, clothes, pottery, clocks, cooking, the wheel, musical instruments and money. She collected information for her text from the writings of early men such as Homer, Aristotle and Cicero, and from the commentaries of recent scholars. Her book is illustrated with her drawings from objects, mostly from Europe and the Near East, stored in the Royal Ontario Museum of Toronto.

Bibliography
•Joynes, Agnes. 1931. *Treasure Seeking in the Store-Rooms of the Past.* Toronto: Ryerson, 237 pp.

Katzmann, Mary Jane See Lawson, Mary Jane Katzmann entry.

Keith, Marian 1874?-1961 pseud. of Mary Esther Miller MacGregor. Esther Miller was born in Rugby, Ontario, to a schoolteacher and his wife, both of Scottish ancestry. The eldest of five children, she was educated in Orillia and at Toronto Normal School, from which she graduated in 1896. She wrote stories and novels and taught public school in Orillia for seven years before marrying Donald MacGregor, a minister, in 1909. She continued to write all her life—several books of non-fiction with religious overtones, and romantic novels full of humour and local colour; *The Forest Barrier* (1930), for example, is set in Ontario in 1837 and focuses on people of Scottish extraction. She was a contemporary and friend of author **L.M. Montgomery**, who also was married to a minister; in 1934 she co-authored a book about women with Montgomery and **Mabel McKinley.** Despite her use of a pseudonym, MacGregor was known as an author in Toronto as early as 1910, and indeed was grouped "with Nellie McClung and L.M. Montgomery as contributors to a revival of writing by women" (Dean 1990).

Keith's *Under the Grey Olives* is the humorous and partially fictionalized account of a visit to the Holy Land by "fifty very ordinary stay-at-homes" including the author, a few other Canadians, some British and many Americans.

The Black-Bearded Barbarian was the Chinese name of George Leslie Mackay, the first missionary sent out by the Presbyterian Church of Canada to a foreign land. He served in northern Formosa from 1872 until his death in 1901. Keith, who obtained much of her information from relatives of Mackay and from another minister from Formosa (now Taiwan), wrote for children, hoping they would be inspired by the great religious spirit of Mackay.

Bibliography
•Dean, Misao. 1990. Marian Keith. *Dictionary of Literary Biography: Canadian Writers, 1890-1920,* s.v. Keith, Marion.
•Keith, Marian. 1927. *Under the Grey Olives.* Toronto: McClelland and Stewart, 175 pp.
•_____. 1930. *The Black-Bearded Barbarian: Mackay of Formosa.* Toronto: McClelland and Stewart, 288 pp.

Kells, A. Edna 1880-? Edna Kells was a Canadian author.

Kells's short biography *Elizabeth McDougall, Pioneer* is about a Quaker, born in England, who would spend most of her life in a distant country surrounded by Indians, know sacrifice and hardship, sorrow and tragedy, loneliness and long anxious waiting—and often sore grief at the end. After emigrating to York (Toronto) with her parents, in 1842 she married George McDougall who would serve as a Methodist preacher in many areas of Canada and finally become a pioneer missionary of the Northwest Territories. McDougall helped her husband in all these missions to Indians and pioneers while bearing and raising a large family. She died a widow in Morley, near Calgary.

Bibliography
• Kells, Edna. 1933. *Elizabeth McDougall, Pioneer*. Toronto: United Church Publishing House, 49 pp.

Kendrick, Mary Fletcher BA. Mary Kendrick was a graduate of Truro Normal College in Nova Scotia and of Boston University.

Kendrick's material for *Down the Road to Yesterday* came from stories of Springfield inhabitants and from old letters and other library resources. Her book has chapters on Springfield and area topography, settlement, education, military connections, customs, transportation, stories, hunting and fishing, Indians, lumbering, fraternal lodges, churches, agriculture, mining and the genealogies of early settlers.

Bibliography
• Kendrick, Mary F. 1941. *Down the Road to Yesterday: A History of Springfield, Annapolis County, Nova Scotia*. Bridgewater, NS: Bridgewater Bulletin, 141 pp.

Kennedy, Ida Mara. Ida Kennedy was among 185 tourists from various parts of Canada and the United States who, in July 1929, joined an organized twenty-day tour called the New Outlook Maritime Special, sponsored by the United Church of Canada. Their aim was to become "better acquainted with people and conditions in the points visited, to the end that a better understanding may be established and a real spirit of good will cultivated."

Kennedy describes in *Touring Quebec and the Maritimes* where the group went, (travelling by train and later bus from Toronto and Ottawa, then east through Montreal), and what it did. At the end, the travellers returned home "with a broader and happier knowledge of our fair Canada, and memories of many pleasant friendships formed, during three of the best weeks of our lives."

Bibliography
•Kennedy, Ida Mara. 1929. *Touring Quebec and the Maritimes*. Toronto: Armac
   Press, 112 pp.

Kenton, Edna 1876-1954.   Edna Kenton is known best for editing the
Jesuit Relations and Allied Documents (*Relations des jésuites*), voluminous
annual reports describing all manner of conditions and experiences sent
home in the 1660s to France by priests of the Society of Jesus stationed in
Canada. She never married.

The subject of Kenton's biography *Simon Kenton* was an important
Kentucky pioneer whom the author felt had been unjustly neglected in history. (One may assume he was also a relative?) Although Kenton himself
was illiterate and left no first-hand material, he was mentioned in many
documents of the period. He trained many boys "in woodcraft, Indian sign,
Indian scouting, and spying and warfare" who later, as men, grew "great as
the West grew great."

With Hearts Courageous has two themes: the way of life of the Montagnais, Huron and Iroquois Indians, and the compelling history of their interaction with Jesuit priests in Canada for about forty years, beginning in 1632
based on the *Jesuit Relations*. Although the Frenchmen had mastered Latin
and Greek easily, they found the Montagnais language, "to their great amaze-
ment, one of infinite variety and richness." Of the priests, she ends her book,
"Men never lived who deliberately dared more, suffered more, enjoyed more,
conquered more and did more than these."

Bibliography
•Kenton, Edna. 1930. *Simon Kenton, His Life and Period 1755-1836*. Garden
   City, NY: Doubleday, Doran, 352 pp.
•_____. 1933. *With Hearts Courageous*. New York: Liveright, 313 pp.

Kinton, Ada Florence 1859-1905.   Ada Kinton was born at Battersea,
England, to middle-class Methodist parents. After a high school education
focused on music and art, she attended art school for five years, earning an
art-master's certificate while at the same time doing charitable work for the
poor. Then she taught art at a ladies' boarding school in England for several
years, at this time meeting General William Booth, founder of the Salvation Army, and attending some Army meetings. She resigned her teaching
position in 1885 to take postgraduate courses at the South Kensington
School of Art. While there, she decided to emigrate to Canada to establish
her own art school. She did so first in Kingston where she became a lifelong friend of **Agnes Maule Machar**, and then in Toronto. Her life
changed in 1889 when she joined the Salvation Army to be of active service to the poor. (This religious organization was the only one at the time

that allowed women to become the equivalent of clergy.) Her superior educational background made her especially useful in writing articles for the Army's *War Cry* and in editorial work. Rather than progress within the Army's ranks, in 1893 she became the private secretary/governess of the wife of the new Salvation Army's head in Canada, Herbert Henry Booth, who was a son of General Booth. She travelled with the family to Australia in 1896 to work for them until she contracted tuberculosis. In 1902 she returned to Canada unwell, dying in her sister's house in Huntsville three years later.

After her father's death when she was twenty-three, Kinton visited her brothers in the Huntsville area for four months, a period described at length in diary entries in *Just One Blue Bonnet.* The title reflects how much can be accomplished by one Salvation Army member. The volume comprises letters, diary entries, and articles written by Kinton, all linked together by her devoted sister, who writes about Kinton: "A spirit high and rare was hers, seeming almost too good for earth. Yet earth needs just such to teach of the possibilities of this humanity of ours."

Bibliography
•Kinton, Ada Florence. 1907. *Just One Blue Bonnet: The Life Story of Ada Florence Kinton, Artist and Salvationist. Told mostly by Herself with Pen and Pencil.* Toronto: Briggs. 192 pp. Edited by her sister, Sara A. Randleson.

Kiriline, Louise de See Lawrence, Louise entry.

Kirkwood, Mossie May Waddington BA MA PhD LLD 1890-1985.
Mossie May Waddington, who was born and raised in Toronto, attended the University of Toronto (Trinity College), graduating with a BA in 1911, an MA in 1913 and a PhD in 1919. Her doctoral studies coincided with the departure of some university teachers to fight in the First World War, so she was hired to instruct "Divinity Greek" and later English at Trinity College. After the war she became Dean of Women at University College (and later at Trinity College), and in 1923 married Trinity professor William Kirkwood. She raised three children while continuing her university teaching and administrative career, which lasted forty years. Her vision was that of a maternal feminist rather than wanting women to have the opportunity for absolute equality with men. She worked hard to establish women's residences at the university, believing that women students should live with an intellectually oriented don who would inspire them with a passion for scholarship and not just monitor their social activities. Her later research dealt with the philosopher and art critic Santayana in her book *Santayana: Saint of the Imagination* (1961). In 1977 she was awarded an honorary degree by Trinity College.

Kirkwood's *The Development of British Thought from 1820-1890* is based on her doctoral thesis. She introduces it by explaining that Coleridge's prose writings indicate that he is more than a man of letters, but not really a trained philosopher; her thesis was undertaken to help the reader with no philosophical background make sense of Coleridge's work. To do this she made an extensive study of both English and German philosophy and literature.

Kirkwood's experience as a Dean of Women gave her the background to write two books. *Duty and Happiness* is a discourse on social ethics, using numerous concrete examples, and addressed "to parents and young people, to teachers and common citizens, and especially to the dwellers of this young continent of North America where all men [*sic*] might live like gods if the capable among them had regard to the facts." She discusses conduct in general, family and other social groups and the behaviour of individuals. She notes: "It appears that in general the celibate man and the sterile woman are equally alien to the purposes of life, and that in a happier society when their numbers are diminished many social evils will automatically disappear" (p. 184). She urges that education bring out in students a fully developed social consciousness as well as a reduction in repression, for people "are now released from the fears of hell, they have tasted of the sweets of pleasure and will no longer accept the code of 'don't' and 'can't'" (p. 200).

In *For College Women . . . and Men*, a book of advice for college students, Kirkwood gives a brief history of universities, then discusses personal problems (whether one should accept "'petting' and those other vulgarities that go with the times"), standards and loyalties, college government and religion. She ends with three talks she had given about the necessity of allowing women as well as men a good education and satisfying work. She believes that women especially must speak out against social evils:

> Accepted standards and popular opinion must no longer be accepted, nor the authority of men be allowed to overwhelm, but the clear intuition of the woman's mind and heart as to the issue for life of any trend or policy must be bravely expressed. However little belief comes in response, it must still be uttered.

Bibliography
•Prentice, Alison. 1989. "Scholarly Passion: Two Persons Who Caught It." *Historical Studies in Education* 1: 7-27.
•Waddington, M.M., BA, MA, PhD. 1919. *The Development of British Thought from 1820-1890 with Special Reference to German Influences.* Toronto: Dent, 194 pp.
_____. MA, PhD. 1933. *Duty and Happiness in a Changed World.* Toronto: Macmillan, 207 pp.

•_____. 1938. *For College Women . . . and Men*. Toronto: Oxford University Press, 81 pp.

Knowles, Lilian Charlotte Anne Tomn BA MA LLM LittD 1870-1926. Lilian Knowles, an Englishwoman, made academic history for women by obtaining a Double First in 1894 at Cambridge University. She eventually was hired to teach at the University of London where, in 1920, she became Dean of the Faculty of Economics, the first woman dean of the university.

After the First World War Knowles was asked to teach a course on the economic development of the British Empire; she found this difficult to do without a textbook, so she set about writing the immense *The Economic Development of the British Overseas Empire*, which involved learning a great deal about Canada as well as other countries. She notes that "someone must first map out the land and then the details would get filled in by special studies and the book itself would be contradicted and amplified and so the subject would grow." Her husband completed the second volume after her premature death.

Bibliography
•Knowles, L.C.A. 1924. *The Economic Development of the British Overseas Empire*. London: George Routledge, Vol. 1, 555 pp; Vol. 2, 616 pp.

Knox, Ellen Mary BA 1858-1924. Ellen Knox was born in Surrey, England, the daughter of a vicar and his wife; her brother would later become a bishop. Her father tutored her for the examinations at Oxford University, even though at that time women were refused admission there. When Oxford finally allowed women to write exams equivalent to the regular ones, Knox received excellent marks. She was granted entrance to, and later graduated from, St Hugh's Hall in Oxford. She taught at Cheltenham Ladies' College, then came to Toronto in 1894 to become first principal of the girls' school Havergal Hall (now College), a post she retained until her death.

Bible Lessons for Schools: Genesis, Knox writes, "form part of a series originally drawn up for the use of my own Class and of the members of my Staff who might wish to avail themselves of them." She lent the notes to teachers in other schools, too, and because the demand for them increased, she decided to publish them to be used as a textbook for students or as outline lessons for teachers. Each lesson contained "the story of one or more chapters of Genesis, together with the moral and spiritual truths most clearly to be deduced from them." She suggests that several lessons could be added for a boys' school which would not be necessary for girls. She rarely gives practical illustrations so that the students' attention is not diverted from the text: "This I have done deliberately, because I have found that those illustrations which come spontaneously from personal experience and reading are those which appeal most to the pupil."

Knox wrote the comprehensive *Bible Lessons for Schools: Acts of the Apostles* for three reasons: first, to transcend individual stories and reach instead "the spiritual power which awakened that knighthood, inspired the character of its leaders and taught the world what Christian love, joy and endurance might be"; second, to show how Jesus' followers "understood and applied the first principles of His teaching and acts to the religious and social problems of their day"; and third, "to show how these same leaders translated the teaching of Jesus, whether given in parable, paradox or precept, into the spirituality and earnest obedience of their own personal life." She analyzes the Acts in the context of history and human behaviour.

Knox has been faulted for not training her students to consider a life beyond that of a "virtuous, charming, middle-class wife and mother" who is dependent on her husband (Bassett 1975, 109), but *The Girls of the New Day* is based on talks about possible careers, full of literary allusions, that she gave to her Havergal students. The book's audience, besides her students, was an isolated family on a ranch in Western Canada whose father had asked her: "We are out of reach of Sunday School and friends—tell me of a book which will give my girl a wider outlook, which will open her eyes to her chances in life." Knox believed that Canada would be ruled in the future, as in the past, not by money, but by men and women who work hard, who understand clean play and who have vision. Chapters, largely devoted to various possible occupations for women, are entitled, for example, "The joy of farming" and "Queen of them all" (who is a mother). Others discuss being a Christian, "A sound mind," "A day dream of Canada," and "The question of boys." An appendix gives the requirements and typical wage of each profession or job.

Bibliography

•Knox, E.M. 1907. *Bible Lessons for Schools: Genesis*. London: Macmillan, 171 pp.

_____. 1907. *Bible Lessons for Schools: Exodus*. London: Macmillan, 401 pp.

•_____. 1908. *Bible Lessons for Schools: Acts of the Apostles*. London: Macmillan, 401 pp.

•_____. 1919. *The Girl of the New Day*. Toronto: McClelland and Stewart, 241 pp.

Lagacé, Anita.   Anita Lagacé was a resident of Grand Falls, New Brunswick.

Lagacé begins *How Grand Falls Grew* with descriptions of the Maliseet Indians and of the St John River on which Grand Falls is situated—"among the wonders of the world, it is after Niagara one of the most imposing sights one can contemplate in the New World" with a seventy-five-foot direct drop and forty-five feet of cascade. The town beside the falls began as a military post in 1791, but town lots were surveyed only in 1847, and the first high school opened only in 1881. Chapter headings include Steamboats, Mail Couriers, Old Ledgers, Old Diaries and Sports.

Bibliography

Lagacé, Anita. 1945. *How Grand Falls Grew*. Grand Falls, NB: n.p., 77 pp.

Langstone, Rosa Willetts BA MA. Rosa Langstone attended the University of Birmingham where she researched the political history of Ontario and Quebec.

History professor Sir Raymond Beazley, Langstone's advisor, writes in the preface of her 241-page book *Responsible Government in Canada* that "This excellent little [*sic*] study of the genesis of Constitutional Government in Canada is one of the best pieces of Historical Research which has been done in the University of Birmingham in recent years." He hopes that Miss Langstone's first historical publication will not be her last.

Bibliography

•Langstone, Rosa W. 1931. *Responsible Government in Canada*. Toronto: Dent, 241 pp.

Langton, Anne 1804-1893. Anne Langton was born in England, the second child of a well-to-do merchant and his wife, and educated largely in Swiss schools. She became a skilled artist, copying the paintings of Old Masters for six years in the cities of Europe. Her ability to paint miniatures helped finance her family when in 1826 it fell on hard times. She immigrated with her family in 1837 to Sturgeon Lake, Ontario, where her brother John had settled in 1833 and where she spent her days housekeeping, teaching children and painting scenes around her. She remained with John and his family for the rest of her life, accompanying them when they moved to Peterborough and then to Toronto in 1855 on John's retirement from the civil service. She kept journals that "present her as a willing, even eager, immigrant" and "have a constant ring of irrepressible good humor, adaptability, and high hopes that make them unique in the literature of settlement" (Thomas 1990). (Her journals, letters and sketches, edited by her great nephew, were published in 1950 as *A Gentlewoman in Upper Canada*.) In 1840 she benefitted the Sturgeon Lake district by buying land with a small inheritance for the first local public school and also by establishing the first circulating local library with the loan to neighbours of volumes from the family's 1,200-book collection.

In *The Story of Our Family*, Langton admits to hardships the family had suffered in the early days, purposely not mentioned in her original letters home. She wrote her "little family record" at the request of her nephews and nieces, but expresses diffidence about the product: "It is much to be feared that my young relatives will be disappointed with the result of their suggestions; however, they will excuse an old woman whose powers they have over-estimated." She notes that the first part is "literally a family record, but as we increased and multiplied, and became scattered, I found it difficult to gather up all the different threads, and consequently my work has very much degenerated into a personal narrative." The book begins with her grandfather Langton and carries forward to her descendants.

Bibliography
•Baker, L. Doris. 1985. *Anne Langton and Pioneers in Upper Canada*. Concord, ON: Irwin.
•Langton, H.H. ed. 1966 [1950]. *A Gentlewoman in Upper Canada: The Journals of Anne Langton*. Toronto: Clarke, Irwin.
•Thomas, Clara. 1990. Anne Langton. *Dictionary of Literary Biography: Canadian Writers before 1890*, s.v. Langton, Anne.
•Langton, Anne. 1881. *The Story of Our Family* (printed for private circulation). Manchester: Sowler, 204 pp.

Lauder, Maria Elise T. Toof. Maria Toof, who was born in St Armand, Quebec, studied theology at Oberlin University, became a linguist and settled in Whitby, Ontario. In 1856 she married Abram Lauder, who later was elected a provincial member of parliament in Ontario; they had a single child, William Waugh, who became a professional pianist. In the 1870s, Lauder, her husband, and a group of Ontario friends visited England for an extended stay, about which she wrote a book, and some years later, she spent the summer in the Harz Mountains of Germany, about which she published a collection of stories in *Legends and Tales of the Harz Mountains, North Germany* (1885).

Evergreen Leaves describes the Lauders's group trip through Britain, complete with ruminations about history and English literature. They visited a number of places in a leisurely fashion, staying for a month in Wales, two months on the Isle of Wight and the winter in London. The text includes not only historical and descriptive material but much congenial banter among the group. In the first printing of her book, Lauder used a pseudonym, "Toofie," based on her maiden name.

Bibliography
•Lauder, Mrs Maria Elise T.T. 1884 [1877]. *Evergreen Leaves; or "Toofie" in Europe*. Toronto: Rose Publishing, 384 pp.

Laut, Agnes Christina 1871-1936. Agnes Laut was born in Huron County, Ontario, to a merchant and his wife. She was raised in Winnipeg and educated at normal school, after which she taught for two years before enrolling at the University of Manitoba. Because of ill health, she withdrew from university after her second year to become an editorial writer for the *Manitoba Free Press* (1895-97); she then travelled around the continent for two years before emigrating to the United States to live permanently. There she wrote many articles and books about North American frontier life.

While researching material for several early novels such as *Lords of the North* (1900), Laut realized the dearth of well-researched history, which she spent most of the rest of her life rectifying. Her books sold so well that by 1902 she commanded the high royalty rate of 20 percent from Briggs, her Toronto publisher. "Laut's best and best-selling books were (in her own words) intended 'To re-create the shadowy figures of the heroic past, to clothe the dead once more in flesh and blood, to set the puppets of the play in life's great dramas again upon the stage of action' " (Gerson 1990). She published three volumes in the prestigious Chronicles of Canada series: *The "Adventurers of England" on Hudson Bay*, *Pioneers of the Pacific Coast* and *The Cariboo Trail*, all based on careful research from original documentation.

Laut remained an outspoken Canadian nationalist despite living in the United States, writing three books to give Americans a better understanding of their northern neighbour: *Canada: The Empire of the North*, which argued that the twentieth century belonged to Canada, *The Canadian Commonwealth*, which summarized some of the current tensions in the country and *Canada at the Cross Roads*. In this third book, she notes that in the ten years before 1921, 450,000 farmers left America to settle in the Canadian prairie provinces. She considers many economic and social questions and their effect on Canada, concluding finally that Great Britain, Canada and the United States must work together to further democracy.

The Fur Trade of America is a factual book about this industry, but also a vindication of the fur trade against people who accused it of cruelty. Other books by her listed below also had significant Canadian content.

Laut was one of the best-known and prolific historians of her time, insisting, unlike some historians, in using primary sources for her information. She notes in *The Conquest of the Great Northwest* that

> Throughout I have relied for the thread of my narrative on the documents in Hudson's Bay House, London; the Minute Books of some two hundred years, the Letter Books, the Stock Books, the Memorial Books, the Daily Journals kept by chief factors at every post and sent to London from 1670. . . . In many episodes, the story told here will differ almost unrecognizably from accepted versions and legends of the same era.

Bibliography
- Gerson, Carole. 1990. Agnes Christina Laut. *Dictionary of Literary Biography: Canadian Writers, 1890-1920*, s.v. Laut, Agnes Christina.
- Laut, A.C. 1902. *The Story of the Trapper*. Toronto: Briggs, 284 pp.
- Laut, Agnes C. 1904. *Pathfinders of the West, Being the Thrilling Story of the Adventures of the Men Who Discovered the Great Northwest: Radisson, La Vérendrye, Lewis and Clark*. New York: Grosset and Dunlap, 380 pp.
- _____. 1905. *Vikings of the Pacific: The Adventures of the Explorers who Came from the West, Eastward*. London: Macmillan, 349 pp.
- _____. 1908. *The Conquest of the Great Northwest, Being the Story of the Adventurers of England Known as the Hudson's Bay Company*. Toronto: Musson, 2 vols., 409 pp. and 415 pp.
- _____. 1909. *Canada, the Empire of the North, Being the Romantic Story of the New Dominion's Growth from Colony to Kingdom*. Boston: Ginn, 446 pp.
- _____. 1914. *The "Adventurers of England" on Hudson Bay: A Chronicle of the Fur Trade in the North*. Toronto: University of Toronto Press, 133 pp.
- _____. 1915. *Canadian Commonwealth*. Indianapolis: Bobbs-Merrill, 343 pp.
- _____. 1915. *Pioneers of the Pacific Coast: A Chronicle of Sea Rovers and Fur Hunters*. Toronto: University of Toronto Press, 139 pp.
- _____. 1964 [1916]. *The Cariboo Trail: A Chronicle of the Gold-Fields of British Columbia*. Toronto: University of Toronto Press, 115 pp.
- _____. 1921. *Canada at the Cross Roads*. Toronto: Macmillan, 279 pp.
- _____. 1921. *The Fur Trade of America*. New York: Macmillan, 341 pp.
- _____. 1926. *The Conquest of Our Western Empire*. New York: Robert M. McBride, 363 pp.

Lawrence, Louise Flach de Kiriline 1894-? Louise Flach was born in Sweden, the daughter of wealthy aristocrats. She trained as a Red Cross nurse, serving at one time in Russia as a translator for an American military mission as well as a nurse before marrying a Russian officer and moving with him during the aftermath of the Russian Revolution until he was killed. She was a delegate of the Swedish Red Cross Expedition to the Volga region during the famine of 1922 before coming to Canada, where she also worked for the Red Cross in northern Ontario. Later, she married and settled down in a remote cabin on the Mattawa River, Ontario, where she was able to observe nature at her leisure. She was the first Canadian woman to be elected (in 1954) to the American Ornithologists' Union. She became increasingly sensitive to the animals and plants around her, writing further nature stories, scientific articles, and a book, *The Lovely and the Wild*, in 1968. The next year she won the prestigious John Burroughs Medal for nature writing. In 1977 her autobiography was published, *Another Winter, Another Spring: A Love Remembered*.

The author was hired to nurse the Dionne quints soon after they were born. In *The Quintuplets' First Year* her work is cited as a paean to all

Canadian nurses, all of whom are said to be well-trained enough to have been able to care successfully for these babies. She notes:

> My intention in writing this book has not been to indulge in wonderment over the biological miracle of five babies, born at the same time to one mother, nor over their unique survival. It has been written in order to share with all mothers and with all those interested in good mothercraft the increased insight into the proper care of the baby which is gained by the mistakes committed and by the success achieved in the rearing and training of the five little sisters.

In the text she makes generalizations about how to care for any baby, as well as how she and other nurses looked after their charges. She decrees that a sick, suffering baby should be in bed, for example (p. 202), and not picked up: "to soothe it in our loving arms by tenderly rocking it to and fro, I am afraid, is but a pitiable admission of our own inability to alleviate its suffering by more efficacious means."

De Kiriline found that her reclusive life brought her in touch with nature in a way she had forgotten since she left Sweden. *The Loghouse Nest* is the story of a year in the life of a wild black-capped chickadee, Peet, who was her friend while she lived at Rutherglen near North Bay, Ontario. Peet and other animals and plants converse as she portrays their way of life.

Bibliography
•Kiriline, Louise de. 1936. *The Quintuplets' First Year: The Survival of the Famous Five Dionne Babies and Its Significance for All Mothers*. Toronto: Macmillan, 221 pp.
•_____. 1945. *The Loghouse Nest*. Toronto: Saunders, 173 pp.
•Lawrence, Louise de Kiriline. 1977. *Another Winter, Another Spring: A Love Remembered*. New York: McGraw-Hill, 267 pp.

Lawrence, Margaret Isabel BA 1896-1973. Margaret Lawrence became interested in the women's rights movement while studying history at the University of Toronto. After her graduation in 1920 she became an author, an editor for *Canadian Home Journal* and a public speaker. In 1932 she toured Canada under the auspices of the Canadian Club, lecturing on the feminist movement. About this time she was secretly in love with a Jew, Benedict (Baruch) Greene, publisher of *Who's Who in Canada*, whom she had met in 1929, but who refused to marry her because she was a gentile. He married instead a Jew, who soon died; then he turned once again to Lawrence. Despite her devotion to feminism, Lawrence's involvement with Greene changed her perspective so much that "she came to believe that a woman's true fulfilment lay in children and the home." After her marriage to him in 1943 she gave up her career and never again wrote professionally (Lawrence 1973).

In *Mediums and Mystics*, the poet Albert Durrant Watson and Lawrence are sceptical of psychic forces. They write in the Proem/Preface, "within each of us is a ladder on which we may climb to the Heart of Love, but our faith must be built into our own life and deed, our own prayer and aspiration; otherwise the storms of time will shatter it." They "hold strongly to the view that all mediate approach to the heavens is unsatisfactory, involving dangers too serious to ignore."

In *The School of Femininity* (also published as *We Write as Women*), Lawrence discusses the writing of forty-five women novelists, noting in her foreword, "The pattern of thought is this—that women for the first time in history upon a large scale are saying their particular say about themselves, about men, and about life as it treats them separately and together with men."

Bibliography

•Lawrence, Margaret. 1972 [1936]. *The School of Femininity: A Book for and about Women as They Are Interpreted through Feminine Writers of Yesterday and Today*. Toronto: Musson, 382 pp.

•_____. 1973. *Love Letters to Baruch of Margaret Lawrence Greene*. Toronto: Musson.

•Watson, Albert Durrant, MD FRASC and Margaret Lawrence. 1923. *Mediums and Mystics: A Study in Spiritual Laws and Psychic Forces*. Toronto: Ryerson, 65 pp.

Lawson, Maria 1852-1945.   Maria Lawson was born and educated in Prince Edward Island, where her father was editor of the Charlottetown *Patriot*. She taught school in PEI for some years before moving to Victoria, British Columbia, with her parents in 1900, when her father became editor of the Victoria *Colonist*. There she again taught school, becoming principal of the Girls' School in Nanaimo. She wrote for her father's paper and authored several books.

The introduction to Lawson's *History of Canada* reads:

> In compiling a school history for the use of Canadian children, the aim of the writer has been to make its readers feel that the explorers, the missionaries, the soldiers, the pioneers and the statesmen of whom its pages tell, were real men and women. They were engaged in the work of changing half a continent, inhabited by wandering tribes of savages, into a prosperous commonwealth. That work is still going on.

The history is divided into many sections to make it easy to read and understand. It ends:

Canada's future is in the hands of the boys and girls of to-day, and it depends on their industry, intelligence, patriotism and righteousness to advance her another step toward an honorable station in the Imperial household, or it may be to win for her a place among the family of nations.

The introduction of Lawson and Young's *A History and Geography of British Columbia* notes that it was prepared for use in British Columbia "in the hope that the children who study it will derive both pleasure and profit from its perusal. Its aim is to show how, from a wilderness, this province has become the home of civilized men [*sic*], who are preparing the country for a much larger population." The introduction ends:

> If, while reading these pages, the children learn to love better the grand and beautiful province which is their home, and resolve that, by honest work and brave endeavor, they will do their part toward making it a great country, the earnest wish of the authors will have been accomplished.

The history half of the text was written by Lawson and the geography half by Young. (See Young entry.)

Bibliography

•Lawson, Maria. 1908 [1906]. *History of Canada for Use in Public Schools.* Toronto: Gage, 290 pp.
•Lawson, Maria and Rosalind Watson Young, MA. 1906. *A History and Geography of British Columbia for Use in Public Schools.* Toronto: Gage, 148 pp.

Lawson, Mary Jane Katzmann 1828-1890. Mary Jane Katzmann was born near Dartmouth, Nova Scotia, and educated at home, learning to read at age three. When she was twenty-four, she became editor of *The Provincial, or Halifax Monthly Magazine* (1851-53), devoted to "advancing the welfare of mankind, by ministering to their cultural improvement, and consequently, their social happiness" (Kernaghan 1988, 462). Her idealism remained with her after the magazine folded; when she then operated a bookstore in Halifax, one of her ambitions was to make fiction morally acceptable to the public and to have responsible copyright laws. She married William Lawson when she was forty.

Katzmann had written a related series of articles entitled "Tales of Our Village" for *The Provincial*; this formed a good background for her *History of the Townships of Dartmouth, Preston and Lawrencetown* which, according to its editor, "was written rather hastily, in order to compete for the Akins Historical Prize of 1887, which was awarded to it by King's College, Windsor." The book was published after Lawson died.

Bibliography
•Kernaghan, Lois K. 1988. Mary Jane Katzmann (Lawson). *Dictionary of Canadian Biography*, s.v. Katzmann, Mary Jane (Lawson).
•Lawson, Mrs William. 1893. *History of the Townships of Dartmouth, Preston and Lawrencetown, Halifax County, N.S.*, edited by Harry Piers. Halifax: Morton, 260 pp.

Leavitt, Lydia. Lydia Leavitt lived in Ontario, and was wealthy enough to travel extensively. However, she was glad to return from warm climates to Canada, "which for many months is ice-bound and covered with its mantle of snow."

Leavitt wrote her travel book after sailing from San Francisco to Hawaii, New Zealand, Australia, Ceylon, India, Egypt, Italy, Switzerland, France and England. At the start of her trip, she was appalled by conditions in San Francisco, railing especially against the Chinese there, whom she called "the yellow-skinned strangers from the Flowery Kingdom." She notes that about 40,000 Chinese are crowded onto an area "that would be insufficient for five hundred people of more cleanly habits." At the end of her trip, she seems less hostile to the poor of London and efforts to Christianize them, writing: "Tell these poor starving children the story of the crucifixion, and how will it affect them, for are *they* not crucified every day by cold and hunger? The crown of thorns which they wear is on their head at their birth, and is composed of sorrow, shame, hunger, misery and wretchedness."

Bohemian Society is a short book full of homespun philosophy aimed at the average reader. She describes Madam Shoddy who looks a person up and down to estimate the value of what she is wearing (p. 42). Madam Snob talks about her ancestors, "being very careful however, to let the remains of a certain few rest in peace, while she rattles the dry bones of her favored ones in our face, until we are tempted to cry 'peace' " (p. 42). Other homilies include: "the religion which is taught from our pulpits frequently helps to nourish all that is most selfish in our natures" (p. 13); "From the animalculae up to God's noblest work, man, there is the evidence of an all-ruling power and intelligence" (p. 35); and "There are times when we are even inclined to smile at our own misery, but it is the smile which brings wrinkles instead of dimples" (p. 34).

Bibliography
•Leavitt, Lydia. n.d. [between 1886 and 1894]. *Around the World*. Toronto: James Murray, 102 pp.
•_____. 1889. *Bohemian Society*. Brockville: Times Printing and Publishing, 65 pp.

Lecocq, Thelma, later Mrs Winston McQuillan. See Douglas, Frances entry.

Leonowens, Anna Harriette Edwards c.1831-1915. Anna Edwards was born in India to an enlisted man and a local woman, making her of "low class" (which she later counteracted by making up a better life story for herself). When she was seven, her father was apparently ambushed and killed. After she finished her schooling at age fifteen, she avoided her step-father's plan to marry her to a middle-aged merchant by joining a tour of the Holy Land; when she returned to India, she married a young officer of her choice, Major Thomas Leonowens. Leonowens had four children in the next five years, the first two dying in infancy. While the family was posted in Singapore, her husband died of sunstroke suffered during a tiger hunt; she then supported herself and children by setting up a school for officers' children. In 1862 she was asked by the King of Siam (now Thailand) to teach his sixty-seven children and some of his many wives, which she did until 1867. Because of ill health and tired of political infighting at court, Leonowens next sailed to the United States, where she wrote two popular romanticized memoirs based on her exotic experiences, *The English Governess at the Siamese Court* and *The Romance of the Harem*, and taught school on Staten Island, NY. In 1878 she moved with her son-in-law and his family to Halifax, where Thomas Fyshe had been appointed manager of the Bank of Nova Scotia. There she helped found the Pioneer Book Club, the Shakespeare Society, a women's suffrage group and the Victoria School of Art and Design, now the Nova Scotia College of Art and Design, where there is a gallery named for her. She continued to travel and write, visiting Russia in 1881, for example, to write a series of magazine articles. She was an ardent socialist and feminist, exposing exploitation of the poor and of all women in her writing and working to win the vote for Canadian women. She retained her connection with Siam with the marriage of her son to the daughter of a Siamese princess; their children were sent to Leonowens in Halifax to be educated. She spent her last years in Montreal, teaching her final class of Sanskrit at McGill University when she was seventy-five.

The English Governess begins with a letter from the King of Siam, requesting that at his court she teach English language, English literature and science, but *not* religion; he did not want any Christian converts. She then describes the adventures of her young son (her daughter had been sent to England) and herself as they gradually adapted to Bangkok and the palace. She taught her classes despite intrigue and active opposition to her role by many at court; even the king was often angry with her insistence on being independent. She needed six months to obtain his permission to leave

Siam, for example, and the Siamese government tried to prevent her books from being published (Landon 1944, 357). Her story was reenacted in the 1946 film *Anna and the King of Siam* and the 1951 musical *The King and I*, filmed in 1956, all banned in Thailand. An animated film of the story was produced in 1999, as was a new version entitled *Anna and the King*, starring Jodie Foster.

The Romance of the Harem, later republished as *Siamese Harem Life*, focuses mostly on individual women in Siam and the absence of dignity and freedom in their lives where slavery and concubinage were the norm. The first story about the king's new young wife whom Leonowens befriends sets the tone; she escapes from the palace, but is apprehended, publicly whipped and burned to death on order of the king. Leonowens also discusses her teaching, which strongly affected the boy who would next be king; under her influence he later brought religious freedom to the country and abolished slavery and the practice of prostration. In her preface, Freya Stark writes of Leonowens that "few people can have wielded a stronger influence in that corner of Asia."

In *Life and Travel in India*, Leonowens writes: "I have tried to give a faithful account of life in India, as well as of the sights and scenes visited by me, with my husband" in the 1850s. With the aid of "voluminous notes" she made at the time, she describes the many places they visited, along with depictions of jugglers, snake-charmers, dancing-girls, yogees, fakeers, Parsees, Brahmins and Mohammedans. She describes with pride the advances Britain had brought to India (a partial or complete end to sutteeism, infanticide, self-immolation, Thuggism and slavery), but was not an advocate of colonialism or of sending missionaries from Britain to convert Buddhists and Hindus to Christianity.

In *Our Asiatic Cousins*, Leonowens devotes chapters to human races and religions (Hindoos, Parsees, Phoenicians, Jews, Arabs) and countries (Egypt, China, Korea, Tibet, Japan and Southeast Asian countries), describing briefly their histories, the lives of important men and how contemporary peoples lived and died. Her migration hypotheses are faulty, given that she believes Central Asia was the cradle of the human race and that the settlers of Africa south of the Sahara were the descendants of the biblical Ham, but her observations about Jews piquant: "There is no doubt that the primal instinct of nationality throbs in every drop of living Ibrhi [Hebrew] blood, and that this great race-force preserves them as a people, who, scattered one from another over the face of the globe, wanderers and set apart, yet are to rush together and fulfill their part in God's plan for the nations of the Earth" (p. 142).

Bibliography

•Dow, Leslie Smith. 1991. *Anna Leonowens: A Life Beyond The King and I*. East
   Lawrencetown, NS: Pottersfield.
•Davies, Gwendolyn. 1990. Anna Leonowens. *Dictionary of Literary Biography*,
   s.v. Leonowens, Anna.
•Landon, Margaret. 1944. *Anna and the King of Siam*. New York: Day.
•Leonowens, Anna Harriette. 1870. *The English Governess at the Siamese Court:
   Being Recollections of Six Years in the Royal Palace at Bangkok*. Boston:
   Fields, Osgood, 321 pp.
•_____. 1953 [1872]. *Siamese Harem Life*. New York: Dutton, 228 pp.
•_____. 1884. *Life and Travel in India: Being Recollections of a Journey
   before the Days of Railroad*. Philadelphia: Porter and Coates, 325 pp.
•Leonowens, Mrs A.H. 1889. *Our Asiatic Cousins*. Boston: Lothrop.

Lewis, Ada Maria Leigh d. 1931. Ada Leigh was born and brought up in
a large and wealthy family in England, a descendant of Lord Byron. As a
young woman she spent two years in Paris, where she founded a Bible
group for some of the two thousand single Englishwomen working there.
Eventually she realized their need was greater than occasional meetings:
some had no place to stay and others were exploited at their jobs. She felt a
religious calling to help them, so in 1872 she organized a hostel in Paris
where such women could live. Her Homes were visited and praised by the
Bishop of Ontario, John Lewis (1825-1901), a widower who helped her
work financially and in his preaching and whom she married in 1889. She
returned with him to Ontario to live, where other clergy were annoyed that
the bishop's charity interests were focused on the Paris Homes rather than
on local needs.

In *Homeless in Paris* Lewis describes her adventures with Ada Leigh
Homes—for example, finding that her first building had no gas or water,
seeing a drunk person for the first time, learning about prostitution and rescuing a woman who tried to drown herself in the Seine. When she wrote
this memoir, Ada Leigh Homes had been in existence for over forty years.

Lewis's biography of her late husband, *The Life of John Travers Lewis*,
is set in a background of Anglican politics in Ontario. John Lewis was an
Anglican minister who emigrated to Canada in 1850, serving at Hawkes-
bury and Brockville in Ontario before becoming a Bishop and finally an
Archbishop. Another Archbishop writes in a prefatory note, "I rejoice to
know that so capable a writer as Mrs Lewis is giving us a book which will
be of utmost value in all that deals with the history of the growth of the
Church in Canada, with which the name of John Travers Lewis is intimately associated." An appendix of early days is written by his eleventh
and only surviving child.

Bibliography
•Lewis, Mrs Travers (Ada Leigh). 1920. *Homeless in Paris: The Founding of the "Ada Leigh" Homes*. London: Society for Promoting Christian Knowledge, 147 pp.
•His Wife. 1930. *The Life of John Travers Lewis, DD, First Archbishop of Ontario*. London: Skeffington, 160 pp.

Lewis, Ella N. Ella Lewis, who lived in Elgin County, southwest Ontario, was devoted to local history. Besides her book about local doctors, she wrote three essays printed by the Elgin Historical Society, in *Sidelights on the Talbot Settlement* (1938), which focused on Col Talbot, his homes and on Col Burwell.

In *Early Medical Men of Elgin County* Lewis gives brief biographies of thirty-six Ontario doctors. She is obviously impressed by their service, but she also notes that the "mother of four" mentioned once is her mother, who circumvented doctors during a plague about 1880 that killed many children, including four belonging to one doctor. Lewis continues that her mother "decided to follow the treatment outlined in the old 'Dr Gunn's Doctor Book' . . . and never wavered in her decision to fight for the lives of her four children unaided by doctors or nurses." Lewis credits her mother's success with the nursing care that doctors had no time for, as well as the primitive concoctions and washes prescribed by Dr Gunn. One of the doctors Lewis describes was a woman, Margaret Corlis, who "is still remembered . . . as she drove speedily around town or out on the less frequented country roads, her skill in handling her spirited steeds . . . ever viewed with admiration by all lovers of horseflesh."

Bibliography
•Lewis, E.N. 1931. *Early Medical Men of Elgin County*. St Thomas, ON: Sutherland Press, 62 pp.

Lizars, Kathleen Macfarlane d. 1931. Kathleen Lizars was born in Stratford, Ontario, the daughter of a judge and his wife, and educated in Toronto and in Scotland. She was for a time the private secretary of the premier of British Columbia. Later, when she and her sister **Robina Lizars** lived in Toronto, they published several books together with Kathleen as junior author.

Kathleen Lizars wrote about the Humber River in Toronto on her own. She includes in *The Valley of the Humber* a number of historical chapters as well as information on geology, fish, other animals and plants. She notes in the preface:

> To gather, condense, and again sift, to reconsider translations and intermediate synopses, is a delightful occupation known to the initiated; there

is a pleasant field waiting for the worker who has ability to develop it; and an earnest cartographer might even make a valuable history that would be unburdened by paragraphs.

Bibliography

•Lizars, K.M. 1913. *The Valley of the Humber 1615-1913*. Toronto: Briggs, 170 pp.

Lizars, Robina d. 1918. Robina, like her sister **Kathleen Lizars**, was born in Stratford, Ontario. She became a novelist as well as a collector of historical data, and married Robert Smith.

The Lizars sisters wrote *In the Days of the Canada Company* about the settlement of the Huron Tract in Ontario founded by John Galt, obtaining their information from the anecdotes and reminiscences of sixty-two people listed by name, including relatives. They state in the preface that "there is no attempt made at historical writing; that will be a matter for the future, after condensation of many similar works," citing Professor Ramsay Wright, who wrote that "Histories of individual families should therefore be collected, and the accounts of various local enterprises carefully noted" so that general histories could be based on these data. In the introduction, Principal Grant of Queen's College in Kingston praises the book heartily: "Their racy descriptions give vivid glimpses of the good old times, and many Canadians will join with me in thanking them for allowing us to sit beside one of the cradles of our national life."

This book was followed a year later by *Humours of '37*, the history of the Rebellion in the Canadas of 1837, the "Humours" of the title used in the sense of incongruity. The Lizars wrote in the preface that it is assumed "that every Canadian is familiar with Canadian history, and that some one or other of its masters is well fixed in school memories." They do not include footnotes to prevent "many unsightly pages," but rather commend readers to the works of many other historians for more information. They are diffident, writing "The work of the humble ant is to gather fragments, and, as the humblest in the tribe, the collectors of the data from which this mélange has risen offer it to the public."

Bibliography

•Lizars, Robina and Kathleen Macfarlane. 1896. *In the Days of the Canada Company: The Story of the Settlement of the Huron Tract and a View of the Social Life of the Period 1825-1850*. Toronto: Briggs, 494 pp.
•_____. 1897. *Humours of '37, Grave, Gay and Grim: Rebellion Times in the Canadas*. Toronto: Briggs, 369 pp.

Lloyd-Owen, Frances.   Frances Lloyd-Owen, born in Prince Edward Island, was a novelist and author of tales about animals.

Working from Charles Masson's anecdotes and his written notes on his life, Lloyd-Owen wrote his life adventures in *Gold Nugget Charlie*. Masson ran away from home as a boy in 1874 to become a soldier, mail-rider, sailor and finally a successful Yukon gold miner during the Yukon gold rush; one of his claims was eventually sold for $35,000.

Bibliography
•Lloyd-Owen, Frances. 1939. *Gold Nugget Charlie: A Narrative Compiled from the Notes of Charles E. Masson*. London: George C. Harrap, 260 pp.

Logan, Annie Robertson Macfarlane d. 1933.   Annie Macfarlane was born in St John, New Brunswick. She became a journalist in New York, then married and settled in Montreal where she wrote fiction as well as a book of history.

An Account of the Explorations and Discoveries of Samuel de Champlain, dedicated to Governor General Earl Grey, came out on the three hundredth anniversary of Champlain's founding of Quebec City; the purchase price of twenty-five cents was to be donated in part to the Quebec Battlefields Fund. Logan tells her story in an interesting fashion, albeit with a decided bias: she writes that Champlain was truly great in Canadian history, but that the French Canadians who came after him were unfortunate, being "neglected by their home government and exploited by corrupt officials." She concludes, "It is as British subjects that they have been able to enjoy the land bequeathed to them by Champlain, to increase wonderfully and prosper."

Bibliography
•Logan, Mrs J.E. 1908. *An Account of the Explorations and Discoveries of Samuel de Champlain, and of the Founding of Quebec*. Montreal: Montreal News Co., 50 pp.

Low, Florence B. Florence Low was apparently a British author who wrote books about Canada to appeal to possible British emigrants.

In *Openings for British Women*, whose cover features a woman holding two horses harnessed for farm work, Low notes that "this little book will give British women some idea of the immense field open to them in Canada and of the means whereby they may take possession of it." She states: "The writer ventures to claim that she has endeavoured to state the facts as she saw them in 1919-1920, and that having had exceptional opportunities of making investigations throughout the Dominion, and having no 'axe to grind' she believes she has presented them accurately." She provides great detail about where women are needed in Canada, what they should bring with them and what jobs they might hold, such as household work, teaching, nursing and farming. She states that a middle-aged woman, if active, capable, adaptable and cheerful, may thrive in Canada. However, "She should dress well and have nothing 'old-fashioned' or 'old-maidish' about her" (p. 80). As in her 1925 book, also published by the Canadian Pacific Railway, there is a full-page ad for CPR tickets and sailings.

Education in Canada is aimed at British parents and potential teachers; Low notes that in British Columbia, the maximum salary after eight years for a domestic science teacher (woman), $1,420, was the same as the starting salary of a manual training instructor (man). In Canada domestic science seemed to be an important subject for young women, judging by pictures of them ironing, sewing and cooking. She praises the practice, beginning in 1916 in Manitoba, of the prairie provinces providing instruction only in English, although in Manitoba the population then comprised nineteen different races with over 50 percent not having English as their first language. The foreign immigrants were at first annoyed by this change, Low reports, but the authorities were pleased to see that "the younger generation of foreign descent, but often of Canadian birth, are developing into worthy Canadian citizens."

In the summer of 1925, sixty-two British secondary teachers, under the auspices of the Overseas Education League, visited Canada to study its education system. *Teachers' Trails in Canada*, describing this adventure, contains not only Low's description of the journey but short impressions from other members of the group as well. Low portrays the many places the group visited while travelling by train across Canada and back, and the many people they met. On their return, they sent a telegram to the King, stating that

> The members of the party were received with the warmest hospitality throughout; they have learned to realise, and in their turn will be able to make more widely known, the loyal spirit and the vast resources of Canada, and they believe that their visit will help to draw closer the ties of understanding and affection between the Motherland and the great Dominion.

Bibliography

•Low, Florence B. c.1920. *Openings for British Women in Canada*. London: Canadian Pacific Railways, 96 pp.

•_____. 1923. *Education in Canada: A Handbook for Intending Settlers*. London: Canadian Pacific Railway, 95 pp.

•_____. 1925. Part 1: The Story of Our Trail (83 pp.) in *Teachers' Trails in Canada*. London: Dent, 184 pp.

Lugrin, Nellie de Bertrand 1874-? Nellie Lugrin was born in Fredericton, New Brunswick, moving when she married E.B. Shaw to the Yukon and then to Victoria, British Columbia. She published many stories in Canada, the United States and England, as well as a book.

Lugrin begins *The Pioneer Women of Vancouver Island*:

> The composite story of the pioneer women of this last West is a plain one. It has to do with the great issues of loving and mating, of birth and death, and the struggle for existence under terrible odds. It is the describing of the first unfolding of a nation and it has the simplicity and grandeur of an epic.

She gathered information on the lives of hundreds of women to tell her story.

Bibliography
•Lugrin, N. de Bertrand. 1928. *The Pioneer Women of Vancouver Island, 1843-1866.* Victoria: Women's Canadian Club of Victoria, 312 pp.

Lynch-Staunton, Emma 1885-1949. Emma Lynch-Staunton, who came from a pioneer ranching family in the Pincher Creek area, was a member of the Alberta Women's Institute.

The first page of her *A History of the Early Days of Pincher Creek* notes that the information in it is "as Gathered Together by the Members of the Alberta Women's Institute and Compiled by Mrs C. Lynch-Staunton," although the text reads smoothly rather than as a compilation. Pincher Creek was named in 1868 when tools were scarce and a party of men lost a pincers in this river; it was found by police in 1874. The book deals with Indian inhabitants, the arrival of Europeans, and their various activities, such as gold and coal mining, ranching and growing wheat. Many pioneers are mentioned by name, as are important ranches, towns and local areas. The many diverse sections are given names such as "Interesting Anecdotes," "Forest Fires," "Old Time Dances" (held at the Beauvais Ranch every night of the year), and "Visit of Governor General of Canada to Pincher Creek" by the Marquis of Lorne in 1881.

Bibliography
•Members of the Women's Institute of Alberta. 1926. *A History of the Early Days of Pincher Creek of the District and of the Southern Mountains.* N.p., 55 pp.

Macbeth, Madge Hamilton Lyons 1878-1965. Madge Lyons was born in Philadelphia and raised when young in the United States; as a teenager she attended exclusive Hellmuth College in London, Ontario. While at this school she became acquainted with **Lady Aberdeen** and a civil engineer, Charles Macbeth, whom she married in 1901. The couple relocated to

Ottawa in 1904, where they moved in high social circles which included Prime Minister Laurier and his wife. Within several years, however, her husband died of tuberculosis. She then supported herself and two small sons by writing stories, articles and books, encouraged by author **Marjorie MacMurchy.** When Macbeth felt she needed new experiences to write about, she travelled extensively by herself (France, Italy, Spain, Yugoslavia, western Canada, South America) while her mother looked after her sons. Soon Macbeth lectured widely about her adventures and opinions and became involved in theatre production. She was a force in the Canadian Authors Association, serving first as head of the Ottawa branch and then elected first woman president of the national body in 1939. She served for three terms, until 1942. Her advice to freelance writers was to buy a notebook and jot down everything they saw and that crossed their minds. Toward the end of her life she wrote the two autobiographies noted below. In *Boulevard Career* she emphasized the difficulty Canadians had writing about their country. A Canadian magazine refused her story about winter in Ottawa, noting: "It is difficult enough to persuade our readers to accept the Canadian scene at its best. It would be suicide for us to give any prominence to our winters. Of course, we have cold and snow and ice, but we scrupulously suppress all mention of the fact" (p. 64).

As well as twenty novels, one of which lampooned Ottawa society (*The Land of Afternoon*, 1924), Macbeth wrote a biography of Stephen Leacock and *Over the Gangplank to Spain*, about her favourite country which she visited at least twice for extended stays. It is "not a Guide Book" (as she notes):

> Nor is it history. None would class it under memoirs, and neither is it fiction. Absolutely, it is not fiction! It's just a book—a book inspired largely by the spiritual refreshment I find in Spain, by deep affection for my many Spanish friends and by an eager desire to halt the stream of tourist traffic to Don Quixote's enchanting land.

Bibliography
•Gerson, Carole. 1990. Madge Macbeth. *Dictionary of Literary Biography: Canadian Writers, 1890-1920*, s.v. Macbeth, Madge.
Macbeth, Madge. 1923. Stephen Leacock. Toronto: Ryerson, 176 pp.
•_____. 1931. *Over the Gangplank to Spain*. Ottawa: Graphic, 359 pp.
•_____. 1953. *Over My Shoulder*. Toronto: Ryerson, 170 pp.
•_____. 1957. *Boulevard Career*. Toronto: Kingswood House, 230 pp.

MacCallum, Elizabeth Pauline BA MA PhD LLD OC 1895-? Elizabeth MacCallum, born in Turkey to missionary parents, was fourteen before she saw a four-wheeled vehicle. She attended Calgary Normal School and Queen's University (BA 1916) where she and **Charlotte Whitton** were rivals and the best of friends. She obtained her MA in English and history there in 1919, then taught in Dawson City, earning $2,300 a year. She was conflicted about religion, giving up Christianity when a young woman despite her missionary upbringing. She studied history for her doctorate at Columbia University, worked at New York's Foreign Policy Association, and later joined the Canadian Department of External Affairs (1942-60) as the expert on the Near and Middle East (she spoke Turkish and Arabic). She was appointed Canada's first woman head of mission, as chargé d'affaires in Lebanon, and later was an advisor to Prime Minister Louis St Laurent. Her extensive knowledge of the Middle East enabled her to warn of future Arab-Israeli conflict there long before this became a reality. Queen's University awarded her an honorary degree in 1952, and later she was inducted into the Order of Canada.

MacCallum wrote *The Nationalist Crusade in Syria* about the Syrian rebellion of 1925-27, from its inception to its close, because it illustrated the functioning of the League of Nation's mandate system, in part "a political experiment peculiar to our own generation," as well as the rebellion against the French authorities who had administered the country for the previous nine years. She concludes that Syria could only attain independence through its own efforts, with France being of more potential help than the League.

Twenty Years of Persian Opium was prepared under the direction of the Opium Research Committee. Iran was chosen as a focus of study because it was one of the few countries producing raw opium that was anxious to address international concerns, and because it was the only country "where an international body has made a study of the economic disarrangement and physical difficulties which might be expected to result from limitation of the opium crop," which America favoured. MacCallum focused on Persian opium policy before the First World War and postwar efforts to control it.

In *Rivalries in Ethiopia*, prepared at the invitation of the World Peace Foundation, the introduction notes that:

> Miss MacCallum has set forth, with candor and detachment, the facts necessary to enable an American reader to understand the crisis precipitated by the Italian preparation for war in Ethiopia. The economic and political situations are exhibited in detail and, finally, Italy's claims in justification of her course and Ethiopia's answers are stated.

Bibliography
• Weiers, Margaret K. 1995. *Envoys Extraordinary: Women of the Canadian Foreign Service*. Toronto: Dundurn Press, chap. 3.
• MacCallum, Elizabeth P. 1928 . *The Nationalist Crusade in Syria*. New York: Foreign Policy Association, 299 pp.
• _____. 1928 . *Twenty Years of Persian Opium (1908-1928): A Study*. New York: Foreign Policy Association, 55 pp.
• _____. 1935. *Rivalries in Ethiopia*. Boston: World Peace Foundation, 64 pp.

Macdonald, Dorothy. Dorothy Macdonald was a Canadian interested in archeology.

Fibres, Spindles and Spinning Wheels is about textiles and their production, which "are second in importance only to agriculture and like agriculture, made their earliest appearance during the Neolithic or New Stone Age," when people first started to lead a settled life. Macdonald discusses briefly wool, flax, cotton, silk and synthetic fibres, then focuses on spinning in many cultures and on spinning wheels. The text is typewritten, with line drawings for illustration.

Bibliography
• Macdonald, Dorothy K. 1944. *Fibres, Spindles and Spinning Wheels*. Toronto: Royal Ontario Museum of Archaeology, 49 pp.

MacDonald, Elizabeth Mary BA PhD. Elizabeth MacDonald was a doctoral student at the University of Toronto, whose 1928 thesis was revamped and published as a book.

The Position of Women as Reflected in Semitic Codes of Law, published in the Oriental Series of the University of Toronto Studies, resembles a women's studies project long before women's studies was invented as a discipline. It is based on the Code of Hammurabi, the Assyrian Code and the Hebrew Codes. Because the life and customs of early Semitic women are not known, she extrapolates them from the life and customs of more recent nomads who have inhabited the Arabian peninsula for many centuries.

Bibliography
• MacDonald, Elizabeth Mary. 1931. *The Position of Women as Reflected in Semitic Codes of Law*. Toronto: University of Toronto Press, 79 pp.

MacDonald, Helen Grace BA 1888-? MacDonald was a political scientist who studied at Columbia University, which sponsored the first edition of her book.

MacDonald wrote *Canadian Public Opinion and the American Civil War* (dedicated to "Canada and the United States: May Brotherhood Prevail") because she believed "that the American Civil War left its imprint upon the political institutions of British North America to a greater extent than has been generally recognized." In Canada the Liberals sympathized with the Northern states in general, while the Conservatives identified more with the Southern states, but both realized the importance of preserving amicable relations with the United States to prevent conflict in Canada. MacDonald collected much of her material from the Canadian Public Archives and the Library of Parliament in Ottawa.

Bibliography
•MacDonald, Helen G. 1974 [1926]. *Canadian Public Opinion on the American Civil War.* New York: Octagon Books of Farrar, Straus and Giroux, 237 pp.

MacGill, Helen Gregory BA MA LLD 1864-1947. Helen Gregory was born into a socially prominent family of Hamilton, with her mother one of Canada's first activists in welfare work. Gregory earned her Bachelor of Music at Trinity College, becoming the first woman student there to earn a BA (in 1889). The following year she earned an MA. She travelled to western Canada in part at the instigation of Sir John A. Macdonald to report on foreign settlement there, then on to Japan after a whirlwind marriage to write about its new national constitution. After her husband died in 1901, leaving her with two small children and her mother to support, she married James MacGill; they settled in Vancouver. She carried out volunteer welfare and women's suffrage work until 1917, when she was appointed a Justice of the Peace and Judge of the Juvenile Court, in part because of the book she had written about women and children and the law. During twenty-three years as a judge, none of her decisions was reversed. She was a founder of the Vancouver branch of the Canadian Women's Press Club. Her daughter Elsie would become the first Canadian woman engineer.

Daughters, Wives and Mothers in British Columbia is based on presentations by legal experts to audiences, "to many of whom the status of the wife, the mother and the child in this Province was an unpleasant, ofttimes an incredible revelation." (For example, if the husband of a childless woman died without a will, his estate had to be divided between the widow and his relatives, or lacking them, the Crown). It was produced as a "ready reference for these who know, and proof to those who doubt." Many unjust laws were documented in this text, but after women received the vote in 1917, these laws were often changed, sometimes with the help of MacGill.

Her updated *Laws for Women and Children in British Columbia* thus happily renders much of the information in her earlier book obsolete. MacGill dedicates this later book to those earnest men and women in public and private life who have striven ceaselessly to better the legal status and conditions of our women and children, and to the noble band of suffrage workers, including those nearest and dearest to me, some of whom have passed on. The splendid evidence of their ability and courage is contained in this brief summary.

In 1938 she was awarded an honorary Doctor of Laws degree by the University of British Columbia; a prominent plaque there honours her with the inscription "Let her own works praise her in the gates."

Bibliography
• MacGill, Helen Gregory MA, Mus Bach. 1913. *Daughters, Wives and Mothers in British Columbia: Some Laws Regarding Them*. Vancouver: Moore Printing, 66 pp.
• _____. 1925. *Laws for Women and Children in British Columbia*. Vancouver: Evans and Hastings, 64 pp.

MacGregor, Mary See Keith, Marian entry.

Machar, Agnes Maule 1837-1927. Agnes Machar, author and poet, was the daughter of a Scottish Presbyterian minister, John Machar, who preached at the Kingston church attended by the families of John A. Macdonald and Oliver Mowat; he was also principal for nine years of Queen's College (later University). She lived and wrote all her life in Kingston, "an outstanding crusader for the causes of temperance, labor, reform, feminism, and in the defense of Christianity" (Gerson 1990), as well as the first Canadian life member of the International Council of Women. In articles and speeches she campaigned for higher education for women so that they could attain the highest possible intellectual and moral excellence. As well as books of biography and Canadian history, she wrote many successful novels, among them *For King and Country: A Story of 1812* (1874), a historical romance featuring General Isaac Brock.

In *Faithful unto Death* about one of Queen's early janitors, the preface states:

> In an age like the present [1859], when the general superficiality of the time seems to extend itself even to religion; and the olden type of manly and vigorous piety is becoming unhappily rare;—it has seemed matter of regret that the rising of literature of our young Country should not possess a record of one whose strict unfailing integrity of life and conduct commended to all around him the power of the religion he professed.

John Anderson (1810-59) from Scotland became janitor and bell-ringer at Queen's College in 1851, living and working there until his death. Machar's father gave the funeral address that ends the book; it calls on professors and students alike to renew their Christian beliefs after cogitating on the humble but religious life of the janitor. Machar's name does not appear at all on the title page.

The preface of *Stories of New France* notes that "The object of this volume is to make the past of Canada better known, to those at least who have not leisure or opportunity to study the glowing pages [in many volumes of history] of Parkman." This shortened version of part of Canada's history deals with "all the most interesting details," with Machar's writings both nationalistic and moral. Her patriotism involved race, because she wrote:

> in the simple name of *Canadian* we may well merge the more partial designations of "Anglo-Saxon" and "Franco-Canadian"; for "Norman and Saxon and Celt are we." It is then our true "national policy" to mould, out of our diverse material, a national character enriched by the best traits of the races from which we spring, enriched also by the bilingual character of our composite origin.

In *The Story of Old Kingston*, about Machar's home town, she writes lyrically: "Nurtured in sacrifice and hardship, inured to repeated disappointments, [Kingston] has proved the 'uses of adversity' in teaching lessons of steadfastness and energy, which have developed her growing life and moulded her still plastic institutions." In underlining the importance of history she writes:

> we cannot be said really to *know* our own time, unless we know something of the events that precede it and helped to determine its character. To a community, the consciousness of its past gives the sense of continuity which is the principle of its collective life and the nurse of its patriotism.

Machar is also enamoured of imperialism. In *Stories of the British Empire*, composed of biographies of famous British people, she writes:

> No one, surely, with any adequate belief in the Divine Ruler of the Universe, can study the wonderful Story of our British Empire without being impressed with a sense of its Divine purpose, its final mission to humanity, as the end for which the shoot of Saxon freedom, planted in British soil, has grown into the greatest Empire this world has ever seen.

Bibliography

- Gerson, Carole. 1990. Agnes Maule Machar. *Dictionary of Literary Biography: Canadian Writers, 1890-1920*, s.v. Machar, Agnes Maule.
- Anonymous. 1859. *Faithful unto Death, A Memorial of John Anderson, Late Janitor of Queen's College, Kingston*. Kingston: James M. Creighton, 66 pp.
- Machar, Agnes. 1890. *Stories of New France, Being Tales of Adventure and Heroism from the Early History of Canada*, Series 1. Boston: D. Lothrop, 313 pp.
- Machar, Miss and T.G. Marquis. 1893 . *Stories from Canadian History Based upon "Stories of New France."* Toronto: Copp, Clark, 96 pp.

•_____. 1893 . *Heroes of Canada Based upon "Stories of New France."* Toronto: Copp, Clark, 96 pp.

•Machar, Agnes Maule. 1908. *The Story of Old Kingston*. Toronto: Musson, 291 pp.

•_____. 1913. *Stories of the British Empire for Young Folks and Busy Folks.* Toronto: Briggs, 356 pp.

MacInnis, Grace Winona Woodsworth BA OC LLD 1905-1991. Grace MacInnis was the daughter of socialist J.S. Woodsworth, founder of the Co-operative Commonwealth Federation (CCF) movement, the precursor to the New Democratic Party. She was born in Winnipeg and graduated from the University of Manitoba, where she won a French government scholarship, thanks in part to her bilingual mother. While her father's secretary on Parliament Hill, she met his right-hand man, Angus MacInnis, whom she married in 1932. Like her father and husband, she also devoted her life to politics, serving as a CCF Member of the Legislative Assembly in British Columbia (1941-45) and as a federal CCF Member of Parliament (1965-74). She lobbied tirelessly for better housing, nursery schools, adequate wages for stay-at-home mothers, birth control and legal abortions. In 1953 her biography of her father, *J.S. Woodsworth: A Man to Remember*, won a Governor General's Award. She received the Order of Canada in 1974 and an honorary degree from the University of British Columbia in 1977.

Canada through CCF Glasses, co-authored with her brother who was also immersed in politics, was officially endorsed by the National Council of the CCF and intended primarily

> for use by platform speakers and study groups. It follows closely the lines of the Dominion Manifesto, its purpose being to provide information supplementing and explaining the different planks. In addition it extends discussion over a number of questions necessarily excluded by the reasonable limits of the Manifesto.

The CCF manifesto was aimed "toward greater economic efficiency and a better life for the rank and file of the people." The authors were unalterably opposed to war, arguing that "Capitalism and peace are incompatible. Wars are fought today to make the world safe for capitalism. . . . THE PROFIT MUST BE TAKEN OUT OF WAR" (Lewis 1993, 110).

The same authors write in the preface of *Jungle Tales Retold* that this work will "examine the methods by which Big Business functions and how monopoly affects the welfare of the community," using a number of common industries for examples. "The title indicates a belief that in spite of a veneer of civilization, capitalism forces the adoption of business methods and ethics not far removed from those of the jungle." The book ends with "the CCF way out of the economic maze," which involves "the transference of the productive machine from private to public ownership and control"; the facts and statistics are enlivened by jazzy subheadings such as "With Tooth and Claw," "Tiger Take All," and "Might Is Right." The authors urge that their book be read by laypeople as well as platform speakers and study groups, and hope that it will open up avenues for further study; at fifteen cents, the price was right.

Bibliography

•Lewis, S.P. 1993. *Grace: The Life of Grace MacInnis*. Madeira Park, BC: Harbour Publishing.

•MacInnis, Grace and Charles J. Woodsworth. 1935. *Canada through CCF Glasses*. Vancouver: Commonwealth Press, 88 pp.

•_____. 1936. *Jungle Tales Retold: A Survey of Capitalist Monopoly in Canada*. Ottawa: Labour Publishing, 58 pp.

MacKay, Isabel Ecclestone Macpherson 1875-1928. Isabel Macpherson was born and grew up in Woodstock, Ontario, where, from 1890 to 1900, she was staff contributor to the *Woodstock Daily Express*. She married a court stenographer, Peter MacKay, in 1895, and moved with him in 1909 to Vancouver. There she raised three daughters and published six novels (among them the popular *Blencarrow* [1926]), four books of poetry and five plays, as well as contributing hundreds of poems and stories to Canadian, British and American magazines. Her own creativity and industry helped make her a champion of fiction writing and journalism in Canada; she helped found the British Columbia chapter of the Canadian Women's Press Club, serving as Vice-President in 1914 and President in 1916, and was Vice-President of the Vancouver branch of the Canadian Authors Association from 1922 to 1926.

Shortly before her death, MacKay completed the manuscript of *Indian Nights* which was published posthumously. It is a book of West Coast Indian legends, a topic to which she had been introduced by her friend **Pauline Johnson**; "like Johnson, MacKay accords a place of honor to the wise woman storyteller" (Relke 1990). The foreword states that although she had "to edit slightly certain parts of her stories, they do not suffer on that account. All ring true and are saturated through and through with the genuine psychology of the Indian. Nothing of value has been lost by her emendations." Her stories are judged to be redolent "of the quaint wisdom and philosophy of a fast-vanishing race."

Bibliography

•Relke, Diana M.A. 1990. Isabel Ecclestone MacKay. *Dictionary of Literary Biography*, s.v. MacKay, Isabel Ecclestone.

•Mackay, Isabel Ecclestone. 1930. *Indian Nights*. Toronto: McClelland and Stewart, 199 pp.

MacKay, Janet Winifred LLB. Janet MacKay, a Canadian of Scottish descent and an early feminist, was one of the few women lawyers actively practising in Vancouver when she decided to become instead a traveller and journalist publishing freelance material out of London, England. She seems to have changed her career after seven years, in part at least because of sexual harassment: she notes of her experiences that "Obviously woman's place if not strictly in the home was at least not in the court-room, not for another hundred years or so."

Before she left Canada, MacKay gave "valuable assistance" to L.C. Bernacchi in writing his book on Captain Oates of Antarctic fame. He notes in *A Very Gallant Gentleman* (1933) that "Without her collaboration and her knowledge and experience in writing, the book, in its present form, would not have been possible." However, she is not listed as co-author.

MacKay's *Interlude in Ecuador* describes her travels by boat to South America and her many adventures there—shooting alligators, escaping from lecherous men, visiting her sister and travelling to Quito. She was put off by the many Europeans she met who assumed themselves superior to the Natives.

Catherine of Braganza states that MacKay's "knowledge of people and the variety of her experiences have enabled her to bring to this book human understanding which gives life to her characters, whilst her legal training has given her the powers of selection and deduction so essential in historical biography." Catherine of Portugal was the wife of King Charles II of England.

In *Little Madam: A Biography of Henrietta Maria*, a princess of France who became the wife of King Charles I of England, MacKay writes that "had she been a man, [she] would have been the great Henry's greatest son. Handicapped by her sex and the education considered sufficient for one of her sex, still she was a great woman."

Bibliography
•MacKay, Janet. 1934. *Interlude in Ecuador*. London: Duckworth, 215 pp.
•_____. 1937. *Catherine of Braganza*. London: John Long, 320 pp.
•_____. 1939. *Little Madam: A Biography of Henrietta Maria*. London: G. Bell and Sons, 380 pp.

Mackenzie, Catherine Dunlop. Catherine Mackenzie was the personal secretary of Alexander Graham Bell (1847-1922), working with him from 1914 until his death, "day in and day out in all of his many activities, much of the time compiling and editing [his] biographical material under his direction."

With this background, Mackenzie was the ideal person to write the biography *Alexander Graham Bell*. She made every effort to verify all unsupported or controversial statements, especially those dealing with the discovery of the telephone, whose invention others wanted to appropriate. She tells the story of Bell's life "in terms of the work he did and the way he did it. Much of this work was momentous, some of it trivial, but all of it was animated with the enthusiasm and burning belief that was part of his genius, and, because it was his sole preoccupation, the story of his work is peculiarly the story of his life."

Bibliography

•Mackenzie, Catherine. 1928. *Alexander Graham Bell: The Man Who Contracted Space*. Boston: Houghton Mifflin, 382 pp.

MacLean, Margaret 1871-1931. Margaret MacLean was born into a family of six boys, with a father who was a businessman in Ottawa and later a city alderman. In 1904, MacLean accompanied him, now a widower, to Japan, where he had been appointed by the government as Canada's commercial agent. The next year she visited China for four weeks, writing up her experiences and observations in a book published by the Methodist Publishing Company in Tokyo "for the author." After her father died, she travelled twice around the world before settling in Toronto. There she studied the varied collections of the Royal Ontario Museum, eventually founding the Education Program against the better judgement of the museum directors. In her first year, 1919, she lectured on twenty-one different subjects to 9,128 people as well as giving thirty-one lectures outside museum hours, writing four magazine articles and producing forty press notices about the museum. She resigned her job under pressure in 1923, then travelled again until her death.

In *The Wise Traveller*, MacLean describes the two Chinese cities she visited in 1905, Shanghai and Soochow. She met women with bound feet, went shopping in the streets, visited a temple and the countryside, travelled along the canals and attended a wedding and a ten-course birthday feast. Her editor, Beverley Stapells, writes that her book "reveals the mind of a bright and cultured woman from a middle-class background at the turn of the century. It is her openness of mind, her objectivity as she encounters a foreign culture and her humanity that draws the reader."

Bibliography

•MacLean, Margaret. 1990 [1906]. *The Wise Traveller*. [Originally called *Chinese Ladies at Home*]. Edited by Beverley Echlin Stapells. Ottawa: Oberon Press, 114 pp.

MacMillan, Marion Thayer. Marion MacMillan spent her summers on Georgian Bay north of Parry Sound, Ontario, beginning in 1919. She gloried in the wilderness, particularly when canoeing. During the third summer, her husband and she ("a physician and his psychologically minded wife") noticed that the reflections made from the rocky shore in the water on a still day, especially at sunrise and at dusk, made startling photographs. By holding these "water photographs" on their side, she could make out bilaterally symmetrical images. On one photo she recognized nine characters from *Alice in Wonderland* arranged in a vertical line. She realized that similar images were found on totem poles and in Indian and Mayan designs, where bilateral repetitions and the superposition of motifs take on human and animal forms.

In *Reflections: The Story of Water Pictures*, MacMillan describes how her discovery was accepted by the art world, by anthropologists and by children, who were more able than adults to make out objects in the black and white photographs.

Bibliography
•MacMillan, Marion Thayer. 1936. *Reflections: The Story of Water Pictures*. New York: Greenberg, 82 pp.

MacMurchy, Helen MD CBE 1862-1953.   Helen MacMurchy, sister of author **Marjory MacMurchy** Willison, was born in Toronto and taught briefly in the 1880s at Toronto's Jarvis Collegiate Institute, where her father was principal. She was so distressed by the school's handicapped students that she decided to become a doctor to help them. She enrolled at Ontario Medical College for Women and the University of Toronto, graduating as a doctor in 1901. After further training in the United States, she became the first woman resident intern at Toronto General Hospital and founder of *The Canadian Nurse* magazine. She practised medicine briefly, then worked for the Ontario government (1906-19), largely as a medical inspector. Her chief interests were the prevention of infant deaths, public health standards and the physical and mental health of children. In 1920 she became director of the Division of Child Welfare in the Dominion Department of Health, for which she wrote a number of best-selling books and booklets. She was elected a life member of the Academy of Medicine, awarded a CBE and cited as one of twelve leading physicians of the Western world.

MacMurchy was a maternal feminist who noted in her first book that "Where the mother works, the baby dies." She wrote *The Almosts* after preparing a census of the province's "feeble-minded" for the Ontario government, hoping that her book might "be used to advance the work of awakening public interest and educating public opinion" about this group.

She includes long excerpts about such people from a number of literary authors, including Shakespeare, Bunyan, Scott, Dickens, Hugo and many more recent novelists. She argues, using these fictitious characters as examples, that the "feeble-minded" should be given justice, a fair chance and the opportunity to have their special gifts appreciated: "we must make a happy and permanent home for them during their lives. The only Permanent Parent is the State" (p. 178). As an advocate of eugenics, she was anxious that the feeble-minded not remain in the community to reproduce; she warned of "what feeble-mindedness costs in hard cash, in self-respect, in social degradation—and degeneracy" (p. 176).

The Canadian Mothers' Book, which gives information on everything one should know about a baby and its needs, was immensely successful, with over 800,000 copies sold in many editions. The first page reads in large type:

> This book has been written for you—a Canadian mother. The government of Canada, knowing that the nation is made of homes, and that the homes are made by the Father and Mother, recognises you as one of the Makers of Canada. No National Service is greater or better than the work of the Mother in her own home. The Mother is "The First Servant of the State."

The title page also includes a short quote from "The mother of a Canadian V.C."

MacMurchy's *How We Cook in Canada* is a sanguine book, beginning "Nothing in the house is more important or more interesting than cooking. Mother never looks prettier than when she is presiding over the destinies of her family from her throne in the kitchen. Her hair is always so nice and she smiles her Mother's smile." She includes information on stoves and open fires as well as basic recipes, and urges all Mothers to have gardens to supply food for the family.

The statistics on which *Maternal Mortality in Canada* is based were only collected beginning in 1921. About that time, maternal death was second only to tuberculosis in women of child-bearing age, with a rate of 6.4 deaths for every 1,000 live births. Of the 1,532 Canadian women who died because of their pregnancies in one year, 1925-26, over half were already in poor health from other causes, or exhausted from child care and overwork; nearly one-quarter did not have suitable access to a doctor. As well as a review of the statistics, MacMurchy presents relevant data and information from other countries and recommends ways in which the mortality rate could be reduced in Canada.

Continuing her interest in eugenics, MacMurchy wrote in *Sterilization? Birth Control? A Book for Family Welfare and Safety*:

Out of every thousand of us there are about ten who are the chief cause
of our present enormous expenditure for institutions and other forms of
relief and care. Of these ten about three are suffering from mental defect,
about three or four from mental disease, and the remaining three or four
are suffering from physical disease, often incurable now, though pre-
ventable in earlier life; or they are law-breakers and criminals; or they
are unemployable; or they have become chronic paupers—they do not
want to work.

She advocates sterilization for selected undesirables, and in general is
against birth control for most people except under medical care. She sum-
marizes:

If a married couple decide to practise contraception, medical advice and
supervision are always necessary to preserve health and safety of the
patient and consequently the happiness of the home. Mental health as
well as physical health may be affected by carrying on the practice of
birth control.

Her position "as medical professional and civil servant enabled Mac-
Murchy to play a central role as intermediary between the scientific and
social worlds, a popularizer of science" (McConnachie 1983, 69); her
career reflected the growing importance of doctors as professionals and
experts. When *Sterilization? Birth Control?* was published in 1934, these
two topics were banned from Women's Institute meetings as being too divi-
sive "by reason of their sectarian ramifications" (Ambrose 1996, 131).

Bibliography
•McConnachie, Kathleen, 1983. Methodology in the Study of Women in History:
   A Case Study of Helen MacMurchy, MD. *Ontario History* 75: 61-70.
•MacMurchy, Helen. 1920 . *The Almosts: A Study of the Feeble-Minded*. Boston:
   Houghton Mifflin, 178 pp.
•_____. MD, Chief of the Division of Child Welfare. 1923 [1920b]. *The
   Canadian Mother's Book*. Ottawa: F.A. Acland, Printer to the King, 136 pp.
•_____. 1923. *How We Cook in Canada*. Ottawa: F.A. Acland, Printer to the
   King, 52 pp.
•_____. 1928. *Maternal Mortality in Canada*. Ottawa: Department of Health,
   74 pp.
•_____. CBE, MD. 1934. *Sterilization? Birth Control? A Book for Family
   Welfare and Safety*. Toronto: Macmillan, 156 pp.

MacMurchy, Marjory c.1869-1938 (later Lady Willison). Marjory Mac-
Murchy was born in Toronto, the sister of **Helen MacMurchy.** Their father
was a mathematics teacher and principal in Toronto; their mother was deeply
involved in the Woman's Foreign Missionary Society. Both sisters were
authors: Dr Helen was known as "the Feeble-Minded MacMurchy" to distin-

guish her from Marjory "the Social Worker MacMurchy," who was concerned with problems of women and children; for example, she befriended young **Madge Macbeth**, who was trying to support her family by writing (Macbeth 1953, 53ff). MacMurchy wrote books and articles on educational and other subjects, edited *The Canadian Educational Monthly* and served as President of the Canadian Women's Press Club from 1909 to 1913. In 1911 she was invited to the coronation of King George and Queen Mary as representative of the Publishers' Press. Later, she became head of the Women's Department of the Canadian Reconstruction Association. In 1926, she married newspaperman Sir John Willison to become Lady Willison.

The Woman—Bless Her is

> devoted to studies of women in Canada. The purpose of these studies is to find an answer to such questions as, What are the most promising developments amongst Canadian women; and in what ways are they preparing for the greatest economic and social contribution which they can make to Canadian national life? It reflects social concerns during the first World War—women in the labour force and women as voters.

MacMurchy raises issues such as the economic value of housework and the perspective of the consumer as opposed to that of the producer and merchant. She emphasizes the need for women's organizations so that they can carry out political action (see Zaremba 1974, 131). MacMurchy was not a pacifist, but advocated suitable war work for women, writing (p. 95): "The Canadian country woman has never been as true to herself and her country as when she has given, and is giving, her husband and sons to fight that 'Thy will may be done upon earth as it is done in heaven.' "

MacMurchy's book on work for women was prepared for use in Ontario school libraries. The preface states: "The object of *The Canadian Girl at Work* is to assist girls in finding satisfactory employment. The further aim of showing them what constitutes a right attitude toward work and toward life through work, underlies the account of each occupation." MacMurchy writes that most women have two periods of work during their life, "that of paid employment and that of home-making," the latter being vital: "Lack of training in home-making is probably the greatest drawback which a girl in paid employment can have." The book is upbeat, noting that "The most important fact for the girl to learn about employment is that when she does well-chosen work in the right spirit, she will find in it happiness and usefulness. . . . She may feel sure that there is work for her to do, that she will find work good, and the world a friendly place."

MacMurchy is anxious for boys and girls to be active readers. She notes in *Golden Treasury of Famous Books* that "This book which you are reading now is meant to help you to find books that you will enjoy." She describes a wide variety that might please a young person, works as varied as *Ivanhoe, The Iliad, The Divine Comedy* and Plato's *Republic*, which would dismay most young readers nowadays. She includes comments on essays, diary entries, letters and poetry, and details briefly the lives of men such as Dickens, Scott, Shakespeare and Homer. Eight pages are devoted to Jane Austen, George Eliot and the Brontës and their books, but otherwise women are virtually ignored.

Bibliography

• MacMurchy, Marjory. 1916. *The Woman—Bless Her: Not as Amiable a Book as It Sounds*. Toronto: S.B. Gundy, 155 pp.
• _____. 1919. *The Canadian Girl at Work: A Book of Vocational Guidance*. Toronto: King's Printer, 152 pp.
• Willison, Marjory. 1929. *Golden Treasury of Famous Books: A Guide to Good Reading for Boys and Girls, and for the Enjoyment of Those Who Love Books*. Toronto: Macmillan, 264 pp.

Macnaughtan, Sarah Broom d. 1916. Sarah Macnaughtan was the fourth daughter of a British Justice of the Peace and his wife. After being educated at home, she became a well-known novelist and traveller, visiting South America, South Africa (where she helped with Red Cross work), Turkey, Palestine, Egypt, Greece, India, Nepal, Burma and North America. She had not finished writing up her experiences in Canada just prior to the First World War before she volunteered as a nurse to work in Belgium; later she left with an ambulance party for Russia, which badly needed medical help. She fell so ill on the way that she returned home to Britain where she died. She was awarded the Belgian Order of Leopold.

Macnaughtan's friend Beatrice Home agreed to edit her unfinished manuscript, which became *My Canadian Memories*. Home notes: "The work is substantially as the author left it, for it was thought better to leave things somewhat unfinished rather than spoil the atmosphere of the book. Miss Macnaughtan always put her own stamp upon her writing, investing it with her own personality in a very marked degree." Macnaughtan not only travelled across Canada by train but discusses the building of the CPR and the CNR and the men who supervised their construction. She has chapters dealing with shipping, reciprocity, the Royal North-West Mounted Police and Quebec—"For it is around Quebec that almost the whole of the heroic history of Canada centres." Macnaughtan had intended to write additional chapters on immigrants and other topics, but her notes were too fragmentary to be used.

Bibliography
•Macnaughtan, S. 1920. *My Canadian Memories*. London: Chapman and Hall, 248 pp.

Macpherson, Annie c. 1842-? Annie Macpherson, the evangelical daughter of Scottish Quakers, was brought up in Glasgow, one of seven children; her father was a schoolteacher and her mother also raised two foster children, "a task that was to impress their eldest daughter, Annie, and through her affect the lives of countless thousands of other children throughout Britain in that century and the one to come" (Bagnell 1980, 19). She moved to London in 1865 to work among the poor, providing first shelter and work for destitute boys and girls who had no place to go, then arranging emigration for them to farms and homes in Canada. She herself spent many winters in Ontario (Belleville, Galt and Stratford) and Quebec (Knowlton), organizing placements for these children. All her effort was inspired by religion and God, whom she thanks in her book for his goodness; her labours in turn motivated Dr Thomas Barnardo to arrange emigration for yet more impoverished young people.

Canadian Homes for London Wanderers describes a trip with English boys immigrating to Ontario, and includes grateful letters from the boys and from people who employed them and helped them settle down in their new country. The book urges "Clergymen and Christian ladies" to collect money—"£6 with outfit, or £10 without an outfit"—so that young children might be allowed to emigrate (p. 57). Every effort was made to keep the boys free from drink and tobacco, "the ruination of this country" (p. 54).

Bibliography
•Bagnell, Kenneth. 1980. *The Little Immigrants*. Toronto: Macmillan.
•Macpherson, Annie. 1870. *Canadian Homes for London Wanderers*. London: Morgan, Chase and Scott, 60 pp.

Macpherson, Charlotte Holt Gethings 1828-1890. See the entry for **Charlotte Holt** for a sketch of Charlotte Macpherson's life.

Reminiscences of Old Quebec, also called *Quebec and Its Vicinity*, was written just before Macpherson died. It describes in many short chapters people and buildings Macpherson knew, sometimes from fifty years earlier. For example, the old Payne's Hotel reminds her of the famous Siamese twins, Chang and Eng, who were exhibited there, joined together side by side. She writes: "As they never conversed together, they had nearly forgotten their native tongue." The Ursuline Convent recalls to mind her childhood, when she loved this school so much that she forced her way in one day when she was late and should have been locked out. One chapter, on nursing, notes that a woman was cured of cancer by having pure lemon juice applied to her tumour. Five hundred copies were bought in the first few weeks after publication.

Old Memories was published in the same year and also deals in short chapters with places, people or stories connected with her home province of Quebec, some from scores of years earlier, and some more recent. She describes a French driver with a sick son who would not trust an English doctor because he wouldn't know anything or might even kill his son at once. After some conversation, the driver decided he *might* go to such a doctor if he were a Roman Catholic. In each book, Macpherson lists the hundreds of subscribers who gave money so that her work could be printed.

Bibliography

•MacPherson, Mrs Daniel. 1890 . *Reminiscences of Old Quebec: Subterranean Passages under the Citadel—Account of the Old Convent of the Congregation of Notre Dame, that does not now exist, Prominent Old Quebecers, etc., etc.* Montreal: Lovell, 123 pp.
•_____. , an Old Quebecer. 1890 . *Old Memories: Amusing and Historical.* Montreal: author, 130 pp.

Macpherson, Katharine Livingstone. Katharine Macpherson was born in Toronto of Scottish descent, but lived her adult life in Montreal where she wrote many stories, articles and books which were often historical in nature.

Pictures from Canadian History has seventy-three short chapters, beginning with Christopher Columbus and ending with A Notable Event, which was the driving in of the last spike in 1885 to complete the Canadian Pacific Railway across Canada. Each paragraph of each chapter is numbered for ease of group study. The book is dedicated with permission to Earl Grey, the late Governor General of Canada, "whose inspiring faith in and zeal for the dominion will long be remembered by a grateful and affectionate people."

Scenic Sieges and Battlefields of French Canada describes seven confrontations that took place in French Canada from 1660 to 1760, again apparently for a readership primarily of children.

In Days of Old retells stories from the Old Testament, complete with conversation and descriptions of time and place to give them context. The chief heroes of the book are Joseph, called The Food Controller of Egypt, and Moses, who lived three and a half centuries later and would lead the Jews out of Egypt and back to Israel.

Bibliography

Macpherson, Katharine Livingstone. n.d. [c.1899] *Pictures from Canadian History for Boys and Girls*. Montreal: Renouf, 230 pp.

• _____. 1908. *Scenic Sieges and Battlefields of French Canada*. Montreal: Valentine and Sons, 126 pp.

• _____. 1928. *In Days of Old: Stories from the Bible*. Philadelphia: Dorrance, 254 pp.

MacWhirter, Margaret Grant d. 1940.   Margaret MacWhirter was an author who lived in eastern Canada.

In the introduction to her book *Treasure Trove in Gaspé and the Baie des Chaleurs*, MacWhirter writes:

> This country of Gaspésia and northern New Brunswick abounds in historical and legendary interest, and it has been my effort to preserve this from oblivion. Already at this lapse of time it is difficult to tell where history ends and tradition begins, because of the overlapping of the one with the other.

However, she is also (surely overly) humble: "In presenting this volume to the public, I realize how inadequately I have performed the task, although the collecting of material and putting it into its present form has been a labour of love." She describes, among other things, geographic regions, wildlife and fish, pioneers, mail service, and Micmac Indians.

Bibliography
•MacWhirter, Margaret Grant. 1919. *Treasure Trove in Gaspé and the Baie des Chaleurs*. Quebec: Telegraph Printing, 217 pp. 3rd edition.

Manning, Ella Wallace Jackson 1910-? Ella Manning was a Canadian.

Manning describes in *Igloo for the Night* the two and a half years (1938-40) she spent with her new husband, Tom Manning, in the Canadian Arctic, mapping the coastline and collecting biological specimens; he was the leader of the British Canadian Arctic Expedition, 1936-41. In one winter the two travelled over one thousand miles by dog team, wearing clothes she had made from animal skins under the tutelage of Inuit women. In winter they slept in freshly made igloos and in summer in a tent.

Bibliography
•Manning, Mrs Tom. 1946 [1945]. *Igloo for the Night*. Toronto: University of Toronto Press, 234 pp.

Maritain, Raïssa Oumansoff 1883-1960. Raïssa Oumansoff was born and lived her early years in Russia. When she was ten, her family emigrated to Paris because of antisemitism. There she learned to understand and accept the "scientism, determinism, positivism, and materialism" espoused by her parents. When she was seventeen, she enrolled in the Sorbonne, where she met fellow student Jacques Maritain (1882-1973). The idealistic couple, who took part in countless philosophical debates and social controversies, agreed that unless they found the answer to the apparent meaninglessness of life, they would both commit suicide. Luckily, they soon became involved with spiritual matters, which cheered them up. In 1904, she and Maritain were married; in 1906, they and her sister Vera, who would always live with them, were baptized as Roman Catholics. Jacques Maritain became a teacher/professor, world famous for his studies on the philosophy of Thomas Aquinas. Because they had Jewish blood, the group spent the Second World War years in Canada, where Jacques taught at the University of Toronto. After the war they moved to Rome and then to Princeton. When Raïssa died, her husband published excerpts from the diary she had kept for fifty-four years under the title *Raïssa's Journal.*

The Maritains' first book, *Prayer and Intelligence* (initially printed privately), they note, "is but an attempt to disentangle and state as clearly as possible, in the spirit of Christian tradition and of St. Thomas, the main directions which seem suitable to the spiritual life of persons living in the world and occupied in intellectual pursuits." It has a section on Sacred Doctrine and another on The Spiritual Life; both have subsections headed by titles in Latin. It argues that the contemplative life is better than the active life.

Raïssa Maritain's deeply religious *Saint Thomas Aquinas* was produced in large print for children. Because St Thomas (1225-74) was especially interested in education, she notes that his anniversary is celebrated in universities (p. 13):

> before an assembly of professors and their pupils, two students take part in a great combat of eloquence and learning, one supporting the *affirmative* and the other the *negative*; it is what is called a *scholastic dispute*, the only kind of a dispute in which each taking part in it is polite and kind to his enemy.

Maritain began her autobiography, *We Have Been Friends Together*, in low spirits, after fleeing from her beloved France to North America to escape the war. The first (translated) volume deals briefly with her early years, then describes in detail the many intellectuals she met at the Sorbonne, where her interests changed from natural history to philosophy to religion.

She wrote the sequel to this volume, *Adventures in Grace*, in a much happier frame of mind, as the war was going well for the Allies. This book extends her story until 1917, focusing on the Maritains' religious life and their acquaintances as well as her husband's early philosophical work.

Bibliography

Maritain, Jacques and Raïssa. 1942 [1922]. *Prayer and Intelligence, Being La Vie d'Oraison of Jacques and Raïssa Maritain*. London: Sheed and Ward, 56 pp.

Maritain, Raïssa. 1942. *Saint Thomas Aquinas: The Angel of the Schools*. New York: Longmans, Green, 127 pp.

• _____. 1942. *We Have Been Friends Together*. New York: Longmans, Green, 208 pp.

• _____. 1945. *Adventures in Grace*. New York: Longmans, Green, 262 pp.

Marsh, Edith Louise d. 1960. Edith Marsh grew up and lived most of her life on Peasemarsh Farm, a bird sanctuary near Clarksburg, Ontario. She never married, so perhaps had more time than most women to write a number of books, to become an expert on birds and write many articles on them and to be a sought-after public speaker. The archives at the University of Guelph contain her papers and some of her artwork.

Marsh, who designed *The Story of Canada* to be read by children (for thirty-five cents), divided it into four parts, each with many subheadings: Canada under French rule, Canada under British rule, Rupert's Land: the great west, and Canada under Confederation. It ends stirringly:

> May [the school children of Canada] be as brave and noble as those who made Canada what she is, honoring the Maple Leaf and the Union Jack, and leaving to those who come after, an example of true loyalty. Thus may they do their part in guiding their country, ever onward and upward, through the years to come.

Marsh dedicates *Birds of Peasemarsh* "To the Memory of my Mother and Father, the founders of Peasemarsh," which is on the western slope of Georgian Bay at the foot of the Blue Mountains in Ontario. It describes the many birds that nested in the three-hundred-acre area (by the home and orchard of her family) and their varied habits, as well as characteristics of birds in general—their value to people, adaptability, migration, enemies and nesting sites. Marsh provides information on how to attract and protect birds: even in 1919 she bemoaned the decrease in numbers of chimney swifts because of modern roofing and chimneys and heating practices. She worried, too, about the extinction of the barn swallow, but this concern has proven to be far less justified. She often gave talks about birds, illustrated by lantern slides of her own pictures.

Marsh begins *Where the Buffalo Roamed* with a picture of western Canada before the coming of Europeans: "In that land lived the pretty deer and the ugly moose." She continues, "The Indians were dark-colored people, quick and active, strong and brave. They had bright, black eyes that could see ever so far, and ears that could hear clearly sounds that you would never notice. They knew more of the woods and the animals than the white men have ever learned." She has chapters on various explorers, on fur traders, on missionaries and on settlement. She ends on a sanguine note, relating with pleasure that "wildlife preserves are being set aside where animals will be allowed to live in peace." Her final sentence reads: "So long as her people are loyal to the good old Union Jack and true to the highest aims of life will the Canadian West be a great and glorious part of the Empire that girdles the Globe."

Marsh's *With the Birds* books are aimed at children. Although she writes, for example, about Mr and Mrs Robin, Mother Bird and Father Bird, and Madame Goldfinch, she includes solid factual material about many common species. She hypothesizes a conversation with a goldfinch, in which the male describes his other finch relatives and making a nest: "My mate did most of the building, but I sang to her all the time." Marsh gives useful tips on what to feed birds, what birdhouses will be of use, and which species should be discouraged around one's home (including crows, house sparrows and cow-birds).

In writing *A History of the County of Grey*, her home region, Marsh worked "in cooperation with the official committee," which included the sheriff, the county treasurer and several wardens. "The book is entirely a County production, having been written and published within the bounds of Grey." As well as general historical information, it includes sections on each township, village and town, and lists early settlers.

Bibliography

•Marsh, E.L. 1912. *The Story of Canada*. London: Nelson, 208 pp.
•_____. 1919. *Birds of Peasemarsh*. Toronto: Musson, 233 pp.
•_____. 1923. [1908]. *Where the Buffalo Roamed: "The Story of the Canadian West."* Toronto: Macmillan, 257 pp.
•_____. 1929 . *With the Birds for Little Folks*. Toronto: Dent, 63 pp.
•_____. 1929 . *With the Birds in Field and Garden*. Toronto: Dent, 87 pp.
•_____. 1931. *A History of the County of Grey*. Owen Sound: Fleming Publishing, 487 pp.

Marshall, Henrietta Elizabeth 1876-? Henrietta Marshall was a British author of history books for children.

Canada's Story is part of the "Our Empire Story" Series; Marshall also wrote other simplified history readers such as *Our Island Story* and *Scotland's Story*. It is told as an exciting tale—"I will find this land," cried Leif Ericson, "I will find this land and call it mine." It discusses various explorers, adventurers and battles, and ends with the second Riel Rebellion, fought because "the Métis thought that they were being badly treated by the Government. They thought that their land was being taken from them, and that they had not enough power in Parliament."

Bibliography
•Marshall, H.E. 1912. *Canada's Story Told to Boys and Girls*. London: T.C. and E.C. Jack, 121 pp.

Marty, Aletta Elise, BA MA LLD 1866-1929. Aletta Marty was born in Mitchell, Ontario, to Swiss parents who spoke several languages at home. She began teaching school when she was fifteen before first working her way through normal school to become a certified teacher, and then attending Queen's University, where she earned a BA (1893) and an MA (1895) with a medal in Modern Languages. Marty taught French and German in high schools in St Thomas and Ottawa for twenty-five years with such distinction that in 1919 she was appointed the first woman public school inspector in Ontario (and indeed in Canada). Her promotion was strongly recommended by a woman trustee on the Board of Education in Toronto, who insisted she was the best person for the job. While based in Toronto, Marty became a firm friend of fellow author **Elsie Pomeroy.** In 1921 she was given an honorary degree by Queen's University and in 1927 was elected president of the Canadian Home and School Federation. Two years later she died in South Africa while on an educational exchange program.

Marty's *The Principles and Practice of Oral Reading* was authorized by the Minister of Education in Ontario for use in high schools. Most of it comprises sixty-three excerpts from works by well-known authors (nearly all male); she notes in the preface that "Owing to copyright difficulties it has not been possible to include a number of very desirable selections. The titles of some of these, however, are given in Appendix C" where it is noted that mimeographed copies may be made of shorter selections (so much for copyright). Marty has written a long introduction and the material for appendices. The former includes discussions on aims and methods of oral reading; abstract and concrete thinking and emotion; and vocal expression (inflection, pitch, force, stress, emphasis, shading, etc.). The appendices have exercises in vocalization and physical exercises for breathing, for the chest and lungs, for the throat and neck and for the mouth.

Marty, who wrote *An Educational Creed* while Inspector of Public Schools in Toronto, expands briefly on nine statements, beginning with "1. I believe in education as the most profitable investment in the world to-day" and ending with "9. I believe in the school as the place to inculcate the spirit of universal good will, which is the basis for world citizenship and world peace." She compares education in Canada with that in other countries, and urges, among other things, the demise of the little red schoolhouse, the importance of a liberal education for all students, the equal importance of moral and physical education with mental education, the increased co-operation of parents with teachers and education as a life-long process. Unfortunately, she describes all children as "he."

Bibliography

•Marty, Aletta E., MA. 1904. *The Principles and Practice of Oral Reading.* Toronto: Canadian Publishing Co, 250 pp.
•Marty, A.E., MA, LLD. 1924. *An Educational Creed.* Toronto: Ryerson, 48 pp.

Mary Theodore, Sister of Saint Ann 1856-1951, nun.   Sister Mary Theodore was a Sister of St Ann who lived and worked as a nun for more than sixty years in British Columbia.

Pioneer Nuns is the biography of the four members of her order who were asked to help bring Christianity to the Canadian West. These nuns set up their first convent in a log cabin twenty by thirty feet and opened a school for "young ladies" in Victoria in 1858. Later, other Sisters worked in other schools, orphanages and hospitals of British Columbia, Yukon and Alaska. By 1908, a total of 132 Sisters of St Ann had come, ninety-one from eastern Canada, thirty from the United States and eleven from Europe "to consecrate their young womanhood to the welfare of British Columbia."

The Seal of the Cross is the biography of Mother Mary Ann (1809-90), Foundress of the Sisters of St Ann. The Archbishop of Vancouver hopes in the foreword that "This well-written life, the story of the spiritual struggles and victories of a generous and holy soul will prove ... an inspiration especially to the members" of the Sisters of St Ann. Mother Mary Ann was born Esther Blondin in Terrebone, Quebec. After being educated at a convent, she founded her own school and later the Order that would serve British Columbia so well, as the author's earlier book describes.

Heralds of Christ the King, a history of the Roman Catholic missionaries (including the Sisters of St Ann) along the west coast of North America, documents

> the sacrifices willingly made for the love of souls, the shocking living conditions to be endured when lodged in Indian camps, the courage and piety of these extraordinary missionaries, their persevering efforts to obtain priests, their occasional disappointments when the weaker Indian character fell under the spell of the white man's bad example.

The foreword points out that the spread of faith in British Columbia was an especially difficult problem because of "the wealth of scenery and climate and natural resources with which Nature has endowed the province." Whereas immigrants to eastern Canada came mainly for freedom from religious persecution and crushing land rents, those to the west usually came to exploit the area's vast resources or for recreation.

Bibliography
•Mary Theodore, Sister SAA. 1931. *Pioneer Nuns of British Columbia: Sisters of St Ann*. Victoria: Colonist Printing, 146 pp.
•————. 1939 . *The Seal of the Cross*. Victoria: St Ann's Convent, 131 pp.
•————. 1939 . *Heralds of Christ the King: Missionary Record of the North Pacific 1837-1878*. New York: P.J. Kenedy, 273 pp.

Massey, Alice Stuart Parkin 1879-1950. Alice Parkin was born in Fredericton, New Brunswick, the daughter of loyalist Sir George Parkin and his wife. After meeting Vincent Massey in England, she arranged to come to Toronto in 1914 as head of the women's residence in Queen's Hall. They married the following year and soon had two sons. Alice Massey acted as hostess for her husband during the various diplomatic posts he held. During the Second World War, when her husband was Canadian High Commissioner to London, she founded The Canadian Officers' Club where, with the help of volunteers, she cooked and served meals to Canadian officers serving abroad. She also helped run a rural hospital, financed by Massey money, where wounded officers could recuperate. She kept her date of birth a secret, perhaps because she was eight or nine years older than her husband.

Massey wrote *Occupations for Trained Women in Canada* following the First World War to answer two important questions: what occupations in Canada were open to trained women, and what provisions existed for their training. She wanted young women to have opportunities other than the traditional occupations as nurses, teachers, or secretaries; issues around careers had arisen years earlier when she had worked with young university women. To find answers, she sent out questionnaires (but she gives no specifics about her research methods). She lists seventeen possible fields of work for women, describing what is involved in each, suitable training and typical salaries. Under "Scientific Work" she notes that there are few openings for women—"women choosing this line of work are in competition with men in a very limited field." She urges that all women interested in a career obtain a general university education before taking specialized training in their chosen discipline.

Bibliography
•Massey, Alice Vincent. 1920. *Occupations for Trained Women in Canada*. London and Toronto: Dent, 94 pp.

Maura, Sister, alias Mary Power BA MA PhD 1881-1957. Mary Power, the daughter of Lawrence Power (who became Speaker of the Senate) and his wife, was educated at Mount St Vincent Academy, London (BA), Dalhousie (MA), and Notre Dame (PhD) universities. Because she was very religious, she became a Sister of Charity of the Halifax Congregation, with her name changed to Sister Maura. She was also a poet and a professor of English at Mount St Vincent College from 1925 until her death.

Sister Maura wrote several books of distinguished verse as well as plays and a book of non-fiction, *Shakespeare's Catholicism.* She states in her foreword to this book that to many, Shakespeare's religion is not obvious from his writings or from what we know about him. Some think he was a Catholic, some an Anglican: "An admirer from beside the Forth holds the poet for a Puritan, and Auguste Comte, quite as logically, takes him for a freethinker." But, she goes on, "Evidence shows that Shakespeare was bred a Catholic, that he was steeped in the traditions of the medieval Church drama, and that he loved the faith of his fathers with a love that found ample expression. . . . That is what the present thesis attempts to make clear." After commenting freely on Shakespeare's work, she concludes that his drama embodies Catholic doctrine and practice accurately and intimately, that he never disparages but rather praises the Catholic Church and that "The spirit that quickens his drama into glowing moral life is inspired by Catholic teaching," all of which "reveals the great Elizabethan a Catholic in mind and heart."

Bibliography
•Maura, Sister AB(Lond), AM(Dal), PhD(ND) 1924. *Shakespeare's Catholicism.* Cambridge: Riverside Press, 171 pp.

Maxwell, Lilian Mary Beckwith BA LLD 1877-1956. Lilian Beckwith was born and raised in Fredericton, New Brunswick, and in 1898 obtained her BA at the University of New Brunswick, which would award her an LLD in 1946. After training to be a teacher, she taught high school in St John and Boston. She married in 1904, settling with her husband in her hometown to raise their three children and later to write about local history. Shortly before her death she published *'Round New Brunswick Roads* (1951), which described a driving trip around her province along with information about its geography, history and development.

Maxwell's *History of Central New Brunswick* was reprinted in 1984 to celebrate the two hundredth anniversary of this province under the auspices of the York-Sunbury Historical Society, the group that had endorsed the original edition. This earlier edition had in turn been based on a series of articles on local history published during 1933 in the *Fredericton Daily Gleaner.* The first part of the book deals with the Indian and French period and the longer second part with the English period, beginning in 1759. Maxwell includes many long lists of citizens who served in the army or who settled at various places, almost all men. In a census list of fifty-seven Acadian families living near St Anne's Point in 1783, men's names are listed together with the number of their children and their years of residence, but there is no mention of women (p. 33).

Maxwell wrote *How New Brunswick Grew* after the great-granddaughter of the Hon. James Brown, a member of the cabinet that brought New Brunswick responsible government, gave her access to his private papers and to government reports of a century earlier. Brown had emigrated from Scotland to New Brunswick in 1810 and lived there as a farmer and legislator until his death in 1870. From these documents, Maxwell includes chapters on the province's boundaries, natural resources and development of institutions. The longest is on education, which in the 1840s was primitive: one public school had fifteen broken window panes, while one schoolroom was apparently the kitchen of the teacher's private dwelling. More than a third of the children did not attend school at all (which was blamed on apathetic parents) even though the curriculum tended to be practical, with mathematics, for example, usually studied in the context of navigation and land surveying. Women teachers were paid one quarter less than men teachers.

Bibliography
•Maxwell, Lilian M. Beckwith. 1984 [1937]. *An Outline of the History of Central New Brunswick to the Time of Confederation.* Sackville, NB: Tribune Press, 183 pp.
•Maxwell, Lilian M.B. 1943. *How New Brunswick Grew.* Sackville, NB: Tribune Press, 95 pp.

McClung, Nellie Letitia Mooney 1873-1951. Nellie Mooney was born on a farm in Grey County, Ontario, the youngest of six children. When she was seven, the family moved to Manitoba to farm. She graduated from Winnipeg Normal School in 1889, then taught school until 1896 when she married Wesley McClung, a pharmacist. He agreed that as a married woman she should be as independent as possible, working for social causes and writing as well as raising their seven children. When she gave a speech about women's rights, she often prefaced it with a comment, to forestall criticism about her activism, that the audience need not worry, her children were safely tucked into bed. Through her novels such as *Sowing Seeds in Danny* (1908) and other writing, she earned a significant amount of money and made a number of friends among fellow authors, including **Cora Hind**, **Pauline Johnson**, **Agnes Laut** and **Laura Salverson**. After moving to Alberta in 1914, she served as a Liberal member of the Alberta provincial

assembly from 1921-26 (defeated finally in part because of her temperance
views), founded the Calgary chapter of the Canadian Women's Press Club
in 1927, was appointed in 1936 to the first board of governors of the Canadian Broadcasting Corporation and in 1938 was a Canadian delegate to the
League of Nations. In addition she wrote a syndicated newspaper column
about her ruminations. Along with **Emily Murphy, Henrietta Edwards**,
Louise McKinney and Irene Parlby, she won the Persons Case in 1929,
which allowed women to sit in the Canadian Senate.

McClung collected some of her public lectures to produce her feminist
book *In Times Like These*. In it, she argued for the rights of women set in
the context of the First World War; one of her twelve chapters is headed
"What do women think of war? (Not that it matters)." She dedicates it:

> To the Superior Persons Who would not come to hear a woman speak,
> being firmly convinced that it is not "natural;" Who take the rather unas-
> sailable ground that "men are men and women are women;" Who answer
> all arguments by saying, "Woman's place is in the home," and "The hand
> that rocks the cradle rules the world," and even sometimes flash out with
> the brilliant retort, "It would suit those women better to stay at home and
> darn their children's stockings"—To all these Superior Persons, men and
> women, who are inhospitable to new ideas, and even suspicious of them,
> this book is respectfully dedicated by The Author.

Essays about war appeared in *The Next of Kin*, thanks to a group of
farm women she met in northern Alberta. McClung writes: "I got my commission from these women . . . to tell what we think and feel, to tell how it
looks to us, who are the mothers of soldiers, and to whom even now the letter may be on its way with its curt inscription across the corner." These
women wanted to work for future world peace so that soldiers would not
have died in vain.

In 1918, still obsessed with the war, McClung published *Three Times
and Out*, the story told to her by a young Canadian soldier who escaped
from prisons in Germany during the war. However it came out as the war
was ending, so was not a great financial success.

Two 1930s books, *Leaves from Lantern Lane* and *More Leaves from
Lantern Lane*, were collected essays from her syndicated columns named
for Lantern Lane at the edge of Victoria, where she and her husband had
moved in 1932: the path to their retirement home was lit by a lantern
because there were no street lights. They comprise short essays about her
experiences and reflections; according to the 1936 book's jacket, they have
"the familiar McClung touch—humor, pathos, abundance of good sense,
that delicate touch of femininity that is so delightful. They are wholesome,
carry a good moral, and are full of human interest."

McClung wrote *Clearing in the West* about her early years, giving "a lively and generally convincing account of her life up to 1896 ending with her marriage" (Hallett and Davis 1993, xii). Her history intermeshes with the history of Canada, making her book especially valuable today. *The Stream Runs Fast*, which came out ten years later, continued her autobiography.

Bibliography

Benham, Mary Lile. 1984. *Nellie McClung*, rev. ed. Toronto: Fitzhenry.

•Hallett, Mary and Marilyn Davis. 1993. *Firing the Heather: The Life and Times of Nellie McClung*. Saskatoon: Fifth House.

Hancock, Carol. 1996. *Nellie McClung: No Small Legacy*. Kelowna, BC: Northstone.

•Thomas, Hilda L. 1990. Nellie Letitia McClung. *Dictionary of Literary Biography, 1890-1920*, s.v. McClung, Nellie Letitia.

•Warne, Randi R. 1993. *Literature as Pulpit: The Christian Social Activism of Nellie L. McClung*. Waterloo, ON: Wilfrid Laurier University Press.

•McClung, Nellie L. 1919 [1915]. *In Times Like These*. Toronto: George J. McLeod, 218 pp.

•_____. 1917. *The Next of Kin; Those Who Wait and Wonder*. Toronto: Allen, 257 pp.

•_____. 1918. *Three Times and Out: A Canadian Boy's Experience in Germany*, with Mervin C. Simmons. Boston: Houghton Mifflin, 247 pp.

•_____. 1935. *Clearing in the West: My Own Story*. Toronto: Allen, 378 pp.

•_____. 1936. *Leaves from Lantern Lane*. Toronto: Allen, 199 pp.

•_____. 1937. *More Leaves from Lantern Lane*. Toronto: Allen, 201 pp.

•_____. 1945. *The Stream Runs Fast: My Own Story*. Toronto: Allen, 316 pp.

McCulloch, Mercy Emma Powell BA 1880-? Mercy Powell was born in Edgar, Ontario, the daughter of Toronto physician and teacher Dr Newton Albert Powell. She was educated at Harbord Collegiate and Victoria College in Toronto, graduating in 1901. After she married Dr Edward McCulloch in 1905, she produced two children who would themselves become doctors, was active in Methodist church work, and wrote stories, poems (*Rhyming through the Years* [1951] is the story in verse by her and her husband of their long life together, written for the fiftieth anniversary of the class of 1901 of Victoria College), and a biography of her father. When a student said to her, "Your Father seems almost a legendary person to me. Why not write out some of his witticisms?" she proceeded to do so.

That Reminds Me of N.A.P. is a series of sketches and anecdotes about Powell. One of his jokes involved the introduction of a clerical speaker: "We have no time limit for you, but we have a feeling that no souls are saved after the first twenty minutes." Powell was the nephew of Hart A. Massey, so that McCulloch was a relative of **Alice Massey.** Proceeds from the sale of her book (fifty cents) went during the Second World War to the Committee for Medical Equipment for Britain and Russia.

Bibliography

•McCulloch, Mrs E.A. 1942. *That Reminds Me of N.A.P.* Toronto: Ryerson, 78 pp.

McCully, Elizabeth A. 1862-1941. Elizabeth McCully, who was born in Truro, Nova Scotia, to a postmaster and his wife, attended normal college there and Missionary Training College in New York because she wanted to be a missionary. As family responsibilities then kept her in Truro, as well as teaching she and her sister Louise (b. 1864) set up a small home mission. She also wrote a biography of one of the first protestant missionaries to Korea, W.J. McKenzie, who had been engaged to her sister but who had died before she could join him at his mission (Brouwer 1990, 55). When she was forty-six, McCully herself was appointed a Presbyterian missionary to Korea. After learning the Korean language, she taught Korean girls and founded with Louise a training school to prepare their charges for church work. She also organized a choir and taught music. She retired in 1934, moving with her sister to Toronto in 1940, the year before her death.

McCully wrote in the preface of *A Corn of Wheat* that the life and works of the Rev. McKenzie would never be forgotten, but that she would fill in its details: "The task of writing should be that of a master pen, and not of a novice; but in the long delay of others who could have done it worthily, I have been impelled to the attempt." McKenzie (1861-95) was a Presbyterian missionary from Nova Scotia who worked first in Labrador and then in Korea, where he lived as far as possible like the Koreans; he died within two years during a local war from bad food and exposure. The book includes some of McKenzie's letters and diary entries.

McCully reached the mission field of Korea herself in 1909; her co-author of *Our Share in Korea* arrived with his nurse wife five years later. Together their aim as authors was to

> tell the story of the Korea Mission of The United Church of Canada; to show how our Mission relates itself to the life of Korea as a whole, and to other Missions and their work; and to encourage and inspire its readers by showing what has already been accomplished, and to challenge and arouse our Canadian Church by indicating what still remains to be done.

It was intended to supplement the more general survey text by J.D. Van-Buskirk, *Korea, Land of the Dawn.* Their book ends: "The ever-new old Gospel of Jesus Christ has made an entry into these open doors [of Korea's mind and heart and soul], and it alone carries the power to right wrongs, and to solve the great problems that confront us in building a right Way of Life for Korea."

Bibliography
- McCully, Elizabeth A. 1903. *A Corn of Wheat or the Life of Rev. W.J. McKenzie of Korea*. Toronto: Westminster, 290 pp.
- McCully, Elizabeth A. and E.J.O. Fraser. 1932. *Our Share in Korea*. Toronto: Woman's Missionary Society, United Church of Canada, 63 pp.

McDougall, Margaret Dixon 1826-1898. Margaret Dixon was brought up in the north of Ireland among "Conservatives of the strongest type," then emigrated to North America to live for years in White River, Ontario, and in Michigan, writing novels and poetry. She remained devoted to Ireland, espousing the cause of Irish nationalism after revisiting her homeland. Her book about this trip, *The Letters of "Norah,"* fed into her creativity; the year after it appeared she published a novel about Ireland (*The Days of a Life*, 1883) based on the current unrest about Home Rule.

The Letters of "Norah" on Her Tour through Ireland is a chatty but political book based on her letters sent home to a newspaper from a return visit to her native land. The Irish people she met spoke Gaelic, but she understood a fair bit of what they said. She had believed until that time that "landlords were lords and leaders, benefactors and protectors to their tenants in my imagination." She had sympathized with the poverty of many Irish people, but had "never dreamed that the tenure of land had anything to do with it" (p. 297). By travelling through Ireland in the early 1880s, she saw "the evils arising from the existing tenure of land. I met with testimony everywhere of how often and how fatally the will of a lord interfered to prevent prosperity" (p. 298). She urges that conciliation, not coercion, be used by the British for Ireland. As the title page (which lacks her name) indicates, this book was published thanks to the help of seventy-four subscribers whose names and contributions are listed; most donated between $1 and $5, although one gave fifty cents and another $10; this type of financing removed all risk from the publisher.

Bibliography
- [McDougall, Mrs A.]. 1882. *The Letters of "Norah" on Her Tour through Ireland, Being a Series of Letters to the Montreal "Witness" as Special Correspondent to Ireland*. Montreal: Published by Public Subscription as a token of respect by the Irishmen of Canada, 303 pp.

McEwen, Jessie Evelyn 1911-? Jessie McEwen was a Canadian author who wrote for children, mostly books of history, but also tales such as *Taltrees* (1949) about pioneer life in the Quebec forest industry.

For *A Picture History of Canada*, McEwen and Kathleen Moore were given the task of writing about Canada's history in such a way that the text described forty-eight coloured pictures by well-known artists (all apparently men). The prose, written for children, includes conversation by various characters in the forty-seven short chapters.

The first half of McEwen's *Short Stories of Great Lives*, comprising short biographies, is devoted to individuals of the Old World, but the second half features sixteen stories of Canadian heroes, beginning with the Cabots and ending with Lord Strathcona. One is a woman—Laura Secord. The stories, aimed at children, are told with lively conversation and anecdote. She records, for example, that Madame Champlain wore at her waist a little mirror: "An Indian would look at it and then exclaim, 'Madame must indeed love me very much, for she wears my image'" (p. 128).

Bibliography
- McEwen, Jessie and Kathleen Moore. 1933. *A Picture History of Canada.* Toronto: Thomas Nelson, 103 pp.
- McEwen, Jessie 1936. *Short Stories of Great Lives.* Toronto: Nelson, 228 pp.

McIlwraith, Jean Newton 1859-1938.   Jean McIlwraith was born in Hamilton to Scottish immigrant parents, one of seven children. She attended Hamilton Ladies' College, then took correspondence courses from Glasgow University while she wrote and looked after her mother. After her mother's death in 1901, she moved to the United States to become a publisher's reader from 1902 to 1919, but her heart remained in Canada where she retired, dying in Burlington, Ontario. As well as non-fiction, she wrote many stories and novels such as *The Curious Career of Roderick Campbell* (1901) and *A Diana of Quebec* (1912), which dramatizes Haldimand's years in Quebec.

In *A Book about Shakespeare*, McIlwraith placed Shakespeare in the context of the awakening of Europe, one hundred years before his birth, from the "bad dream of the Middle Ages." Italy was the first country that "opened her eyes to the fact that life upon this earth is of interest and value for its own sake; that neither church nor state has the right to keep a man [*sic*] from developing every power of his mind." England belatedly followed Italy's lead, and its jewel in the time of Queen Elizabeth I was Shakespeare. The author describes his life, his plays and how they were connected to the events of the day.

Canada is a history of that nation which she wrote before moving to the United States. It ends on a sanguine note:

> The strongest nations have been built up with a mixture of races, and the time is at hand when French and English will remember only that they are Canadians, will glory alike in the deeds that the ancestors of either tongue have done upon this continent, and, resolving not to be unworthy of the noble heritage left them, will look hopefully into the future, will "Greet the unseen with a cheer."

A Book about Longfellow, a companion to her first literary book, discusses Henry Wadsworth Longfellow in the context of North America, which had at its beginning first no written language, and then no creative literature, even though the potential for such literature was present: "bobolinks, orioles, blue-birds are in themselves fully as poetical as skylarks and nightingales" (p. 18). She argued that it was only a settled society that could produce a poet such as Longfellow, "the first poet to gain the hearts of the American people as a whole."

The biography *Sir Frederick Haldimand* (1718-91) was one of the prestigious Makers of Canada Series; (one of her novels, purportedly narrated by Haldimand's private secretary during his years in Quebec, also focuses on this army officer). Haldimand, who was born and died in Switzerland, was the governor of Quebec from 1777 to 1786. Canadian historians have commented that no important events happened during his rule, prompting McIlwraith to state that "to him belongs the credit that they did not occur."

Bibliography

•Dean, Misao. 1990. McIlwraith, Jean Newton. *Dictionary of Literary Biography, Canadian Writers, 1890-1920*, s.v. McIlwraith, Jean Newton.
•M'Ilwraith, J.N. ("Jean Forsyth"). 1898. *A Book about Shakespeare Written for Young People*. London: T. Nelson, 222 pp.
•McIlwraith, J.N. 1899. *Canada*. Toronto: Briggs, 252 pp.
M'Ilwraith, J.N. ("Jean Forsyth"). 1900. *A Book about Longfellow*. London: T. Nelson, 165 pp.
•McIlwraith, Jean N. 1904. *Sir Frederick Haldimand*. Toronto: Morang, 356 pp.

McKinley, Mabel Burns. Mabel Burns grew up in Ingersoll, Ontario, and attended normal school and the Toronto Conservatory of Music. After marrying a doctor she spent several years with him in China before returning to Ontario. She was an ardent nationalist and a member of the Canadian Authors Association and the Canadian Women's Press Club. In 1934 she co-authored with **L.M. Montgomery** and **Marian Keith** a book about remarkable women.

Canadian Heroines was the first book in the Maple Leaf Series of Longmans Green, "especially dedicated to you, the Boys and Girls of Canada," to illustrate the "Heroism, Hardship and Loyalty" endured by Canadian pioneers. Ten women are profiled, beginning with Madame de la Tour and ending with Elizabeth McDougall (see **Kells** entry). An exciting incident in the life of each is described complete with conversation—for example, rescuing sailors from a Lake Erie storm (Abigail Becker), eluding enemies (Laura Secord), existing under perilous conditions (Marguerite de Roberval, Mrs Shubert) or outwitting Indians (Madeleine de Verchères, Marie Anne Lagemodière).

The publication of *Canadian Heroes*, also "endorsed by the Imperial Order Daughters of the Empire," was made possible by the success of McKinley's *Canadian Heroines*. It too endeavoured "to try and convey to the school children of today the great hardships, and sacrifices that were endured by the early settlers to this country; the cruel battles with the Indians, the loss of many loyal, brave and staunch settlers through suffering from cold and hunger." She notes that details of battles and politics, along with "differences of theory and opinion, official mistakes and shortcomings, are purposely left out. Stress is laid upon the real unity of will and purpose which bound together the many early settlers of Canada."

Famous Men and Women of Canada was also one of the Maple Leaf series of books. The preface states that:

> In the guise of biographical sketches, the author has dealt with the period of settlement that followed exploration in what is now Canada, and has endeavoured to portray the hardships that our forbears experienced. A description of the social life and customs of the time has been woven into the stories.

McKinley records many lively anecdotes, focusing on almost as many women as men—Catharine McPherson of the Red River Settlement, **Nellie McClung**, **Elizabeth Simcoe**, **Susanna Moodie** and **Pauline Johnson.**

Bibliography
•McKinley, Mabel Burns. 1929. *Canadian Heroines of Pioneer Days*. Toronto: Longmans, Green, 66 pp.
•_____. 1930. *Canadian Heroes of Pioneer Days*. Toronto: Longmans, Green, 119 pp.
•_____. 1938. *Famous Men and Women of Canada*. Toronto: Longmans, Green, 128 pp.

McLaurin, Katherine Sarah 1869?-1951.   Katherine McLaurin, born in India to missionary parents, became a missionary herself to India in 1893. **Flora Clarke** (1939, 281) describes her as "A highly gifted woman of magnetic personality . . . inspiring and encouraging the people as they entered the Christian fold while the caste women with whom she came in contact overcame their natural timidity and received her as a true friend." She idolized her mother, writing her biography so that she would be remembered.

The Enterprise is the history of the Baptist mission founded by her parents in 1874; fifty years later, when the book was written, there were over 1,000 Indian workers, 17,000 Christians, a fine hospital and 400 village schools, as well as other specialized schools. Co-author and missionary Orchard wrote two sections for the book, the Maritime Provinces contribution (1874-1912) and the Canadian Baptist Mission (1912-24), while McLaurin wrote the third, the Ontario and Quebec contribution (1874-1912). She states that "The truly wonderful story of how God led the Baptists of Ontario and Quebec into the great foreign mission enterprise—the greatest and most daring of them all—is pre-eminently a story of personalities," some of whom were, of course, her relatives.

Mary Bates McLaurin (1846-1938) was a biography of the author's mother, who was living in Woodstock, Ontario, when she married a Baptist missionary and went with him in 1869 to India. She spent most of the rest of her life there, aside from long leaves in Woodstock and Toronto. **Flora Clarke** writes (p. 649) that Mary McLaurin "placed before all with whom she came in contact a high ideal of Christian womanhood"; as well as her daughter, her son (Rev. J.B. McLaurin, DD) also became a missionary in India.

Bibliography

• Orchard, Rev. M.L., MA, BD and Miss K.S. McLaurin. 1924. *The Enterprise: The Jubilee Story of the Canadian Baptist Mission in India, 1874-1924.* Toronto: Canadian Baptist Foreign Mission Board, 348 pp.
• McLaurin, K.S. 1945. *Mary Bates McLaurin.* Toronto: Women's Baptist Foreign Missionary Society of Ontario West, 142 pp.

McLennan, Mary Louise 1879-1938.   Mary McLennan who lived in Stratford, Ontario, was a devotee of art, eager to share her interest with children.

McLennan's book, *Children's Artist Friends*, focuses on the work of twenty-five painters, all but one (Rosa Bonheur) a man, and only one a Canadian (Tom Thomson); she reminds her readers that Thomson lived close to Toronto. She divides the artists into six groups according to what they painted (Landscapes, Seascapes, Portraits, Holy Pictures, Animal Pictures and Allegorical Pictures). The artists are introduced in turn with a brief description of their lives and of their style of painting; there are two paintings by each painter in black and white, underneath which are a relevant poem and a critique of the work.

Bibliography

• McLennan, Mary Louise. 1931. *Children's Artist Friends.* London: Dent, 99 pp.

McNaughton, Margaret Peebles. Margaret Peebles was born in Scotland and emigrated with her family to New Westminster, British Columbia, in 1888. Two years later she married Archibald McNaughton (1843-1900) who was one of the Overlanders of '62, a group of about two hundred men who travelled by ox- and horse-drawn carts from Fort Garry (later Winnipeg) to British Columbia, where they hoped to mine for gold. They arrived too late to make their fortunes in mining, so some carried on to the coast and left Canada, while others such as her husband remained as settlers. When he became paralyzed in 1894, Margaret nursed him until he died six years later.

During the first two years of her husband's illness, McNaughton wrote *Overland to Cariboo*, based on stories he told her about his early adventure. Until 1931, her book was the only account available of the 1862 trek across Western Canada.

Bibliography
•McNaughton, Margaret. 1973 [1896]. *Overland to Cariboo: An Eventful Journey of Canadian Pioneers to the Gold Fields of British Columbia in 1862.* Vancouver: Douglas, 176 pp.

McWilliams, Margaret May Stovel BA DLitt LLD 1875-1952. Margaret Stovel was born in Toronto and received her BA from the University of Toronto in 1898, the first woman graduate in political science. She became a journalist in the United States, then married Roland McWilliams in 1903. They moved to Winnipeg in 1910; thirty years later, he became Lieutenant-Governor of Manitoba. Margaret McWilliams was an active club woman, involved for forty years in the Winnipeg University Women's Club, the Women's Canadian Club, and the Local Council of Women. She was the first president of the Canadian Federation of University Women, founded in 1919, and later a vice-president of the International Federation. In the summer of 1926, she and her husband attended conferences in Europe and then, because of their interest in political and economic movements, visited Russia, which would inspire her second book. McWilliams became Winnipeg's first woman alderman in 1932, serving for four consecutive terms. During her years in Winnipeg she led morning and evening classes in current events, which attracted audiences of up to 1,200 people a week. In 1943 she was appointed by the Canadian government to chair a subcommittee on the problems Canadian women would face after the war; this work provided information for her 1948 book *This New Canada*. She received honorary degrees from the Universities of Manitoba (1946) and Toronto (1948) for her public service, and the Manitoba Historical Society continues to award the Margaret McWilliams Medal for Institutional History for suitable books. Among her friends were **Kennethe Haig** and **Kathleen Strange.**

Manitoba Milestones discusses the history of the province, beginning with chapters on Explorers, Fur Traders and Settlers, and ending with The Test of War and New Times, New Forces (including information on the wheat pool, wheat rust, power development and new mining). Although it has many illustrations, virtually none include women, so that the development of the province seems to be an entirely masculine effort, an impression bolstered by long lists of premiers (all men), lieutenant-governors (all men) and military men. She also lists eighteen early spellings of "Winnipeg," beginning with the 1734 "Ouinipigon" of La Vérendrye.

Russia in Nineteen Twenty-Six was published in part to give "our observations in the form of a woman's impressions of what she saw and heard." Roland, listed as senior author, wrote the thirty-one-page introduction and the summary; Margaret wrote the eighty-eight-page text describing what they saw. Roland concluded that the future Russia "will depend more on the course taken by the other nations than on anything that happens within. The policy of the American government, and in a less degree the attitude of the present British government, are well calculated to produce a Russia which will be a menace to every Western nation."

The McWilliams's book *If I Were King of Canada* is the authors' assessment of what Canada could do to combat the disastrous effects of the Great Depression. They fantasize that on February 30, 1930 or 1931, a horde of Canadians from all walks of life advanced on Ottawa demanding: "We will have a king to rule over us. As we did in war time, so now in our distress we shall have one leader and follow him faithfully and eagerly. To Ottawa to choose a king!" The people chose the authors, who jointly style themselves Oliver Stowell, to be in charge of their future. The chapters comprise sixteen proclamations, each summarizing some facet of Canadian life, and envision ways in which the future can be improved. Their solutions are idealistic, sometimes hierarchical and sometimes prescient, such as "As for the Senate, it might as well be abolished at once" (p. 122).

Bibliography

•Kinnear, Mary. 1991. *Margaret McWilliams: An Interwar Feminist*. Montreal: McGill-Queen's University Press.
•McWilliams, R.F. and M.S. 1927. *Russia in Nineteen Twenty-Six*. London and Toronto: Dent, 128 pp.
•McWilliams, Margaret. 1928. *Manitoba Milestones*. Toronto: Dent, 249 pp.
•Stowell, Oliver. 1931. *If I Were King of Canada*. 1931. Toronto: Dent, 173 pp.

Member of the Community—Ursulines. The author was an Ursuline nun living in Quebec.

The anonymous author dedicates *Glimpses of the Monastery* (called by her a "little sketch of [her convent's] history" [418 pp!]) to its joint foundresses. She wanted to introduce to anglophone readers "those 'valiant women' who shared the courage and long suffering of the holy priests and missionaries of the 'heroic age' of Canada," as well as present a picture of the lives of the Ursuline nuns, although as she notes she had little leisure to write because she was not excused from her teaching duties nor from following the religious exercises of the community. She based the history on the *Jesuit Relations* published in France from 1632 to 1672, documents and letters relating to the first Mother Superior of the convent (Venerable Mother Marie Guyart who died in 1672) and subsequent convent annals and documents. The first edition was well received, with readers "interested to find that while the country was yet in its infancy, a feeble colony struggling for existence, the sacred fire, destined to enlighten the intelligence of future generations was carefully maintained in the religious institutions already founded."

A second volume, *Reminiscences of Fifty Years*, was written by the same nun twenty years later, updating the history from 1839 to 1889 using eyewitness accounts. She writes: "no longer the mingled threads of tradition we have to unravel, nor the brief records on the pages of the annals that will be our sole guide, but we can now tell of what we have seen and testify to what we have known." Before it was published, the author was pleased to submit it to a priest for perusal. *Reminiscences* is more playful than her first book, including, for example, a description in a seventeen-verse poem of an academic examination in 1874 of twenty-three pupils.

Bibliography
•Member of the Community. 1897 [c. 1877]. *Glimpses of the Monastery: Scenes from the History of the Ursulines of Quebec during the Two Hundred Years 1639-1839*. Revised edition. Quebec: L.J. Demers et Frère, 418 pp.
•Member of the Community. 1897. *Reminiscences of Fifty Years in the Cloister 1839-1889. A Sequel to Glimpses of the Monastery*. Quebec: L.J. Demers et Frère, 184 pp.

Member of the Institute of the Blessed Virgin Mary, Toronto. The anonymous author was a Blessed Virgin Mary nun who lived with her order at the Loretto Abbey in Toronto.

In 1847, five members of the order of the Blessed Virgin Mary, also known as the "Loretto Nuns," sailed from Ireland to Toronto at the invitation of the Bishop of Toronto. The leader, who died four years later, was succeeded in office by Rev. M. Teresa Dease (1820-89), the subject of *Life and Letters of Rev. Mother Teresa Dease*. Dease was born in Dublin, received a good schooling and became a nun in the order in which she would spend her life. She founded Ontario branches of the Institute of the Blessed Virgin Mary for convents and/or for the education of children in Toronto, Brantford, London, Belleville, Guelph, Kingston, Niagara Falls, Hamilton, Lindsay and Stratford as well as in Joliet, IL. The preface notes that the chapters are "principally religious, but there are some that are secular and occasionally humourous. Without doubt the writing and compilation of the book was, for the author, a labour of love."

Bibliography
•Member of the Community, A. 1916. *Life and Letters of Rev. Mother Teresa Dease, Foundress and Superior General of the Institute of the Blessed Virgin Mary in America.* Toronto: McClelland, Goodchild and Stewart, 282 pp.

Meredith, Alden G. Alden G. Meredith, whose maiden name is unknown, was interested in social history.

In *Mary's Rosedale* Meredith describes, using both private letters and other contemporary sources, members of the wealthy Jarvis family who lived in this expensive part of Toronto between 1827 and 1861. The Jarvises were United Empire Loyalists and members of the politically conservative Family Compact of Ontario.

Bibliography
•Meredith, Alden G. 1928. *Mary's Rosedale and Gossip of "Little York."* Ottawa: Graphic Publishers, 280 pp.

Merkley, E. May. May Merkley lived in Williamsburg, Ontario, and was cared for medically by Dr Mahlon William Locke, whose biography she wrote.

Merkley was inspired to write her laudatory book *Our Doctor* because she felt he had "more than his share of notoriety," perhaps from envy of his fame. Locke was born near Williamsburg in 1880 and educated at Queen's University from which he graduated as a doctor in 1905. He then practised in his hometown, specializing in surgery and ailments of the hands and feet. He became world famous for his care of feet, which included manipulations and designing special shoes for patients: "The attention and interest of much of the world is centered on Williamsburg. It has become more and more thronged with the noble, and fashionably dressed—attracted by the doctor's fame as a healer—a fame which has spread thence in ever-widening circles." He gave as many as 1,800 patients three manipulations daily, working from 7.30 AM until 9 PM. To accommodate his patients, many buildings were constructed as the village increased dramatically in population.

Bibliography
•Merkley, E. May. 1933. *Our Doctor.* Morrisburg, ON: Leader Publishing, 61 pp.

Merrill, Helen M. Helen Merrill, the daughter of a judge and his wife, was born in Napanee, Ontario. As a journalist, she wrote articles, but she also wrote stories and poems. When she lived in Toronto she worked in the Ontario Archives and was prominent in women's literary circles. Merrill wrote *Picturesque Prince Edward County* to increase summer tourism in this area near where she grew up. She notes in the preface, "Though conscious of my inability to do it anything like justice, I am endeavoring in carefully compiling and giving this phamplet [*sic*–of 126 pp!] proper circulation, to make it a means to that end." The book includes descriptions of places such as Picton and the local sandhills, shorts trips in the area and beyond, poems by various authors, legends and long anecdotes. She ends with the log kept on a ten-day cruise around the County in a thirty-three-foot yacht.

Bibliography
•Merrill, Helen M. 1892. *Picturesque Prince Edward County*. Picton: Gazette Book and Job Printing, 126 pp.

Meyer, Bertha BA 1899-? Bertha Meyer was a member of the Department of Germanic Languages and Literature at McGill University.

For *Salon Sketches*, Meyer wrote biographies of Dorothea Mendelssohn (1763-1839), Rahel Lewin (1771-1833) and Henriette Herz (1764-1847). The year of publication, 1938, is significant, for these women were in their day "outstanding figures in German-Jewry." Meyer continues, "That hyphenated term, then as now, spelled an unhappy union and contained within itself the elements for bitter conflict, which these brave and earnest women sought to overcome, each in her own way." These women each became Christians during their lifetime which Meyer considered inevitable given their circumstances (to be able to marry, to lessen an individual barrier, to gain equality in society). Meyer concludes her book: "The loss to any cause or any community of its high-minded members is always incalculable, and that Jewry recognizes its loss is clear from the insistence with which it now would claim for its own all three of these outstanding women who contributed so much to the period of the greatness of the Berlin Salons."

Bibliography
•Meyer, Bertha. 1938. *Salon Sketches: Biographical Studies of Berlin Salons of the Emancipation*. New York: Bloch, 207 pp.

Miller, Bessie See Cary, Elizabeth Marguerite.

Miller, Maud Henderson 1866-? Maud Miller of Upper Woodstock, New Brunswick, was interested in local history. Because of this, the president of the York and Sunbury Historical Society urged her for years to write a history of Upper Woodstock where she lived, but she doubted her own ability.

Miller changed her mind when she discovered an 1876 map of the village which gave details of the seventy-two houses present. She found that "my memory of houses and names had been exact and that I could verify every item." For *History of Upper Woodstock* she obtained information from early village residents and their families, history books, provincial legislative material, early newspapers and her own diary. She describes the development of Upper Woodstock, which began about 1830, devoting chapters to the iron works, railways and bridges, furniture factory and the inhabitants along the main roads and in the Presbyterian graveyard. She recalls the old days with regret, concluding that the earlier settlers were less mercenary, more self-reliant, more temperate about alcohol, more honourable in politics and decidedly more religious.

Bibliography

•Miller, Maud Henderson. 1940. *History of Upper Woodstock*. Saint John, NB: Globe Printing, 165 pp.

Miller, Muriel BA, MA 1908-1987. Muriel Miller was born in Hartland, New Brunswick, and educated at the Universities of New Brunswick (BA 1931) and Toronto (MA 1933). Her master's thesis centred on Bliss Carman (1861-1929), a poet who interested her because he had been born in her hometown and had studied at her alma mater, UNB. Miller later wrote a biography of Homer Watson, and *G.A. Reid, Canadian Artist* (1946), so she was obviously attracted to creative people. After marrying Julian Miner, she lived for years in Peterborough and Timmins. Miller rounded out her life's interest in Canadian art with the publication of *Famous Canadian Artists* (1983), which comprises brief biographies complete with original quotes of twenty-three painters she knew personally. About this time she was a cultural activist: John Meisel, a member of the Canadian Radio-television and Telecommunications Commission, reports that she was instrumental in expanding the range of a classical music radio station based in Peterborough.

For her book *Bliss Carman*, Miller "had the advantage of knowing intimately many of the sources of his inspiration." She was also "guided by wise counsellors who had shared his companionship." She hopes that it "will offer a small but useful lamp to those who wish to explore further into the poet's mind and art." As well as giving information about Carman's life, she quotes and critiques many of his poems.

The foreword to Miller's *Homer Watson* states that her work "was undertaken in a systematic spirit, and shows a keen appreciation of the effect of environment upon an impressionable artist of reflective type." Homer Watson (1855-1936) was born in Doon, near Kitchener. He worked in the brickyard six days a week, then hid on Sundays from his religious mother so he could teach himself to paint the landscape around him. Even-

tually he became a full-time artist, whose paintings would be lauded by
Oscar Wilde and James Whistler, among others.

Bibliography
•Miller, Muriel MA. 1935. *Bliss Carman: A Portrait*. Toronto: Ryerson, 136 pp.
•_____. 1988 [1938]. *Homer Watson, the Man of Doon*. Toronto: Summerhill
   Press, 160 pp.

Millichamp, Helen Dorothy A. BA MA 1908-? Dorothy Millichamp was
born in Toronto but studied in England, receiving her BA in 1929 in economics and languages from Oxford University. Her career in child education began in 1931 when she left her job as an assistant in the biology
department at the University of Toronto to study for her MA with Dr. W.
Blatz at his Institute of Child Study. She soon became Blatz's main deputy,
not only running the school with **Margaret Fletcher**, **Helen Bott** and others but helping him organize the lives and environment of the Dionne quintuplets when they were on public display in northern Ontario. During the
war, she helped him found a training school in Birmingham to teach supervisors how to set up daycare centres in Britain, which would serve women
workers and their children. The five women experts for the Canadian Children's Services wore uniforms with ties, which **Alice Massey,** wife of
Canada's High Commissioner to Britain, bought for them from Harrod's.
When she returned to Canada, Millichamp took over the administration of
daycare nurseries in Ontario, which also were being set up to free women
for war work, and shared the position of Assistant Director at the Institute
of Child Study. She was headmistress of Bishop Strachan School from
1948 to 1952 before again joining the Institute until it closed in 1968. She
then founded, with **Mary Northway**, the Brora Centre, where research in
child development could continue (Raymond 1991).

    The three authors of *Nursery Education* all worked at the St George's
School for Child Study at the University of Toronto, William Blatz as
Director, Dorothy Millichamp as Assistant Director of the Nursery School
Division, and Margaret Fletcher as Principal of the Nursery School. The
information in their book was developed over ten years in their school,
which was founded in 1926 with Rockefeller Memorial money. They per-
ceive the nursery school to be a place where children "should start to learn
certain social skills and attitudes which they cannot learn at home." The
authors discuss work and play habits of pre-school children, social and
emotional adjustments and suitable routines—for dressing, washing, eat-
ing, sleeping and elimination. They advise parents to establish an early
morning routine for bowel elimination so it "need not concern the school
except when the home routine is upset, at which times the parent can be
asked to notify the school" (p. 71).

Bibliography
•Blatz, William E. MA, MB, PhD, Dorothy Millichamp MA and Margaret Fletcher. 1936 [1935]. *Nursery Education: Theory and Practice*. New York: Morrow, 365 pp.

Mirsky, Jeannette BA 1903-1987. Jeannette Mirsky was born in New Jersey and raised in New York City, where she graduated from Barnard College in 1924. After marrying Edward B. Ginsburg, an industrial engineer, the couple moved to South Carolina until 1950, then to Princeton for the rest of their lives. Because they seem to have had no children, Mirsky, a historical geographer, could devote her time to writing articles and ten books, all dealing with frontier places or with people who were trailblazers; to do this she received grants from the Guggenheim and Rockefeller foundations. All were published under her maiden name.

Mirsky's first book, *To the North!* focuses on Europeans in the Arctic, including the Canadian Arctic, "the best history of northern exploration so far written," Vilhjalmur Stefansson notes in the introduction. Mirsky had been given free range of Stefansson's northern library of 17,000 titles, many of them original sources, which she had read and studied for three and a half years. In 1937, her book was withdrawn by the publisher because Dr Frederick Cook filed a lawsuit against it on the grounds that it discredited his claim of having in 1908 been the first man to visit the North Pole. Despite this, the book was republished in 1946 and again in 1970 under the title *To the Arctic!*

Bibliography
•Mirsky, Jeannette. 1970 [1934]. *To the Arctic!* Chicago: University of Chicago Press, 352 pp.

Mitchell, Margaret Knox Howell BA 1901-1988. Margaret Howell studied biology and geology at the University of Toronto, graduating in 1924, then worked as a secretary in the palaeontology department of the Royal Ontario Museum until she married in 1927. When she volunteered for unpaid museum work in ornithology, she was given a project studying the passenger pigeon, and became the first woman research affiliate of any natural history museum in Canada. In the years 1950-54, when she was stationed with her husband in Rio de Janeiro, she carried out a comprehensive study of local bird behaviour and distribution (289 species positively identified), which was published by the Royal Ontario Museum to acclaim in 1957 as *Observations on Birds of Southeastern Brazil*. The following year she was elected a member of the prestigious American Ornithologists Union.

To collect information on passenger pigeons, the Museum had sent out a questionnaire in 1926 across Ontario asking for information about this species which had become extinct when Martha, the sole remaining individual, died in 1914 at the age of twenty-five in the Cincinnati Zoo. *The Passenger Pigeon in Ontario* is based on the data collected, together with information from other reliable sources in the literature. It was published under a special bequest as Contribution No. 7 of the Royal Ontario Museum of Zoology.

Bibliography
•Mitchell, Margaret H. 1935. *The Passenger Pigeon in Ontario.* Toronto: University of Toronto Press, 181 pp.

Monck, Frances Elizabeth Owen Cole d. 1919.   As the wife of the brother of the Governor General of British North America from 1861 to 1867 (Lord Monck), Frances Monck visited Canada in 1864-65. Her almost daily account of her experiences were sent back to her home as letters; they describe the trip from Ireland to Quebec and then on to Ottawa, where she spent most of the winter, and visits to other parts of the Canadas as well.

These letters were gathered together to produce *My Canadian Leaves*, of which ten copies were printed in 1873 for "private circulation." It was subsequently republished, most recently by the University of Toronto Press in 1963, which version includes information previously deleted.

Bibliography
•Monck, Frances E.O. 1891 [1873]. *My Canadian Leaves: An Account of a Visit to Canada in 1864-65.* London: Richard Bentley, 367 pp.

Montgomery, Doris.   Doris Montgomery gathered impressions of the Gaspé area of Quebec while driving around it with her photographer friend Mary Van Nest. Both of them had trouble conversing with the many people they met who spoke only French.

In *The Gaspé Coast in Focus*, Montgomery devotes chapters to the coast, the "big hills," fishing villages, flowers and birds and Percé Rock. The prose is lyrical, in keeping with the romantic accompanying photographs. She ends her book philosophically: "The task of adopting the best of the new ways and preserving the best of the old is not an easy one but our Gaspé friends are equal to it. To know the Gaspé Coast and its people is to love both."

Bibliography
•Montgomery, Doris. 1940. *The Gaspé Coast in Focus.* New York: Dutton, 88 pp.

Montgomery, Lucy Maud OBE 1874-1942. Lucy Maud Montgomery was born and raised by her strict Presbyterian grandparents on Prince Edward Island, where she studied to be a teacher at Prince of Wales College. She taught, worked briefly on a Halifax newspaper and then cared for her grandmother, using her spare time to write first poems and short stories which she sold to newspapers and magazines. She then turned to novels, beginning with *Anne of Green Gables* (1908), which are still world famous. In 1911, after her grandmother died, she married Rev. Ewan Macdonald and moved with him to Ontario, where he was a minister. She continued to write and raised her two sons there, as well as acting as a minister's wife, nursing her husband through intense bouts of melancholia and encouraging other writers in the Canadian Women's Press Club and the Canadian Authors Association. She herself was resentful because her husband never commended her for her writing although she paid most of the family's bills. In 1935 she became an officer of the Order of the British Empire; she was also a Fellow of England's Royal Society of Arts. Throughout her life she kept a personal journal which is currently being published in a number of volumes (Rubio and Waterston, 1985 on).

Montgomery wrote her short autobiography, *The Alpine Path*, originally published serially in the Toronto magazine *Everywoman's World*, because of the immense interest in her books and therefore in their author. In it, "Montgomery shows a remarkable memory for details and stresses her happier memories, shading them only slightly with the inevitable fears and pains of a sensitive youngster." Frazer (1990) also notes that although "posthumous revelations do not contradict her autobiography, they do fill in gaps and help to explain the apprehensions, anger, and rebelliousness that make her most powerful books something more than pleasantly flavored pabulum for the young." Montgomery notes in *The Alpine Path* (p. 52) that she always meant to be an author: "To write has always been my central purpose around which every effort and hope and ambition of my life has grouped itself. I was an indefatigable little scribbler, and stacks of manuscripts, long ago reduced to ashes, alas, bore testimony to the same."

Courageous Women, written with two friends, comprises the short biographies of twenty-one women. Only six are non-Canadians (including Joan of Arc, Florence Nightingale, Queen Victoria and Helen Keller), so it is strongly nationalistic. Four are Canadian authors—**Catharine Parr Traill, Pauline Johnson, Aletta Marty** and **Marshall Saunders.** The text is written with conversation and anecdotes, which will especially interest young readers.

Bibliography
- Bruce, Harry. 1994. *Maud: The Life of L.M. Montgomery*. Toronto: Seal.
- Frazer, Frances. 1990. Lucy Maud Montgomery. *Dictionary of Literary Biography: Canadian Writers, 1890-1920*, s.v. Montgomery, Lucy Maud.
- Gillen, Mollie. 1983. *The Wheel of Things: A Biography of Lucy Maud Montgomery*. Halifax: Goodread Biographies.
- Rubio, Mary and Elizabeth Waterston. *The Selected Journals of L.M. Montgomery*, Vol. I (1889-1910) 1985; Vol. II (1910-1921) 1987; Vol. III (1921-1929) 1992; Vol. IV (1929-1935) 1998. Toronto: Oxford University Press.
- Rubio, Mary and Elizabeth Waterston. 1995. *L.M. Montgomery: Writing a Life*. Toronto: ECW Press.
- Montgomery, L.M. 1990 [1917]. *The Alpine Path: The Story of My Career*. Don Mills: Fitzhenry and Whiteside, 96 pp.
- Montgomery, L.M., Marian Keith and Mabel Burns McKinley. 1934. *Courageous Women*. Toronto: McClelland and Stewart, 203 pp.

Moodie, Susanna Strickland 1803-1885. Like her sister **Catharine Parr Traill**, Susanna Strickland was born in England to a retired couple. She wrote professionally before marrying John Moodie, a half-pay officer, and emigrating in 1832 to backwoods Upper Canada (Ontario), where most of their seven children were born. Unlike her sister, however, she was a reluctant immigrant who disliked much of the hard life that homesteading for eight years entailed. Clara Thomas notes (p. 58) that "Susanna [also unlike her sister] was, in fact, not a diarist, not a writer of calm expository prose, certainly not an instructress of prospective emigrants, but a gifted recorder of character, dialogue and incident, especially of a humorous nature."

In 1852, Moodie published *Roughing it in the Bush*, describing her pioneering experiences, which has sold well ever since, although a Canadian edition appeared only in 1871. "It is a settlement narrative consisting of sketches in a basically chronological order and reflecting the Moodies' experience of and responses to the culture shock, the trials, and the pleasures of immigration and pioneer life." (Ballstadt 1990). Although the Strickland family into which Susanna was born produced many authors, they were not all proud of her success. Her sister Sarah wrote from England in 1875, "The publication of that disgusting book *Roughing it in the Bush* made the very name of Canada hateful to us all. It was very mortifying to have a book like that going the round of low vulgar upstarts." Many Canadians were also upset with her often negative depiction of their country.

Moodie wrote *Life in the Clearings* at the suggestion of her London publisher, Richard Bentley, who wanted her to update her story by describing life in Canadian towns at mid-century. It focuses around a trip from her home in Belleville to Niagara. "In dealing with the institutions and traits of a young society she is able to amplify her view of human progress by conveying a sense of the vitality and liberty of the people and celebrating the advancement resulting from their mechanical genius and industrious habits" (Ballstadt 1990).

Bibliography

•Ballstadt, Carl. 1990. Susanna Moodie. *Dictionary of Literary Biography: Canadian Writers before 1890*, s.v. Moodie, Susanna.

Gray, Charlotte. 1999. *Sisters in the Wilderness: The Lives of Susanna Moodie and Catharine Parr Traill*. New York: Viking.

•Thomas, Clara. 1966. The Strickland Sisters, pp. 42-73. In Mary Quayle Innis, ed. *The Clear Spirit*. Toronto: University of Toronto Press.

•Moodie, Susanna. 1962 [1852]. *Roughing it in the Bush, or Forest Life in Canada*. Toronto: McClelland and Stewart, 237 pp.

•————. 1989 [1853]. *Life in the Clearings versus the Bush*. Toronto: McClelland and Stewart, 340 pp.

Moore, Irene 1876-1947.   Irene Moore seems to have been a Canadian author.

Moore was obviously an ardent admirer of the subject of her biography, *Valiant La Verendrye*, who was a fur trader, soldier and adventurer who explored the Lake Winnipeg area in 1739. After describing his exploits in detail, she ends her book, "His graces of mind and person and the vastness of his performance earned for this well-nigh incomparable voyageur to the last syllable of recorded time the love and remembrance of the dwellers in the country of his birth and the lands of his discovering."

Bibliography

•Moore, Irene. 1927. *Valiant La Verendrye*. Quebec: King's Printer, 383 pp.

Moore, Kathleen See McEwen, Jessie entry.

Moore, Theodora Cornell 1846-1923 See Bugeia, Julia entry.

Morley, Margaret Warner 1858-1923.   Margaret Morley and her friend M., a female artist, travelled together through Nova Scotia, spending most of their time in Acadia and Cape Breton.

Morley's book *Down North and Up Along* describes their adventures, as well as including titbits of regional history. They especially enjoyed talking to the local inhabitants and watching them at work and when relaxing.

Bibliography

•Morley, Margaret Warner. 1900. *Down North and Up Along*. New York: Dodd, Mead, 304 pp.

Morris, Elizabeth Keith. Just before the First World War, Elizabeth Morris and her sister visited Canada from Great Britain, travelling by train across the country.

Morris's *An Englishwoman in the Canadian West*, which describes their experiences, seems aimed at possible immigrants to Canada with Morris portraying homesteading, bush life, education, climate and agriculture, among other things. She notes:

> The primitive element pervading everything, the vastness of the country, the habit of taking people at their own valuation, the simplicity of living, the presence of work amongst all classes, and the exhilarating atmosphere, all combine to make that intangible quality which belongs only to a country in the making.

Bibliography
•Morris, Elizabeth Keith. 1913. *An Englishwoman in the Canadian West*. London: Simpkin Marshall, 192 pp.

Morrison, Edith Lennox. Edith Morrison was an Ontario author.

Morrison's biography *William Tyrrell of Weston* focuses on Tyrrell (1816-1904), known locally as the "first citizen" or civic leader of Weston, now a suburb of Toronto. Over a long life he evolved from being a self-trained carpenter to becoming an architect and engineer, an amateur scientist, and someone conversant in municipal law. Her book is based on his papers and on old workbooks discovered in 1927 and preserved by his sons. Supplementary information came from letters and public records, and from people still living in York County who remembered him.

Bibliography
•Morrison, Edith Lennox and J.E. Middleton. 1937. *William Tyrrell of Weston*. Toronto: Macmillan, 152 pp.

Morrissey, Sister Helen, RHSJ, nun. Helen Morrissey was a nun who was "a keen student of the inspirational early days of our Province [Quebec]. She has ever been wishful to make English-speaking Canadians more fully aware of French Canada's illustrious past," as the introduction to her book states.

The book, *Fanny Allen*, reflects this interest. Fanny Allen was not famous in her own right but in that of her father. The first part of the book is devoted to Ethan Allen (1737-89), a Vermont general who tried to capture Montreal from the British in 1775. He was arrested there and sent to jail in England. After returning to North America he married Fanny Montressor, his second marriage, in 1784. Their daughter, Fanny Allen, attended the convent boarding school of the Sisters of the Congregation of Notre Dame in Montreal, where she was converted to Roman Catholicism. Then she became a nun, called "The Beautiful American Nun," in the Montreal Hotel Dieu Hospital. Long after she died young, in 1819, a Fanny Allen Hospital under Hotel Dieu administration was established in 1894 in Vermont on land once owned by her father.

Bibliography
• Morrissey, Sister Helen RHSJ. 1940. *Fanny Allen, Ethan Allen's Daughter*. Gardenvale, QC: Garden City Press, 135 pp.

Morton, Irene Elder 1849-1921. Irene Elder was born in Hantsport, Nova Scotia, and educated at Acadia Seminary before marrying Albert Morton. She wrote articles, stories and poems as well as a book.

The Coming of the French is the story of Champlain taken from his diaries. The foreword says it was written "as a labor of love for the children of Canada, [the author's] earnest desire being that they should have a more thorough knowledge of the early history" of her beloved country. The book, published eight years after Morton's death, was edited by her daughter, Alberta Irene Morton, who kept the copyright. Champlain is praised because "He never broke faith with the Indians, and retained their confidence and affection until the last." The author gives thanks to the French Canadians who "brought us our first civilization" and cleared the ground for agriculture. "To-day they furnish us a background of romantic and tragic history."

Bibliography
• Morton, Irene Elder. 1929. *The Coming of the French*. Toronto: McClelland and Stewart, 59 pp.

Mowat, Grace Helen 1875-1964. Grace Mowat was an expert on the history of St Andrews, New Brunswick, where she lived. The foreword of the 1953 reprint edition of her book notes that "Miss Mowat is an authority on the traditions of Charlotte County and scarcely a week goes by but the Registry Office sends on to her a visitor who has called to enquire about his ancestry. Miss Mowat is tireless in her activities on behalf of these strangers."

St Andrews was founded in 1783 by United Empire Loyalists exiled from the United States. *The Diverting History of a Loyalist Town* describes in detail St Andrews' development over the years.

Bibliography
• Mowat, Grace Helen. 1976 [1932]. *The Diverting History of a Loyalist Town: A Portrait of St Andrews, New Brunswick*. Fredericton: Brunswick Press, 152 pp.

Mugglebee, Ruth E. 1903-? Ruth Mugglebee was apparently an American author.

The introduction to her book, *Father Coughlin*, states that she has written a detailed and interesting biography. "Miss Mugglebee pictures life in a small Canadian town of forty years ago, as well as the requirements of the religious life, with skill and charm." The first 120 pages describe the early life of Rev. Charles E. Coughlin (b. 1891), who was born and grew up in Hamilton. He attended St Michael's College at the University of Toronto before entering the priesthood. For seven years he served near Windsor, Ontario, both teaching at Assumption College and ministering in a parish, before leaving in 1923 to work in the United States. He was to become famous for his missionary work by radio from Royal Oak, a suburb of Detroit.

Bibliography
•Mugglebee, Ruth. 1933. *Father Coughlin the Radio Priest, of the Shrine of the Little Flower*. Garden City, NY: Garden City Publishing, 358 pp.

Mullins, Janet Elizabeth. Janet Mullins, who lived in Liverpool, Nova Scotia, was a devotee of local history. She collected "historical notes partly dictated to, partly written in long hand for, a teacher on the Liverpool Academy staff to be used in conjunction with printed historical matter in giving a course in local history to her class of the year 1938." (Liverpool, Nova Scotia, had been founded in 1759 and incorporated in 1897.) After she organized and published this material serially in the *Liverpool Advance*, the editor of this newspaper suggested the articles be produced in book form.

Each chapter of *Some Liverpool Chronicles* is filled with facts and figures. Mullins notes optimistically in her section entitled Slaves that:

> The term "slave" as applied to them had not the meaning that it bore in the South, for here negroes had freedom in every respect and their children were as free as any other children. The adults however, considered themselves bound to remain with their employers—the men working on their farms, at their fisheries and as seamen on their vessels, the women, as domestics. (p. 28)

Bibliography
•Mullins, Janet E. 1980 [1941]. *Some Liverpool Chronicles*. Liverpool, NS: Lancelot Press, 297 pp.

Munday, Luta. Luta Munday married her Mountie husband in Toronto in 1905, then joined him in the West the following year. Her husband and she were later posted to many other parts of Canada, including the Arctic.

In *A Mounty's Wife*, Munday tells the story of the lives of the "Mounties" from a woman's perspective. Her foreword begins:

> There have been many histories, many romances, and many tales written and woven about the members of that famous body of men 'The Royal North-West Mounted Police,' but no mention has been made of the help-mates of these men, and this is my excuse for telling of my life for over twenty years as the wife of one of these members.

Bibliography
•Munday, Luta. 1930. *A Mounty's Wife, Being the Life Story of One Attached to the Force but Not of It*. Toronto: Macmillan, 217 pp.

Murphy, Emily Gowan Ferguson 1868-1933. Emily Ferguson was born in Cookstown, Ontario, to a well-to-do business family with six children. At fifteen she became a boarder at Bishop Strachan School in Toronto, where she further developed her "encyclopedic mind." The headmistress there showed that it was possible to memorize several pages from any book read aloud, a skill acquired by Murphy that enabled her to quote freely from a variety of sources. She married an Anglican minister, Arthur Murphy, when she was nineteen and moved with him every few years to a new Ontario town where her husband had a call. They had four daughters, two of whom died young. In 1898, the family sailed to England, where Arthur had been invited as a missionary. On the voyage, she met English people who disparaged Canadians as being half-educated, mean, petty, bad-mannered and boastful. (She herself would be appalled by the poverty in Great Britain.) Murphy was so annoyed that she resolved to record her observations of the "old world" to be made into a book. Murphy continued to write for the rest of her life—essays, book reviews, articles, books—preferring to do so after midnight when her chores were done, her family asleep and the house quiet. Her articles and books were vital in supporting the family when her husband became sick with typhoid fever.

In 1903, following the death in Ontario from diphtheria of their six-year-old daughter, the family moved to Manitoba, where they hoped for a more healthy life. They settled in Swan River north of Winnipeg, but a few years later moved on to Edmonton. In Alberta, Murphy took on many worthy causes and founded, led or joined several writing groups—Canadian Women's Press Club (of which she was National President from 1913 to 1920), Canadian Society of Women Journalists of English and the Canadian Authors Association. During this time she was heavily involved in feminist causes, entertaining Emmeline Pankhurst and becoming friends with **Nellie McClung**, who moved to Edmonton in 1914. In 1916, thanks to her interest in women, she was made the first woman magistrate in the British Empire and a judge of the Juvenile Court in Edmonton. As such, she was compassionate toward female drug addicts and prostitutes who came into conflict with the law. She further publicized problems of drug addiction by lecturing on the subject throughout Canada and the United States. However, she believed that the mentally unfit should be sterilized so that they could not produce children who would be a drain on the state; to this end she aroused public opinion for the passing in 1928 of the Alberta Sexual Sterilization Act which has recently come into public disrepute. Her writings also are sometimes racist, especially against Chinese and blacks. Murphy was instrumental in organizing the Persons Case in 1927 (which also involved **Henrietta Edwards** and **Nellie McClung**) to determine if Canadian women could be members of the Senate, a point on which her own authority as a police magistrate had been questioned. When the case was won, many hoped that she would be appointed as the first woman senator, but politics being what they are, this did not happen. She was proud of her busy life, claiming that "The only truly contented women are those who have both a home and a profession."

For her first book, *The Impressions of Janey Canuck Abroad*, Murphy chose the protagonist's name as the feminine counterpart to "Johnny Canuck." In the preface she notes that the book is composed of "diary-scraps and letters" rather than being "a glorified guide book." She admits that it contains little that is new "for the well-informed traveller, except perhaps a different insight, for we all see through our own particular prejudices and temperament. We LOOK physically but SEE mentally. This must be my plea for the re-weaving of old materials." Sections of this book also appeared in the general-interest magazine *National Monthly of Canada*, for which Murphy later became Women's Editor.

Emily Murphy was one of the million people to settle on the Canadian prairies between 1901 and 1911. In *Janey Canuck in the West* she describes the "hundreds of thousands of newcomers representing a cross-section of races, religions, nationalities, occupations, and backgrounds" she encountered. She filled "her notebooks with her impressions of what she had observed and understood," but changed the name of her town of Swan River to Poplar Bluff "to protect the innocent."

Open Trails describes various trips Murphy took across the prairies from her Edmonton base and as far east as Ottawa. She met a Norwegian woman on a homestead who had last been to the nearest town six years earlier, when she had gone to the hospital, miners and prospectors, Natives, nuns and even black people when she visited the United States south of Winnipeg. This book was accompanied by a flyer of laudatory comments about the book and its author from sixty-four different publications, far more than usually review a book nowadays.

The format of *Seeds of Pine* is similar to that of *Open Trails*, but this time she travels to the north and northwest, visiting Jasper, Banff and Athabaska Landing and boating on the Lesser Slave River and Lesser Slave Lake. She describes coal-mining, horse races, gardening in the north, hero priests and a Ruthenian community. She concludes that the North "is an exacting mistress, this white-bodied, rude-muscled North, and, of times, she breaks and hurts a man till he drags his brokenness away to die. Yet, is she beautiful and passionately human; full of vigour and drunken with life, and her house stretches from the dawn to dayfall" (p. 300).

Murphy's interest in the drug problem led her to research the subject in depth, despite threats on her life. Her articles on drugs, first appearing in *Maclean*'s magazine, were expanded to produce *The Black Candle* which, she noted, "deals with the moral, physical, mental, social, curative, legal, criminal, punitive, causative, historical, tragical, medical, financial, and even grimly humorous phases of the subject" (Mander 105). She urged stiffer jail sentences, corrective lashes and, if they were aliens, immediate deportation for drug offenders. She does not blame the victims of drug abuse but rather the "palmerworms and human caterpillars who should be trodden underfoot like the despicable grubs that they are." She states that "while facing the drug evils without blinkers, I have endeavored to discuss it without offending the sensibilities of the readers."

Bibliography

•Coates, Donna. Emily Murphy. *Dictionary of Literary Biography: Canadian Writers before 1890*, s.v. Murphy, Emily.
•Mander, Christine. 1985. *Emily Murphy, Rebel*. Toronto: Simon and Pierre, 150 pp.
•Sanders, Byrne Hope. 1945. *Emily Murphy, Crusader*. Toronto: Macmillan, 355 pp.
•Ferguson, Emily. 1902 [1901]. *The Impressions of Janey Canuck Abroad*. Toronto: n.p., 186 pp.
•_____. 1975 [1910]. *Janey Canuck in the West*. London: Cassell, 306 pp.
•_____. 1920 [1912]. *Open Trails*. London: Dent, 250 pp.
•Canuck, Janey. 1922 [1914]. *Seeds of Pine*. Toronto: Musson, 301 pp.
•Murphy, Emily F. "Janey Canuck." 1922. *The Black Candle*. Toronto: Thomas Allen, 405 pp.

Murray, Hon. Amelia Matilda 1795-1884. Lady Murray, the daughter of Bishop Murray, a friend of Lady Byron and a maid of honour to Queen Victoria, visited North America both as a tourist and as an amateur botanist, carrying with her a huge container for plants. She travelled in Canada for two months in the fall of 1854, then journeyed through Upper Canada to Niagara by train and steamer to begin a much longer sojourn in the United States. The letters she wrote during her trip were soon made into a book. She continued during her life to study plants, to sketch and to promote the education of women.

Lady Murray states in the preface to *Letters from the United States, Cuba and Canada* that her correspondence was not written with publication in mind, that she is not a partisan, and that she wants to avoid controversy and pain, but feels that facts (such as hers) should always be welcome. She asks the indulgence of the reader because the letters "were hastily written, sent off by post uncopied, and generally uncorrected." She attended the Canadian parliament in Quebec City (noting the odd effect of conducting affairs in two languages when many members seemed to understand only one), and sought out many species of plants, new to her, which she identified by their scientific name. Noting a number of black people near Chatham, she comments on the regrettable actions of Abolitionists in urging that American slaves be freed, believing that the slaves' "ill-judging friends have proved worse than enemies"; she seemed to be annoyed that so many blacks would not work for pay even though "people are in distress for both out-of-door and in-door servants" (p. 119). At the end of her book she invited readers to apply if they wished for a set of her sketches to illustrate the text.

Bibliography
•Murray, Hon. Amelia M. 1969 [1856]. *Letters from the United States, Cuba and Canada*. New York: Negro Universities Press, 410 pp.

Murray, Frances Elizabeth c. 1831-1901. Frances Murray was born into a prominent New Brunswick family. Her father, a lawyer, died when she was about three, so she was apparently raised in the St John home of her uncle whose biography she would later write. He was president and she vice-president of the Eclectic Reading Club of Saint John from 1880 to 1888, an organization devoted to "the mutual improvement of the members in reading and their knowledge of general literature" (Davies 1994). When he died in 1888, she was elected president, later writing that the meetings had "done more than we imagine to promote thought, research, discussion, or literary subjects and thus they have helped to free us a little from the everyday cares of our busy lives and to raise us to a higher plane of thought and being." She was deeply involved in many charitable organizations concerned with the Anglican church, orphans, young people and treatment of animals. After **Lady Aberdeen** visited St John in 1894, Murray also fought for women's rights as an executive member of the local Council of Women.

Memoir of LeBaron Botsford, MD is about Murray's uncle, who practised medicine for fifty years. She writes in her preface that because hers is the first book to be written about a St John citizen, it will be of special interest to all his fellow citizens. Her aim

> has been to narrate the moulding circumstances which surrounded Dr Botsford's [1812-1888] childhood and youth, vividly to depict him as he walked among us for so many years—a physician, friend, and citizen—and partially to reveal the hidden motor-power of Christian principle which impelled the various professional, social, and benevolent activities of his life.

It includes a lecture by Botsford on evolution and the thumb.

Murray honoured the memory of a second friend with her book *In Memoriam: Fred Hervey John Brigstocke*. Brigstocke had been archdeacon of St John and rector of Trinity Church, with whom she had dined every Sunday after service.

Bibliography

•Davies, Gwendolyn. 1994. Murray, Frances Elizabeth. *Dictionary of Canadian Biography*, s.v. Murray, Frances Elizabeth.
•Murray, Frances Elizabeth. 1892. *Memoir of LeBaron Botsford, MD*. Saint John, NB: J. and A. McMillan, 285 pp.
_____. 1899. *In Memoriam: Fred Hervey John Brigstocke*. St John, NB: J. and A. McMillan, 159 pp.

Nannary, M.A. Nannary, who apparently never married, was a deeply religious woman who lived in St John, New Brunswick.

Nannary's *Memoir of the Life of Rev. E.J. Dunphy* tells us that Dunphy immigrated from Ireland to Canada, where he studied to become a Catholic priest. After his ordination in 1849 he spent twenty-seven years as a pastoral priest, mostly in St John, New Brunswick; he died in 1876. Nannary notes that he was not a *great* man, but "a good man, a faithful servant of God, a holy priest." She writes, "It is to keep alive this memory that I have undertaken, with many misgivings, a short and I fear very imperfect sketch of his energetic, hard-working life. I have done so at the urgent request of my many friends and his, knowing him as I did from childhood."

Bibliography
•Nannary, M.A. 1877. *Memoir of the Life of Rev. E.J. Dunphy*. St John, NB:
Weekly Herald, 127 pp.

Nase, Edith Rowena. Edith Nase was a resident of Westfield, New
Brunswick, who was interested in local history.

When the Maritime Library Association "revived an interest in parish
histories by its competition last year," Nase writes, "I undertook joyfully
the task of collecting and compiling the history of the Parish of Westfield,"
a Loyalist settlement in Kings County, New Brunswick. In *Westfield* Nase
describes mostly early pioneers, including her relative Col. Henry Nase
who, in 1783, was the first United Empire Loyalist to arrive in the area.
Short sections are devoted also to churches, lumbering, schools, bridges,
roads and anecdotes.

Bibliography
•Nase, Edith Rowena. 1925. *Westfield: An Historical Sketch*. N.p., 80 pp.

Neatby, Hilda Marion BA MA PhD LLD LLD FRSC OC 1904-1975.
Hilda Neatby was born in England, the second youngest of eight children,
in a family that emigrated to Canada when she was two. She studied at the
University of Saskatchewan, graduating in honours history in 1924 and
then earning her master's degree. She studied for a year in Paris on a scholarship provided by the Province of Saskatchewan before beginning her
career as a professor, mostly at the University of Saskatchewan. She earned
her PhD from the University of Minnesota in 1934. Neatby went on to
become a member of the Massey Royal Commission on National Development in the Arts, Letters and Sciences, which in 1951 recommended government support for these activities and the formation of the Canada Council. She was also a noted critic of Canadian education with her 1953 book
So Little for the Mind; her call for a return to basics and an emphasis on
traditional education was strongly criticized by educational bureaucrats.
She received honorary degrees from the University of Toronto (1953) and
Brock University (1967) and was made a companion of the Order of
Canada in 1967.

Neatby's doctoral thesis was made into her first book, *The Administration of Justice under the Quebec Act*, in which she addressed the question
of the judicial system in Quebec after 1775: "Were the bitter complaints of
the English party justified, or were they merely the petulant expression of a
disappointed desire for race domination?" She concluded that "It has been
impossible to find any short or simple answer to this question."

Bibliography

•Neatby, Hilda M. 1937. *The Administration of Justice under the Quebec Act.*
  Minneapolis: University of Minnesota Press, 383 pp.
•_____. 1983. *So Much To Do, So Little Time: The Writings of Hilda Neatby.*
  Edited by Michael Hayden. Vancouver: University of British Columbia Press.

Newbigin, Marion Isabel DSc (Lond) 1869-1934.   Marion Newbigin,
born and raised in Scotland, was educated at university primarily as a geographer, although she also studied zoology and botany. She lectured at Bedford College in London and wrote books mainly about the geography of
parts of Europe which she visited, usually with her sister; in the 1920s she
toured eastern Canada and wrote about the geography and its implications
of the St Lawrence River. Her last book, published posthumously, was
Plant and Animal Geography (1936).

    In *Canada, the Great River, the Lands and the Men*, Newbigin writes:
"Of all the new experiences which such a visit yields perhaps none is more
memorable than the preliminary journey from the entrance of the Gulf of
St Lawrence to the river, and up its tranquil waters." The book deals with
various geographical areas of eastern Canada from a historical perspective
of the French and English populations. It is intended both for people familiar with Canada and for those who only know it by repute whom she hopes
will be encouraged by her words to visit it.

Bibliography

•Newbigin, Marion I. 1926. *Canada, the Great River, the Lands and the Men.*
  London: Christophers, 308 pp.

Nichols, Marie Leona Hobbs 1880-?   Marie Nichols was an American
author.

    In *Ranald MacDonald*, Nichols tells his story with verve and conversa-
tion. The subject (1824-94) was born to a Chinook Native woman and a
Scot fur trader at the Hudson's Bay post in Fort George. His mother died
shortly after his birth, so he was raised primarily as a European, being sent
away to school at Red River. He led a life of adventure, both in North
America and in Japan.

Bibliography

•Nichols, Marie Leona. 1940. *Ranald MacDonald, Adventurer.* Caldwell, ID:
  Caxton Printers, 169 pp.

Nielsen, Dorise Winnifred Webber 1902-? Dorise Webber grew up in London in part during the air raids of the First World War. She became a teacher, then emigrated to Saskatchewan where she taught school briefly before marrying a farmer, Peter Nielsen, in 1927. Because they were unable to make ends meet during the Depression, the family was on relief for three years—$11.25 a month to feed a family of five. Being politicized by this experience, she became active in the CCF, which seemed like the best party to represent the poor, then became a Unity candidate in her riding of North Battleford to try to defeat the Liberal member of parliament. She had no organized campaign for the 1940 election, but managed to win because she successfully represented the many dispossessed. As the only woman elected to the House of Commons in that year, she was very popular, attracting 8,000 people to hear her speak at Maple Leaf Gardens in Toronto. She championed democracy, castigating the wartime government in Canada for eroding civil liberties. Nielsen had to struggle with all the problems facing a woman politician: her husband left her because he was unable or unwilling to look after their children while she was in Ottawa, so she had to board them in Saskatoon, then Winnipeg and finally Ottawa. She was not re-elected in 1945 in part because she had become a communist. She moved to Toronto to work for the Communist Party's Educational Department, then left Canada permanently to live in communist China.

Democracy Must Live! comprises Nielsen's collected addresses, mostly focused on ending poverty: "As long as people are living in poverty Canada is not a great nation. Actually the most subversive thing in Canada is poverty. I shall never forget why I was sent here [to Ottawa] and whom I represent."

New Worlds for Women, written after she joined the Labor-Progressive Party, discusses the status and role of women in Canada from a woman communist's perspective. Among the thirty-seven sketches are: Union activity in wartime, Baby bonuses, Children under foot, and What can a poor woman do?

Bibliography
•Nielsen, Dorise W., MP. 1940. *Democracy Must Live!* Toronto: Canadian Tribune Publishing, 62 pp.
•_____. 1944. *New Worlds for Women.* Toronto: Progress Books, 110 pp.

Northway, Mary Louise BA MA PhD DLitt 1909-1978. Mary Northway was born in Toronto to a businessman and his wife and attended Bishop Strachan School and the University of Toronto (BA 1933, MA 1934, PhD 1938 in psychology). She also studied at Cambridge University. She taught psychology at the University of Toronto from 1934 to 1968 (although she was designated an Assistant Professor only in 1946) as well as working in the Institute of Child Study where she was supervisor of research from 1953 to 1968. Like the others at the Institute, she was insistent that no kind of fear impede a child's learning. There was never any punishment for the children, nor even competition among them. The Institute tried instead to give the students the gift of time: "The unhurried mind rarely breaks; on the contrary, it often achieves. Creativity arises more often from serenity than from confusion. Education must delight as well as instruct the mind; children must experience not merely the jobs, but the joys of human living" (Northway 1966, 26). When the University of Toronto shortsightedly decided in 1968 to discontinue funding the longitudinal research for which the Institute had become famous, Northway was annoyed. She resigned to co-found the Brora Centre, carrying on her research there until her death. She was awarded an honorary degree by Trent University.

Northway's own research focused on measuring the development of social relationships. Since she loved outdoor life and camping, she carried out one study, written up in her book *Appraisal of the Social Development of Children*, using sociometric techniques on eighty children at Glen Bernard summer camp where she was program director; she asked them who were their preferred companions in various situations and noted how their friendships changed over a three-week interval. Northway states in her introduction to this book that "appraisal" is one of the most important problems of modern education. New methods of teaching and new theories of child development can be adopted, but they must be evaluated to see if they are worthwhile. She discusses the methodology of appraisal, indicating how it could be used in an elementary school setting. Along with over one hundred journal articles and reviews, Northway also wrote a basic text on sociometry (1952), the study of social relationships, based on her work with children.

Bibliography

•De la Cour, Lykke. 1987 (Winter). The 'Other' Side of Psychology: Women Psychologists in Toronto from 1920 to 1945. *Canadian Woman Studies* 8,4: 44-46.

•Northway, Mary L. PhD. 1940. *Appraisal of the Social Development of Children at a Summer Camp*. Toronto: University of Toronto, 62 pp.

•Northway, Mary L. 1966. *Laughter in the Front Hall*. Toronto: Longmans.

Norton, Sister Mary Aquinas BA PhD, nun. Mary Norton was a nun, a Sister of Saint Francis, who obtained her PhD from the Catholic University of America in Washington, DC. Her base was in Rochester, Minnesota.

Although her book *Catholic Missionary Activities in the Northwest*, a version of her PhD thesis, defines the Northwest as the terrain later incorporated into the states of Minnesota, North Dakota and South Dakota, the text deals extensively with the mission of St Boniface (now part of Winnipeg), established on the Red River in 1818. The mission of Pembina, of more ephemeral importance, was founded the same year under British auspices. The Hudson Bay Company soon realized, because of a boundary adjustment, that this mission was on American soil, so it was ordered evacuated. A Catholic missionary at this time, Norton writes, served mainly Indians and Métis, and "spent his days in a wilderness, travelling over hills and valleys, forests and prairies, marshes and swamps, rivers and lakes, and fallen trees. On foot, on snowshoes, on horseback, by dog train or canoe, he covered the vast expanse of territory under his care" (p. 139). His charges "felt his influence and profited by it in varying degrees."

Bibliography
•Norton, Sister Mary Aquinas. 1930. *Catholic Missionary Activities in the North-west 1818-1864.* Washington: Catholic University of America, 154 pp.

Nute, Grace Lee BA PhD 1895-1990. The American scholar Grace Nute, who taught history at Hamline University in St Paul from 1927 to 1960, was also a member of the Minnesota Historical Society's staff from 1921 to 1957.

In her extensive reading, Nute became so steeped in the ambience of the fur trade that her first book was *The Voyageur.* As she notes in her preface:

> Though he is one of the most colorful figures in the history of a great continent, the voyageur remains unknown to all but a few. This little [289 pp.] book seeks to do justice to his memory for the romance and color he has lent to American and Canadian history, and for the services he rendered in the exploration of the West.

The introduction to the reprint of Nute's *Caesars of the Wilderness* states that:

> Based on many years of research in repositories throughout France, England, and North America, [this book], with its skilful presentation of new evidence, settled many of the questions that had long puzzled scholars. Where others had been content to speculate, Grace Lee Nute grounded her book in authentic though obscure manuscript sources and thereby managed to separate theory from verifiable fact.

Nute was so captivated by Lake Superior that she visited it many times. In *Lake Superior*, as the editor notes, "she provides almost everything one could wish to know about Lake Superior, from its first fashioning in the workshop of Nature uncounted millions of years ago to the current year of 1944." It was one of a series of five books on the five Great Lakes.

Bibliography
- Nute, Grace Lee. 1931. *The Voyageur.* New York: Appleton, 289 pp.
- _____. 1978 [1943]. *Caesars of the Wilderness: Médard Chouart, Sieur des Groseilliers and Pierre Esprit Radisson, 1618-1710.* St Paul: Minnesota Historical Society Press, 386 pp.
- _____. 1944. *Lake Superior.* Indianapolis: Bobbs-Merrill, 376 pp.

Nutt, Elizabeth Styring FSAM, AMD, ARCA 1870-1946. Elizabeth Nutt was born in England and educated in Sheffield, where she studied and taught art from 1904 to 1919. Like Frederick Varley and Arthur Lismer before her, two members of the Canadian Group of Seven who had also studied at the Sheffield School of Art, she emigrated to Canada to serve as principal of the Victoria School of Art and Design in Halifax (which later became the Nova Scotia School of Art and Design). She was an activist, in 1922 helping found the Nova Scotia Society of Artists of which she was president in 1925. She was eager to share her experiences of art, founding the Citizens' Society in 1933 and writing extensively about it. She was a member of the Canadian Authors Association and of many art groups, with her art works exhibited throughout Canada and the United States.

The seventeen art lessons making up *"Significance"* first appeared in a series entitled "The Teaching of Pastel Work" in the English educational journal *The Schoolmistress.* She sees her book as "a plea for the rational appreciation of Drawing as a most valuable means whereby we may aid in unfolding the God-like in our children." She argues that drawing is not merely the perfection of the mechanical but the training of the mind: "if we begin with the emotion and interest ... uppermost in our minds, the mechanical will take care of itself, the mind will seek means whereby to express itself beautifully." Section titles include "The harmony of shapes" and "The dog-ness of the dog." Her title comes from her observation that "Line, Form, Tone and Colour all have Significance."

In the preface to *The World of Appearance Part II*, whose contents also in part appeared in *The Schoolmistress*, Nutt states "The War instead of paralysing effort has stimulated it and urges us to the sincere contemplation of the great Principle of Harmony which governs all that is permanent; and in no subject is its government more apparent than in art work." Her book endeavours "to state briefly and clearly some of the truths underlying the world of appearance, a knowledge of which is the birthright of every child." The eighteen chapters deal with such things as Light, shade and shadow; Surface appearances; Dull or lustreless objects; and Characteristics of glass. She includes a great deal of theory as well as sophisticated practical instruction.

Bibliography
•Nutt, Elizabeth Styring. 1916. *"Significance," or Flower Drawing with Children*. Sheffield: J.W. Northend, 111 pp.
•_____., FSAM (Eng) AMD (Sheffield, Eng), ARCA (Canada). 1935. *The World of Appearance Part II. The Representation of Solidity and of Surface Appearances and of Textures*. Sheffield: Parker Bros, 111 pp. (In this volume Nutt states that Parts I and III have not yet been published.)

O'Hara, Margaret MD LLD KIH 1855-1940. Maggie O'Hara was born on a farm in Lanark County, Ontario, and later based in Smiths Falls. She taught school before studying medicine, graduating from Queen's University (1891) and taking postgraduate study in New York. She served as a medical missionary for the Presbyterian Church of Canada in central India from 1891 to 1927; this area, when she graduated, had nine million people but only fourteen missionaries to work with them. Because of her medical knowledge and attractive personality she became close friends with the Dhar royal family and an adoptive mother to several Indian girls (Brouwer 1990). She received an LLD from Queen's University in 1932 and was awarded the Kaiser-i-Hind medal for her long and valued service to India. Despite being a doctor, her four main interests in life were the Presbyterian Church, Queen's University, the British Empire and India.

The introduction to O'Hara's *Leaf of the Lotus*, which comprises mostly her letters from the mission field written between 1891 and 1914, notes that "The people she was going among were not savages, they had an older civilization than our own, but they were the hardest class to reach with the gospel because of their polite indifference." It emphasizes her importance in aiding the sick, saving many lives, and being "a vital factor in helping to establish the Kingdom of God in Dhar, and in persuading men and women to yield allegiance to Christ."

Bibliography
•O'Hara, Margaret. 1931. *Leaf of the Lotus*. Toronto: John M. Poole, 188 pp.

Paget, Amelia Anne MacLean 1867-1922. Amelia MacLean was born and grew up in the North-West, spending eight years in Qu'Appelle, Saskatchewan, where her father was a factor with the Hudson's Bay Company. She learned to speak both Cree and Ojibway fluently. In 1885, during the second Riel Rebellion, the MacLean family was captured at Fort Pitt and held hostage by Indians for over a year. Much later, the Dominion Government gave a small amount of money to Paget, now married to a man in the Department of Indian Affairs, to document information about Indians.

In *The People of the Plains*, Paget is a staunch advocate of aboriginal peoples, describing their way of life as she had observed it for many years and recounting some of their myths and legends.

Bibliography

•Paget, Amelia M. 1909. *The People of the Plains*. Toronto: Ryerson, 199 pp.

Palk, Helen. Helen Palk, an educator interested in Canadian history, published *The Book of Canadian Achievement* in 1951.

Palk's *Pages from Canada's Geography* was written for children of grades 5 and 6. She states that "In this book an attempt has been made to vitalize the study of [history and geography] by uniting them in the real social experience of travel." She invites her readers to join her in her tour of Canada, beginning in Nova Scotia and ending in British Columbia, with the north omitted. She describes only those places and industries that appeal in some way to young readers, with history suggested rather than detailed.

My Country's Story Book 1 is composed of many short items, each about a page long. In "Women of New France" (p. 204), the authors announce that:

> Canadian women have, from the earliest times, been the partners and comrades of their husbands. Canadian wives have always helped their husbands out of doors; and Canadian husbands help their wives in the house. It is this fine comradeship between the fathers and mothers which makes Canadian homes the happiest in the world.

Book 2 focuses on English-Canada; in keeping with its revision for use by Catholic schools, the section entitled "Builders of the Church in Western Canada" deals only with the Roman Catholic Church. It comprises chapters on the Church of St Boniface in Manitoba, the Mission of the Oblate Fathers to Native peoples, and the Grey Nuns.

Bibliography

•Palk, Helen. 1939. *Pages from Canada's Geography*. Toronto: Dent, 383 pp.
•Dickie, D.J., Helen Palk and E.C. Woodley. 1952 [1941]. *My Country's Story. Book 1, The French Colonial Period*, 224 pp; *Book 2, English Colonial Period and the Dominion of Canada*, 294 pp. Toronto: Dent, 224 pp. Revised and adapted for use in Catholic Schools.

Peat, Louisa Watson d. 1953. Louisa Peat was an American who lived in Canada during the Second World War.

Because Peat was aware that Canada was composed of many contradictions, she felt it important that these be explained to neighbouring Americans: "It is imperative that Canada be understood, as a people, as a country, a nation, a potential world power, an ally and a friend." She describes the Canada she experienced while at war in *Canada: New World Power* in twenty chapters with titles such as "Her Twelve Million People," "Our Distinctive French," "Drama of the Doukhobor" and "Canadian Women See It Through."

Bibliography

•Peat, Louisa W. 1945. *Canada: New World Power*. New York: National Travel Club, 293 pp.

Peck, Anne Merriman 1884-?   Anne Merriam Peck was born in New York State, the daughter of a clergyman and his wife. She attended art school and later taught drawing and writing at the extension division of the University of Arizona. With the birth of her son, she became interested in writing children's literature; she herself illustrated many of her children's books, some of which focused on different regions of the world she had visited, such as Germany, Europe, America and Mexico, as well as Canada.

Young Canada is less a history of the country than a description of its various regions as they existed just before the Second World War. She focuses on individual children in each region to make the book especially pertinent to young readers. It thus begins with Peter and Johnny, two boys she met while in Canada, helping a Lunenburg fisherman mend nets. Her major aim was to make Americans better friends with Canadians: "to become really acquainted with our neighbors we must visit them, learn to know their customs, the land they live in, and to share their interest."

In *The Pageant of Canadian History*, Peck envisions Canada as a panorama so she does not describe it chronologically but "in big sweeps of movements"—French exploration and social life, other explorers and traders, the growth of British settlements, etc. It was written "for my fellow Americans, to pass on my discovery of the vivid history of our northern neighbors and my admiration for them." She also, of course, hopes her book will be bought and read by Canadians.

Bibliography

•Peck, Anne Merriman. 1943. *Young Canada*. New York: Robert M. McBride, 248 pp.
•_____. 1943. *The Pageant of Canadian History*. New York: Longmans, Green, 370 pp.

Pellerin, Maude Gage 1884-? See Price, Bertha Weston entry.

Pepper, Mary Sifton d. 1908. Mary Pepper was a Canadian author interested in history.

Pepper was annoyed that the nineteen pioneer women who landed as Pilgrim mothers at Plymouth Rock in the United States in 1620 have been celebrated in romance and poetry, while those who helped found Canada are virtually forgotten. She describes in *Maids and Matrons of New France* the four important periods of pioneering women in Canada: the first attempts beginning in 1604 of colonization in Acadia, Quebec's struggles to gain a foothold between 1608 and 1660, the founding of Montreal in 1642, and the advent of the Carignan regiment into Canada in 1665.

Bibliography
•Pepper, Mary Sifton. 1901. *Maids and Matrons of New France.* Boston: Little, Brown, 286 pp.

Perkins, Charlotte Isabella 1878-? Charlotte Perkins was so interested in local history, especially that of her hometown Annapolis Royal, Nova Scotia, that she prepared pamphlets describing it.

Perkins's *The Romance of Old Annapolis Royal* comprises an updated compilation of these pamphlets which had been "favourably received." She gives an overview of the town's past, then discusses the history of the important houses, churches and schools using material she obtained from archival sources and old-timers. She notes that early private schools were

> conducted by maiden ladies who were anxious to eke out a living from their scanty store of knowledge. They taught girls and small boys and usually in a room in their own home where it would be convenient "to watch the pot boiling" at the same time. It was not considered necessary for girls to have too much education; if they mastered the "Three R's" and worked a sampler they were sufficiently finished scholars.

Bibliography
•Perkins, Charlotte Isabella. 1934. *The Romance of Old Annapolis Royal, Nova Scotia.* N.p., 101 pp.

Pickford, Mary 1892-1979. Gladys Louise Smith, later known as Mary Pickford, became the best-known woman in the world in the 1920s because of her acting roles in over 190 movies. She was born in Toronto to a working couple. Her father died when she was six, leaving her mother, invalid grandmother, brother, sister and herself almost destitute. Because she was a theatrical child, Gladys was delighted to act in melodramas on Toronto stages such as the Royal Alexandra, beginning when she was seven. She had often been sick when younger so she was as yet unable to read, meaning that her mother had to read her lines to her which she then memorized. Gladys took part in a number of plays, eventually touring for five years around the continent with her family in a repertory company, her adult height of five feet allowing her to play children's roles for many years. When she was seventeen, she began to act in silent movies where she was a great success as "America's Sweetheart." She married Douglas Fairbanks in 1920, setting up with him a Hollywood house, Pickfair, which became widely celebrated. The couple, along with Charlie Chaplin and director D.W. Griffith, formed United Artists, which would make and distribute films. With the arrival in the late 1920s of talking movies, which did not suit her, Pickford's movie career ended. After her marriage also broke down, she wed actor Buddy Rogers in 1937, a marriage which lasted forty-three years. She was unable to have children, so they adopted a son and a daughter. Although her interest in Christianity was sparked by evangelist Mary Baker Eddy, her later years were spent as an alcoholic recluse; she hoped to have the films in which she acted destroyed so that she would not be remembered by modern viewers as ludicrous. In 1935 Pickford published her autobiography, *My Rendezvous with Life*, to give her own perspective on her career; this was followed in 1956 by another, *Sunshine and Shadow*, which appeared a year after her booklet called *Why Not Try God?*

Bibliography

•Whitfield, Eileen. 1997. *Pickford: The Woman Who Made Hollywood*. Toronto: Macfarlane Walter and Ross.
Pickford, Mary. 1935. *My Rendezvous with Life*. New York: H.C. Kinsey, 441 pp.

Pincock, Jenny O'Hara 1890-1948.   Jenny Pincock, who lived in St Catharines, Ontario, and was the author of stories and poems, was distraught after her husband, Robert Newton Pincock, died in May 1928. She desperately wanted to keep in touch with him, so she and some friends persuaded a medium, William Cartheuser (who had a wide reputation and was endorsed by the Society for Psychical Research of New York City), to come and help them organize seances, many of which were held at her home. About seventy individuals were involved, all but two listed in her book by name; nearly all were convinced that communication with the dead was possible. She later was involved with the Radiant Healing Centre of St Catharines, an institution founded on a belief in the ability of the spirit to promote healing, and was the first editor between 1932 and 1935 of a number of issues of its journal, *Progression*.

Pincock's book *The Trails of Truth* is made up of accounts of seances giving time and place, who attended, and what happened, including conversations among "Spirit," named spirits and witnesses; Pincock states that she talked with her dead husband on ten occasions. The foreword states that it is "the voice of multiplied testimony from a body of educated and truth-loving witnesses to events that happened in their presence and in which they took an active part, proving conclusively that the so-called dead are consciously alive and often in close contact with us, are deeply interested in us, loving and helping, and retain their old-time characteristics, affections, manners and peculiarities." Many of us would like this to be true.

Bibliography
•Pincock, Jenny O'Hara. 1930. *The Trails of Truth*. Los Angeles: Austin, 396 pp.

Pinkerton, Kathrene Sutherland Gedney BA 1887-1967. Kathrene Gedney grew up in Milwaukee, one of four children, and graduated from the University of Wisconsin in 1909 with a degree in public health. In 1911 she married Robert Pinkerton, a journalist and outdoorsman whose uncertain health necessitated that they live, with their newborn daughter, for five years in the backwoods of western Ontario near Atikokan. The couple survived mainly on the money they earned from the articles and books they wrote. During the next twenty-five years of their marriage they travelled west and lived in a number of states, primarily California, and later cruised by yacht in the north Pacific Ocean. Pinkerton's books about their adventures were published years later, after they had settled down.

Woodcraft for Women is a distillation of what Pinkerton learned from her years of living in the wild because she wanted to encourage women to enjoy the outdoors as men did. She notes (p. 13): "Resolved to its essentials, woodcraft is a game, and, like all games, becomes most fascinating when we win. Nature is our opponent. To force from her comfort and pleasure means victory. The greater our ease and skill and power of adaptation, the quicker and the sweeter the rewards." Her book gives women the information they need to appreciate the wilderness.

In *Wilderness Wife*, Pinkerton describes her life in the Canadian backwoods north of Lake Superior when she and her husband first moved north. They built a cabin miles from the nearest town and pioneered there for three years, making money by writing stories and articles. This book was republished in 1976 as *A Life in the Wilds*.

In *Three's a Crew*, Pinkerton describes cruising in two successive yachts in the waters of British Columbia and Alaska over a seven-year period, the three being her husband, her nine-to-sixteen-year-old daughter Bobs, and herself. She recounts dodging whales in case their boat should be overturned, avoiding icebergs, feeding seals, and visiting rivers choked with salmon.

Two Ends to Our Shoestring is the story of the Pinkertons' first thirty years of marriage, during which the couple lived first in wilderness Canada north of Lake Superior, and then travelled to and through many parts of the United States, including Alaska. Their story is told with humour, although there is a tension between being productive writers, being good parents and maintaining a wandering lifestyle.

Bibliography

•Pinkerton, Kathrene. 1916. *Woodcraft for Women*. Outdoor Handbooks No. 41. New York: Outing Publishing, 174 pp.

•_____. 1939. *Wilderness Wife*. New York: Carrick and Evans, 327 pp.

•_____. 1940. *Three's a Crew*. New York: Carrick and Evans, 316 pp.

•_____. 1941. *Two Ends to Our Shoestring*. New York: Harcourt, Brace, 362 pp.

Platt, Harriet Louisa Williams d. 1914. Harriet Platt, who was married, was the President of the Bay of Quinte (Ontario) Branch of the Woman's Missionary Society of the Methodist Church.

Platt was asked to write *The Story of the Years* about this Society because of her "well-known literary ability." She notes in the preface:

> To save from oblivion the record of brave deeds and patient endurance, is to furnish our Church with an added motive for earnest, aggressive work in the future; hence it is our hope and prayer that the story of our twenty-five years may stimulate to loving, sympathetic service, not only our present Woman's Missionary Society membership, but a much wider circle of Christian woman.

This history is based on missionaries' letters and on annual reports. The introduction explains that women's missionary work has been instrumental in expanding the lives of many white women, especially those unmarried:

> Their ideals have changed; individual responsibility for the betterment of the world, both at home and abroad, has been borne in upon them, and the growing power of being able to bring things to pass, of planning and of being responsible for the carrying of such plans to successful completion, has given to them an added dignity, a new courage, a more intelligent devotion, and a deeper spiritual life.

Missionary women benefitted others as well as themselves, bringing "female education" and respect for women to many cultures.

Bibliography

•Platt, Harriet Louise. 1908. *The Story of the Years: A History of the Woman's Missionary Society of the Methodist Church, Canada, 1881-1906*. Vol. 1—Canada. 2nd ed. Toronto: Woman's Missionary Society Methodist Church, Canadian Wesley Buildings, 154 pp.

Plummer, Mary Wright 1856-1916. Mary Plummer was an author who visited Canada to gather material for a children's book.

Plummer wrote *Roy and Ray in Canada* because her earlier book about the twelve-year-old twin boys, *Roy and Ray in Mexico*, had proven successful. Its successor is a "record of a summer recently spent in the eastern part of the Dominion of Canada." The text, most of it stilted conversation among the family, tells the story of the twins setting off from New Jersey with their father and sister (Dora) to see what eastern Canada is like and to learn something about its history. They travel mostly by train, enlightened as they go by their intellectual father.

Bibliography

•Plummer, Mary Wright. 1908. *Roy and Ray in Canada*. New York: Henry Holt, 395 pp.

Pomeroy, Elsie May 1886-? Elsie Pomeroy was born in Fullarton, Ontario, and educated in nearby Mitchell and at Stratford Normal School. She was a teacher at King Edward Public School in Toronto, a friend of school supervisor **Aletta Marty**, and an ardent supporter of Canadian literature. She was also active in teacher organizations and in the Canadian Authors Association, where she came to know and admire Charles G.D. Roberts (1860-1943); it was he who persuaded her to join this group of which he was president from 1927 to 1929, and to write his biography. Just before he died in 1943, the year her biography was published, Roberts married a woman fifty years younger than he, which upset Pomeroy. She went on to write several other books, including *William Saunders and His Five Sons* (1956), about the Marquis wheat family. (In the introduction to this book she is lauded because she approaches biogaphy "in a serious mood and not as a pastime.")

Roberts was anxious that his biography be written, but that it not be written by his son Lloyd, whom he did not trust to put the correct slant on his life. He therefore worked closely with Pomeroy on her authorized biography, *Sir Charles G.D. Roberts*, noting in a letter that "it is almost a sort of *camouflaged autobiography*" (Adams 1986, 195). She consulted members of his family, former students, and friends who showed her hospitality when she visited places associated with his early life. Although Roberts was over twenty-five years older than Pomeroy, he was known to be attracted and attractive to women and feared that there would be gossip about them when Pomeroy's highly laudatory book was published. He therefore asked her to have her name appear as E.M. Pomeroy on the title page, which she agreed to do.

Bibliography
•Adams, John Coldwell. 1986. *Sir Charles God Damn*. Toronto: University of
    Toronto Press.
•Pomeroy, E.M. 1943. *Sir Charles G.D. Roberts: A Biography*. Toronto: Ryerson,
    371 pp.

Poole, Evelyn Lavina 1907-? Evelyn Poole from Wilton Grove, Ontario,
graduated in 1926 from London Normal School while specializing in
English, then taught in Dorchester Township, where she was active in
United Church work with young people.

Poole was a member of the MacFarlane clan, about which she writes in
History of the MacFarlanes, compiling descriptions of how clan members
had spent their lives. The brief biographies begin with those of John
(1802-81) and Isabella Henderson (1810-95) MacFarlane, who came to
southwest Ontario from Argyllshire, Scotland, in 1842. They continue with
a brief history of each of their children, and in turn of their offspring. Some
descriptions are brief—as one member remarked, "The Scotch strain in us
makes us too canny to reveal our weaknesses and too modest to reveal our
accomplishments!" The book had a limited printing of one hundred copies.

Bibliography
•Poole, Evelyn Lavina. 1931. *History of the MacFarlanes 1831-1931*. London,
    ON: private, 79 pp.

Portlock, Rosa Elliott 1839-1928. Rosa Portlock was a religious woman
who came from Woodstock, but lived as an adult in nearby Berlin (Kitchener), Ontario. One of her books was a novel set in England, *The Head
Keeper* (1898), the title referring to God, who is an integral part of the
story.

Portlock wrote about her neighbours and their activities in *Twenty-five
Years of Canadian Life*, interlarding her observations with philosophical
comments and quotes taken from the Bible. She notes in her introduction,
"There are questions of the day to answer, and I feel I should be a coward
if I did not try to meet them. Yet the attempt to do so may be considered
presumptuous on the part of one in so humble a position, but most things
come from small beginnings." She ruminates on the Boer War, noting "the
Boers have no sense of honor; they will keep no oath of loyalty one
moment beyond their own convenience, but will take the first chance to
make an attack in spite of it. It is hard to make peace with an enemy of that
kind, or with those who hate us as the Boers do. Yet South Africa is
Christ's, and must be added to His kingdom. A patched-up peace would be
in vain. We must be patient, then, until God is pleased to put down our enemies."

Bibliography

•Portlock, Mrs Rosa. 1901. *Twenty-five Years of Canadian Life with a Study on Bible Prophecy*. Toronto: Briggs. 195 pp.

Powell, M. Viola. Viola Powell was a member of the Women's Institute in Ontario who was asked to write a history of the movement.

Laura Rose Stephen, the first government lecturer and organizer of Women's Institutes, writes about *Forty Years Agrowing* that "Miss Powell has the keen mind, the exceptional ability, the rare sympathetic understanding and quiet perseverance, that has made her well-fitted for the task of giving to the world this concise account of the Women's Institute Movement in Canada"—"the largest and most wide spread single organization for women, that we know of, in the world." Women's Institutes, founded by **Adelaide Hoodless**, were initially considered a feminine version of Farmers' Institutes for men, but gradually they acquired their own agenda (Ambrose 1996, 34). Viola Powell describes, along with their history, their contribution to rural women in matters of health, culture and recreation.

Bibliography

•Powell, M. Viola. 1941. *Forty Years Agrowing: A History of Ontario Women's Institutes*. Port Perry, ON: Port Perry Star, 96 pp.

Pratt, Viola Leone Whitney BA DLittS 1892-1984. Viola Whitney grew up in Atherley, Ontario, and attended Victoria University in Toronto, where she was editor of the student newspaper *Acta Victoriana* and winner of the gold medal in English. She taught school for five years, then married E.J. Pratt, the poet and later professor at her alma mater. Her religious nature was reflected in her activity in the United Church as editor of the young people's magazine *World Friends* (from 1929 to 1955) and as author of one of its study guides for the young, *One Family*. She was also an essayist and public speaker, focusing on biblical themes, history through the ages and literary criticism (Pratt 1990b). In 1956 Victoria University honoured her with a Doctorate of Sacred Letters. Among her literary friends were **Mary Quayle Innis** and **Margaret Laurence**, whom she and her daughter, her only child and herself a poet, artist and editor, visited in England. The Pratts also visited **Jenny Pincock** in St Catharines to attend a seance where they believed that two children from her miscarriages contacted them; she wrote up this experience for Pincock's *The Trails of Truth*. Viola Pratt loved all living things, but especially gardens and birds, which she commemorated by collecting bird poems and bird stamps.

Because the overall study topic of the United Church in the mid-1930s was the family atmosphere it hoped to create among its many missions, Pratt wrote her book on this theme using the title *One Family*; she wanted children in their study sessions to "increase in wisdom and stature and in favour with God and man" [*sic*]. Each chapter, comprising material for one meeting, focuses on a particular subject, including mission stations in Africa, India, China, Japan, Korea and Trinidad; to accompany each lesson, Pratt includes ideas for plays, games, posters and projects. She hopes her book will be fun for children and "that it may help to forge a link in that golden chain which will eventually bind together all the children of the earth in loving fellowship within the Family of God."

Bibliography
- Pratt, Viola Whitney. 1937. *One Family*. Toronto: Woman's Missionary Society, 96 pp.
- _____. 1990 . *Viola Whitney Pratt: A Testament of Love*. Edited by Mildred Claire Pratt. Toronto: Lugus Productions.
- _____. 1990 . *Viola Whitney Pratt: Papers and Speeches*. Edited by Mildred Claire Pratt. Toronto: Lugus Productions.

Price, Bertha Maud Weston 1872-1955.   Bertha Weston was born and educated in the Eastern Townships of Quebec, becoming a journalist with training in music and French. She married George Price in 1891 and had five children, but continued writing articles and children's stories from her home in Sherbrooke. She was on the staff of *The Sherbrooke Daily Record*, which shortly before her death published a series of articles on local history collected into a book entitled *Glimpses into the Past* (1950). In keeping with her literary interests, she was a member of the Canadian Authors Association and the Canadian Women's Press Club.

Price wrote the stories that make up *Legends of Our Lakes and Rivers* at her cottage on Lake Massawippi; this book was a revised and enlarged version of the earlier *Legends of Our Lakes* (1923). In her preface, she notes that these legends from Old Quebec come "from the keen minds and love of adventure evident in earliest dwellers in our lands, some of them filled with weird imaginings, others of a practical tone, but all showing the desire to pass on to coming generations real, or fancied stories of Nature and her children." She obtained the legends in part from early residents of the Eastern Townships in Quebec and is also indebted to "quaint traditions treasured by the Indians, the first dwellers in Canada." She regrets in her finale "that in many parts of Canada there have not been retained more of the 'whims and fancies' of the old days when people were prone to think of, talk of, and to pass on to their children quaint stories of their own long ago."

Price and her friend Maude Pellerin (from Hatley, Quebec) published *The Trail of the Broad Highway*, a compilation of prose and poetry, themselves, because they wanted to share with their readers "the wonderful heritage in Beauty and History, and the unlimited possibilities in Industry which the Counties of Stanstead and Sherbrooke [in the Eastern Townships of Quebec] possess." They write:

> If we have so far succeeded as to inspire in the hearts of residents of these, our own counties, a greater love and loyalty; if we have created in the minds of those not already familiar with this locality a desire to view the unsurpassed scenery along the Trail of the Broad Highway [the Derby Line-Sherbrooke Highway], and to enjoy the pleasures and hospitality awaiting them here on every hand, we are indeed happy and the purpose of this book has been accomplished.

They end the acknowledgements, after thanking the many people who provided them with information: "Throughout the volume we have aimed to be sincere."

Bibliography
- Price, Bertha Weston. 1937 [1923] *Legends of Our Lakes and Rivers*. Lennoxville, QC: Beck Press, 58 pp. Rev. ed.
- Price, Bertha Weston and Maude Gage Pellerin. 1929. *The Trail of the Broad Highway*. Sherbrooke: Authors, 121 pp.

Price, Elizabeth Bailey 1885-1944. Elizabeth Bailey Price, born in Winnipeg, began her career as a teacher, but soon switched to journalism. She served as an editor, then moved to Calgary where she wrote syndicated articles about pioneer life in the West. Price was elected national president of the Canadian Women's Press Club in 1932.

Price worked closely with **Martha Black** to ghost write her 1938 autobiography *My Seventy Years*.

Price, Enid Margaret BA MA. Enid Price was born in Toronto to a Canadian Pacific Railway employee and his wife. She attended school in many parts of Canada before enrolling at McGill University. For her master's degree, she studied with economist Stephen Leacock, who was doubtful that women could be scholars, but allowed her to follow her own interest in the experience of women who entered the labour force during the First World War. She was supported by the Canadian Reconstruction Association (whose head of the Women's Department was **Marjory MacMurchy**), which in 1918 offered three scholarships for Canadian women graduates at three Canadian universities—Toronto, Manitoba and McGill:

> The scholarships were offered in the belief that the careful, sympathetic and trained investigation of women's work by women graduates is one of the most effective methods by which the economic and industrial well-being of women may be secured. The data collected and presented will

lead, it is believed, to further study and a clearer understanding of women's employment.

The topics for research had to deal with homemaking or industrial employment for women. In 1922 Price married Allan Turner Bone, a construction engineer she had met at McGill, with whom she travelled extensively before settling down in Montreal to raise a family. She was president of the National Council of Women from 1951 to 1956, beginning her service in the local council of Montreal, where she worked in both French and English for causes such as votes for women.

Using statistics and interviews in her master's research, Price investigated the relative number of males and females employed before and during the war, women's wages before and during the war, the background of working women, the number of French Canadians in industrial work, and the proportion of married and unmarried women workers. She found among other things that women's wages were less than men's for the same work, and concludes simplistically that "The experience gained through the war period has shown woman her shortcomings and her attributes. If she profits by her knowledge, the future holds all that she may desire in the variety of occupation and adequate compensation." Her analysis appears in her short book *Changes in the Industrial Occupations of Women*.

The same year Price published *Industrial Occupations of Women*, which also was based on material from her thesis.

Bibliography
•Price, Enid M., BA. 1919 . *Changes in the Industrial Occupations of Women in the Environment of Montreal during the Period of 1914-1918*. Montreal: Canadian Reconstruction Association, 86 pp.
•_____. 1919 . *Industrial Occupations of Women*. Montreal: Canadian Reconstruction Association, 86 pp.

Pringle, Gertrude Edwina Seton Thompson. Gertrude Pringle, a long-time believer in social niceties, was educated in Toronto and Switzerland. As a journalist she was active in the Canadian Authors Association and in writing articles and columns for magazines and newspapers. She kept lodgers, two of whom were **Mazo de la Roche** and her cousin Caroline Clement. Because she was impressed by de la Roche's writing, she acted informally as her social secretary and guardian of her privacy during 1927, when de la Roche rose to fame by winning the *Atlantic Monthly* prize for her novel *Jalna*. In keeping with her social standards, Pringle perceived de la Roche as of aristocratic European ancestry (rather than someone born in Newmarket, whose parents had belonged to the working class), and treated her accordingly (Givner 1989, 117-18).

Pringle begins the preface to *Etiquette in Canada*: "That there is real need of authentic information on etiquette, as followed by representative society in Canada, has been proved conclusively by my ten years' experience in conducting an information column in leading Canadian magazines and in a daily newspaper." This book is the first to consider social usage in Canada; Pringle felt that etiquette described in American books was not entirely suitable, although it had gained exposure thanks to moving pictures, and that British etiquette was too general. She emphasizes that "the information in this book has been obtained from many Canadian sources—social, official, judicial and literary."

Bibliography
•Pringle, Gertrude. 1932. *Etiquette in Canada: The Blue Book of Canadian Social Usage*. Toronto: McClelland and Stewart, 447 pp.

Pullen-Burry, Bessie FRAI, FRGS 1858-1937   Pullen-Burry, a British imperialist educated in Brighton and Germany, devoted her life to travel, visiting Europe, the Holy Land, Africa, India, Japan, Australasia, the West Indies, the United States and Canada. Because of her experiences, which she described in her books, she was made a Fellow of the Royal Anthropological Institute and of the Royal Geographical Society, and president (1912) of the first union of women interested in geography. She lectured widely about foreign countries and about the "Negro Race" under British and American rule.

Her 1911 trip to Canada depicted in *From Halifax to Vancouver* lasted several months. She sailed from Liverpool, disembarking in Quebec, then visiting the Maritime provinces before taking the train west. Her aim for her large volume of impressions was to promote "a greater interest in, and a better understanding of the vast and magnificent Dominion of Canada." She gives many opinions on the status of women, possible immigration, economic development and other issues. During her trip she was introduced to many fellow authors, including **Katherine Hughes, Margaret McNaughton, Emily Murphy, Amelia Paget** and **Marshall Saunders.**

Bibliography
•Pullen-Burry, B. 1912. *From Halifax to Vancouver*. London: Mills and Boon, 352 pp.

Putnam, Ada MacLeod.   Ada Putnam was a religious woman living in Prince Edward Island.

Putnam's *The Selkirk Settlers* is about St John's Presbyterian Church (completed in 1824) in Belfast, PEI, and its adherents. The founder of the colony that erected the church was Thomas Douglas, born in 1771 in Scotland, who as a young man was a friend of Walter Scott. Following the death of six older brothers, Douglas became, at twenty-six, the fifth Earl of Selkirk and decided to use his inheritance to help destitute Scottish farmers immigrate to a large tract of land in Prince Edward Island. As the British government was uninterested in his scheme, he himself chartered three sailing vessels to transport eight hundred men, women and children to North America. Putnam describes the settlers, their church, and its ministers, ending her book with a list of ten men from the parish who entered the Christian ministry and "one medical missionary, Dr Annie Young, who labored for many years in India."

Bibliography
•Putnam, Ada MacLeod. 1939. *The Selkirk Settlers and the Church They Built at Belfast*. Toronto: Presbyterian Publications, 57 pp.

Radforth, Isobel. Isobel Radforth was a scientist interested in fish.

Radforth's *Considerations on the Distribution of Fishes in Ontario* is a scientific treatise beginning with a geological history of the lakes and rivers of the province following the final retreat of the glacier from 20,000 to 35,000 years ago. She lumps together kinds of fish with similar distributions in the province; for example, about one-sixth of the species, twenty-four, are found virtually everywhere in Ontario, while other groups include species found potentially everywhere, or only in restricted regions. Some fish are derived from saltwater species, and some have been introduced into Ontario by human beings.

Bibliography
•Radforth, Isobel. 1944. *Some Considerations on the Distribution of Fishes in Ontario*. Toronto: University of Toronto Press, 116 pp.

Ratcliffe, Dorothy Una 1891-1967. Dorothy Ratcliffe, a popular British poet (for example, her book of children's poetry *Nightlights* [1929]) and author of a number of books about northern England, visited Canada in autumn to write a book about this experience.

To the Blue Canadian Hills, dedicated in part to her children, describes a week in early October that she and her reluctant husband spent near Timiskaming, travelling by foot, canoe and motorboat and staying in rustic camps. She elected to donate the profits from her travelogue to the Canadian Red Cross Society.

Bibliography
•Ratcliffe, Dorothy Una, FRAS, FRGS. 1928. *To the Blue Canadian Hills: A Week's Log in a Northern Quebec Camp*. Leeds: North Country Press, 90 pp.

Ravenhill, Alice 1859-1954.   Alice Ravenhill lived and worked for fifty years in Britain before moving with her sister in 1910 to Vancouver Island to help look after her nephew who wanted to homestead there. Her British professional career was "a story of constant growth and change: she moved from the teaching of public health and sanitation into administrative work in nursing; thence into the opening field of home economics, in schools and universities; and finally into the study of Indian life and culture." In all these areas she published books and articles. In her first years in Canada, Ravenhill carried on her earlier work to some extent, publishing informational bulletins for the British Columbia Department of Agriculture and giving lectures to Women's Institute groups and others. In general, however, she found Canada very conservative and sexist, with no institutions willing to take full advantage of her extensive knowledge and experience. In 1926 she became so interested in the arts and crafts of Native tribes of the province that she began to reproduce tribal designs in needlework on hooked rugs, cushions and bags; ten years later, when her work was well-known, she was asked to introduce the subject of Native crafts to students at the Victoria Normal School. On enquiring into this request, she learned that an eight-week course on B.C. Indians had recently been included in the grade school curriculum, although no appropriate book to teach it was available; she therefore volunteered to write a textbook. Later she produced a book on Indian crafts. She completed her memoirs when she was ninety-two.

Following her arrangement with the Provincial Department of Education to write a text on Indians, Ravenhill produced *The Native Tribes of British Columbia*, based on her many years of study.

Ravenhill was commissioned by the Indian Affairs Branch to prepare *A Corner Stone of Canadian Culture* along with twenty large wall charts "showing examples of the arts and crafts formerly practised by the Indian Tribes of this Province," including information on mythical beings, masks, paintings, carvings, basketry and weaving; it was intended to give teachers and students "a record of former tribal decorative arts and crafts which have possibilities of further development and utilization in modern life." Interest in the book was so great that it was also made available to other institutions and to the general public. The Indian Affairs Office in Ottawa believed "that Canadian Indians have a real contribution to make to the prosperity of the Dominion . . . by the exercise of their innate gifts of conception, technique and intelligence."

Bibliography
•Ravenhill, Alice. 1938. *The Native Tribes of British Columbia*. Victoria: C.F. Banfield, 142 pp.
•_____. 1944. *A Corner Stone of Canadian Culture: An Outline of the Arts and Crafts of the Indian Tribes of British Columbia*. Victoria: British Columbia Provincial Museum, 103 pp.
•_____. 1951. *Alice Ravenhill: The Memoirs of an Educational Pioneer*. Toronto: Dent, 241 pp.

Rayleigh, Clara Elizabeth La Touche Vicars Strutt, baroness d. 1900. Lady Clara Rayleigh was the wife of Lord Rayleigh, president-elect of the British Association, a group of male scientists; (Lord Rayleigh was noted for his mathematical work on the dynamics of blue sky). In 1884, the annual gathering of this association was held in Montreal, the first time it had met outside the United Kingdom, with an attendance of about 750, many subsidized by the British government. Following the meetings, the group travelled by train to western Canada before visiting the United States.

Rayleigh's book *The British Association's Visit to Montreal* is a collection of letters that she wrote home to her mother in England, the first six describing Canada, and the rest detailing the United States. It begins with a description of the meetings themselves, at which Sir John A. Macdonald spoke. She then depicts the journey across most of Canada, pausing near Winnipeg when a trestle bridge gave way, and ending at the Columbia River where they saw track being laid which would soon complete the cross-Canada railway.

Bibliography
•Rayleigh, Clara Lady. 1885. *The British Association's Visit to Montreal, 1884; Letters by Clara Lady Rayleigh*. London: Whitehead, Morris and Lowe, 119 pp.

Raymond, Ethel T. d. 1960. Ethel Raymond, who lived in Hamilton, was a member of the Hamilton Branch of the Canadian Women's Press Club and researched topics of interest in Canadian history.

Raymond's biography *Tecumseh*, of the great Shawnee war chief, is part of the thirty-two-volume Chronicles of Canada series. Tecumseh (1768-1813) fought with the British in the War of 1812, but "it was for the lost cause" of his own people for which he and his thousand warriors were really fighting, and of course in vain. He was killed in battle at what is now Thamesville, Ontario, after the British had broken ranks and fled. Unlike Brock, who also died while fighting, Tecumseh was not given a state funeral but was buried without ceremony by his friends in an unmarked grave.

Bibliography
•Raymond, Ethel T. 1915. *Tecumseh: A Chronicle of the Last Great Leader of His People*. Toronto: University of Toronto Press, 159 pp.

Read, Blanche Goodall 1866-? See Johnston, Blanche Read entry. Blanche Read's *The Life of John Read* is the biography of her husband John (1862-98) who died young and was, like her, an officer in the Salvation Army. She notes in the preface of her "little volume":

> My story is told—simply and I fear imperfectly—but if this perpetuation of my now sainted husband's memory proves a stimulus to his comrades in the holy warfare, and an incentive to more devoted service, and inspires our readers to more fully consecrate their lives to the Lord, I shall feel that the two purposes which activated me in attempting to write this biography have been realized.

Bibliography
•Read, Blanche J. 1899. *The Life of John Read*. Toronto: Salvation Army, 181 pp.

Reid, Edith Gittings 1863-? Edith Gittings was born and lived in Baltimore, where she married when she was twenty. Because of her interest in medicine, she wrote several biographies of medical doctors.

The Great Physician is the story of the famous Dr (later Sir) William Osler (1849-1919) who was born in Canada, trained at McGill University and worked in Montreal until 1884. The book is based in part on a longer, more chronological and definitive life, but as Reid states, "there are those who did not know him who might be deterred by its length, and it has been thought desirable to publish a shorter 'Life.' " She quotes mainly from his addresses and essays, finding them more intimate than his letters. Reid's later book was *The Life and Convictions of William Sydney Thayer, Physician* (1936).

Bibliography
•Reid, Edith Gittings. 1931. *The Great Physician: A Short Life of Sir William Osler*. New York: Oxford University Press, 299 pp.

Reid, Helen Richmond Young BA LLD CBE 1869-1941. Helen Reid was born in Montreal, received a BA and gold medal in 1899 from McGill University (where later she would serve as a governing fellow for fifteen years), and also studied in Germany and Switzerland. She became director of the Montreal School of Social Work and of the Montreal Child Welfare Association, as well as maintaining connections with many other related associations. During the First World War she organized Montreal's Patriotic Fund, and afterward was appointed a member of the federal Repatriation Committee. She was awarded an LLD from Queen's in 1916 for her civic work, and in 1935 a CBE.

Reid co-authored *The Japanese Canadians* based on her involvement with the National Committee for Mental Hygiene in Canada which studied first the problems of Ukrainian Canadians and then those of Japanese Canadians. Her co-author was Charles Young, who had carried out extensive work with Japanese people in British Columbia. Reid is thanked in the preface for her effort in seeing Part 1 of the book through the press.

Bibliography
• Young, Charles H., and Helen R.Y. Reid. 1938. *The Japanese Canadians*. Toronto: University of Toronto Press, 295 pp., edited by H.A. Innis.

Repplier, Agnes DLitt 1855-1950. Agnes Repplier was an American, born in Philadelphia to a middle-class Roman Catholic family. She did not learn to read until she was nine, when her mother stopped reading aloud to her to force her to read for herself. When she was twelve, she was sent to school for the first time; she was expelled for disruptive behaviour four years later. From then on she occupied herself by reading and writing, glorying in her "passion for words." She soon began to sell stories, sketches and poems to newspapers and magazines to help support her family following her father's bankruptcy. From 1884 on, she became primarily an essayist and writer of non-fiction, for which she eventually was awarded an honorary degree. Two of her books dealt largely with Canada, *Père Marquette* and *Mère Marie*.

Père Marquette tells the story of Jacques Marquette (1637-75), who was born in France and studied in Jesuit schools to become a Jesuit priest (1666). He was anxious to bring religion to the New World that he had read about each year in the annual volume of *Jesuit Relations*—letters and diaries sent home by missionaries in New France to their superiors in France. Marquette spent years in Quebec City, Sault Ste Marie, and St Ignace, where he taught Christianity to the Natives he settled amongst; later he was the first European, with Louis Jolliet, to explore the Mississippi River.

Marie Guyard (1599-1672), the subject of *Mère Marie*, was born in Tours, France. She felt compelled to marry when she was seventeen, although she wanted instead to enter a convent. Soon after she had a son, her husband died. At age thirty-two, when her son was more or less self-sufficient, she entered the Ursuline convent in Tours to become Mère Marie de l'Incarnation. In 1639, she sailed with four other women to Quebec City to establish a convent there. For the rest of her life she taught Native and French girls and published spiritual treatises and dictionaries for Algonquin and Iroquois peoples.

Bibliography
- Stokes, George Stewart. 1949. *Agnes Repplier*. Philadelphia: University of Philadelphia Press, 274 pp.
- Repplier, Agnes. 1929. *Père Marquette*. New York: Book League of America, 181 pp.
- _____. , Litt.D. 1931. *Mère Marie of the Ursulines: A Study in Adventure*. New York: Literary Guild of America, 314 pp.

Richardson, Evelyn May Fox BA 1902-1976. Evelyn Fox was born in Nova Scotia and educated at Dalhousie University. When she married Charles Richardson in 1926, they bought Bon Portage Island near Shag Harbour, the island neighbouring that on which she had been born and where her husband was appointed lighthouse keeper. Later she wrote other related books, including *My Other Islands* (1960) and *Living Island* (1965).

Richardson's book *We Keep a Light* tells the story of her new way of life that has since vanished. "So here I am," she writes, "a lightkeeper's wife on a small island three miles from the mainland, isolated much of the year, and living [with three children] under conditions that most of the country outgrew fifty years or more ago." She describes in loving detail rebuilding and maintaining the lighthouse where they lived, bringing in and raising animals for food and farming, silly mistakes they made and occasional successes. This first book about her island life won the Governor General's Award in 1945 for non-fiction. *We Keep a Light* is still in print and in demand.

Bibliography
- Richardson, E.M. 1985 [1945]. *We Keep a Light*. Toronto: McGraw-Hill Ryerson, 271 pp.

Ridley, Hilda M. d. 1960. Hilda Ridley was born in Sparta, Ontario, and, along with her sister Laura who would also become an author, was educated in a private school in England. Ridley wrote stories and poems for many magazines, several of which won national prizes. As well, for twelve years she was on the contributing staff of *Saturday Night*. With Alan Creighton, she collected and edited poems, mostly from women, to publish them in *A New Canadian Anthology* (1938) put out by her own Crucible Press.

Ridley's *The Story of L.M. Montgomery* was published in Canada shortly after Montgomery's death in 1942 (see Montgomery entry). Most of it is devoted to Montgomery's early life before her marriage, including extracts from her letters and journals as well as some conversation. Montgomery's books were published from 1908 on, but they began to sell exceptionally well only after 1924—in the next twenty years, over three million copies of her novels were purchased. They continue to be popular around the world, especially in Japan.

Bibliography

•Ridley, Hilda M. 1956 [c. 1944]. *The Story of L.M. Montgomery*. London: George Harrap, 143 pp.

Rijnhart, Susanna Carson MD 1868-1908.   Susanna Carson grew up in Chatham and Strathroy, Ontario, the daughter of a school principal and later school inspector and his wife. She was a devout Methodist who early decided to become a medical missionary; she attended the Woman's Medical College in Toronto from which she graduated in 1888 in the second class of doctors. She and her sister Jennie, also a doctor, set up practice in London and then in Strathroy. In 1894 she married the Dutch missionary Petrus Rijnhart, newly dismissed from missionary work in China as an imposter, and headed with him for Tibet, unsponsored by any missionary society. It took them six months to cross China by houseboat and mule-cart. They made no Christian converts during four years of practising medicine in rural Tibet, so they decided that preaching in the capital might be more effective; they set off for Lhasa with their infant son, three guides, horses with food for a year, and five hundred New Testaments. During this journey their young son died and her husband was murdered, leaving Rijnhart to struggle back as best she could to Canada. She returned in 1902 to China "to devote the remainder of her days to the welfare of the barbarians who slew her husband." She did so almost alone and then with the Rev. James Moyes of the China Inland Mission whom she married in 1905; he had to resign from this Mission because of her past connection with Petrus Rijnhart. In 1907 they came back to Canada to stay near her sister in Chatham while she was pregnant; she died there two months after childbirth. Her husband applied to rejoin the China Inland Mission but it refused him, as did the Canadian Methodist Mission in Sichuan.

Rijnhart describes the couple's adventures and their disastrous expedition to Lhasa in *With the Tibetans in Tent and Temple*, which she wrote after her return to Canada and while "under the stress of many public engagements." She wanted to "arouse the interest of Christendom in the evangelization of Tibet, and to create a sure possibility of her own return to that land," as the introduction states. The book was successful in both aims.

Bibliography

•Hacker, Carlotta. 1984. *The Indomitable Lady Doctors*. Halifax: Goodread, pp. 98-113.

•Rijnhart, Susie Carson, MD. 1911 [1901]. *With the Tibetans in Tent and Temple: Narratives of Four Years' Residence on the Tibetan Border, and of a Journey into the Far Interior.* New York: Fleming H. Revell, 406 pp.

Ringland, Mabel Crews BA MA 1890-? Mabel Crews, the daughter of a minister and his wife, was born in Winnipeg and educated in Toronto, receiving her BA in modern languages from the University of Toronto in 1910. She married Hans Ringland in 1916, but carried on her career as journalist, lecturer and freelance household advisor for T. Eaton Co; in this connection she criticized the advertising industry for treating women as "morons" and for not taking their complaints seriously. Ringland later became interested in child psychology and education, earning her MA at the University of Toronto in psychology and anthropology in 1930. She was a member of the Toronto Heliconian Club and club historian of the Canadian Women's Press Club.

Ringland's *Tested Methods for Teachers of Juniors*, aimed at Sunday school classes, was written

> to discuss with teachers the various problems and aspects of their work with boys and girls between the ages of nine and 12, in the hope that from these practical experiences of a fellow-teacher, they may gain some inspiration and help in their very vital task of leading the Junior to become a "Doer of the Word," and of bringing him [*sic*] into conscious relationship with Jesus Christ as his personal saviour.

The thirty-seven chapters include: The boy who makes trouble in class, The boy who will not study his lesson, and Rivalry amongst juniors.

Ringland's co-authored *A Study of Tics in Pre-School Children* is based on her MA thesis research, carried out at St George's School for Child Study at the University of Toronto, although Dr Blatz is honoured as first author. She observed twenty-five nursery school and forty-six public schoolchildren for tics—a tic being described as "any circumscribed muscular activity, exclusive of gross random movements, that is not necessary to or relevant for the immediate adjustment to the apparent motivating situation." Ringland found that tics were extremely common forms of reaction in young boys and girls, especially of the mouth. They occurred particularly when gross bodily movement was inhibited, as when the children sat at tables and desks. This book was the third volume in the Child Development Series of the University of Toronto.

Bibliography
•Ringland, Mabel Crews. 1924. *Tested Methods for Teachers of Juniors.* Toronto: Ryerson, 155 pp.
•Blatz, W.E., and Mabel Crews Ringland. 1935. *A Study of Tics in Pre-School Children.* Toronto: University of Toronto Press, 58 pp.

Ritchie, Mary Christine. Mary Ritchie appears to have been a Canadian author.

As Ritchie's biography *Major General Sir Geoffrey Twining* attests, she was a great admirer of her subject, writing that "none achieved more valuable and varied work, with more invariable success than did Sir Geoffrey Twining, and none was finer and simpler in character than he." Twining (1862-1920) was born in Halifax, attended Royal Military College, joined the Royal Engineers in India, and then helped survey a railway line in East Africa. For six years he taught military engineering at RMC in Kingston, before serving in the British army in India, China and Europe.

Bibliography
•Ritchie, Mary Christine. 1922. *Major General Sir Geoffrey Twining KCMG, CB, MVO: A Biographical Sketch and the Story of His East African Diaries.* Toronto: Macmillan, 102 pp.

Ritson, Lady Kitty See Vincent, Lady Kitty entry.

Robertson, Gladys See Vant, Margaret Josephine entry. Robertson lived in Winnipeg, where she was principal of Sir Sam Steele School.

Robertson, Jessie Ewart 1859-1888. Jessie Ewart, born in Strabane, Wentworth County, Ontario, grew up in a religious household, reading Milton's *Paradise Lost* when she was eight years old. She attended Hamilton Collegiate Institute, then taught with piety and dedication for eleven years before marrying James Robertson and moving to Welland in 1888. She died later that same year of dyspepsia.

A Teacher's Life comprises many of Robertson's writings, including letters of inspiration from "Uncle Tom" from a column aimed at young readers of an agricultural journal. Her sisters and friends oversaw the publication of this collection as a tribute to the memory of one who died far too young.

Bibliography
•Robertson, Jessie E. 1890. *A Teacher's Life, with Extracts from Diaries, Essays and Letters.* By her Sisters and Friends. Hamilton: Griffin and Kidner, 218 pp.

Robson, Elizabeth. Elizabeth Robson's grandfather emigrated from Britain to Ontario, where she grew up in the 1860s in the backwoods near Acton with one thousand acres of nearby forest to wander in and Indians as neighbours. Her family attended Methodist meetings early on because there was no Presbyterian church close enough to reach with their oxen (they had no horses). Later, a Presbyterian church and then an Anglican church were built nearby. Robson had few books as a young girl, but did read *Jane Eyre*, which was thought unsuitable by her elders. Nor was card playing allowed in her family. She remembers the safety she felt when young, even when lost in the woods, compared to the later worry of traffic accidents and other dangers. Elizabeth Robson's small book of memories, *Early Days in Canada*, which relates these events, was written for her grandchildren so they would have some idea of her life as a pioneer. She usually omits dates and places in her chronicle, which lessens its value as history.

Bibliography
•Robson, Elizabeth. 1939. *Early Days in Canada: A Grandmother's Tale*. London: Stockwell, 108 pp.

Rockley, Alicia Margaret (Tyssen-Amherst) Cecil, Baroness MBE, CBE d. 1941. Lady Rockley, the wife of the first Baron Rockley, was a social activist and, because of a passionate interest in flowers and gardens, the author of many books on the subject, including an early *History of Gardens* (1896). When she landed in Auckland in 1926 on her way from Canada to Australia on behalf of the Society for Oversea Settlement of British Women and the Victoria League, she found that her New Zealand friends had kindly decorated her room with flowers, each with its native name attached.

Because Rockley did not recognize these blooms, nor the ones she later saw in Australia, she decided to write a book, *Wild Flowers of the Great Dominions*, complete with sketches. In the preface she thanks many botanists, the staff at Kew Garden and the Chelsea Physic Garden, and High Commissioners and Agents-General of the Dominions for their assistance.

Some Canadian Wild Flowers comprises in part the notes Rockley made for her earlier book. As well as an overview of Canadian flowers, incorporating sections on ferns, conifers and edible berries, she includes chapters on Newfoundland, the prairies and British Columbia, as well as sketches she made of many species.

Bibliography
•Rockley, The Lady, CBE. 1935. *Wild Flowers of the Great Dominions of the British Empire*, London: Macmillan, 380 pp.
•_____. 1937. *Some Canadian Wild Flowers Being the First Part of Wild Flowers of the Great Dominions*. Toronto: Macmillan, 107 pp.

Rogers, Grace Dean McLeod BA MA 1865-1958. Grace McLeod was born in Westfield, Nova Scotia, the daughter of a lawyer and his wife, who attended Dalhousie University before marrying a lawyer. She did research in early local history, and in 1911 was the first woman to be awarded an honorary degree, in her case an MA, from Acadia University. Five years later, because of her interest in writing and in history (she would be the first woman admitted to the Nova Scotia Historical Association), she prepared Canadian missionary **Matilda Churchill's** letters from India for publication because Churchill was too ill to do so. Among her novels she wrote *Joan at Halfway* (1929).

Rogers dedicates *Stories of the Land of Evangeline*—fourteen tales from old Acadie of people and historical events complete with conversation—to her grandfathers. The first story is about a hunchbacked boy from Port Royal and a buried treasure; the last is about Brook Watson, an English orphan who had his leg cut off after a shark attack in Cuba, worked for a time in Nova Scotia where he learned about business, then returned to England where, in 1796, he was elected Lord Mayor of London.

Pioneer Missionaries in the Atlantic Provinces tells the histories of six male missionaries, most of whom were born before 1800, emigrated to Canada, and ministered to people in the Atlantic provinces. It was one of a large number of Ryerson Canadian History Readers endorsed by the Imperial Order Daughters of the Empire and the Provincial Departments of Education.

Bibliography
- Rogers, Grace McLeod. 1923 [1893]. *Stories of the Land of Evangeline.* Toronto: McClelland and Stewart, 341 pp.
- _____. 1930. *Pioneer Missionaries in the Atlantic Provinces.* Toronto: Ryerson, 64 pp.

Rose, Hilda 1880-1967. Hilda Rose was born in Illinois and trained to be a teacher. She had hoped to go to university, but instead went west to recover from tuberculosis; there she married a man twenty-eight years older than herself. They homesteaded in Montana, where conditions were so poor that they were barely able to make ends meet on their "stump farm." Never one to give up, she organized a women's group that met regularly to raise money to help neighbours in particular distress, of whom there were many. From 1918 on, Rose wrote letters to acquaintances about her desperate life; these letters were eventually published in *The Atlantic Monthly.* When she was forty-five, she realized that her family would have to start over if it hoped to survive, so with her elderly husband and young son she moved in 1926 to Alberta, near Fort Vermilion. There they again homesteaded, living at first in a tent. She had hoped to make money from trapping, but there were too few furbearers where they settled. Luckily, when they most needed it, she received cheques for her published letters.

Rose's book *The Stump Farm* comprises material from these and subsequent letters which amazed readers: for example, she writes (p. 118) "A tent is such a draughty place to live in, when it gets 40 degrees below zero." Her publisher notes about her book:

Here is an insight clarified rather than dimmed by hard manual toil, a sympathy broadened rather than extinguished by solitude, a spiritual craving refined rather than coarsened by primitive surroundings and rigorous disciplines. Here is another proof of the underlying romance and inspiration that can be found in the lives of the "Forgotten Millions."

Bibliography

•Rose, Hilda. 1928. *The Stump Farm: A Chronicle of Pioneering.* Boston: Little, Brown, 178 pp.

Ross, Anna d. c.1904. Anna Ross was a deeply religious woman, the second wife of John Ross (1821-87) whom she married in 1874.

Ross's book about her husband, *The Man with the Book*, is pious, concerned largely with church history and one man's involvement with it. She writes from Clinton, Ontario, in the preface: "This little book is not a biography. It is only an attempt to preserve a memory that is blessed, and to extend an influence that has been for good. . . . The fact that [the book] has been brought to completion confirms the hope with which it was started, that 'The Lord hath need of it.' " She ends her preface, "If, in any measure, this little [264 pp.!] book is 'meet for the Master's use,' it shall, in that measure, prove a power for good; if not, it might better never have been written." She was able to document in detail her husband's role in the formation of the Presbyterian Church of Canada.

The New Covenant addresses an argument with three parts:

> 1st. That we, as Christ's, have fallen heir to a covenant with God, which gives us legal right before Him to all the privileges covered by the three terms of that covenant. 2nd. That the failure to utilize this tremendous fact is the cause of the feebleness and failure of the Church of Christ. 3rd. That the way to actual power and victory in Christian life and service is to apprehend and utilize this covenant.

Ross continues: "Are these things true, or are they not? These are weighty questions." After long discussion she ends her book enigmatically: "The fruits shall shew whether there is a real message from God in this little book or not."

Bibliography

•Ross, Anna. 1897. *The Man with the Book, or Memoirs of John Ross of Bruce-field.* Toronto: R.G. McLean, 264 pp.
•_____. 1901. *The New Covenant: A Lost Secret.* Toronto: Briggs, 193 pp.

Ross, Margaret c.1846-1935. Margaret Ross attended the University of Toronto and much later in her life wrote a biography of Sir George Ross, possibly a relative given their same names. She had two private interviews with him, one as an undergraduate and the second twenty years later.

The subject of Ross's biography, *Sir George W. Ross*, was a statesman, educator, writer and orator, serving from 1872 to 1914 in the Ontario legislature, the House of Commons, and the Senate. After describing Ross's career, she copies tributes on his life from a large number of sources. She writes in a high-minded way in the preface:

> If [the author] should be fortunate enough to contribute encouragement even in a small degree, to any of the youths of our Province, to press forward because of her effort in trying to show them what industry, perseverance, energy and courage with high ideals did for the subject of this book, the author will ever cherish a deep sense of gratitude to the overruling hand that guided her, at the age of seventy-seven, through difficulties which had to be met in its preparation.

Bibliography
- Ross, Margaret. 1923. *Sir George W. Ross: A Biographical Study*. Toronto: Ryerson, 195 pp.

Rothery, Agnes Edwards Pratt 1888-1954. Agnes Rothery lived in Boston, but upon marriage to Harry Pratt moved with him frequently before settling in Charlottesville, VA, where he became a professor of music. They had no children, so Rothery, who published under her maiden name, had time to write a large number of books, including biography, juvenile fiction, and novels, but mostly books of travel about countries and places in Europe and North America. A memoir of her early married life is entitled *A Fitting Habitation* (1945).

In *The Ports of British Columbia*, Rothery focuses on the two largest cities, describing Victoria mainly from a historical perspective and Vancouver from an economic and resource one.

Bibliography
- Rothery, Agnes. 1943. *The Ports of British Columbia*. Garden City, NY: Doubleday, Doran, 279 pp.

Rourke, Louise. Louise Rourke grew up in Britain and arrived in Canada in 1924 to marry the accountant of the Hudson's Bay Post at Fort Chipewyan in northeastern Alberta. She spent two years there before the railway reached this outpost—one of the first non-missionary women to live in the Canadian north in all seasons. She was a writer who sent articles from her new northern home to various children's annuals, a linguist who translated a Norwegian book into English, and an idealist: she refused to wear "trapped fur," even in the north, on conscientious grounds.

Rourke wrote *The Land of the Frozen Tide* as a record of her stay at Fort Chipewyan with her husband, describing the business of the fur trade and the problems of surviving so far north. She ends her book with an appendix called "The North through a Man's Eyes," which gives short extracts from her husband's private diary of daily events at the fort.

Bibliography
•Rourke, Louise. 1928. *The Land of the Frozen Tide*. London: Hutchinson, 352 pp.

Roy, Jennet. Jennet Roy was an early teacher in Lower Canada (Quebec) who wrote her school texts because there were no suitable history books in English for her students.

Both *Text-book of Canadian History* and *History of Canada* were widely used in Lower Canada and authorized for schools in Upper Canada, too, with the seventh edition of the former being published in 1863. She notes humbly in the latter that

> having been favoured with the assistance of some gentlemen of literary standing, and the free use of the ample materials contained in the Library of the Legislative Assembly, she has ventured to put forth this little work [278 pp.], pleading, as her excuse, the absolute necessity of providing such a source of information for British American Youth.

The first two hundred pages are devoted to the history of Canada and the rest to a description of central and eastern Canada, including their main cities and geographical features. Each paragraph is numbered and many questions are posed to facilitate study, such as (p. 13): "What is said of Sebastien Cabot? What southern country is he said to have discovered? What did he explore? . . . what pension did he receive?" Gerson (1994, 25) writes: "The lack of available information about this obviously successful author signals the double marginalization of children's literature and women authors within the Canadian literary canon."

Bibliography
Roy, Mrs Jennet. 1847. Text-book of Canadian History. Montreal: Charles G. Dagg. 232 pp.
•Roy, J. 1861. *History of Canada for the Use of Schools and Families*. Montreal: Charles G. Dagg, 278 pp. 6th ed.

Royce, Marion Victoria BA MA LLD OC 1901-1987. Marion Royce was born in St Thomas, Ontario, and educated at McMaster University, the Ontario College of Education, and the Universities of Toronto (MA) and Chicago. She was principal of Moulton College for Girls in Toronto, then a staff member of the Young Women's Christian Association in Montreal, and later at national and international YWCA levels. In 1954 she became the first Director of the federal Department of Labour's Women's Bureau, in which role she worked for better daycare, for more part-time jobs for married women with children, and for better education for women. She retired in 1967, but continued her efforts to improve conditions for women by consulting for the Commission on the Status of Women and writing books such as *Continuing Education for Women in Canada* (1969) while affiliated with the Ontario Institute for Studies in Education. She was awarded an honorary degree by Acadia University in 1975. Her literary friends included **Mary Quayle Innis.**

The Effect of the War on the Life of Women was based on information from YWCAs in many countries, gathered in response to a questionnaire sent out in 1942 from the Washington YWCA. "The questionnaire provided an excellent basis for a general survey including three main areas of investigation: home and family life, economic status and social and legal status." These data were augmented by other information, including cogitation of a small group of Canadian women "thinking and planning for postwar reconstruction." She concludes that, just as after the First World War, women's "capacity in the eyes of men has grown, and their own inferiority feelings are vanishing." She notes that the war had given women wider job opportunities and more family responsibilities, but it also caused increased suffering and sexual promiscuity. She looks forward to a society in which men and women are equal and "full partners in the world-wide struggle for justice, mutual respect and cooperation, not only in the family but in every sphere of human relationships."

Bibliography
•Royce, Marion V. 1945. *The Effect of the War on the Life of Women*. Geneva: World's Young Women's Christian Association, 72 pp.

S., A. A.S., a British woman who describes herself as having uncertain health and limited powers, sailed in June 1883 with a small party from Liverpool to Quebec City, where they planned to start their quick trip to Canada. They visited Montreal, Niagara Falls by way of New York City, then Toronto and back to Quebec. (This truncated journey described as visiting "Canada" contrasts with trips taken several years later, when the Canadian Pacific Railway allowed tourists readily to cross the entire continent.) A.S. was back home in Britain on July 22 after her exhilarating (and surely exhausting) holiday.

A.S. wrote *A Summer Trip to Canada* "to induce ladies to go to Canada, or the States for their summer trips, instead of confining themselves to the Continent, or the British Isles," assuring the reader that "There are no difficulties that ladies cannot overcome." She hopes that her descriptions of the places her group visited and the people they met will pique the interest of potential tourists.

Bibliography

•S., A. 1885. *A Summer Trip to Canada*. London: City of London Publishing, 112 pp.

Sadlier, Mary Anne Madden 1820-1903. Mary Anne Madden was born in Ireland and educated there by tutor. Following the death of her father and her subsequent impoverishment, she immigrated in 1843 to Canada. In 1846 she married James Sadlier, who, with his brother, owned a bookbinding business and later a publishing firm, D. and J. Sadlier and Company, in Montreal. This business thrived in large part because it published dozens of novels and other books by Mary Anne Sadlier. She produced six books (and six children) between 1846 and 1860. Lacombe (1990) notes that she "was famous in her day for didactic, sentimental romances promoting the causes of Catholicism and Irish culture in North America," with novels such as *The Flanagans: A Tale Illustrative of Irish Life in the United States* (1855) popular in Europe, Canada and the United States. In 1860, the family moved to New York. After her husband's death in 1869, she helped manage the family firm until her brother-in-law's demise sixteen years later. She then returned in poverty to Canada to live with her daughter Anna Teresa Sadlier, also a well-known novelist. As she grew older she produced biblical and Catholic school texts which appealed to a more religious readership. Before she died, a Sadlier Testimonial Fund was created for her by her friends, and she was given recognition by Notre Dame University and the Pope for her writing and services to the Church.

Sadlier wrote *Catechism* because there was no book on this subject in the schools that was not too large, too elaborate for junior classes, or too long "so as to fatigue the memory of the young learners." Her text comprises over six hundred questions and answers relating to the Bible. The First Epoch of the Old Testament (embracing we are told 1,656 years, the beginning of the world until Noah's time), begins: "Q. How did God create the world? A. God created the world of nothing, and by His word alone." Presumably school children had to memorize this material.

Sadlier was prompted to write *Purgatory* in her sixties, when "we are happily drawn more and more towards the eternal truths of the great untried world beyond the grave." She stated that "Of all the divine truths which the Catholic Church proposes to her children, assuredly none is more acceptable to the pilgrim race of Adam than that of Purgatory," a statement that will bemuse non-Catholics. She sees it as a link between the living and the dead, which keeps the memory of the dead alive and gives the living the joy of helping them in "that shadowy border-land through which, in pain and sorrow, they must journey before entering the Land of Promise." She felt that there was a void in "English Purgatorial literature": there were many doctrinal works and works of devotion, but few books directed toward the general reader. She focused her book on anecdotes, legends and poetry, with enough doctrinal and devotional matter to make it theologically legitimate. She includes extracts from many authors, most of them Catholics; some of the poetry is by Canadians.

Needless to say, Sadlier's *Catholic School History of England*, printed in the Dominion Catholic Series, also has a religious bias: "The following pages were written to provide our Catholic Schools of all grades with such a record of the main facts of English History as, viewed from a Catholic standpoint, would present them before the pupils with fairness and impartiality." The preface notes that in treating controversial questions, "the author has studiously avoided all remarks that could offend the most fastidious, and has given merely a necessary and clear view of the facts related." One such controversial subject is the rise of Protestantism and the reign of King Henry VIII; she describes in detail the agonizing death of this "spoiler" king whose body was "one mass of disease and corruption," and how his blood was lapped up by a dog (p. 172).

Bibliography

Lacombe, Michèle. 1990. Mary Anne Sadlier. *Dictionary of Literary Biography: Canadian Writers Before 1890*, s.v. Sadlier, Mary Anne.

•Sadlier, Mary Anne. 1885 [1866]. *A New Catechism of Sacred History; Compiled from Authentic Sources for Catholic Schools*. Montreal: Sadlier, 178 pp.

•_____. 1886. *Purgatory: Doctrinal, Historical and Poetical*. New York: Sadlier, 500 pp.

•A Catholic Teacher. 1891. *Catholic School History of England*. Montreal: Sadlier, 316 pp.

St Maur, Susan Margaret Mckinnon, Duchess of, (formerly Duchess of Somerset) d. 1936. In the late 1880s, English aristocrat Susan St Maur travelled for seven months with her husband by train across Canada and then by other means up and down the west coast of the continent. Unfortunately, they were both keen on indiscriminate hunting, shooting at various mammals and birds they encountered, sometimes just for target practice. Despite this, they lamented the earlier slaughter of bison that had left piles of bones up to a metre high alongside the railway track.

The Duchess notes diffidently that although she has tried to describe their adventures accurately in *Impressions of a Tenderfoot*, "from lack of literary skill, the following pages may not suggest to the reader all the wonder and pleasure I experienced among the strange and beautiful scenes they describe." She writes:

> To me the mental exhilaration of fresh scenes and fresh faces was a continual delight, and in recalling those scenes and faces I have been prompted to put memories and notes together, and, with the addition of my few hastily-drawn sketches, I now venture to offer the result to any one who, in lenient mood, will care to accompany me over the many leagues of our travels in this, my first essay in literature.

Bibliography

•St Maur, Mrs Algernon. 1890. *Impressions of a Tenderfoot during a Journey in Search of Sport in the Far West*. London: John Murray, 279 pp.

St Paul, Mother M., OSU. Mother St Paul was a long-time member of the Ursuline Community of Chatham, Ontario. During her life she watched her community grow physically, and rejoiced as hundreds of young women became nuns and thousands of students graduated from the community's school.

Mother St Paul wrote the history of her order in *From Desenzano to "The Pines"* at the behest of its Alumnae Association. She describes the order's founder, Angela Merici, born in Desenzano, Italy, in 1417, as a young woman known for her piety and consulted by many on temporal and spiritual matters. When she was fifty-seven, Merici formed with twelve devout young disciples the Order of St Ursula, the first teaching order of women ever established in the Roman Catholic Church, which would eventually comprise twenty thousand nuns. Members of the order moved to Sault Ste Marie in 1853, and to Chatham in 1860, where they bought property which would house the Ursuline Academy of Chatham at "The Pines." The foundress there was Mother Mary Xavier Le Bihan.

Bibliography

•St Paul, Mother M., OSU. 1941. *From Desenzano to "The Pines": A Sketch of the History of the Ursulines of Ontario, with a Brief History of the Order Compiled from Various Sources*. Toronto: Macmillan, 387 pp.

Salter, Mary Dinsmore BA PhD. Mary Salter was a student at the University of Toronto who became interested in child development on taking a course in this subject from Dr W. Blatz, head of the Institute of Child Study; Blatz was an excellent teacher who gave his students answers to upcoming exam questions so that no one would fail. After earning her doctorate, in 1947 she became an assistant professor in psychology at the University of Toronto, working alongside her husband, Len Ainsworth. In the 1950s they began pioneering work on the attachment bonds between mothers and newborn babies in London, Uganda and Baltimore where she was hired by Johns Hopkins University (Raymond 1991).

In her pioneering study *An Evaluation of Adjustment*, based on work done at the Institute of Child Study, Mary Salter devised a way to evaluate characteristics "of an individual's adjustment by means of a series of scales all based upon the common concept of security," both within and outside the family. The security could be viewed objectively—an observer judges whether an individual's behaviour meets the demands made by the environment, or subjectively—an individual answers questions about whether he/she is satisfied with his or her own activity. When she examined teens who smoked and did not smoke, and who had and did not have parents who objected, she found that the least secure teens were those who smoked and had objecting parents, while the most secure were those who did not smoke and whose parents would not have objected anyway.

Bibliography
•Salter, Mary D. 1940. *An Evaluation of Adjustment Based upon the Concept of Security*. Toronto: University of Toronto Press, 72 pp.

Salverson, Laura Goodman 1890-1970. Laura Goodman was born in Winnipeg to poor Icelandic immigrants who moved frequently (to North Dakota, Minnesota, Mississippi and back to Manitoba) so that her father could find work. Her mother produced many babies, but most soon sickened and died; indeed, because of illness Laura herself did not go to school (or speak English) until she was ten. "As a result of her childhood experiences she developed a sympathy for the poor and an awareness of the plight of women that inform her writing" (Hjartarson 1990), which often interpreted Icelandic life for English-speaking readers. Laura Goodman wanted to go to normal school, but the family could not afford this. In 1913 she married a railway dispatcher with whom she lived in a number of small towns across the prairies; she often kept boarders, writing verse and stories in her free time and continuing to study English syntax, grammar and composition. She was encouraged by **Nellie McClung**, whom she met at the literary society that gathered regularly in the Regina Public Library. In 1916 her only child, George, was born; he would eventually adapt some of her books for radio. Her writing career was finally launched in 1922 when she won a Women's Canadian Club of Saskatchewan prize for a short story. She went on to write many stories, articles and novels, one of which (*The Dark Weaver*) won a Governor General's Award in 1937.

Salverson also won a Governor General's Award for non-fiction in 1939 for her autobiography, *Confessions of an Immigrant's Daughter.* Buss (in Neuman and Kamboureli 1986) notes that this book is composed of separate short episodes

> to gather together the strands of her identity, divided as they are between her close identification with her mother and her father, and her need to take into account her Icelandic heritage, her Canadian childhood and her American experience. Most of all, she wants to find strong, female figures who will help her define herself as wife, mother and writer at the same time. (p. 156)

Bibliography

- Hjartarson, Paul. 1990. Laura Goodman Salverson. *Dictionary of Literary Biography: Canadian Writers, 1890-1920*, s.v. Salverson, Laura Goodman.
- Salverson, Laura Goodman. 1939. *Confessions of an Immigrant's Daughter.* London: Faber and Faber, 523 pp.

Sanders, Byrne Hope CBE, CC 1902-1981. Byrne Sanders was born in South Africa and came to Canada with her family when she was eleven. She began her career as a reporter in Woodstock, Ontario, when she was seventeen, switched to working for Eaton's (1923-26), then became editor of *BusinessWoman* (1926-29) and of *Chatelaine* (1929-52), based in Toronto. In 1932 she married Frank Sperry, with whom she had two children, but she continued to work outside the home. During the Second World War she headed the Consumer Branch of the Wartime Prices and Trade Board (receiving a CBE for this) which would, after the war, form the basis of the Canadian Consumers' Association. In 1951 she joined her brother in Sanders Marketing Research, organizing polls such as the Gallup Poll in Canada and other work until she retired in 1971. She always began her work day by greeting each employee personally (Fraser, 1997). Her later writing included co-authoring *Hey Ma! I Did It* (1953), a description of the election campaign of her friend Margaret Aitken, M.P.

Sanders met **Emily Murphy** only a few times, so her biography *Emily Murphy, Crusader* is based in large part on Murphy's thousands of letters and many articles and books. As an editor, Sanders was offered the chance to write this book in 1938, five years after Murphy's death, and was delighted to undertake the task. Sanders's niece is politician Pat Carney.

Bibliography
- Fraser, Sylvia, ed. 1997. *Chatelaine: A Woman's Place: Seventy Years in the Lives of Canadian Women*. Toronto: Key Porter.
- Sanders, Byrne Hope. 1945. *Emily Murphy, Crusader ("Janey Canuck")*. Toronto: Macmillan, 355 pp.

Sanderson, Camilla. Camilla Sanderson was brought up in Peterborough, Ontario, the daughter of an Irish minister and his much younger English wife. She wrote not only a biography of her father but also books of poetry such as *If I Could Sing* (1913).

Sanderson's father, as described in *John Sanderson the First* (d. 1880), was an Irish-born minister of the Wesleyan Methodist Church of Canada. The "Rev. Prof." F.H. Wallace of Victoria College in Toronto notes in the introduction:

> Their daughter has most lovingly and charmingly depicted their life and character. The style is fresh, naive, vivacious; the book abounds in graphic descriptions of places, persons and events; there are many touches both of humor and of pathos; there are frequent glimpses into the details of the daily life not only of the parsonage, but also of the general community fifty years ago which make that period and that phase of our history live over again to the reader.

Bibliography
- Sanderson, Camilla. 1910. *John Sanderson the First, or A Pioneer Preacher at Home*. Toronto: Briggs, 237 pp.

Sansom, Mary J. Sansom was a working-class Englishwoman who sailed to Canada for her vacation in 1911, something few people like herself had previously had the time or money to do. Even fewer had written about their experiences, unlike the many wealthy British tourists who had travelled widely across the country.

Sansom begins *A Holiday Trip to Canada* with her departure by ship from Bristol in June for her three-week vacation. She depicts at length the vessel and life aboard it, which she enjoyed with the three women who shared her inside cabin. She stayed in Montreal for a few days, then visited Niagara Falls and Toronto by train, returning from Toronto to Montreal by boat. She was greatly impressed by Canada compared to England, noting in Canada less poverty, less alcoholism, much care in screening new arrivals, and more patriotic feeling toward their own country and the homeland of Britain.

Bibliography
•Sansom, Mary J. 1916 [1912?]. *A Holiday Trip to Canada.* London: St Catherine
    Press, 120 pp.

Saunders, Margaret Marshall BA MA CBE 1861-1947. Marshall Saunders was born in Milton, Nova Scotia, where her father would be a Baptist
minister. She was educated at home until she was fifteen, then at a boarding
school in Edinburgh, finishing her studies in France and at Dalhousie University. She taught for a few years in Canada before deciding that she preferred writing; she started with exciting and romantic stories before turning
in large part to tales about the animal friends she loved. Her many fictionalized books and talks fostered a love of animals in millions of children in
America (where she lived for years) as well as in the British Empire; *Beautiful Joe* (1894) was the first Canadian book to sell more than a million
copies—Saunders transposed the story from around Georgian Bay to
Maine so that she would have a better chance of winning an American
Humane Educational Society literary competition and attracting an American readership. She never married, and felt that those who did not have
children "should at least assist in the rearing of some created thing, if it is
only a bird. Otherwise they become egotistical and absorbed in self"
(p. 35). Saunders travelled a great deal, noting "that it was absolutely necessary that I should be on the scene where my story was laid," but distinctive local colour is not apparent in most of her books (Gerson 1990). She
was an ardent supporter of the Society for the Prevention of Cruelty to Animals, the Anti-Vivisection Society, the Humane Society, the National
Council of Women and the Women's Christian Temperance Union. While
living in Halifax, she and **L.M. Montgomery** founded the Maritime branch
of the Canadian Women's Press Club. In the 1920s Saunders moved to
Toronto, where she and her sister built a house to accommodate themselves
and their animal friends. Saunders received an honorary MA from Acadia
University in 1911 and was made a Commander of the Order of the British
Empire in 1935. The Canadian Writers' Foundation helped keep her from
poverty when she grew old.

About *My Pets*, her only book of non-fiction, Saunders writes, "While
the most of my stories are partly true, I have never before written one that
is entirely and wholly true in every particular. The story of my aviary and
the pets in it is taken from my diaries, and many of the birds are still living
and moving and having their being." She began her aviary with four baby
screech owls, given to her in California. There followed a hawk, a chip-
munk, and hundreds of other wild and domestic animals that she describes
lovingly from her home in Halifax. At that time caged migratory song birds
sent from Europe could still be purchased in pet stores, but native birds

could no longer be so treated, to Saunders's satisfaction. Although she purchased some caged birds and mammals, many of her pets were orphans who would have died had they been left in the wild.

Bibliography
•Gerson, Carole. 1990. Margaret Marshall Saunders. *Dictionary of Literary Biography: Canadian Writers, 1890-1920*, s.v. Saunders, Margaret Marshall.
• Saunders, Marshall. 1908. *My Pets*. Toronto: Ryerson, 251 pp.

Saxby, Jessie Margaret Edmondston 1842-1940. Jessie Edmondston was born in Scotland, the daughter of a doctor and his wife, and educated at home. She married Dr Henry Saxby, after whose death she wrote and published many stories, poetry and novels, such as *Geordie Roye* (1880), becoming the Shetland's most famous writer. In 1888 she travelled alone to Canada by ship, then journeyed by Canadian Pacific Railway through Quebec and Ontario to the prairies and beyond.

Saxby writes about some of her Canadian experiences in *West-Nor'-West* in an opinionated and depressing way, quoting a correspondent who refers to Chinese "allowed to carry on all their vile practices, morally and physically, and sanitary, which they have been accustomed to do in their own country," and to an older generation of women "who screamed when a spider ran over their skirts, and fainted at a pin's scratch." She is, however, religious: "Happy is that people whose God is the Lord." She hopes that her observations will prove useful to prospective immigrants, especially women who were then in great demand in the New World.

Bibliography
• Saxby, Jessie M.E. 1890. *West-Nor'-West*. London: James Nisbet, 154 pp.

Schäfer, Mary Townsend Sharples 1861-1939. Mary Sharples was born into a wealthy Quaker family in Philadelphia. About 1890 she married a much older botanist and physician, Charles Schäfer, with whom she explored the Rocky Mountains; they were friends there with R.B. Bennett, later Prime Minister of Canada (1930-35). Charles Schäfer died in 1903, the same year as her parents, but Mary Schäfer had enough money to be able to complete her late husband's book about wildflowers in the Rocky Mountains. To this end she travelled by horse and foot through the mountains, painting and photographing plants; while there, she met **Julia Henshaw** whose flower book of the same area would be published a year earlier. Schäfer married her English guide, Billy Warren, in 1915, and lived the rest of her life in Banff.

Schäfer enjoyed outdoor life so much that she camped in the Rocky Mountains with friends during the summers of 1907 and 1908, with never "a thought that the daily happenings of our ordinary camplife would ever be heard of beyond the diary, the family, the few partial friends." For her acquaintances with "aches and pains, with sorrows and troubles," however, she decided to write *Old Indian Trails* about these trips "to bring to them the fresh air and sunshine, the snowy mountains, the softly flowing rivers,—the healers for every ill." On her second trip, her party "discovered" Maligne Lake, which the Canadian government then asked her in 1911 to survey. Her adventures doing so were included in a 1980 volume, *A Hunter of Peace*, which also included a reprint of her earlier book. She noted in one of her journals "Civilization! How little it means when one has tasted the free life of the trail!" (Wylie 1995, 152).

Bibliography

Schäfer, Mary T.S. 1911. *Old Indian Trails: Incidents of Camp and Trail Life, Covering Two Years' Exploration through the Rocky Mountains of Canada.* New York: Putnam, 364 pp.

————. 1980. *A Hunter of Peace and Old Indian Trails of the Canadian Rockies.* Edited by E.J. Hart. Banff: Whyte Museum.

Schofield, Emily M. McAvity. Emily Schofield married her husband in 1904, three years before he became Dean of Fredericton. Later, when he was Bishop of British Columbia, they lived in Victoria.

Schofield wrote *Charles Deveber Schofield*, the biography of her husband (1871-1935), shortly after his death, so that memories of him might be kept alive. He was born into a large Anglican family of St John, New Brunswick, and educated at King's College and at theological institutions in Great Britain. After his ordination, he preached in Hampton parish, New Brunswick, and in Nova Scotia, organizing the building of a cathedral in Fredericton as he would later do in Victoria.

Bibliography

•Schofield, Emily M., his wife. 1941. *Charles Deveber Schofield: Late Bishop of British Columbia.* Victoria: author, 69 pp.

Schwartz, Julia Augusta 1873-? Julia Schwartz was an American writer greatly interested in the Arctic.

Schwartz's *Westward Ho!* "is the story of an explorer, Vilhjalmur Stefansson, who has helped to gather facts about our arctic coast"; she recounts his Arctic adventures based on his books and papers (the subtitle of the book belies her contribution). She describes the ten winters and thirteen summers he spent in the Arctic, travelling thousands of miles by boat, snowshoe and dogsled, and the life of the Inuit whom he encountered. Schwartz is every bit as optimistic as Stefansson about the possibilities of the Arctic, envisioning not "barren grounds" in the north, but "arctic

prairies" which will "provide forage for immense herds of these self-sup-
porting animals [caribou or reindeer]. From this huge supply, meat will be
sent to all the markets of the world." Stefansson estimated that Canada
could sustain between twenty and forty million caribou, and that these,
together with caribou/reindeer from Alaska and Siberia, would make "rein-
deer one of the chief meats of the world."

Bibliography
•Schwartz, Julia Augusta. 1928. *Northward Ho! An Account of the Far North and Its People*. Selected from the writings of Vilhjalmur Stefansson and adapted for boys and girls. New York: Macmillan, 181 pp.

Scott, Bertha Isabel. Bertha Scott, a native of Springhill, Nova Scotia,
was interested in its history.

Scott's book *Springhill* is an enlarged version of a prize-winning essay
she entered in a contest, sponsored by the Maritime Library Association, to
"stimulate local research, to recover and preserve the facts and traditions
relating to early history and first settlers of various localities." Because of a
lack of available records, Scott notes that her research "required much personal enquiry, and it has been necessary to sift, balance and arrange a great
amount of material thus acquired"; she secured much information "just on
the point of being forgotten." She describes the fifty-year history of the
town in detail—location, pioneer settlers and development. The town grew
up because of the coal deposits underneath it, but the mines themselves are
only mentioned. She includes many statistics and many lists—of male settlers, lacrosse team members (all men), members of the dramatic company
which included several "young ladies," the male Springhill Band, soldiers
and ministers.

Bibliography
•Scott, Bertha Isabel. 1926. *Springhill: A Hilltop in Cumberland*. Springhill, NS: n.p., 119 pp.

Segall, Jean Brown. Jean Segall grew up in Portage la Prairie, Manitoba.

Segall tells in *Wings of the Morning* the story of her younger brother
who was "one of Canada's greatest aces—Wing Commander Mark Henry
Brown, Distinguished Flying Cross and bar, Croix de Guerre, Military
medal and Military Cross of Czechoslovakia." He was born in Portage la
Prairie in 1912, and grew up in small-town Manitoba. Having learned to fly
in 1932, he sailed to England four years later to join the Royal Air Force;
this seemed a wonderful opportunity when jobs were scarce during the
Depression. He became a fighter pilot whose efforts helped win the 1940
Battle of Britain; he himself was shot down and died in Italy in 1941.

Segall notes about the Battle of Britain that "Little has been said of the individual men who spent those trying months stemming the tide of enemy bombers and fighters which sought to vanquish the Royal Air Force. Who were these valiant men?" Copies of some of his letters are included in her book.

Bibliography

•Segall, Jean Brown. 1945. *Wings of the Morning*. Toronto: Macmillan, 151 pp.

Shack, Sybil Frances BA MEd LLD 1911-? Sybil Shack, who was born in Winnipeg, earned a BA from the University of Manitoba and an MA in education. She became a well-known teacher at both elementary and secondary school levels, as well as the first woman high school principal in Winnipeg. She was also a leader in various professional organizations involving education, among them as director of the Canadian Teachers' Federation for three years. She disputed **Hilda Neatby**'s hypothesis, set out in her book *So Little for the Mind*, that education in Canada was deficient. Her later books included *Armed with a Primer: A Canadian Teacher Looks at Children, Schools and Parents* (1965), *The Two-Thirds Minority: Women in Canadian Education* (1973), and *Saturday's Stepchildren: Canadian Women in Business* (1977). Shack was awarded an LLD from the University of Manitoba in 1969 for her service to education.

Both authors of *Early Life in Canada* were teachers at Winnipeg schools when their book was published, Shack at Laura Secord School. It is one of the Guidebook Series in Social Studies, a school history with a difference, the story of how the boys and girls of Pleasant Valley School learned about early Canada. Each chapter begins with school incidents, then continues with what the students learn about some facet of Canadian history—how America was found, living in New France and New England, the unknown west and new homes in east and west. There is a great deal of conversation between the teacher, Miss Gordon, and her eager pupils, as well as lists of exercises that will appeal to students. The book ends with the perspective of a new Polish immigrant, father of one of the boys, who urges that new Canadians be well treated: "Do not look on them as 'foreigners.' A foreigner is a person who is *visiting* in the country. Remember that even the Indians did not treat your ancestors as foreigners. Ignorant as they were, they saw that the white men had something that would make their country a better place in which to live."

Bibliography

•Chafe, J.W., assisted by Sybil Shack. 1946 [1943]. *Early Life in Canada*. Toronto: Ryerson, 135 pp.

Shadd, Mary Ann Camberton 1823-1893. Mary Ann Shadd was the first of thirteen children, five of whom lived to adulthood, born to a free black (mixed-race) couple living in Wilmington, Delaware. Her father, owner of a shoemaking business, was an outspoken abolitionist; the family house was one of the stops on the Underground Railroad for slaves headed to freedom in the north. About 1833 the family moved to Pennsylvania, where black children could obtain an education. After Mary Ann Shadd graduated from a private Quaker boarding school at the age of sixteen, she moved back to Wilmington to establish a school for free black children. She taught in several American cities for the next ten years. When the United States in 1850 passed the Fugitive Slave Act, which made it easier for slaveowners to hunt down and reclaim runaway slaves and put free blacks at risk of being kidnapped, she moved to Canada, settling in Windsor.

With an influx of blacks from the south seeking safety, Shadd was able to start a new school open to whites as well as blacks. She wrote *A Plea for Emigration* which she sold during many lecture tours in Ontario and the United States. In 1853 she gave up teaching to start a newspaper, the *Provincial Freeman* "devoted to anti-slavery, temperance, and general literature," soon moving it to Toronto and then to the Chatham area where members of her family joined her and helped run the paper. The newspaper faltered when it became known its publisher was a woman, but it apparently appeared sporadically until 1859, three years after Shadd had again returned to teaching. About this time she saved a fugitive slave from being captured by ringing the bell of the Chatham Town Hall. In 1856 she had married Thomas Cary, a Toronto barber and widower who had helped found her paper; they had two children together before he died four years later. During the American Civil War she acted as a recruiting officer for several states, receiving $15 for each slave man she could bring forward who was willing to fight. After the war she returned to live in Washington, DC, where, during the rest of her life, she studied at Howard University and became a lawyer, taught, wrote and worked for women's rights and suffrage. She is remembered by plaques describing her life and work in Toronto and Chatham and by a school bearing her name in Scarborough.

Shadd wrote *A Plea for Emigration* to provide information about relocation and settlement for American blacks who, before the age of mass communication, knew little about the possibilities. Because she believed that Ontario was the best option, she devoted most space to it, describing its climate, topography, agriculture, job opportunities, political rights and laws protecting blacks. She argued that "segregation (whether in school, church, or community), was a retrograde step for Black emigrants." She ended with a consideration of emigration to other areas, praising the West Indies and Vancouver Island over Africa, Mexico and South America.

Bibliography

Bearden, Jim and Linda Jean Butler. 1977. *Shadd: The Life and Times of Mary Shadd Cary.* Toronto: NC Press.

•Shadd, Mary A. 1998 [1852]. *A Plea for Emigration, Or, Notes of Canada West.* Edited, annotated and with an introduction by Richard Almonte. Toronto: Mercury Press, 55 pp.

Sharples, Alice 1906-? Alice Sharples was a broadcaster and author from Quebec who wrote travel books and later, under her married name Baldwin, narrative histories such as *The Price Family: Pioneers of the Saguenay* (1978) and a 1981 novel, *High, Wide and Handsome.*

In order to write *Ports of Pine—Labrador, Newfoundland, Gaspé,* Sharples visited the three areas mentioned in the title of her book, describing and giving information on their geography, history, sights and inhabitants and using conversation written in phonetic dialect. When she visited the International Grenfell Mission, Wilfred Grenfell found her "a very understanding visitor," as he mentions in the foreword. Her book is unusual in that if you turn it over and open it from the back, you find another book by the same author, this one called *Ports of Palm—Haiti, Jamaica, Cuba, Nassau,* which is 121 pages long. Since the book(s) was published by a steamship line, it was undoubtedly written to encourage tourism.

Bibliography

•Sharples, Alice. 1939. *Ports of Pine—Labrador, Newfoundland, Gaspé.* Montreal: Steamship Co., 89 pp.

Shearwood, Mary Howard Henderson. Mary Shearwood was employed at the Dominion Bridge Company.

Shearwood's *A Dominion which Spans a Dominion* is a history of this company—"the simple story of some of the happenings of the Company during the last fifty odd years," a company "which is endeavouring to give to Canada truth and beauty of design in meeting the demands for structural steel in all its forms." The history is detailed, beginning in the 1880s with a description of the steel industry. Other chapters deal with the development of the company, the shop, the erection department, the engineering department and the divisions, branches and subsidiaries. She concludes the book, in considering the place of women, by noting joyfully that the company not only has hired women but that the wives of the employees are deeply interested in the company "and are convinced that every new bridge erected means more than the mere crossing of a river. It means to them the joy of a creator in his efforts to be constructive."

By Water and the Word, describing the life of the Right Reverend Newnham during his missionary service in the Diocese of Moosonee, is based on his diary from 1891 to 1904; during his term in the north he travelled over four thousand miles by canoe, 1,700 by dog train and sled and five hundred by snowshoe. Although the title page says that her book is "a transcription of the diary of" this is not so, as most of the bishop's adventures (he was made a bishop in 1893) are told in her own words. The Primate of the Church of England in Canada hopes in the preface that Newnham's story will be "a means of leading more of our people to understand better the glory and greatness of the missionary work of the Church of England in Canada."

Bibliography

? Shearwood, Mrs F.P. 1936. *As It Was in the Beginning.*

•_____. 1937. *A Dominion which Spans the Dominion.* Montreal: Dominion Bridge Co., 57 pp.

•_____. 1943. *By Water and the Word: a Transcription of the Diary of the Right Reverend J.A. Newnham, MA, DD, LLD while Plying the Waters and Ice Fields of Northern Canada in the Diocese of Moosonee.* Toronto: Macmillan, 216 pp.

Shenton, Mary J. d. 1915.   M.J. Shenton was married to the Rev. Job Shenton.

A Biographical Sketch of the Late Rev. Job Shenton by His Widow comprises about fifty pages of this book; although Shenton's name is not on the title page, it appears after the dedication: "To all those who have loved him;" she regrets that the book will miss "the touch of his hand in revision" and the inspiration of his voice. Shenton writes:

> In this brief sketch I make no attempt to be otherwise than desultory, as I can only wander through the garden of memory and pluck here and there a leaf, a bud or blossom, as they present themselves to my hand; and these I venture to offer my readers, although loosely tied together and crude in their arrangement, and sometimes, I fear, losing much of their fragrance and beauty in the handling.

Job Shenton (1838-1901) was born in England and sailed in 1858 to the Maritimes, where he preached as a layperson and studied to become a Methodist minister. With his wife, he served for the rest of his life on a number of circuits and in churches in the east; he was praised as both a caring pastoral worker and an inspiring speaker, as presumably his included sermons and lectures attest.

Bibliography

•His Widow. 1902. *A Biographical Sketch of the Late Rev. Job Shenton by His Widow with Some of His Sermons and Lectures*. St John, NB: J. and A. McMillan, 236 pp.

Shoolman, Regina Lenore 1907-1999. Regina Shulman was born in Czernowitz in eastern Europe, and emigrated in 1920 with her Jewish family to Canada, where they changed the spelling of their name. Her father supported them by selling dry goods from a pushcart in rural Quebec, and then by opening a bookstore in Quebec City. Later they moved to Montreal where Regina studied French and German at McGill University. On graduating, she received a scholarship from the French government which enabled her to study art in Paris and become an expert on eighteenth-century drawings. When back in Canada she worked as a social worker for the Jewish community and as a journalist for the *Montreal Star*; in her spare time, she taped folk songs from rural Quebec on a primitive recording machine, translated French poetry, published her own poetry (her 1932 chapbook is called *Uncertain Glory*) and wrote articles on painters such as Krieghoff for *Canadian Forum*. In 1936 she married an American art critic, Charles Slatkin, with whom, after they had moved to New York state, she later wrote other important books on art, including *Treasury of American Drawings* (1947) and *Six Centuries of French Master Drawings in America* (1950). They had two daughters.

The painter Arthur Lismer wrote in the foreword to their book *The Story of Art*:

> the work which the authors here present is doubly valuable. Their careful analysis of art and its background affords us a synoptic view not only of great art periods, but also of the changing character and ideals of mankind. In making these behind-the-scene stories of art palatable to the general reader, a genuine service has been rendered. The economic setting, the surge of historical forces, are revealed and clarified, while the life stories present the masters at their work in candid-camera fashion.

The Enjoyment of Art is "A survey of the permanent collections of painting, sculpture, ceramics and decorative arts in American and Canadian museums: being an introduction to the masterpieces of art from prehistoric to modern times." The many illustrations of works of art from over one hundred museums are discussed nationally, beginning with I: Art of Ancient Egypt and ending with XVI: American School and XVII: Pre-Columbian Art of the Americas. The book was heartening because it was published during the war when no works of art could be shipped from overseas; it showed art lovers how rich North America was in world treasures.

Bibliography
- Shoolman, Regina, and Charles Slatkin. 1940. *The Story of Art: The Lives and Times of the Great Masters.* New York: Halcyon House, 332 pp.
- _____. 1942. *The Enjoyment of Art in America.* Philadelphia: Lippincott, 792 pp.

Sibbald, Susan Mein 1783-1866.   Susan Mein was born and raised in southwest England, the fifth daughter of a physician in the Royal Navy and his wife. She was educated in Cornwall and then at a fashionable boardingschool in Bath; after her debut, she spent winters in London and summers on her father's estate in Scotland. She married William Sibbald in 1807 and had two daughters and nine sons, eight of whom held military commissions during their lives. In 1836, after her husband died, she emigrated to Canada, buying Eildon Hall and surrounding property on Lake Simcoe, Ontario, which is now remembered in Sibbald Point Provincial Park. There she entertained in style many important people, including Bishop Strachan and other members of the conservative Family Compact. Although she went back to Britain in 1843, she returned to Toronto in 1856 to spend the last ten years of her life. She is buried beside her Lake Simcoe church, near the grave of **Mazo de la Roche**, who later summered in the area.

When she was in her seventies, Sibbald wrote *The Memoirs of Susan Sibbald* describing her first twenty-nine years of life. As a staunch supporter of British customs and institutions, she believed firmly in class distinctions and lamented the rise during her lifetime of the middle class.

Bibliography
- Fowler, Marian E. 1976. Susan Mein (Sibbald). *Dictionary of Canadian Biography*, s.v. Mein, Susan (Sibbald).
- Sibbald, Susan. 1926. *The Memoirs of Susan Sibbald (1783-1812).* Edited by her great-grandson Francis Paget Hett. London: John Lane, Bodley Head, 339 pp.

Simcoe, Elizabeth Posthuma Gwillim 1762-1850.   Elizabeth Gwillim became an orphan and an heiress several hours after her birth when her mother died; her father had died earlier in the year. She was raised in England by her aunt and uncle, and was well educated for the time, learning French and German and how to paint and sketch. After she married Lt-Col John Graves Simcoe when she was sixteen and he thirty, they settled down in Devonshire, where she enjoyed an active social and outdoor life. In 1791 she accompanied her husband to Upper Canada (Ontario), where he would be the first lieutenant governor, leaving behind four of her six young children (she would eventually have eleven) and taking only two-year-old Sophie and the baby Francis. The Simcoes stayed first in Quebec City, then moved to Niagara; they also visited York (Toronto) and other areas before returning to England in 1796. Wherever possible, she established a daily routine of taking tea, dancing, playing cards, chatting and making trips by foot or sleigh to local places of interest. Her husband died in 1806, forty-four years before she did. Although she was only five feet tall, she became an autocrat, insisting that her seven daughters remain with her rather than marry.

Simcoe's *The Diary of Mrs John Graves Simcoe*, first published in 1911, describes the people she met while in Ontario and her surroundings: "She was an enthusiastic reporter of the natural world in all its manifestations, from rattlesnakes to blossoming orchards, and her talent for the telling detail gives her writing its lasting appeal" (Thomas 1990). Thomas also notes that she "was not universally popular, some contemporary critics calling her excessively rank-conscious, demanding, and formal, but for her part she was ready to accept both the land and its inhabitants, particularly the Indians, with remarkable equanimity, even enthusiasm."

Bibliography

•Firth, Edith G. 1988. Elizabeth Posthuma Gwillim (Simcoe). *Dictionary of Canadian Biography*, s.v. Gwillim, Elizabeth Posthuma (Simcoe).

Fryer, Mary Beacock. 1989. Elizabeth Posthuma Simcoe, 1762-1850: A Biography. Toronto: Dundurn Press.

•Thomas, Clara. 1990. Elizabeth Simcoe. *Dictionary of Literary Biography: Canadian Writers before 1890*, s.v. Simcoe, Elizabeth.

•Simcoe, Elizabeth Posthuma. 1965. *The Diary of Mrs John Graves Simcoe*. Toronto: Macmillan (first edited in 1911 by John Ross Robertson). Edited by Mary Quayle Innis.

Sime, Jessie Georgina 1868-1958. Jessie Sime was born in Scotland but grew up in London, educated by her parents who were both writers; she was also related to the English novelist Mrs Oliphant and the University of Toronto president Sir Daniel Wilson. After attending Queen's College, London, she studied singing in Berlin, becoming briefly a public singer; her knowledge of languages enabled her later to do both French and German translations. She then worked in publishing and herself became a writer of short stories, magazine columns, reviews and eventually books. In 1907 she came to Canada: "By far the bulk of her writing was done in Canada, for Montreal and the countryside of Quebec stimulated her literarily [her popular novel *Our Little Life* (1921), for example, portrays the poverty of Catholic immigrants in a city based on Montreal]. More fundamentally, Canada also gave her recognition and a career" (New 1990). Her writing was successful enough that she was able to invest money during the 1930s. Sime became vice-president for Quebec of the Canadian Women's

Press Club, president of the Montreal Branch of the Canadian Authors Association, secretary of the Montreal P.E.N. group, and president of the Montreal Centre of the International Club for Authors.

Sime's *The Mistress of All Work* is about housekeeping—"in the making of the home woman normally finds her true profession." Sime, who was not married, continues, "The home must always be deeply at the root of a woman's life, if only because of its intimate connection with motherhood; and into its creation there should normally go all the art in her that is not exhausted in motherhood." (Her feminist work of fiction, *Sister Woman* (1919), however, shows why a homemaking role is not the answer for many women.)

Sime's *Thomas Hardy of the Wessex Novels*, of which one hundred copies were printed, is really an essay discussing and giving her opinion of his novels. She had seen and been impressed by Hardy, an acquaintance of her father, when she was a young girl. She praises him as a democrat, but feels that although he has "sympathy" for the world, he fails to connect adequately with it (New 1990).

In a Canadian Shack recounts trips Sime made in successive summers to a rural Quebec poultry farm. She discusses the people she came to know and their way of life, realizing eventually that she felt more at home with a French-Canadian neighbour than with her English hostess. She finds that one can put down real roots in Canada only after a period of slow acclimatization and reception. She philosophizes about the dichotomy in many people between the sophisticated and the primitive, which she feels is the basis of much of the violence and anxiety in the world.

The Land of Dreams gives accounts of some of Sime's dreams which she recorded over seven years, tracing their origins and significance. Her perspective is not that of an acknowledged expert; indeed, she writes, "I have sedulously and of set purpose refrained from questioning the few scientists and psychologists of my acquaintance who were in touch with recent dream-investigations and I have also refrained from reading anything that dealt specifically with the subject." She believes that dreams can foretell the future.

Bibliography
•New, W.H. 1990. Jessie Georgina Sime. *Dictionary of Literary Biography: Canadian Writers, 1890-1920*, s.v. Sime, Jessie Georgina.
•Sime, J.G. 1916. *The Mistress of All Work*. London: Methuen, 146 pp.
•_____. 1928. *Thomas Hardy of the Wessex Novels: An Essay and Biographical Note*. Montreal: Louis Carrier, 58 pp.
•_____. 1937. *In a Canadian Shack*. Toronto: Macmillan, 241 pp.
•_____. 1940. *The Land of Dreams*. Toronto: Macmillan, 273 pp.

Simms, Florence Mary. Florence Simms was an anglophone author.

Etoffe du Pays is a low-key book of vignettes about the lower St Lawrence River, specifically the area around Cap à l'Aigle and Murray Bay, which Florence Simms visited. She writes about French Canadians from a British Canadian's perspective.

Bibliography
•Simms, Florence Mary. 191?. *Etoffe du Pays: Lower St Lawrence Sketches.* Toronto: Musson, 87 pp.

Sisters of Providence. No individual is mentioned on the title page, although the foreword indicates that the author is a nun of the Sisters of Providence Order who had earlier written *The Sisters of Providence in Chili.*

The Institute of Providence was founded by the fourteenth and youngest child of the Taverniers of Montreal—Emmélie, born in 1800. In 1823 she married Jean Gamelin of Montreal, who died at age fifty-three four years later. Immediately she and her friends set up the Association of Charity to help the poor in the cold winter of 1827-28. Shortly after this, the last of her three children died. From then on she devoted her life to religion and to helping those in need through asylums, refuges and orphanages. Her group became the Ladies of Providence in 1841, under the auspices of the Roman Catholic Church, from which in 1843 the religious body of nuns was formed. The five-volume proposed work was a monumental historic effort.

Bibliography
Sisters of Charity of Providence. 1927-1949. *The Institute of Providence: History of the Daughters of Charity, Servants of the Poor Known as the Sisters of Providence.* Montreal: Providence Mother House, 566 pp., 5 vols.
•_____. Volume l: *Preliminaries and Foundations 1800-1844.*

Skelton, Isabel Murphy BA MA c.1880-1956. Isabel Murphy, born in Fitzroy, Ontario, was an early student at Queen's University, obtaining her MA in 1901. In 1904 she married fellow student Oscar Skelton (1878-1941) who later became a professor at Queen's and then a public servant in Ottawa. Together they raised three children. After 1945 she wrote other biographical sketches and a book, *William Bell, Parson and Pioneer* (1947).

The Backwoodswoman was written "to present briefly some characteristic glimpses of Canadian women pioneers. They not only met the needs of their own day, but laid lasting foundations for ours." Skelton states:

> Few women are enrolled among the Makers of Canada. Yet in all save the earliest years they have formed nearly half the population and have

done almost half the work. But historians, absorbed in the annals of war and politics and business, tell us little of the part they have played. The woman's stage was set not in the limelight, but in the firelight. Only rarely would the glare of battle light up for an instant the heroic daring of a Madame de la Tour or a Laura Secord and etch their names on history's page.

She ends her preface, "The women of Canada to-day have a proud heritage in the memories of their pioneer predecessors. We owe them homage as we owe devotion to the land they helped to make."

After visiting archives and libraries in Canada, England, Ireland and the United States, Skelton wrote *The Life of Thomas D'Arcy McGee*, the first comprehensive biography of this politician (1825-68) who came from Ireland and the United States to spend the last decade of his life in Canada. Skelton feels he was a vital spark for the nation:

> He gave us the conception of a Canada which national memories, history and legend could adorn, and around which national song and poetry, a national literature and a national art could grow. His speeches, his writings, his poetry, D'Arcy McGee dedicated to one purpose—to intensify our patriotism and to extinguish among us the party fires of sectional strife.

Bibliography
- Skelton, Isabel. 1924. *The Backwoodswoman: A Chronicle of Pioneer Home Life in Upper and Lower Canada.* Toronto: Ryerson, 261 pp.
- _____. 1925. *The Life of Thomas D'Arcy McGee*, Gardenvale, QC: Garden City Press, 554 pp.

Skinner, Constance Lindsay 1877-1939.   Constance Skinner was born and raised in the small fur centre of Quesnel, British Columbia, where her father was a Hudson's Bay factor. Despite, or perhaps because of, the isolation of her family, she was a precocious author, writing her first story at five years of age and her first novel at eleven. At fourteen, the year her family moved to Vancouver, she produced the libretto and score for a children's operetta, which was performed to raise money for charity. At sixteen, Skinner was sent to live with an aunt in California; she remained in the United States for the rest of her life, writing plays, poems, stories, articles, novels and histories of pioneer life that were strongly influenced by her observation of Natives and fur trading in Canada when she was young. The novel *Red Willows* (1929), for example, explores relations between Indians and whites during the British Columbia gold rush.

Beaver, Kings and Cabins, about Canada's early history and the fur trade, is based on both primary and secondary sources; Skinner especially thanks Vilhjalmur Stefansson in the preface for giving her access to his large private library. She used her father's letters and notes for specific information about Indian lore.

Bibliography
•Relke, Diana M.A. 1990. Constance Lindsay Skinner. *Dictionary of Literary Biography: Canadian Writers, 1890-1920*, s.v. Skinner, Constance Lindsay.
•Skinner, Constance Lindsay. 1933. *Beaver, Kings and Cabins*. London: Lovat Dickson, 273 pp.

Slatkin, Regina Shoolman See Shoolman, Regina entry.

Smith, Gertrude P. Gertrude Smith of Toronto, a member of the Wardell clan, was interested in genealogy.

Smith begins the preface of her book by noting that to some its title, *A Brief History of the Wardell Family*, "may sound presumptuous, a straining after unearned greatness," while to others the book may seem unnecessary— what have the Wardells done? She agrees that there are no great Wardells, but continues that:

> civilization would be impossible, were it not for the mighty efforts of men like old Joseph Wardell [born 1734 in Wales and emigrated to Canada from the United States as a Loyalist in 1785] and his sons. What man is greater than the hardy pioneer, who goes alone into the silent places, and by the power of his own unaided effort, smooths the way for the countless thousands who come after?

Women are included in Smith's text, even though they are absent from her generalizations. The decision to undertake this history was made at the Wardell Annual Picnic in Hamilton in 1908 by an appointed committee, including the author, Miss Emma Wardell of Smithville, and Mr Isaac Wardell of Smithville, who provided most of the information. Smithville was named for a brother of Isaac Wardell's wife.

Bibliography
•Smith, Gertrude P. 1910. *A Brief History of the Wardell Family from 1734 to 1910*. Toronto: Jackson, Moss, 104 pp.

Smith, Marjorie J. BA MA 1907-1957. Marjorie Smith was born in Minnesota and attended the Universities of Minnesota (BA) and Chicago (MA). She taught at Smith College of Social Work and did welfare work in the United States from 1929 until 1943, when she became a professor and Director of the School of Social Work at the University of British Columbia. She remained there until 1956, the year before her death.

Rural Case Work Services discusses social work cases in general from an American, specifically Washington State, perspective; it gives many examples of families experiencing problems "of personal, social, and economic adjustment" and relates how these problems were or could be addressed and solved by professionals.

Bibliography
•Smith, Marjorie J. 1943. *Rural Case Work Services*. New York: Family Welfare Association of America, 62 pp.

Smith, Olive Willett. Olive Willett was born in the Gaspé, Quebec, a land that she adored. On her marriage she became Olive Smith.

In *Gaspé the Romantique*, Willett wrote a book "to bring to the public a deeper appreciation of the traditions, customs and simple beauty of the lives of these people and the grandeur of the country in which they live." She describes towns and villages along the new highway around the peninsula, which "has been the means of bringing the world of today to this isolated coast and more firmly uniting a people who for centuries have lived in social and religious harmony." Her observations include a gamut of topics such as eel fishing, shrines, provincialisms and jails, as well as historical details.

Bibliography
•Smith, Olive Willett. 1936. *Gaspé the Romantique*. New York: Crowell, 159 pp.

Somerset, Susan Margaret, Duchess of See St Maur entry.

Speight-Humberston, Clara E. 1862-? Clara Speight-Humberston, who lived in Toronto, spent the first part of her life helping her husband, Humberston, with his political career. After thirty-five years and his death, she turned her attention to biology, her main interest, preparing over 1,900 pictorial charts of Canadian flowers and animals for Canadian schools. Then she became engrossed in the evolution of the earliest forms of life.

Her book *The Origin of the Chemical Elements and of Cell Life* explores possible connections between electrical energy and cell multiplication. She announces, "The electrical constitution of matter forces the recognition that *motion* is *life*, and the control of motion determines the length of time the material form shall live." She concludes from her studies with a microscope and from reviewing the work of many scientists that she proves "the elements are products of growth as living activities, and that growth is the result of a process of 'pushing' crystalline particles together into definite groups, through the government of motion by the force known as 'rotating electricity' or magnetism." She finds that "Bacteria are therefore rotating groups of electric charges, and they evidence all the motions found to govern the earth itself."

In *Spiritism*, she explains how she came at a late age to investigate the origin of celllife:

> The quickening of the mind, at a definite time of life may be traced to a resurrection of some part of the physical organization, that had been supporting a field of latent energy, which could not come into spiritual expression before a certain age of the life-form—thus "time" as a fourth dimensional control of light took on its active condition and forced the woman out of her pathway, into a new domain of thought.

She notes, "Certain discoveries of the fixation of numbers and their multiples characterising every reaction undertaken by the scientific investigator [herself] under direct experimentation, caused the writer [herself] to seek out the Professors at the University, and lay before each, the import of those numbers." Unfortunately, she found the professors at the University of Toronto in each discipline too narrow to be able to understand her ideas, which include in point form:

- Spiritism is now proven through the mathematics of the radium element;
- Man cannot cease to exist, as his life is a space phenomenon, making him one with Universal space itself;
- The Bible is supreme under Newton's law of gravitation;
- Secret of the transmutation of zinc into copper explains the functions of vacuoles in the human body.

Bibliography
•Speight-Humberston, Clara E. 1914. *The Origin of the Chemical Elements and of Cell Life*. Acton: Acton Free Press, 60 pp.
•Speight-Humberston, Clara E. 1922. *Spiritism: The Hidden Secret in Einstein's Theory of Relativity*. Kitchener: Commercial Printing, 232 pp.

Spence, Mary Ellen (Nellie) BA, LLD c.1868-1953. Nellie Spence, who was born in Whitby, Ontario, to a clerk and his wife, was in the first class of women to.enter the University of Toronto in 1884. After graduation she became a history teacher in Toronto, remaining at Parkdale Collegiate for thirty-eight years until her retirement in 1928. During the First World War she organized the Parkdale Knitting Brigade to make sweaters, caps, mufflers and socks for Parkdale servicemen. She was awarded an honorary degree from the University of Toronto in the 1930s for her historical writings, which included articles as well as a book.

Spence's *Topical Studies in Canadian History* was "the course of lessons which my classes have taken in Canadian history," prepared "at the suggestion of a number of ex-pupils." She notes it "may be of some value," although the lessons "are, of course, not intended to take the place of a text-book." Her sources include English and American historians, as well as a man called Garneau—"how good a thing it is with our race prejudices still so absurdly strong, to read the pages of that true-hearted French-Canadian!" she writes in her preface. Historical facts are set out in lists, charts and note form to make them readily available, so that the book is reminiscent of a fulsome and erudite Coles Notes.

Bibliography
•Spence, Nellie, BA. 1897. *Topical Studies in Canadian History Covering the Work Prescribed for Primary Leaving, and Matriculation Examinations in Ontario*. Toronto: Musson, 187 pp.

Spence, Ruth Elizabeth BA PhD 1890-1953.   Ruth Spence was largely educated in Ontario, but obtained her PhD from Columbia University, studying under the renowned John Dewey. She then taught as a professor of education at Smith College.

Ruth Spence wrote and dedicated her academic book *Prohibition in Canada* as a memorial to Francis Stephens Spence, her father. She quotes him liberally, stating that "he who was pre-eminently the authority on the temperance movement in Canada is the virtual author of this history," although this is certainly a great overstatement. Spence largely ignores for lack of space the contributions of individuals (except her father) and the growth of opinion, but includes the activities concerning prohibition of organizations, successive federal governments, provincial governments and various countries of the world. There is relatively little information on drinking and its deleterious effects on families.

Spence wrote *Education as Growth*, derived from her PhD thesis earned at Columbia University, "to present to Ontario readers the theory of Education as Growth, as formulated by Professor John Dewey (1859-1952) of Columbia University; to examine the secondary school system of the province from the point of view of that theory; and to make suggestions as to desirable lines of advance." Spence was in an excellent position to apply theory to school practice in Ontario, with whose system she was familiar. She discusses at length the aim of education, the secondary school system of Ontario, curricula, the centralized control of the curriculum, and the departmental examination system. Her recommendations for improvement include: a single system of schools with more comprehensive and purposeful criteria; methods of testing that will take into account wider education outcomes than are dealt with by the present departmental exams; subject matter that meets the needs of students; and more self-directed learning, which will entail less uniformity and more respect for individual differences. Ruth Spence Arndt (now married) was also the ideal person to write *John Dewey's Philosophy of Education*, which was aimed at improving the human condition. His theory of education was pragmatic—what works is right. "It abandons the rationalist scheme of verbal solutions, *a priori* reasons, fixed principles, closed systems and pretended absolutes and origins, and works with specific facts and concrete conditions of experience." He urged that children solve problems that interested them, because "when we are most interested, we put forth most effort." Arndt describes a rural school in which children learned only what they wanted to know, yet after four years they knew the standard curriculum better than pupils from non-experimental schools.

Bibliography

- Spence, Ruth Elizabeth. 1919. *Prohibition in Canada*. Toronto: Ontario Branch of the Dominion Alliance, 624 pp.
- _____. 1925. *Education as Growth: Its Significance for the Secondary Schools of Ontario*. Toronto: private, 183 pp.
- Arndt, Ruth Spence, PhD, sometimes Assistant Professor of Education, Smith College, USA. 1929. *John Dewey's Philosophy of Education*. Pretoria: J.L. Van Schaik, 105 pp.

Spragge, Ellen Elizabeth Cameron 1854-1932. Ellen Spragge, who travelled on the first through-train of the Canadian Pacific Railway that left Montreal in June 1886, wrote a series of articles on this adventure that were published in the magazine Toronto *Week*; she concluded her travelogue four months later in Victoria. After the addition of further material, her reports were published as a book.

Spragge hoped that her book *From Ontario to the Pacific by the CPR* might "in some degree supply an existing deficiency of information about a most interesting part of the Dominion—especially the district of Kootenay, with the mining interests of British Columbia." She praised the CPR highly, recommending the trip across Canada to all tourists.

Bibliography

- Spragge, Mrs Arthur. 1887. *From Ontario to the Pacific by the CPR*. Toronto: C. Blackett Robinson, 186 pp.

Springett, Evelyn Cartier Galt. Evelyn Springett was a Canadian of British stock who was named in part for Sir George Cartier, a friend of her father, and for her grandfather, John Galt. She met her future husband while visiting her brother in Winnipeg. After marrying Arthur Richard Springett in 1893, she spent her next years raising a family on his ranch in southern Alberta.

Springett wrote her memoir, *For My Children's Children*, for her six grandchildren, at the suggestion of her eldest sister, Amy Grant. The first part describes her various relatives; the rest comprises her own autobiography. The Springetts, she notes (p. 16), "belong to that upper middle class of England which, with its fine manners, sound morals, loyalty and energy, has done so much to maintain and extend the Empire." She, like another of her seven sisters, "ventured into the realms of literature" (p. 32) with this work.

Bibliography
•Springett, Evelyn Cartier. 1937. *For My Children's Children*. Montreal: Unity Press, 204 pp.

Steen, Ragna d. 1962.   Ragna Steen was a long-time resident of Bardo, Alberta.

Ragna Steen and Magda Hendrickson's book *Pioneer Days in Bardo, Alberta*, "just happened. It started at a time when we were asked to prepare some material about the pioneers for the local school and the Women's Missionary Federation." They began to consult pioneers for accurate information and to record the stories they heard for the children and grandchildren of the district pioneers. They collected so many narratives that they decided to make a book, which they did over the course of four years. It begins with the movement of Europeans into the Canadian West, specifically in 1894 when many settlers from Crookston, Minnesota, often of Norwegian stock, came to Bardo to begin a new life. The authors recount in detail information on social life, education, transportation, and various activities. Both seem to have been married.

Bibliography
•Steen, Ragna and Magda Hendrickson. 1944. *Pioneer Days in Bardo, Alberta, including Sketches of Early Surrounding Settlements*. Tofield, AB: Historical Society of Beaver Hills Lake, 228 pp.

Steeves, Helen Isabelle Harper 1873-?   Helen Steeves was the great-granddaughter of Moncton's first storekeeper, William Harper (1764-1834), although she downplays this connection in her book lest it detract from her story.

For *The Story of Moncton's First Store and Storekeeper*, Steeves obtained her information largely from two books owned by Harper, one, Ledger G, in use from 1815 to 1820 and the other, about 1830, for copying business letters. Steeves describes the cultural context of the store, begun in 1809 and burned down in 1834, and particular transactions from the early account book. There is little information on women; accounts were usually in the name of men, with farm wives seldom coming to the store to buy supplies.

Bibliography
•Steeves, Helen Harper. 1924. *The Story of Moncton's First Store and Storekeeper: Life around "The Bend" a Century Ago*. St John, NB: McMillan, 178 pp.

Stephenson, Annie Devina Watson 1862-1939.   Annie Watson of Mimico, Ontario, was educated at private schools and at Jarvis Collegiate, Toronto, before travelling in Europe. She was active in Toronto in Methodist Church work, where she met and married Frederick Stephenson, MD, DD, the Secretary of the Young People's Forward Movement. She helped to publish missionary textbooks, edited *The Missionary Bulletin* and prepared programs for the Sunday schools and Young People's Societies. In addition, she travelled several times across Canada, and kept in close touch with Methodist missionaries in the mission fields of Canada, Japan and China, often inviting them when on furlough to stay in her home.

When Frederick Stephenson was asked to produce a history suitable for young people about his church's missionaries, he persuaded his wife to write *One Hundred Years of Canadian Methodist Missions*, a task she was well-fitted to do, given her long and intense involvement with the movement. On its publication he kept the copyright while she made a "free-will offering," to quote his words. The book was fittingly published just as the Methodist Church in Canada disappeared to become part of the United Church of Canada.

That They May Be One is an introduction to the work of the Board of Home Missions of the United Church, written by Stephenson and Sara Vance for study groups of church youth so that they could learn about "the history, traditions and culture of some of the sixty-eight different nationalities now represented in our Canadian population." Stephenson notes that these diverse people will obviously be in contact daily: "When they come to understand and trust each other, our racial prejudice will disappear, and the day of real Canadian unity will begin to dawn." The book includes chapters on United Church work in Canada with Chinese, Japanese, French, Indians, Doukhobors, Finns, Ukrainians, Italians and Anglo-Saxons. The authors hoped that their book would inspire young people to dedicate their life "to the service of the Master and our country, in some needy school, hospital, mission home, or church, in the strategic newer centres of the Dominion." This book, like her first, was published through Stephenson's husband.

Bibliography
•Stephenson, Mrs Frederick C. 1925. *One Hundred Years of Canadian Methodist Missions 1824-1924*. Toronto: Missionary Society of the Methodist Church, 2 vols.
•Stephenson, Mrs and Sara Vance. 1929. *That They May Be One*. Toronto: F.C. Stephenson, Secretary Young People's Missionary Education, 222 pp.

Stevenson, Mabel McLuhan. Mabel Stevenson was an author living in Ontario.

Stevenson wrote *Our Government*, a "little book," really a handbook, to explain the Canadian system of self-government. The foreword notes that lack of space precluded discussion on most detailed exceptions or on public questions of the day, but Stevenson hopes that "the reader will pass from an acquaintance with the elements of Canadian government to that serious realization of our country's problems which ought to characterize every man and woman who has entered into full Canadian citizenship." In the year the book was published, no Canadian woman was allowed to vote. Provincial examples focus on Ontario, so this book would be implicitly less useful to people from other provinces.

Bibliography
•Stevenson, Mabel McLuhan. 1917. *Our Government: A Book for Canadians*. Toronto: George J. McLeod, 178 pp.

Stewart, Frances Browne 1794-1872. Frances Browne was born in Ireland to an Anglican clergyman and his wife, orphaned when thirteen and adopted by a great-uncle who introduced her to the writer Maria Edgeworth, soon her correspondent. In 1816 she married Irishman Thomas Stewart, with whom she would have eleven children. Their family of then three children and servants immigrated to Canada in 1822, settling on 1,200 acres of grant land on the Otonabee River in Ontario, near where **Anne Langton** and **Catharine Parr Traill** and their families would also settle. Thomas Stewart became a justice of the peace and a member of the Ontario Legislative Council, but died young in 1847, twenty-five years before his wife. Stewart had studied some botany, which enabled her to help Traill in the identification of plants; Traill (1885) "was deeply indebted for many hints and for the cheering interest that she [Stewart] always took in my writings, herself possessing the advantages of a highly cultivated mind, educated and trained in the society of persons of scientific and literary notoriety in the Old Country."

The first entries of Stewart's *Our Forest Home* describe her voyage by ship to Canada; the last were written shortly before her death. A friend of Stewart requested as early as 1833 that Stewart publish her letters so that others could enjoy them, but they were only collected after her death from friends and family in Ireland and Canada. These, along with journal entries, were edited by her daughter, Eleanor Susannah Dunlop, who wrote: "My first idea was that this volume should only be for members of our own family, but so many incidents and events of great public interest are recorded by my mother relating to the early days of the town and country about

Peterboro, that I have been persuaded to give it to the public." Glazebrook (1972) notes that "although unskillfully edited, the book is one of the best in the long list of accounts by immigrants and travellers." The second edition, prepared by Dunlop's niece, Frances Browne, contains additional letters and related appendices.

Bibliography

•Glazebrook, G. de T. 1972. Frances Browne Stewart. *Dictionary of Canadian Biography*, s.v. Stewart, Frances Browne.
•Stewart, Frances. 1902 [1889]. *Our Forest Home, Being Extracts from the Correspondence of the Late Frances Stewart*. Compiled and edited by her daughter E.S. Dunlop. Montreal: Gazette Printing, 300+xci pp. 2nd ed.

Stirling, Emma M. Emma Stirling, a Scotswoman, was the founder of the Edinburgh and Leith Children's Aid and Refuge Society, spending her own money and energy until 1893 to find shelter and placements for homeless children. With so many in distress, she decided to move to Nova Scotia and prepare a home for them in the Annapolis Valley, where they would have a better chance of building a future for themselves. In the 1890s, she felt forced by conflict with her work to retire to Pennsylvania.

The first part (1877-86) of *Our Children in Old Scotland and Nova Scotia* describes Stirling's social welfare work in Scotland with destitute children, who eventually numbered three hundred. The second part (1886-92) describes her life with up to three hundred more children whom she cared for and settled in Nova Scotia. It ends bitterly with the dissension that led her to give up her life's work.

Bibliography

•Stirling, Emma M. 1898. *Our Children in Old Scotland and Nova Scotia with Sequel Being a History of Her Work*. Coatesville, PA: C.N. Speakman, 184 pp.

Stone, Maud Morrison. Maud Stone was an author living in Toronto.

This Canada of Ours traces in sixty-three short chapters the history of Canada from the time of its earliest inhabitants to the First World War. Stone writes in her introduction, "My aim is to make this wonderful study of the Canadian people more interesting to the boys and girls, who to-morrow will have the destiny of the country in their own hands; for on the past of a nation her future is built." She states that she has attempted to trace the development and steady progress of the two races in Canada, and the growth of the Dominion of Canada "until it has become the great nation of to-day, with an Ambassador at Washington and a place in the League of Nations."

Bibliography
•Stone, Maud Morrison. 1937. *This Canada of Ours*. Toronto: Musson, 376 pp.

Strachan, Mrs E.S. Mrs Strachan, from Hamilton, was the Corresponding Secretary, Field (named Foreign in 1909), of the Methodist Woman's Missionary Society from 1881 to at least 1917; her mandate included visiting missions in the field.

In the introduction to *The Story of the Years* about Canadian Methodist missions and missionaries, Strachan is called "an eyewitness and minister of the word from the beginning." In her book she interweaves historical events "with the charm of her own personality." Her book is a continuation of the twenty-five-year history written by **Mrs H.L. Platt** of the WMS, which "considers the missions in the same general order, only striving to mark their development and the opening of new stations." It deals with overseas missions (Japan and China), missions for aboriginal peoples and Quebec protestants and Home missions. In describing urban hospitals and schools and their functioning, the text seems less than welcoming, entitling the relevant section "Strangers and Foreigners" which is in turn divided into "Asiatic Foreigners," "European Foreigners," and "Many Nationalities," comprising other new Canadians. One picture of aboriginal girls in Port Simpson, British Columbia, is entitled "Future Canadian Home-Makers."

Bibliography
•Strachan, Mrs E.S. 1917. *The Story of the Years: A History of the Woman's Missionary Society of the Methodist Church, Canada, 1906-1916*. Toronto: Woman's Missionary Society, Methodist Church, 338 pp.

Strange, Kathleen Redman 1896-? Kathleen Redman was born in London, England, and while working there during the First World War met and married Major H.G.L. Strange, with whom she immigrated to the Canadian West and raised four children. Within three years of settling on a farm, without any previous experience of agriculture, they won the World's Wheat Championship at the Chicago International Grain Exposition. They cultivated three hundred acres of virgin sod and as much again of soil already in production, building up a reputation across Canada for producing good seed. Strange wrote film and radio scripts, stories for various magazines and books, and was a member of the Canadian Women's Press Club, as well as other writing groups.

Strange describes in *With the West in Her Eyes* (which won a Canadian Book Contest) the over ten years she and her family spent on a western Canadian prairie farm. She explains that she was not one of the early pioneers, but arrived "when the slow-moving oxen had long since disappeared and time and labour-saving horses and tractors toiled upon the land in their stead; when the old log and sod houses were rapidly supplanted, in many instances, by pretentious frame dwellings."

Never a Dull Moment is a biography of her husband, Harry Strange, whose life stories his wife recorded as nearly as possible in her husband's own words, using first person pronouns. He grew up in England and France, and after apprenticing in engineering, travelled extensively—the Boer War, gold mining in the Klondike, Honolulu, the First World War, then agricultural work in western Canada until the Second World War.

Bibliography

• Strange, Kathleen. 1937 [1936]. *With the West in Her Eyes: The Story of a Modern Pioneer*. New York: Dodge, 292 pp.
• Strange, Harry and Kathleen. 1941. *Never a Dull Moment*. Toronto: Macmillan, 373 pp.

Strong, Margaret Kirkpatrick PhD. Margaret Strong was an early public policy analyst.

Strong's *Public Welfare Administration in Canada* was inspired both by her previous research into social problems in Canada and by encouragement from faculty of the Graduate School of Social Service Administration of the University of Chicago, where she had been a student. At the time the book was published as one of the Social Service Monograph series of that university, the development of public social service policies in both the United States and Canada was in a state of uncertainty, so that resource works such as Strong's were badly needed.

Bibliography

• Strong, Margaret Kirkpatrick. 1930. *Public Welfare Administration in Canada*. Chicago: University of Chicago Press, 246 pp.

Stuart, Arabella Mary (pseud.) Arabella Stuart travelled from Quebec to Scotland in 1823 and spent the next six years living in England, France and Malta.

Stuart described her low-key adventures in her diary and in her letters, many of them addressed to her mother. *Arabella's Letters* includes both her correspondence and that of friends in Canada, all compiled by her granddaughter.

Bibliography

• Stuart, Arabella M., ed. 1927. *Arabella's Letters together with the Contents of Her Small Diary 1823-1828*. Toronto: Musson, 300 pp.

Sykes, Ella Constance d. 1939. Ella Sykes was an Englishwoman who travelled from Britain to western Canada in 1911 to investigate possible job openings for educated women, since there were reportedly a million surplus women in the United Kingdom who could not earn enough money to support themselves. She decided that her six-month trip would be most useful if she worked as a home-help or maid, so she could have first-hand experience of what this entailed.

After toiling in five different households, Sykes concludes that a free life in Canada could easily be preferable to one in overcrowded England. In her *A Home-Help in Canada*, she states that a woman must be willing and able to work very hard in Canada if she is to succeed, but that if she has skills in teaching, stenography, dressmaking, some aspects of farming or domestic arts, she will be better off than the drudges who become home-helps: "Canada is a Land of Opportunity for the young, strong, and resourceful, who can cheerfully adapt themselves to entirely new conditions of life, in which they must divest themselves of many an English prejudice." She ardently desires "that British women shall help to build up the Empire, and the sisters of the men who are doing such splendid pioneer work in the Dominion are surely fitted for the task."

Bibliography
•Sykes, Ella C. 1912. *A Home-Help in Canada*. London: G. Bell and Sons, 304 pp.

Taylor, Monica, SND DSc. Monica Taylor was a scholar, author and nun.

Taylor writes that her biography *Sir Bertram Windle* is "a comprehensive, albeit a short [428 pages!], account of his life story." Windle (1858-1929) grew up in Ireland, and studied at Trinity College in Dublin where he became a devout Roman Catholic. He taught at the University of Birmingham from 1882 to 1905, then returned to Ireland to work for higher education. He came to St Michael's College at the University of Toronto in 1920 to spend the last years of his life studying, lecturing and writing. Taylor includes many letters from Windle; as she notes in her introduction, he believed that a biography "should never be undertaken by a near relative and that the subject of a biography should be allowed to tell his own story by means of letters and extracts from his own writings and utterances. These principles have been acted upon whenever it was possible to do so."

Bibliography
•Taylor, Monica, SND DSc. 1932. *Sir Bertram Windle*. London: Longmans, Green, 428 pp.

Textor, Lucy Elizabeth BA PhD 1871?-1958. Lucy Textor was an American who obtained her PhD from Yale University, writing her thesis on a number of French citizens who emigrated to Canada. She then taught as a professor at Vassar.

Textor's book *A Colony of Emigrés in Canada*, based on her PhD thesis, tells the story of a group of people who escaped during the French Revolution from France to England, where they were welcome for a few years. Forty-four of them then set out with the help of the British government for Upper Canada, to become settlers under the leadership of the Marquis de Brecourt. Based on original letters and first-hand records, Textor describes how and why the group came together and where various members settled in Canada.

Bibliography
•Textor, Lucy Elizabeth. 1905. *A Colony of Emigrés in Canada, 1798-1816*. Toronto: University of Toronto Studies, 86 pp.

Thornhill, Mary Elizabeth 1865-? Mary Thornhill was born and grew up in Toronto, where she attended a convent school and took great pleasure in music. As an adult, she helped found a business in the buying and selling of lace; she also, with her sister, sold fashion designs to retailers such as Eaton's. She made a number of buying and touring trips to Europe.

Between Friends is Thornhill's account of her life in business and of her various hobbies which included bridge, golf and riding.

Bibliography
•Thornhill, Mary Elizabeth. 1935. *Between Friends*. Toronto: Reginald Saunders, 252 pp.

Timlin, Mabel Frances BA PhD LLD OC 1891-1976. Mabel Timlin, the eldest of four children, was born and grew up in Wisconsin. Her father, although not a good provider for the family, inspired in his daughter an interest in politics and economics. She attended Normal College and taught school for a few years, moving in 1917 to Saskatoon, where four years later she became a secretary and later an administrator at the University of Saskatchewan. She was highly ambitious, studying part-time at this university for a bachelor's degree, which she obtained with "Great Distinction" in 1929. She earned her PhD at the University of Washington in 1940, when she was nearly fifty. She had become an instructor at the University of Saskatchewan in 1935, working her way up to full professor in 1950 and receiving an honorary degree there in 1969. Later work by Timlin included the books *Does Canada Need More People?* (1951) and *The Social Sciences in Canada* (1968), a study of the "institutional structure for the support of research in the social sciences in Canada." Her late-blooming success in academia was only possible because of her great ability and determination, but I remember that she also had a great enthusiasm and zest for life.

Timlin's doctoral work focused on Keynes's thought. A review states that her revised thesis, *Keynesian Economics*, "makes plain on every page the high competence of the author and the very great and sustained care she has used in writing it. In its possession of clear-cut purposes and method, in its detailed thoroughness, and in consistency, good architecture, and exactness and clearness of statement, it is outstanding." Keynes himself bought the book and wrote Timlin that it looked to be an "excellent piece of work," although he indicated he was too busy in wartime to give it much attention. The book, which has been translated into Japanese and used as a university textbook, was reissued in 1977.

Bibliography
- Spafford, Shirley. 1997. No Ordinary Academics: Teaching and Research in Economics and Political Science at the University of Saskatchewan, 1910-1960. Unpublished paper.
- Timlin, Mabel F. 1977 [1942]. *Keynesian Economics*. Toronto: McClelland and Stewart, 198 pp.

Toofie See Lauder, Maria entry.

Traill, Catharine Parr Strickland 1802-1899. Catharine Parr Strickland, named after the last queen of King Henry VIII who was a distant ancestor, was born near London. She was educated at home and was a published author of stories by the time she was sixteen years old; of the nine children in her family, six would become writers. She became interested in Canada when her younger brother, Samuel, emigrated there in 1825. When she was thirty and had published nine books, she married Lt Thomas Traill and emigrated with him to backwoods Upper Canada (Ontario) near Peterborough; she was soon followed by her sister **Susanna Moodie** and her family. Like her mother, Catharine bore nine children. When her husband died in 1859 she was left almost destitute, so to earn money for herself and her family she continued to write and publish what she could. In her spare time, she collected and studied local plants, encouraged by her neighbour, **Frances Stewart.** She ended her life in penury, when she was ninety writing to a publisher to beg him to make her an offer for her "little book with original drawings" (Theberge 1976, 31); she wanted to sell him publishing rights for twenty-five dollars, while she herself would pay for the illustrations. In recognition of her service to Canada, she had a variety of fern she discovered named after her and a small island in Stony Lake given to her by the government. She was also awarded British funds as the oldest living "authoress" in the British empire.

Traill's first book (1836) describes positively her new pioneer life in Canada, based on letters written back to England to her mother, sisters and friends. Peterman (1990) writes, "*The Backwoods of Canada*, which went through numerous editions and was translated into French and German, reveals the strength of her middle-class, English values even as it offers one of the most perceptive personal accounts of early settlement in Upper Canada." It earned her £150.

In 1854, she published *The Canadian Settler's Guide*, which gave useful information on housekeeping for prospective immigrants; it originally was titled *The Female Emigrant's Guide*, but the next year's reprint was aimed at all settlers, presumably to reach a wider market. In the preface, Traill writes that it is "devoted for the use of wives and daughters of the future settler, who for the most part, possess but a very vague idea of the particular duties which they are destined to undertake, and are after totally unprepared to meet the emergencies of their new mode of life." It includes details on such things as what to bring to Canada, how to choose a ship and buy a ticket, gardening, cooking, curing meat, the weather and making jam, soap, bread, candles and carpets.

Because of Traill's love of nature, she wrote a number of monographs, articles and books on this subject. *Canadian Wild Flowers* was illustrated with lithographs by Agnes Moodie FitzGibbon, daughter of **Susanna Moodie**, as was her 1885 book (her niece now remarried and become Agnes Chamberlin). Traill notes in it that her niece, "with a patriotic pride in her native land," wanted the book to be produced entirely in Canada. She adds pragmatically, however, that "Any short-comings [in the book] that may be noticed by our friends, must be excused on the score of the work being wholly Canadian in its execution."

Studies of Plant Life in Canada, her second botanical "little work [227 pp.!] on the flowers and native plants of Central Canada is offered to the Canadian public with the hope that it may prove a means of awakening a love for the natural productions of the country, and a desire to acquire more knowledge of its resources"; Traill explains that with the spread of civilization across the country, many plant species will disappear. Although she aims her book at the general reader rather than the expert, she gives the scientific as well as the common names of plants. She hopes her book will inspire in readers a love of God, "who has pointed us to that love which has clothed the grass of the field and cared for the preservation of even the lowliest of the herbs and weeds."

In *Pearls and Pebbles*, which presents mainly information on Ontario animals and the environment, she addresses the reader: "if you glean but one bright glad thought from the pages of my little volume [241 pp.!], or add but one pearl to your store of knowledge from the experience of the now aged naturalist, she will not think the time wasted that has been spent in gathering the pebbles from note-book and journals written during the long years of her life in the backwoods of Canada."

Bibliography

•Eaton, Sara. 1969. *Lady of the Backwoods.* Toronto: McClelland and Stewart, 175 pp.

Gray, Charlotte. 1999. *Sisters in the Wilderness: The Lives of Susanna Moodie and Catharine Parr Traill.* New York: Viking.

•Peterman, Michael A. 1990. Catharine Parr Traill. *Dictionary of Literary Biography: Canadian Writers before 1890,* s.v. Traill, Catharine Parr.

Theberge, C.B. 1976. *Canadiana on Your Bookshelf.* Toronto: Dent.

Traill, Catherine Parr. 1996. *I Bless You in My Heart: Selected Correspondence of Catherine Parr Traill.* Edited by Carl Ballstadt et al. Toronto: University of Toronto Press.

•[anonymous]. 1836. *The Backwoods of Canada, Being Letters from the Wife of an Emigrant Officer.* London: Charles Knight, 351 pp.

•_____. 1969 [1854, 1855]. *The Canadian Settler's Guide.* Toronto: McClelland and Stewart, 247 pp.

•_____. 1972 [1868]. *Canadian Wild Flowers.* Toronto: Coles Publication, 86 pp.

•Traill, Mrs C.P. 1906 [1885]. *Studies of Plant Life in Canada: Wild Flowers, Flowering Shrubs, and Grasses.* Toronto: Briggs, 227 pp.

•_____. 1894. *Pearls and Pebbles, or Notes of an Old Naturalist.* Toronto: Briggs, 241 pp.

Trevelyan, Katharine See Götsch-Trevelyan entry.

Tucker, Sarah 1774-1859?   Sarah Tucker, who never married, was a British historian who specialized in writing about Anglican missionary activity; her books centred on mission work in south India, Nigeria and New Zealand, as well as Canada (Gerson 1994, 12).

Tucker states in the preface of *The Rainbow in the North* that "This little volume was undertaken from the twofold conviction that, while the interest felt in Missionary work must very much depend on a knowledge of its details, the length of time that has elapsed since the commencement of many of our Missions renders their early history almost inaccessible to general readers." She describes in detail Indian inhabitants, the arrival and work of missionaries from 1820 to 1850, especially Rev. William Cockran, and characteristics of northwestern Canada. The Rainbow in the title is the bringing of a knowledge of "GOD" to this country's aboriginal inhabitants.

Bibliography
•Tucker, S. 1851. *The Rainbow in the North: A Short Account of the First Establishment of Christianity in Rupert's Land by the Church Missionary Society.* London: James Nisbet, 216 pp.

Turnbull, Elizabeth M. Elizabeth Turnbull was a Canadian interested in the outreach work of the United Church.

Turnbull was the editor of *The Missionary Monthly*, which gave her a wealth of material for her book *Through Missionary Windows*, a "snapshot" of one year in United Church mission life, with chapters devoted to work in Africa, central India, China (3), Japan, Korea, Trinidad and Canada (6). Each describes services provided for women and girls and items of current interest, as well as the names of those providing the services in the scores of mission centres. One missionary woman was heartened when she noticed a cross on the grave of a Native child who had recently died rather than a sewing machine which had previously been placed on many graves for use by the dead in their spirit home (p. 107).

Bibliography
•Turnbull, Elizabeth M. 1938. *Through Missionary Windows: A Story of the Home and Foreign Work of the Woman's Missionary Society of the United Church of Canada, 1937-1938.* Toronto: Woman's Missionary Society, 128 pp.

Turnbull, Jane Mason BA MA PhD 1896-? Jane Turnbull was a bilingual scholar of literature.

Turnbull's book *Essential Traits of French-Canadian Poetry* is based on her PhD thesis written for the University of Chicago. She states that Quebec in the 1930s had a great wealth of written material and "claims to be creating a 'national' literature" and "in so far as her progress can be measured in literature, has climbed well up on the ladder." She examines poetry that experts judged to be outstanding to see if it is distinct from poetry of France and concludes that it is indeed distinct: "there was one absorbing purpose to which poets were earnestly devoted, namely, the creation as well as the preservation of a national consciousness, based upon the traditions established by the example of devout and courageous ancestors."

Bibliography
•Turnbull, Jane Mason MA, PhD. 1938. *Essential Traits of French-Canadian Poetry.* Toronto: Macmillan, 225 pp.

Turner, Alice Willard BA MA PhD LLD. Alice Turner was born in the Norval, Ontario, manse where **Lucy Maud Montgomery** lived for many years. She received her MA from McGill and her PhD from the University of Toronto, then worked as a statistician with government and business before becoming a founding professor of mathematics at York University, Toronto. When she received an honorary degree from that university in 1977, she argued in her address to the graduates for the multiple importance of mathematics:

> In recognizing the striking challenge for advanced mathematics and research, however, it would seem to be a great pity to under-emphasize the importance of mathematics as a humanistic study.... Such study could heighten our sense of individual values and thereby help to counterbalance the seemingly impersonal thrust of technological progress. (University Women's Club, 1978, 50)

Turner's *We All Own Canada* argues against socialism by documenting the already wide distribution of wealth among the Canadian population, and makes a reasoned case for private enterprise. She notes, in keeping with her philosophy, that "This booklet has been prepared on my own responsibility as a private citizen, and is published independently as such."

Bibliography
•Turner, Alice Willard. 1944. *We All Own Canada*. Toronto: Collins, 63 pp.

Tyrrell, Mary Edith Carey 1870?-1945. Edith Carey, who was born in the Baptist parsonage in St John, New Brunswick, grew up in St John, England, and southwestern Ontario before moving to Ottawa, where she met the man she would marry in 1894. J.B. Tyrrell was an explorer and mining geologist working for the Geological Survey. During their engagement and first years of marriage, she spent months while he was away in the field studying geology so that she would understand his work. She finally joined him permanently when they moved to Dawson City following the Klondike gold rush. Before the First World War they returned to settle permanently in Toronto, where Tyrrell became president of the Women's Canadian Club, the Women's Historical Society, and, related to her husband's career, founded the Women of the Mining Industry in Canada Association.

Tyrrell's autobiography, *I Was There*, describes the couple's life together in the Yukon in the aftermath of the gold rush and ends shortly after they returned to Ontario.

Bibliography
•Tyrrell, Edith. 1938. *I Was There: A Book of Reminiscences*. Toronto: Ryerson, 131 pp.

Vant, Margaret Josephine MA. Margaret Vant lived in Winnipeg and taught at Lord Roberts School.

Living in Canada, a social science text for grades five and six, is written in a folksy manner, describing how Miss VanRob of Sunnivale School, "one of the best teachers in the district," teaches her pupils about Canada. By way of conversation among teacher and eager scholars, Vant and Robertson describe farming, mining, lumbering, trapping, fishing, manufacturing, transportation and community living. For a short skit (p. 94), they introduce Spirit of Communication, a character who seems now sorely dated: "She is dressed in a long blue or black robe. On the robe are pasted pictures of aeroplanes, telephones, buses, horses, ships and trains. She may have a bandeau of aeroplanes. She carries a silver wand." Among other men in the skit, they introduce Pierre from Quebec, who sings "Alouette."

Bibliography
•Vant, Margaret Josephine MA and Gladys Robertson. 1944. *Living in Canada.* Toronto: Ryerson Press, 157 pp.

Vincent, Ethel Gwendoline Moffat, Lady Howard 1861-1952. Lady Ethel Howard, the daughter and wife of British Members of Parliament, devoted much of her time to travelling and writing books about her trips. Before visiting Canada in 1891, she had been around the world with her husband, who had been Director of Criminal Investigation; she published their adventures in *Forty Thousands Miles over Land and Water: The Journal of a Tour through the British Empire and America* (1885).

She notes in her preface to *Newfoundland to Cochin China* (Cochin China was the French name for central and south Vietnam) that the favourable reception of her first travel book "has induced me to yield to the kind wishes of many Friends and Constituents and to record the impressions of my second circle round the world." The boat docked in Newfoundland, from where her party sailed to the Maritime provinces and then travelled by train across Canada, a trip she documents in journal form. She ends the section on Canada (p. 104): "Canada languishes for the want of population and capital. Give them to her, and she will become the finest country in the world, and our most prosperous as well as most loyal colony—British to the heart."

Bibliography
•Vincent, Mrs Howard. 1892. *Newfoundland to Cochin China by the Golden Wave, New Nippon, and the Forbidden City.* London: Sampson, Low, Marston, 374 pp.

Vincent, Kitty, Lady 1887-1969. Lady Kitty Vincent, the daughter of the Earl of Airlie and his wife, was educated at home, and married Lt-Col Ritson in 1926 (although she did not use her married name as an author). Her interests in life were dogbreeding, writing and travelling, so she asked her friend Eira, on four days' notice, to join her on a winter trip to central Canada that combined these interests. Eira agreed to go, dazzled by Vincent's descriptions of deep snow, packs of wolves and endless forests. Before they returned to Britain, they travelled to New York City to watch dog team races.

Two on a Trip, the story of their adventures, is full of sprightly vignettes and anecdotes:

> Personally, I never understand how Canadian women stand a winter in a town where life is one long struggle between the weather and the fashions. The girls display their knees in silk stockings although they envelop their feet in snow-boots; their feet remain warm and hideous and their knees are lovely and frost-bitten.

Vincent starts with tales of seasickness on the Atlantic, then recounts mostly their life near Metagama, where the two women stayed in a bush hut, enjoyed the cold weather, and ran a trapline briefly with their dog. She describes with good humour the problems of lighting a stove, using snowshoes, taking a bath and catching mice.

Bibliography
• Vincent, Lady Kitty. 1930. *Two on a Trip*. London: Herbert Jenkins, 253 pp.

Wales, Julia Grace BA MA PhD 1881-? Julia Wales, a native of Quebec, graduated as a gold medallist from McGill University in 1903. She earned her MA at Radcliffe and her PhD at the University of Wisconsin, then joined the faculty of English at Wisconsin, doing research on Shakespeare, but spending her summers in St Andrews East, Quebec.

Wales began to write *Democracy Needs Education* in the summer of 1939, when "Recent events have brought home with force the value of the democratic heritage and the responsibility of our generation to conserve its ideals." She notes in the foreword that she felt it essential that students should learn about how democracy operated under normal conditions, "in order that they may clearly know both what it is that they stand on guard to defend in an emergency and how they may carry on a no less loyal service when they are permitted to return to the ways of peace." There are fifteen short chapters on such topics as the principle of democracy, honesty, training of politicians and voters, thrift, leisure and the home. Each ends with a number of questions to elicit discussion, i.e., "What are the dangers of trying very hard to 'Keep up with the Joneses'?"

Bibliography
•Wales, Julia Grace PhD. 1942. *Democracy Needs Education.* Toronto: Macmillan, 107 pp.

Walker, Gertrude E. Gertrude Walker was an author living in Winnipeg.

Walker's name appears not on the title page of her book, *Romantic Winnipeg,* but under the short preface to a new edition. The small book begins with a historic overview of the city that is soon intertwined with anecdotes of the past and a description of Winnipeg as if the reader were visiting various parts of it in the present. It ends with detailed information from the 1930s. One section is indeed romantic (p. 46), beginning "I AM WINNIPEG! I stand at the gateway to the new Empire and my gates are open on all sides," and ending with "Romantic Winnipeg salutes you in the words of the old voyageur: 'It is not farewell for he who drinks of the Red River returns to drink again.' " The book includes advertising, indicating that it was used as a guide for tourists.

Bibliography
•[Walker, Gertrude E.]. 1938 edition. *Romantic Winnipeg.* N.p., 68 pp.

Walworth, Ellen Hardin 1858-1932. Ellen Walworth was an American author living in Albany, NY, who as a girl travelled around the world with her uncle and published an account of their trip in *An Old World as Seen Through Young Eyes, or Travels Around the World* (1877). Later, her uncle, who was investigating Jesuit manuscripts in Montreal, encouraged her to do research on the Native woman Tekakwitha, who was born near Albany.

In *The Life and Times of Kateri Tekakwitha,* Walworth recounts the story of this Native woman (1665?-89) who had an Algonquin mother and an Iroquois father, but because both died when she was young, was brought up in the Mohawk Valley in New York state by an aunt with whom she did not get along. After being baptized a Christian and refusing to marry, she escaped her relatives in 1677 and travelled to Sault St Louis (Kahnawake) near Montreal where there was a mission village with three Jesuit priests. She was known there as La Bonne Catherine, a devout woman much given to prayer who made herself a bed dotted with thorns so that during Lent she would suffer as Christ had suffered. Eventually she became sick and died when she was twenty-four. After her death she appeared as a vision to several friends and to a priest; as well, people who prayed at her grave attributed miracles to her. Recently she was accorded beatification by the Roman Catholic Church, and she may in future be canonized as its first Native American saint.

Bibliography
• Walworth, Ellen H. 1893. *The Life and Times of Kateri Tekakwitha, the Lily of the Mohawks*. Buffalo: Peter Paul and Bros., 314 pp.

Washburne, Heluiz Chandler 1892-1970. Heluiz Chandler was born in Ohio and worked as a home fashion adviser and travel columnist for the *Chicago Daily News* before becoming a full-time author. In the 1930s she worked closely with an Inuit woman to write the story of her life.

Anauta, the subject of Washburne's book *Land of the Good Shadows*, was from Baffin Island. She spent her early life as a traditional Inuit before marrying a trapper living in Labrador. After he died, she joined her children in Newfoundland and then in mainland United States. She worked in a factory for five years and then became a professional lecturer, speaking about the north. She also translated the Psalms into Inuktitut. Anauta had often been told she should write a book about her exotic life, but because she couldn't write very well, she didn't do so. Finally, when she was about fifty, she asked her friend Washburne to write it for her, a process that took four years. The first year, Washburne made typewritten notes of everything Anauta told her of her past life. Then they arranged the notes in chronological order, which was difficult because Anauta hadn't kept track of dates. Finally, Washburne typed the book, asking in the margin questions that Anauta should answer when she went over the text; Anauta also suggested additions or deletions.

Bibliography
• Washburne, Heluiz Chandler and Anauta. 1940. *Land of the Good Shadows: The Life Story of Anauta, an Eskimo Woman*. New York: John Day, 329 pp.

Watson, Mary Urie BA d. 1950. Mary Watson was raised in Ayr, Ontario, and graduated from the Philadelphia College of Domestic Science and Columbia University. She was principal of the Ontario Normal School of Domestic Science and Art in Hamilton, then a member of the Home Economics Department of the Ontario Agricultural College as well as first principal of Macdonald Institute, founded in 1903 in Guelph in part thanks to the efforts of **Adelaide Hunter Hoodless**; it was empowered to grant certificates to teachers of domestic science. During her tenure of this position, Watson organized a library of clippings and articles dealing with household affairs that she offered on loan to members of Women's Institutes; as early as 1909, two years after announcing this resource, she had received 350 requests for information (Ambrose 1996, 50). She was very earnest about her work, claiming that sewing was a skill that could "give honesty, for when you express yourself by making things, and not by using words, it becomes impossible to dissimulate your vagueness or ignorance by ambiguity" (Ross 1974). Watson taught in Guelph from 1903 to 1920, then retired to live in her hometown of Ayr. The University of Guelph has an extensive archival collection of her papers.

Watson who, unlike Hoodless, had university training in domestic science, worked together with Hoodless to update the textbook called *Public School Household Science* (1905) that Hoodless had published seven years earlier as *Public School Domestic Science* (1898). (See Hoodless, Adelaide entry.)

Bibliography

•Ross, Alexander M. 1974. *The College on the Hill*. Toronto: Copp, Clark.

Watt, Gertrude Balmer Hogg 1882-1963. Gertrude Hogg, who was born in Guelph and educated at Loretto Academy in Hamilton and at Brantford Collegiate, married A.B. Watt, a fellow journalist from Brantford. They lived in Woodstock, Ontario, writing for the *Sentinel-Review* until 1905, then moved to Edmonton to work for the Edmonton *Saturday News*. She was a charter member of the Canadian Women's Press Club and a good friend of fellow journalist **Kit Coleman.**

In Edmonton Gertrude Watt was a staff contributor, writing a column entitled "The Mirror" under the pseudonym "Peggy." *A Woman in the West* comprises extracts from her columns between 1905 and 1907 that "would serve a useful purpose in giving those in other parts of the globe a glimpse of the Canadian West, as viewed from a woman's stand point." Her writing did not reflect a superficial traveller's point of view, but the ideas "of one who has lived her daily life in the centre of the activity that has been exciting the interest and the wonder of the world and whose good fortune it has been to come into touch with many of the men who are making history in our midst." Each short chapter is a lively vignette based on her ruminations or on what she had done or seen.

This book was so well-received that she prepared a second volume, *Town and Trail*, also largely from her published articles and from columns in *Saturday News* and *The Alberta Homestead*. In it she included observations mostly about Alberta but also other topics for variety. She hopes this book will give "the world at large some idea of the charm of life in Alberta, of the spirit which animates our citizens and of the opportunities which this wonderful province, so dear to the hearts of its sons and daughters, has to offer to the right kind of men and women."

Bibliography

•Watt, Gertrude Balmer. 1907. *A Woman in the West*. Edmonton: News Publishing, 52 pp.

•_____. 1908. *Town and Trail*. Edmonton: News Publishing, 85 pp.

Watt, Madge Robertson BA MA MBE. Robertson, the daughter of a lawyer and his wife, was born and raised in Collingwood, Ontario. She attended the University of Toronto, receiving the first master's degree awarded to a woman. She worked on a newspaper in New York before marrying Alfred Watt and moving with him to Victoria, British Columbia, where she became a member of the Women's Institute and continued to write articles and also a book on southern Vancouver Island. When the First World War broke out, she was stranded in England as she was arranging for the education there of her two sons. During the war, realizing the need for women to help in the war effort by producing more food and keeping up morale, she became the founder and chief organizer of the Women's Institute movement in Great Britain. She organized the first one hundred Institute branches herself, then trained others to do this job; by 1921 there were over two thousand branches in Britain, more than in the founding nation of Canada. **Lady Byng** became patroness of the Women's Institutes, and Watt was awarded an MBE (Matron of the British Empire) for her work.

Watt's book *The Southmost Districts, Vancouver Island: Colwood, Metchosin, Sooke* was written "with special reference to [these districts'] desirability as sites for pleasant homes and their suitability for three special lines of agriculture—sheep, fruit and poultry." It reads like a booster document, with sections headed for example "Sheep Profitable," "Climate Right for Chickens," and "A Paradise for Fruit Growers," which is no surprise because it was authorized by the Vancouver Island Development Association. It has a section on Women Farmers, because "Agriculture for women is too little practised here," although she notes, "It is true that women are not so easily satisfied as men. They require more in the way of environment and possibilities." Watts claims that women like especially beautiful scenery including water; neighbours and social life; nearby shopping, churches, post office, doctors and public transportation; and a good climate that allows them to produce their own food. Watt includes many quotations from local residents, praising Vancouver Island and giving advice.

Bibliography
• Watt, Madge Robertson. 1910. *The Southmost Districts, Vancouver Island: Colwood, Metchosin, Sooke.* Victoria: Victoria Colonist, 64 pp.

Weaver, Emily Poynton 1865-1943. Emily Weaver was born in Manchester, England, and educated at a private school. When she came to Canada with her parents at the age of fifteen, they settled on a farm in southwestern Ontario. In 1889 she moved to Toronto and lived there and in Halifax as an adult, writing mainly historical novels (such as *Only Girl: A Tale of 1837* [1938]) and books of Canadian history.

In *A Canadian History for Boys and Girls*, Weaver writes that she has "endeavored to tell the story of Canada simply, and to choose subjects for illustration which would help boys and girls to understand the conditions of life prevailing in former times and in different parts of our widely-extended country." It won $200 in a Dominion history competition.

In *Builders of the Dominion*, Weaver "sketched for school children, as nearly as possible in chronological order, the lives of a number of men who have had a share in making the Dominion of Canada what it is to-day." All had some connection with the Maritime provinces, and she is partial to Empire Loyalists, noting that "The Dominion of Canada probably would not have existed but for the Loyalists." The paragraphs in each chapter are numbered for ease of study by pupils.

Weaver writes of *Old Quebec* that "This little book aspires, neither to the utility of a guide-book, nor to the dignity of a history. It is designed rather as a reminder of the great events which have given to the old city of Quebec a world-wide fame." The historical overview is accompanied by many sketches.

The Stories of the Counties of Ontario devotes a chapter to each of Ontario's forty-three counties and eleven districts, detailing when and how each was settled and initially developed. Some were easy to write about because of the work of earlier historians, but for others "the material had to be gathered with arduous labour, here and there, far afield." All represented a story of conquest, "of men, with little resource save their own strong arms, iron wills and alert intelligence, pitted against wild, beautiful, prolific Nature, and prevailing to subdue the earth." She again states partiality to settlers driven from the United States because of the American Revolution: "This Province had not, of course, a monopoly of all the Loyalist settlers who came northwards after the revolution, but it had enough to bring it into being with a distinctive character of its own, enough, exclusive of other brave and useful pioneers, to furnish it with heroes—and heroines—for the early days of stress and strain and struggle."

In *Canada and the British Immigrant*, her audience is the prospective immigrant, so this book gives "a general idea of the Dominion as a whole, and of each of the provinces a little more in detail, touching their history only as it seems likely to help to the understanding of what they now are, and of the attitude and ideals of the Canadian people." She urges that people not immigrate if they lack the possibility of a job, given "the financial stringency of 1913."

In *The Book of Canada for Young People*, Weaver blends together the two kinds of people who came to Canada—those who were explorers, adventurers and forceful leaders, and those "of a quieter type, who crossed the seas to make new homes, bringing with them a love of order and settled government, and laying the foundations, wherever they went, for churches, school, and all they stand for."

Bibliography

•Weaver, E.P. 1900. *A Canadian History for Boys and Girls*. Toronto: Copp, Clark, 312 pp.

•Weaver, Emily P. 1904. *Builders of the Dominion: Men of the East*. Toronto: Copp, Clark, 116 pp.

•_____. 1907. *Old Quebec: The City of Champlain*. Toronto: Briggs, 60 pp.

•_____. 1913. *The Stories of the Counties of Ontario*. Toronto: Bell and Cockburn, 318 pp.

•_____. 1914. *Canada and the British Immigrant*. London: Religious Tract Society, 311 pp.

•_____. 1928. *The Book of Canada for Young People*. Toronto: Doubleday, Doran and Gundy, 267 pp.

Weekes, Mary Loretto 1885-? Mary Weekes, who was born in Nova Scotia, trained and worked as a nurse in Boston hospitals from 1910 to 1914 before she married and moved to Regina. She loved the West, living part-time in a cottage in the Qu'Appelle Valley and researching information on prairie history and regional Native peoples, which she published in books and in articles for such magazines as *Saturday Night* and *Canadian Forum*. Later she moved to Toronto.

Round the Council Fires has nine chapters, each devoted to an Indian chief who had significant interaction with Europeans in what is now Canada. Her material, gathered and often quoting from early letters, journals and statements, is presented in adventurous episodes that provide some perspective from the Native point of view.

The Last Buffalo Hunter is a biography. At a 1932 party in Lebret, Saskatchewan, she joined a group of pioneers celebrating Norbert Welsh's birthday and talking about the olden times on the prairies at Fort Qu'Appelle; the most fascinating man was the oldest, former buffalo hunter Norbert Welsh himself, who was then eighty-seven and completely blind. Because he liked the sound of Weekes's voice, he agreed to tell her the story of his life so that she could make it into a book. He was born on the Red River, the son and grandson of Hudson's Bay Company men, and worked when he was young for board and one cent a day. When he grew up he went West to trade with the Indians and hunt buffalo, an activity that declined each year as more buffalo were wiped out. Weekes writes, "Norbert Welsh was not an educated man judged by modern educational standards, yet he spoke seven languages—English, French, Cree, Sioux, Blackfoot, Assiniboine and Stoney." She later wrote a novel about Welsh's life, *Painted Arrows* (1941), and other books about Native peoples.

Bibliography
- Weekes, Mary. 1935. *Round the Council Fires*. Toronto: Ryerson, 113 pp.
- _____. 1945 [1939]. *The Last Buffalo Hunter as Told to Her by Norbert Welsh*. Toronto: Macmillan, 304 pp.

Wetherell, Margaret Hubner Smith d. 1933. Margaret Wetherell was an Ontario author interested in local history.

Although the comprehensive *Jubilee History of Thorold* is catalogued as having been written by Wetherell, I could not find her name anywhere in the book. In the preface "The writer" thanks many individuals by name for information received, but nowhere is she herself identified. The Township of Thorold began as a United Empire Loyalist settlement; its tranquillity was disrupted over the years by an American occupation in the War of 1812, the construction of the Welland Canal, and Fenian Raids in 1866. Wetherell includes chapters on these events as well as on canal towns, agriculture, churches, schools, libraries and newspapers. There are twelve appendices, most listing men belonging to various groups, but one naming owners of the agricultural prize winners for 1897 for categories such as "Aged Sow, with pigs under 8 weeks."

Bibliography
- [Wetherell, Margaret]. 1898. *Jubilee History of Thorold Township and Town from the Time of the Red Men to the Present*. Published by John H. Thompson for the Thorold Beaverdams Historical Society. Thorold: Thorold Post Printing, 289 pp.

Wetmore, Jessie Helen Louise BA MA. Jessie Wetmore was a scholar who earned her master's degree from the University of Alberta, her studies financed by a trust fund.

Wetmore's *Seneca's Conception of the Stoic Sage* is devoted to the Roman philosopher Seneca, the Stoic philosophy that he preached and how they both perceived the Sage or Wise Man. She hoped thus to arrive "at a better understanding of ancient thought" and to attempt "an estimate of the permanence of the ideal enshrined in that exalted character, the Stoic Sage." She goes into great depth about the context of Seneca's life, the history of his times and the extent to which Seneca followed his own ideal of the Sage, believing that the Stoic ideal lives on in the self-imposed discipline and honour present in modern-day scholars.

Bibliography
•Wetmore, Jessie Helen Louise, BA. 1936. *Seneca's Conception of the Stoic Sage as Shown in His Prose Works*. Edmonton: University of Alberta, 66 pp.

Whiting, Lilian 1847-1942.   Lilian Whiting grew up in Illinois, where both parents served as principals of the local school; she was mostly educated at home, however, reading in the family's large library. She became a journalist, soon settling in Boston where in 1890 she became editor-in-chief of the Boston *Budget*. She made many trips to Europe, gathering material for her many books about Europeans and European cities and about spirituality. Her reputation was so great that in 1897 a Lilian Whiting Club was formed in New Orleans for people interested in the arts and sciences. She hated to grow old, so gave her date of birth as 1859 rather than 1847.

Canada the Spellbinder describes Canada, starting in the East and moving to the newly settled West, focusing especially on regions served by railways, which she considers a magnificent invention. She includes many historical details, but her real focus is "spiritual truth": "The Call of the North-West is to art, to science, to poetry, to religion. It is the call to the great spiritual realities of the spiritualised life, 'the power of conduct, the power of intellect and knowledge, the power of beauty, and the power of social life and manners.' "

Bibliography
•Whiting, Lilian. 1917. *Canada the Spellbinder*. Toronto: Dent, 322 pp.

Whitton, Charlotte Elizabeth BA MA CBE OC DCL LLD 1896-1975.
Charlotte Whitton was born in Renfrew, Ontario, to an Anglican father and a Catholic mother. She earned a BA (1917) and an MA (1918) from Queen's University, along with many medals and the Governor General's prize; in 1941, Queen's gave her an LLD. She was interested in child welfare and, as director of the Canadian Council on Child Welfare for many years, helped to put it on a scientific footing that it had not enjoyed earlier. She was also an author and long-time member of the Canadian Women's Press Club. She began to lecture and write in earnest, often on a contract basis, after she felt forced in 1941 to resign from the Council. From 1950 on she was involved in Ottawa politics, serving for many years as mayor and voted Canada's Woman of the Year six times. She was also made a Commander of the British Empire. She lived for almost thirty years with her dear friend Margaret Grier, a federal civil servant.

Canadian Women in the War Effort recounts the myriad works that women accomplished, much of it voluntary, during the first part of the Sec-

ond World War. Women actively participated in the Armed Forces including medical work, long-time organizations which focussed on the war
effort and voluntary war organizations. One section is entitled "Possible
demands upon them for further full-time mobilization," which may imply
why the book was written. Women are urged by HRH Princess Alice in a
foreword to give all they can to relieve the suffering in Britain: "It is just as
true to-day as ever that the hand that rocks the cradle rules the world, so let
us be up and doing."

Whitton's name is not on the title page of *A Hundred Years A'Fellin'*,
her book on forestry, presumably because she was retained on contract to
write it. It commemorates the centenary of the Gillies Brothers Ltd lumber
company, including an account of the "whole trade in all its many facets
from the timber cruising, the river driving, the saw mill to the world trade
conditions. In fact it is an authentic history of the Ottawa Valley of that
time, 1842 to 1942, opening the way for the early pioneers in the settlement
of the country."

The Dawn of Ampler Life, undertaken on behalf of the federal government, is a critique of planning documents from Canada, the United States
and the United Kingdom for human welfare after the war. Whitton was
asked to make a comparative analysis of these reports "and to comment
upon their possible adaptability to Canadian needs." Her review, published
as *The Dawn of Ampler Life*, was to be practical and non-political.

Bibliography

•Rooke, P.T. and R.L. Schnell. 1987. *No Bleeding Heart: Charlotte Whitton, A
   Feminist on the Right*. Vancouver: University of British Columbia Press, 243 pp.
•Whitton, Charlotte. 1942 *Canadian Women in the War Effort*. Toronto: Macmil-
   lan, 57 pp.
•[Whitton, Charlotte]. 1974 [1943]. *A Hundred Years A'Fellin'*. Ottawa: Runge
   Press, 172 pp.
•Whitton, Charlotte, CBE. 1943. *The Dawn of Ampler Life*. Toronto: Macmillan,
   154 pp.

Williams, Helen Ernestine. Helen Williams was born in Knowlton, Quebec, and educated at Knowlton Academy and Dunham Ladies' College.
Among her writings are short biographies of early French-Canadian heroes.

In *Spinning Wheels and Homespun* Williams writes about rural and small
town life in the Eastern Townships of Quebec, emphasizing nostalgia and literary allusion. She also travelled to some extent, describing the people and
scenes she encountered.

Three Churches begins: "Anglicans of St Paul's Church, Knowlton,
have had the unique, if bitter-sweet, privilege of building three churches
within a hundred years, in 1843, 1892, and 1941." The first church was

taken down because of its age and inconveniences, while the second burned down. Williams describes all three churches and the people who worked and worshipped in them.

Bibliography
• Williams, Helen E. 1923. *Spinning Wheels and Homespun*. Toronto: McClelland and Stewart, 314 pp.
• _____. 1941. *Three Churches*. Knowlton, QC: St Paul's Church, 50 pp.

Williams, Mabel Berta 1878-? Mabel Williams was passionately interested in Canada's western national parks, which she knew thoroughly. As well as the two books described below, in 1948 she published *The Banff-Jasper Highway* (revised in 1963) in which she gives a history of the area and a mile-by-mile report of what can be found along this scenic route.

The Heart of the Rockies, aimed at tourists, gives a general description of the Rockies and of their large National Parks, plus activities there and short descriptions of vegetation and wildlife. She comments that mountain goats are apparently "dominated by feminine influence, because groups are often seen on dangerous heights led by a sagacious old nanny." Otherwise, all animals are referred to as "he."

In *Guardians of the Wild*, Williams tells the story of the National Parks of Western Canada. Soon after their proclamation, wildlife species that had been heavily shot and trapped began to reappear; Williams describes the return of bison and other game animals to Alberta National Parks, and the building of highways to service the parks.

Bibliography
• Williams, M.B. 1924. *The Heart of the Rockies*. Hamilton: H.R. Larson, 97 pp.
• _____. 1936. *Guardians of the Wild*. London: Nelson, 147 pp.

Willison, Marjory See MacMurchy, Marjory entry.

Wilson, Idele Louise BA MA. Idele Wilson, a graduate of the University of British Columbia, was an authority on trade union agreements and bargaining procedure, and Director of Research and Editor of the Workers' Educational Association's *Labour News*. She focused her research on labour law, labour legislation and social and economic problems, particularly as they affected workers.

Wilson's small book *Union Security* argues, with the use of examples and statistics, the importance of closed union shops to prevent the exploitation of workers.

Bibliography

•Wilson, Idele L. MA. 1944. *Union Security*. Toronto: Workers' Educational Association of Canada, 64 pp.

Wood, Ruth Kedzie. Ruth Wood was a Fellow of the Royal Geographical Society who wrote a number of tourist handbooks, two of which include information on Canada.

The Tourist's Maritime Provinces begins with general information about eastern Canada (climate, language, methods of transportation) and specific data for the tourist (hotels, cuisine, sports, amusement and festivals). After a brief history, it discusses in great detail the various regions in the east, what highlights each offers the visitor, and exact information on distances (still useful), on prices (startling), and on trivia—"It is said that Acadian children rarely kissed their mothers after the first communion, it being a Brittany custom to restrain emotion" (p. 113).

The second part of *The Tourist's Northwest* discusses British Columbia and Alberta, giving first basic information on travel, and then specific details about four regions. A foreword describes the benefit of learning about a place one plans to visit before the actual trip, taken from an article in a 1915 issue of *Geographical Journal*.

Bibliography

•Wood, Ruth Kedzie. 1915. *The Tourist's Maritime Provinces, with Chapters on the Gaspé Shore, Newfoundland and Labrador and the Miquelon Islands*. New York: Dodd, Mead, 440 pp.
•_____. 1917. *The Tourist's Northwest*. New York: Dodd, Mead, 528 pp.

Wooster, Julia Louise 1914-? Julia Wooster was a Research Assistant in the Farm Credit Administration of the United States who worked under the direction and with the collaboration of a Senior Agricultural Economist. This Administration prepared and published a series of books on agricultural credit systems in foreign countries, of which that on Canada was the third.

Agricultural Credit in Canada describes Canada's system before the Second World War, noting that "It is particularly interesting to see how that country, a neighbor with similar cultural background and tradition as well as a topography and natural conditions not far different from those of the northern United States, has attacked the problem of extending credit to the farmer."

Bibliography

•Wooster, Julia L. and Walter Bauer. 1941. *Agricultural Credit in Canada*. Washington, DC: United States Department of Agriculture Bulletin, 63 pp.

Wright, Esther Isabell Clark BA PhD LLD 1895-1990. Esther Clark, the daughter of a businessman and future Lieutenant-Governor of New Brunswick and his wife, was born and raised in a well-to-do Baptist household. She was determined to go to university, the first in her immediate family to do so, and earned her BA (1916) at Acadia University and her PhD (1931) at Radcliffe College. She married an Englishman, Conrad Payling Wright, in 1924, and taught sociology at Stanford and Harvard Universities. She returned to Nova Scotia to teach at Acadia University from 1943 to 1947; this academic position activated her to publish over the years a number of books about her native province, such as *The Loyalists of New Brunswick* (1955) and *The St John River and Its Tributaries* (1966). David Cruise and Alison Griffiths (1997) describe Wright: "A sociologist by education, a social reformer by passion, a writer by inclination and an enthusiastic and caustic gossip by avocation, Wright let no aspect of the human condition pass without judgment." She received an honorary degree for her scholarly activity from Acadia University in 1975.

Most of the chapters of *The Miramichi*, a book focused on the watershed of the Miramichi River, describe particular men, beginning with Richard Denys, whose father had been given vast holdings in New Brunswick in the seventeenth century by the Company of New France. The last man considered is Dr John Vondy, who nursed immigrants arriving in New Brunswick with typhus and himself fell sick of this disease, dying in 1847.

Wright gathered historical information for her companion volume, *The Petitcodiac*, from many sources, including the Public Archives in Ottawa, registries of deeds in the Maritimes, libraries, memoirs and personal sources, paying special attention to early pioneers and their descendants. She notes, "It has been a peculiar pleasure to be able to dig out and to assemble this much of the history of the Petitcodiac region, not only because it was a peculiarly tantalizing problem historically, but also because it was the story of my Mother's country and of her people."

Bibliography
•Cruise, David and Alison Griffiths. 1997. *On South Mountain: The Dark Secrets of the Goler Clan*. Toronto: Penguin.
•Moody, Barry M. 1995. Esther Clark Goes to College. *Atlantis* 20,1: 39-48.
•Wright, Esther Clark. 1944. *The Miramichi: A Study of the New Brunswick River and of the People Who Settled along It*. Sackville, NB: Tribune Press, 79 pp.
•Wright, Esther Clark. 1945. *The Petitcodiac: A Study of the New Brunswick River and of the People Who Settled along It*. Sackville, NB: Tribune Press, 76 pp.

Wrong, Margaret Christian BA MA 1887-1948. Margaret Wrong was the daughter of University of Toronto professor George Wrong and his wife. She was educated at this university (BA, MA) and at Oxford University, then served in Toronto as secretary to the Young Women's Christian Association, and from 1916 to 1921 as Dean of Women at University College. In 1921 she moved to Geneva as Secretary of the World Student Christian Federation, travelling widely through Europe. She then became interested in Africa, making a number of trips south of the Sahara in British, Belgian, French and Portuguese territories and in Liberia, most undertaken in her capacity as Secretary of the International Committee on Christian Literature for Africa (1929-48), a sub-committee of the International Missionary Council which comprised about forty missions working in Africa. Supported by British, Canadian and American missionary, and some philanthropic, bodies, she became a pioneer and expert on Africa-wide literature and literacy. She died in Uganda in 1948.

Wrong's *Ideals and Realities in Europe* was written while she was Travelling Secretary of the World's Student Christian Federation. She writes that it is "merely an outline of some of the destructive and creative forces at work, the aim being to show the relation of the individual to these forces both as victim and as the explorer of a new way." She wants the explorer "to hear still small voices which in the din of traffic often go unheard"; hope lies in following paths that lead to life rather than death, "following with the open mind of the scientist and with that freedom of spirit which makes it possible to see the significance of things called small and insignificant, and the insignificance of much which by common report is magnificent and great." Chapters discuss Europe before and after the First World War, postwar cooperation between countries and peoples, religion and the life and prospects of individuals. She concludes with the importance of spiritual values between nations, and the "willingness on the part of the individual to lose his life for the sake of life."

Africa and the Making of Books "is based in part on information obtained during a seven-months' tour made in 1933 when in my capacity as secretary of the Committee I visited West, Central and East Africa." The aim of this committee was "to promote the preparation, publication and distribution of literature for use in connexion with missionary work in Africa." Wrong discusses the types of books wanted by Africans, especially Christian books, and the many problems with providing them. For example, there were between eight and nine hundred languages spoken in Africa; governments often wanted their citizens to use only the official national language(s) while the missionaries favoured religious books in the vernacular; a language was written sometimes with different symbols;

books could be printed either in correct or pidgin English; the population was largely illiterate; there was usually only poor light for reading after dark; and books were often destroyed by mildew or insects.

Wrong writes in the preface of *The Land and Life of Africa* that her book will be only "a small fire throwing a feeble light," because Africa was so complex and full of variety and had been going through rapid change. She notes that:

> The West has grave responsibilities in Africa for the destiny of over 100,000,000 people of many tribes and races. These responsibilities are largely unrealized. It is hoped that this book may help to interest citizens, including older schoolboys and schoolgirls, in the peoples of Africa who have been swept so suddenly into all the devious currents of modern life and upon whom we make such heavy demands.

She elucidates problems and solutions as far as possible by letting Africans speak in their own voices.

With financial help from the Carnegie Corporation, Wrong travelled through Kenya, Uganda, Sudan, Nigeria and the Gold Coast for six months from December 1938 to continue her inquiry "into the need of literature for African peoples, and to discuss with those on the spot how that need could best be met." *Across Africa* gives impressions of the places she visited as well as conclusions about literature development and needs. She writes, "Evidence received since the outbreak of war indicates that the war is increasing the desire for reading among African peoples and that in these days of anxiety, danger, and shortage of staff it is more than ever necessary to supply food for the minds and spirits of men [*sic*] through the written word."

Five Points for Africa discusses necessities for the continent established by a church conference: the abolishment of extreme inequality in wealth; the need for equal opportunity in education for all children; the safeguarding of the family as a social unit; the need for a sense of divine vocation in daily work; and the wise use of resources by all people now and in the future.

In 1942, the Foreign Missions Conference of North America voted to form a study group "to consider how the total resources of African churches and missions may be utilized to better advantage."

After several years of planning, Wrong and two male colleagues visited seven countries in west-central Africa for six months of study; their report, *Africa Advancing*, was published the following year.

Bibliography

•Davis, Jackson, Thomas M. Campbell and Margaret Wrong. 1969 [1945]. *Africa Advancing: A Study of Rural Education and Agriculture in West Africa and the Belgian Congo*. New York: Negro Universities Press, 231 pp.

- Wrong, Margaret, MA. 1925. *Ideals and Realities in Europe*. London: Student Christian Movement, 148 pp.
- _____. 1934. *Africa and the Making of Books, Being a Survey of Africa's Need of Literature*. London: International Committee on Christian Literature for Africa, 56 pp.
- _____. 1935. *The Land and Life of Africa*. London: Edinburgh House Press, 144 pp.
- _____. 1940. *Across Africa*. London: International Committee on Christian Literature for Africa, 104 pp.
- _____. 1942. *Five Points for Africa*. London: Edinburgh House Press, 150 pp.

York, Eva Rose Fitch 1858-1938. Eva Fitch was born into a Baptist family in Norwich, Ontario, attended Woodstock Collegiate, then studied music until she married Winford York, a doctor, in 1879. After he died the following year, she prepared for a career in music by studying the organ in the United States. About this time she became a born-again Christian who would devote much of her life to religion as well as music and literature. She founded and conducted the Philharmonic Chorus and Orchestra in Belleville, then moved to Toronto where she was an organist and choir leader at Grace Church. She gave up her music in 1899 to help girls and women, both practically and spiritually, "who have fallen into sin," as her two books describe. Her other writing included a religious novel, *The White Letter: A Tale of Retribution and Reward* (1903), copies of which she gave free to anyone who might accept its "Gospel message." She was remembered by the Eva Rose York Bible Training School for women established in 1922 in India (at Palkonda and then Tuni).

York's *Feathers with Yellow Gold*, with the help of excerpts from annual reports, describes her founding of Redemption Home to help girls and women in need and its functioning until 1914. She shows "that change kept pace with its needs and with the development of its founder's belief in the unfailing providence of God."

When My Dream Came True, a book of autobiography and religious rumination, includes her next fifteen years when she travelled over North America to bring the Word of God to those in rural and urban groups who needed her spiritual guidance, her efforts supported financially by those who knew and believed in her and her work. She notes that the title refers to "heart rest, the pathetic quest of the world, the dream of mankind" which few attain and claims that "On yonder, somewhere, sometime, somehow, one's heart-hunger is to be satisfied. How this can be accomplished may be learned from the pages that follow."

Bibliography
• York, Eva Rose. 1920. *Feathers with Yellow Gold: The Story of Redemption Home, Toronto, Canada.* Toronto: Evangelical Publishers, 235 pp.
• _____. 1935. *When My Dream Came True: A Brief Autobiography in Which the Author Is Seen Seeking and Finding Abiding Joy.* Toronto: Evangelical Publishers, 62 pp.

Youmans, Harriet Phelps. Harriet Youmans was a religious woman living in Grimsby, Ontario.

Grimsby Park on Lake Ontario was renowned as an old-fashioned camp-meeting place where first mammoth temperance rallies (in 1846 for example) and then revival meetings were held the last week of each August from 1859 on. "The camp-meeting seems to have been a prominent feature of the early religious life of Canada. Long before there were towns or villages, the scattered settlers were wont to gather occasionally in those primitive meetings." Youmans describes in detail in *Grimsby Park, Historical and Descriptive* the park and the men who were chiefly responsible for the revivals' successes; although she devotes an entire chapter to each of the few important men, only Phelps, surely a relative, is mentioned in the book's title. She ends her book: "Grimsby Park has a noble past which these imperfect pages have utterly failed to depict."

Bibliography
• Youmans, Harriet Phelps. 1900. *Grimsby Park, Historical and Descriptive, with Biographical Sketches of the Late President Noah Phelps and Others.* Toronto: Briggs, 75 pp.

Youmans, Letitia Creighton 1827-1896. Letitia Creighton was raised a Methodist on a pioneer farm near Cobourg, Ontario, by an American mother and an Irish father. She finished her education at Cobourg Ladies' Seminary and at Burlington Academy in Hamilton, where she remained for two years as a teacher to pay off her tuition. When she was twenty-three, she married Arthur Youmans, a farmer and widower with eight children, and moved with them to a farm near Picton, Ontario. As well as raising and home-schooling this family, she taught Sunday school. She and her family had little acquaintance with alcohol, but so many of her young students had suffered from the indirect effects of alcoholism that she founded at Picton a Canadian branch of the Women's Christian Temperance Union; in 1885 she was elected president of the newly organized Dominion WCTU. She spoke so passionately against alcohol (in the United States as well as Canada) that by 1891 her organization had over nine thousand members. "Her oratory electrified her audience" Crowley (1990) writes, "where her long, turgid but emotionally inspired speeches based on biblical themes were enthusiastically received." Youmans soon emerged "as Canada's foremost female temperance organizer." Her group had a broad social mandate that included visiting prisons (she declared inmates "privileged to be in an environment free from accursed beverages") and threatening to publish the names of prostitutes' clients, to the consternation of many men. Youmans was against universal suffrage, a right which she felt would weaken the temperance crusade. When her husband died in 1882, she moved to Toronto and increased her temperance efforts, visiting Great Britain, California and British Columbia in the cause.

Youmans's autobiography, *Campaign Echoes*, which recounts her social activism, was undertaken "by request of the Provincial Woman's Christian Temperance Union of Ontario" (of which she had been president) three years before her death, when she was already bedridden and forced to dictate her remembrances: "My own feelings shrank from writing an 'autobiography,' and it was only at the earnest solicitations of friends that this book was ever commenced" (p. 68).

Bibliography

• Crowley, T.A. 1990. Letitia Creighton (Youmans). *Dictionary of Canadian Biography*, s.v. Creighton, Letitia (Youmans).
• Youmans, Letitia. 1893. *Campaign Echoes: The Autobiography of Mrs Letitia Youmans, the Pioneer of the White Ribbon Movement*. Toronto: Briggs, 312 pp.

Young, Rosalind Watson BA MA LLD 1874-c.1962. Rosalind Watson was born in Huntingdon, Quebec, the daughter of a minister and his wife. She attended McGill University earning a degree in geology and a Gold Medal, and then became a teacher. She taught school in Victoria, British Columbia, making field trips in her spare time to gather material for her master's degree. She married Henry Young in 1904 and went with him to the Yukon; there she persisted in studying rocks. As she was unable to continue teaching because of her marriage, she became a popularizer of science and technology, publishing mining and geographical works as an "amateur." In 1911 they returned to Victoria, where her husband served as the Minister of Education for British Columbia. She received an LLD from the University of British Columbia in 1961. (See Lawson, Maria entry.)

A History and Geography of British Columbia, published by the joint authors Maria Lawson (for history) and Rosalind Young (for geography), was aimed at the province's public school students. Young describes the geology of British Columbia briefly, then discusses its various regions, dwelling on their climate, towns, agriculture, natural resources and industries.

Bibliography
•Young, Rosalind Watson, MA. 1913 [1906]. *A History and Geography of British Columbia—Geography* pp. 83-156. Toronto: Educational Book Co.

Ziegler, Olive Irene BA 1894?-1980. Olive Ziegler graduated from the University of Toronto in 1914, and the following year founded with four other women the Canadian Girls in Training (CGIT) movement. Her work with girls continued for many years in her position as Secretary for the national Young Women's Christian Association. In the early 1930s, she was appointed head resident of the University Settlement in Toronto, where she introduced the nursery school; during the Second World War she served as housing counsellor in Halifax.

The foreword of Ziegler's "authorized sketch" *Woodsworth: Social Pioneer*, about J.S. Woodsworth (1874-1942), the first leader of the Co-Operative Commonwealth Federation (CCF) party, notes that his "varied career as minister, social worker, dock labourer, Labour lecturer, inmate of jail, Member of Parliament, leader of a new party with vast possibilities, has been told by Miss Olive Ziegler of Toronto, with sympathetic insight, conciseness, and literary grace." He was the father of **Grace MacInnis.**

Bibliography
•Ziegler, Olive. 1934. *Woodsworth: Social Pioneer*. Toronto: Ontario Publishing Co, 202 pp.

Anonymous. The author of *A Memoir of the Life and Work of Hannah Grier Coome* is not identified other than in the text as a member of the Sisterhood of St John the Divine in Toronto, founded by the subject of her biography.

Her book was written to celebrate the fifty-year jubilee in 1934 of the Community, when "only one of the first little band of Sisters is left to remember the old Chapel, the Novitiate, and the other surroundings of that tiny Convent in St Matthias' Parish." Hannah Grier was born in 1837 near Belleville, the sixth child of a rector and his wife who educated her at home. When she was twenty-two, she married an English engineer, Charles Coome, who was helping to lay track for the Grand Trunk Railway between Belleville and Kingston, their future home. They later moved to Britain for nineteen years, where St John the Divine was Coome's parish church. After her husband died in 1878, Coome decided to "offer her widowhood in complete dedication to God's service" (p. 23). She did this by serving a novitiate at a convent near New York City, in training for founding a Sisterhood in Toronto backed by Anglican church officials. The new convent was based first at two houses on Euclid Avenue, where the three sisters, dressed in black habits, offered dinners twice a week for the poor, a health clinic, a Bible class for boys and clothing for those in need. Contributions of money, goods and volunteer service were requested from those who had the means. As early as 1885, the sisters sent seven women to Moose Jaw to nurse soldiers wounded in the second Riel Rebellion. Then they founded a small women's hospital and a church home for the aged, and in 1893 took over the Bishop Bethune College for girls in Oshawa. By 1901, the sisters numbered twelve hard-working women. Coome died in 1921, but the convent carried on.

Bibliography

• Anonymous. 1933. *A Memoir of the Life and Work of Hannah Grier Coome.* London: Oxford University Press, 294 pp.

Appendix A: Authors Who Received Honorary Degrees from Canadian Universities

Education/Scholarship

Donalda Dickie	1952	University of Toronto
Wilhelmina Gordon	1950	Queen's University
Mary Quayle Innis	1958	Queen's University
	1965	University of Waterloo
Mossie May Kirkwood	1977	Trinity College, ON
Elizabeth MacCallum	1952	Queen's University
Aletta Marty	1921	Queen's University
Lilian Maxwell	1946	University of New Brunswick
Hilda Neatby	1953	University of Toronto
	1967	Brock University
Mary Northway	1979	Trent University
Grace Rogers	1911	Acadia University
Sybil Shack	1969	University of Manitoba
Nellie Spence	1937	University of Toronto
Mabel Timlin	1969	University of Saskatchewan
Alice Turner	1977	York University
Esther Wright	1975	Acadia University
Rosalind Young	1961	University of British Columbia

Literature

Clara Dennis	1938	Mount Allison University
Bertha Dunham	1947	University of Western Ontario
Marshall Saunders	1911	Acadia University

Medicine

| Maude Abbott | 1936 | McGill University |
| Mary Jackson | 1976 | University of Alberta |

Religious work

Matilda Churchill	1923	Acadia University
Margaret O'Hara	1932	Queen's University
Lydia Gruchy	1953	University of Saskatchewan
Eva Hasell	1963	University of Saskatchewan
Viola Pratt	1956	Victoria University

Social Work/Activism

Ishbel Aberdeen	1897	Queen's University
Emily Cummings	1910	King's College NS
Margaret McWilliams	1946	University of Manitoba
	1948	University of Toronto
Helen Reid	1916	Queen's University
Marion Royce	1975	Acadia University
Charlotte Whitton	1941	Queen's University

Agriculture

| Cora Hind | 1935 | University of Manitoba |

Judgeship

| Helen MacGill | 1938 | University of British Columbia |

Politics

| Grace MacInnis | 1977 | University of British Columbia |

APPENDIX B: AUTHORS WHO WERE SCHOLARS AND MEDICAL WORKERS

Scholars

At least nine women included in this work wrote PhD theses in part or entirely about Canada (seven are listed in Dossick 1986):
- Sister Mary Norton in history at Catholic University of America
- Margaret Strong in public policy at University of Chicago
- Jane Turnbull in French at University of Chicago
- Elizabeth Armstrong in history at Columbia University
- Florence Dunlop in psychology at Columbia University
- Ruth Spence in education at Columbia University
- Aileen Dunham in history at University of London
- Hilda Neatby in history at University of Minnesota
- Lucy Textor in history at Yale Univeristy

Other women who had top degrees and wrote scholarly books about Canada were American Luella Gettys (public policy), British Lilian Knowles (economics) and Scottish Marion Newbigin (geography).

At least five Canadian authors did their doctoral work in Canada, all at the University of Toronto: Mossie May Kirkwood in philosophy, Elizabeth MacDonald in Semitic law, Mary Northway and Mary Salter in psychology and Alice Turner in mathematics. Most Canadians who obtained PhDs graduated from non-Canadian universities:
- University of Bonn–Carrie Derick
- University of Chicago–Margaret Strong, Jane Turnbull

- Columbia University–Elizabeth Armstrong, Donalda Dickie, Florence Dunlop, Elizabeth MacCallum, Ruth Spence
- University of London– Dorothy Blakey, Aileen Dunham
- Notre Dame University–Sister Maura
- Radcliffe/ Harvard–Esther Wright
- University of Washington–Mabel Timlin

At least twenty-two other Canadian women earned their masters' degrees in a variety of disciplines.

Some of the scholars included among the authors were or became professors. They are:

- Maude Abbott in medicine at McGill University
- Dorothy Blakey in English at University of British Columbia
- Carrie Derick in botany at McGill University
- Aileen Dunham in history at College of Wooster in Ohio
- Wilhelmina Gordon in English at Queen's University
- Mossie May Kirkwood in English at University of Toronto
- Lilian Knowles in economics at University of London
- Sister Maura in English at Mount St. Vincent University
- Bertha Meyer in Germanic languages at McGill University
- Hilda Neatby in history at University of Saskatchewan
- Marion Newbigin in geography at Bedford College, London
- Mary Northway in psychology at University of Toronto
- Grace Nute in history at Hamline University in St Paul, MN
- Mary Salter in psychology at Johns Hopkins University in Baltimore
- Marjorie Smith in social work at University of British Columbia
- Lucy Textor in history at Vassar University
- Mabel Timlin in economics at University of Saskatchewan
- Alice Turner in mathematics at York University
- Julia Wales in English at University of Wisconsin

Doctors

Five women were medical doctors:

- Maude Abbott taught at McGill University
- Mary Jackson practised in northern Alberta
- Helen MacMurchy worked for health departments in the Ontario and Canadian governments
- Margaret O'Hara worked as a medical missionary in India
- Susanna Rijnhart was a medical missionary in Tibet

Nurses

Seven of the authors were active as nurses:

- Constance Bruce and Mabel Clint nursed in Europe during the First World War
- Annie Foster worked for the Red Cross in England during the First World War
- Alvine Gahagan nursed in rural northern Alberta
- Frances Hasell brought religion and health to rural western Canada
- Louise Lawrence worked for the Red Cross in northern Ontario and nursed the Dionne quintuplets
- Mary Weekes nursed in Boston hospitals from 1910 to 1914

APPENDIX C: PUBLISHING AND SUPPORT OF AUTHORS

Publishing

Most books were written and submitted to a publisher as they are today, a first book submitted on speculation, with subsequent books often requested by the publisher if the first was successful. Over the time period of this study, books by Canadian publishers rose from about 56 percent to 68 percent of the total published, those by American publishers rose from about 13 percent to 23 percent, and those by British publishers fell from about 31 percent to 9 percent. (Percentages are approximate only, as many books were published by several countries, and the ones I counted were those copies I found in libraries.) Only two books were published outside these three countries, in Pretoria and in Geneva. Susanna Moodie's *Roughing it in the Bush* (1852) sold so well that her London publisher, Richard Bentley, asked her to write a follow-up book about pioneer life in the towns of Upper Canada. Mazo de la Roche was so popular as a novelist that her publisher requested a non-fiction book from her on Quebec to take advantage of her fame. Dodd, Mead ran a series of world travel books by Ruth Wood in the 1910s, while McClelland and Stewart published four books of travel in Canada by Kathrine Brinley in four consecutive years (1935-38). In the 1900s Dent was important as a publisher focusing on school books, while Ryerson Press and to a lesser extent Macmillan Press exhibited nationalist zeal which resulted in the publication of many histories of Canada, a subject that they felt had been overlooked (Campbell 1995).

Other methods of publication were available, too (although we have no means of judging how common these were, given that only a few books mention publishing details). In the early days, some writers financed their books by subscription, asking potential readers to give them money to pay for publication. This removed the risk of financial loss. Subscriptions made possible the appearance of books by Margaret McDougall, who collected money from Irish people to publish her letters about her tour through Ireland (1882), by Charlotte MacPherson, who had written her remembrances of sixty years in Quebec (1890), by May Drummond, who wrote the biography of the rector of the local church (1916) and by Mabel Clint (1934), who recalled her experiences as a nurse in the First World War, made possible by the Alumnae Association of the Royal Victoria Hospital in Montreal and other subscribers.

More often authors published their books themselves, as many still do today, often, presumably, because they could not interest a publisher in them. In this study it seems that about six percent of authors did so over most of the time period of the study, with somewhat more in the early days. Self-publication was common for authors of local histories, but happened, too, for books of more general interest, such as the autobiography of Charlotte Führer (1881), a travel book by Grace Denison (1890), who expected "dear five hundred friends" to read the first edition, the biography of Tom Thomson by Blodwen Davies (1935) and a book of Yukon wildflowers by Martha Black (1936). Alice Turner, arguing against socialism, stated publicly that she published her 1944 book from her own pocket to prove her independence.

Royalties from sales are rarely mentioned in books. In those included in this work, authors noted that they would donate them to various causes usually related to their books: the Quebec Battlefields Fund (Annie Logan 1908); the daughters of the biographical subject of a book (May Drummond 1916); the Canadian Red Cross Society (Maude Abbott 1916; Dorothy Ratcliffe 1928); native Chinese evangelists (Rosalind Goforth 1937); poor Scottish fishermen (Bird 1856); and medical equipment for Britain and Russia (Mercy McCulloch 1942). Some books announced that their authors had written them without compensation (Janet Carnochan and Annie Stephenson), and those authors who printed their books privately probably made little or no money on them.

Critical Support of the Author

It is likely that all or most of the authors had the encouragement and support of at least members of their family, but some were fortunate to have outside support as well, both moral and financial; without such support, many of their books would not have been published. These sources are mentioned with appreciation in the book prefaces. Financial support came to some through scholarships, such as those of the Canadian Federation of University Women to Dorothy Blakey (1935), that of the government of Saskatchewan to Hilda Neatby (1937), and money from the Regional Writing Program of the University of Minnesota to Florence Jaques (1944). Encouragement came sometimes from governments; the Ontario Department of Agriculture, for example, urged Women's Institutes to undertake local histories wherever possible (as Sara Campbell 1936). Provincial Departments of Education could also be very influential when they agreed to accept particular books as accredited school texts (as Grace Rogers 1930). Encouragement also came from historical and literary groups such as the Maritime Library Association, which sponsored a history competition (acknowledged by Edith Nase 1925 and Bertha Scott 1926, even though they personally published the work they wrote for the competition), the York-Sunbury Historical Society of New Brunswick (Lilian Maxwell 1937; Maud Miller 1940), and The Canadian History Competition (Dorothy Heneker 1927). Some support was with library help—both Constance Skinner (1933) and Jeannette Mirsky (1934) thank Vilhjalmur Stefansson for the use of his extensive Arctic collection.

The backing mentioned so far was not necessarily connected with publication, however, which always needed specific funds. Publication not underwritten by a commercial press as discussed above was financed (rather than just encouraged) by a number of sources.

Commercial Concerns

The Canadian Pacific Railway and some steamship lines paid for some books, hoping that tourists and immigrants who read them would be persuaded to use their transportation (Marjorie Harrison 1930; Blodwen Davies 1930; Alice Sharples 1939). A forestry company paid Charlotte Whitton by contract to write about their operation, while Madge Watt's book on the marvellous potential of Vancouver Island was backed by the Vancouver Island Development Association.

Governments

Governments were also involved in producing books. Ontario and the federal government, for example, published books about health for its citizens by Dr Helen MacMurchy. The latter also paid money to Amelia Paget to document information about Indians on the prairies; she had lived among them for many years after being kidnapped along with her birth family.

Interest Groups

A variety of groups financed the publication of books to further their work. A good example is the Institute of Child Study in Toronto, which published, via the University of Toronto Press, studies focused on children by psychologists such as Helen Bott, Dorothy Millichamp, Mary Northway, Mabel Ringland and Mary Salter. The Canadian Reconstruction Association financed and published research by Enid Price (1919) on the relationship between women and work during the First World War. Mission groups and church sects authorized and/or published books to stimulate interest in their work (as Eda Green 1912; Annie Stephenson and Sara Vance 1929; Viola Pratt 1937; Marguerite Brown 1938; Muriel Beaton 1941).

Local Committees

A committee of Grey County in Ontario authorized Edith Marsh to write its history, while some churches set up committees to oversee the publication of their history undertaken by women authors.

GENERAL BIBLIOGRAPHY

Books consulted and used in at least two entries are included in this General Bibliography.

Bibliography

Ainley, Marianne Gosztonyi, ed. 1990. *Despite the Odds: Essays on Canadian Women and Science*. Montreal: Véhicule Press.

Ambrose, Linda M. 1996. *For Home and Country*. Guelph: Federated Women's Institutes of Ontario.

Bannerman, Jean. 1977. *Leading Ladies Canada*. Belleville, ON: Mika Publishing.

Bassett, Isabel. 1975. *The Parlour Rebellion*. Toronto: McClelland and Stewart.

Bennett, Jennifer. 1991. *Lilies of the Hearth*. Camden East, ON: Camden House.

Berger, Carl. 1970. *The Sense of Power*. Toronto: University of Toronto Press.

Brouwer, Ruth Compton. 1990. *New Women for God: Canadian Presbyterian Women and India Missions, 1876-1914*. Toronto: University of Toronto Press.

Buss, Helen M. 1986. Canadian women's autobiography: Some critical directions. In Shirley Neuman and Smaro Kamboureli, eds. *A Mazing Space: Writing Canadian Women Writing*, pp. 154-64. Edmonton: Longspoon/ NeWest.

Buss, Helen M. 1990. Women and the garrison mentality: Pioneer women autobiographers and their relation to the land. In Lorraine McMullen, ed. *Re(Dis)covering our Foremothers*, pp. 123-36. Ottawa: University of Ottawa Press.

Campbell, Sandra. 1995. From romantic history to communications theory: Lorne Pierce as publisher of C.W. Jefferys and Harold Innis. *Journal of Canadian Studies* 30: 91-116.

Canadian Encyclopedia. 1985. Edmonton: Hurtig.

Canadian Who's Who (1898 to present). Toronto: Trans-Canada Press/ Who's Who Canadian Publications.

Canadian Women of Note Biographies. 1981. Toronto: MICR Systems. Microfiche MFCL 3269.

Carman, Bliss. 1925 [1908]. *The Making of Personality*. Boston: Page.

Conrad, Margaret, Tony Laidlaw and Donna Smyth. 1988. *No Place Like Home: Diaries and Letters of Nova Scotia Women, 1771-1938*. Halifax: Formac.

Contemporary Authors. 1962-present. Detroit: Gale Research.

Creighton, Donald. 1958. *A History of Canada*. Boston: Houghton Mifflin.

Crosby, Marcia. 1991. Construction of the imaginary Indian. In Stan Douglas, ed. *Vancouver Anthology: The Institutional Politics of Art*, pp. 267-91. Vancouver: Talon Books.

Dagg, Anne Innis. 1992. Canadian voices of authority: Non-fiction and early women writers. *Journal of Canadian Studies* 27: 107-22.

Dagg, Anne Innis and Patricia J. Thompson. 1988. *MisEducation: Women and Canadian Universities*. Toronto: OISE Press.

Dossick, J.J. 1986. *Doctoral Research on Canada and Canadians, 1884-1983*. Ottawa: National Library of Canada.

Doyle, James. 1990. Research—Problems and solutions: Canadian women writers and the American literary milieu of the 1890s. In Lorraine McMullen, ed. *Re(Dis)covering our Foremothers*, pp. 30-36. Ottawa: University of Ottawa Press.

Ford, Anne Rochon. 1985. *A Path Not Strewn with Roses*. Toronto: University of Toronto Press.

Fowler, Marian. 1982. *The Embroidered Tent*. Toronto: Anansi.

Fulford, Robert. 1993, Winter. The trouble with Emily. *Canadian Art*, 33-39.

Gay, Peter. 1984. *The Education of the Senses*. New York: Oxford University Press.

Gerson, Carole. 1994. *Canada's Early Women Writers: Texts in English to 1859*. Ottawa: Canadian Research Institute for the Advancement of Women, Paper No 33.

Givner, Joan. 1989. *Mazo de la Roche: The Hidden Life*. Toronto: Oxford University Press.

Gould, Jan. 1975. *Women of British Columbia*. Saanichton, BC: Hancock House.

Griffiths, Naomi Elizabeth Saundaus. 1993. *The Splendid Vision: Centennial History of the National Council of Women of Canada 1893-1993*. Ottawa: Carleton University Press.

Harding, Les. 1994. *The Journeys of Remarkable Women: Their Travels on the Canadian Frontier*. Waterloo: Escart Press.

Harrington, Lyn. 1981. *Syllables of Recorded Time: The Story of the Canadian Authors Association*. Toronto: Simon and Pierre.

Institute of Child Study, University of Toronto. 1951. *Twenty-Five Years of Child Study: The Development of the Programme and Review of the Research at The Institute of Child Study, University of Toronto, 1926-1951*. Toronto: University of Toronto Press.

Macmillan Dictionary of Canadian Biography. 1978. Toronto: Macmillan. 4th edition.

MacMurchy, Archibald. 1906. *Handbook of Canadian Literature (English)*. Toronto: Briggs.

Montgomery, L.M., Marian Keith and Mabel Burns McKinley. 1934. *Courageous Women*. Toronto: McClelland and Stewart.

Muir, Elizabeth Gillan and Marilyn Färdig Whitely, eds. 1995. *Changing Roles of Women within the Christian Church in Canada*. Toronto: University of Toronto Press.

Noonan, Gerald, ed. 1985. *Guide to the Literary Heritage of Waterloo and Wellington Counties from 1830 to the mid-20th Century*. Waterloo: Wilfrid Laurier University Press.

Parker, George L. 1985. *The Beginnings of the Book Trade in Canada*. Toronto: University of Toronto Press.

Prentice, Alison, Paula Bourne, Gail Cuthbert Brandt, Beth Light, Wendy Mitchinson and Naomi Black. 1988. *Canadian Women: A History*. Toronto: Harcourt Brace Jovanovich.

Raymond, Jocelyn Motyer. 1991. *The Nursery School World of Dr Blatz*. Toronto: University of Toronto Press.

Rex, Kay. 1995. *No Daughter of Mine: The Women and History of the Canadian Women's Press Club 1904-1971*. Toronto: Cedar Cave Publishing.

Rooke, P.T. and R.L. Schnell. 1987. *No Bleeding Heart: Charlotte Whitton, A Feminist on the Right*. Vancouver: University of British Columbia.

Sangster, Joan. 1989. *Dreams of Equality: Women on the Canadian Left, 1920-1950*. Toronto: McClelland and Stewart.

Story, Norah. 1967. *The Oxford Companion to Canadian History and Literature*. Toronto: Oxford University Press.

Tippett, Maria. 1990. *Making Culture: English-Canadian Institutions and the Arts before the Massey Commission*. Toronto: University of Toronto Press.

University Women's Club of Toronto. 1978. *Seventy-Five Years in Retrospect*. Toronto: University's Women's Club.

Waite, P.B. 1995. Journeys through thirteen volumes: *The Dictionary of Canadian Biography. Canadian Historical Review* 76,3: 464-81.

Waterston, Elizabeth. 1989. *The Travellers–Canada to 1900*. Guelph: University of Guelph.

Wylie, Betty Jane. 1995. *Reading between the Lines*. Toronto: Key Porter.

Zaremba, Eve, ed. 1974. *Privilege of Sex: A Century of Canadian Women*. Toronto: Anansi.

INDEX

The subjects addressed by the authors in their books are listed on the left-hand side of the colon. The authors who wrote about each topic, listed on the right-hand side of the colon, are found in the text in alphabetical order, the date or dates referring to the date of their book(s) on the subject. If two authors have the same surname, then the author's initial is given after her surname.

grants, Canadian conditional: Gettys 1938
Greeley, Floretta and Hugh: Greeley 1920
Grenfell, Sir Wilfred: Fox 1941
Grenfell Mission: Greeley 1920
Grey County, ON: Marsh 1931
Grey Owl: Anahareo 1940
Grimsby Park, Grimsby, ON: Youmans, H. 1900
Groseilliers, Sieur des: Nute 1943
Guernsey, Isabel: Guernsey 1943
Haldimand, Sir Frederick: McIlwraith 1904
Halifax: Hallam 1937
Halifax County, NS: Lawson, M.J. 1893
Hall, Mary: Hall 1884
Hamilton, ON: Burkholder 1938
Hardy, Lady Duffus: Hardy 1881
Hardy, Thomas: Sime 1928
Harrington, Charlotte: Geddie 1908
Harrington, Rebie: Harrington 1937
Harrison, Marjorie: Harrison 1930
Hasell, Frances: Hasell 1922, 1925, 1930
Hathaway, Ann: Hathaway 1904
Hawaii: Forsyth Grant 1888
Hayward, Victoria: Hayward 1922
Henderson, Mary: Henderson 1937
Henrietta Maria, Queen: MacKay, J. 1939
Henry, Rev Thomas: Henry 1880
Herring, Frances: Herring 1900, 1903
Herz, Henriette: Meyer 1938
Hind, E. Cora: Haig 1945; Hind 1937, 1939
Hitchcock, Mary: Hitchcock 1899
Hogner, Dorothy: Hogner 1939
holiday names: Foster, A. 1938
Holt, Charlotte: Holt 1875
Holy Land: Keith 1927
household advice: MacMurchy, H. 1920b, 1923
housekeeping: Sime 1916; Sykes 1912
household science: Hoodless 1898, 1905; Watson 1905
Howey, Florence: Howey 1938
Hubbard, Mina: Hubbard 1908
Hudson, Henry: Cate 1932

Humber Valley, ON: Lizars, K. 1913
Huron Tract Settlement, ON: Lizars, R. 1896
Hutchison, Isobel, botanist: Hutchison 1934
illness: Brown, A. 1938
immigrant children: Macpherson, A. 1870; Stirling 1898
immigration, experience/advice: Binnie-Clark 1910, 1914; Cran 1908; Emigrant Lady 1878: Hall 1884; Harrison 1930; Johnstone 1894; Low c.1920, 1923, 1924; Moodie 1852, 1853; Morris 1913; Pullen-Burry 1912; Saxby 1890; Sykes 1912; Textor 1905; Traill 1835, 1854; Weaver 1914
policy: Foster, K. 1926
research: Cowan, H. 1928
India: Leonowens 1884
missions: Archibald, M. 1932; Churchill 1916; Clarke 1939; Duncan, J. 1944; McLaurin 1945; O'Hara 1931
Institute of Providence: Sisters 1927
Inuit woman: Washburne 1940
inventions: Barwick 1932
Ireland, tour: McDougall 1882
Jackson, Mary Percy, doctor: Jackson 1933
Jameson, Anna: Jameson 1838
Japanese Canadians: Reid, H. 1938
Jaques, Florence: Jaques 1944
Jarvis family, Toronto: Meredith 1928
Jephson, Lady: Jephson 1897
Jesuit priests: Concannon 1930; Kenton 1933
Johnson, Amelia, Annie: Johnson 1888
Johnson, E. Pauline, poet: Foster, A. 1931
Johnston, Blanche Read: Dean 1919; Johnston, B. 1919
Johnston, Elizabeth: Johnston, E. 1901
Johnstone, Catherine: Johnstone 1894
Keith, Marion: Keith 1927
Kenton, Simon: Kenton 1930
King, William: Jamieson 1925
Kingston, ON, history: Machar 1908
Kinton, Ada: Kinton 1907

status: Angus, M.I. 1932; Edwards 1908, 1916; Hensley 1907, 1913; MacDonald, E. 1931; MacMurchy, M. 1916; Nielsen 1944; Royce 1945; Sime 1916

Women's Institute, Ontario: Powell 1941; Watt, M.

woodcraft: Pinkerton 1916

Woodstock, Upper, NB: Miller, M.H. 1940

Woodsworth, J.S., politician: Ziegler 1934

work and women: Knox 1919; Low c.1920, 1924; Price, E. 1919a, b; MacMurchy, M. 1919; Massey 1920; Sykes 1912

world tour: Beaton, M.H. 1942; Cowan, M. 1945; Hind 1937, 1939; Leavitt 1886-1894

yoga: Beck 1937

York, Eva: York 1920, 1935

Youmans, Letitia: Youmans, L. 1893

Young Women's Christian Association: Carr-Harris 1892; Royce 1945

Youville, Venerable Mother d': Duffin 1938

Yukon: Black 1936, 1938; Cameron, C. 1920; Davis 1933; Harrington 1937; Hitchcock 1899; Hutchison 1934; Lloyd-Owen 1939; Tyrrell 1938